SITUATING
SALSA

WITHDRAWN FROM
THE LIBRARY

UNIVERSITY OF
WINCHESTER

KA 0272383 2

SITUATING

Global Markets and Local Meanings in Latin Popular Music

SALSA

Edited by **Lise Waxer**

ROUTLEDGE
NEW YORK AND LONDON

Published in 2002 by
Routledge
29 West 35th Street
New York, NY 10001

Published in Great Britain by
Routledge
11 New Fetter Lane
London EC4P 4EE

Routledge is an imprint of the Taylor & Francis Group.
Copyright © 2002 by Routledge

Printed in the United States of America on acid-free paper.

KING ALFRED'S COLLEGE
WINCHESTER

02723832 793.3
WAX

All rights reserved. No part of this book may be reprinted or reproduced or utilized in any form or by any
electronic, mechanical, or other means, now known or hereafter invented, including any photocopying and
recording, or in any information storage or retrieval system, without permission in writing from the publisher.

10 9 8 7 6 5 4 3 2 1

Library of Congress Cataloging-in-Publishing Data

Situating salsa : global markets and local meanings in Latin American popular music / edited by Lise Waxer
        p. cm.
    Includes index.
    ISBN 0-8153-4019-2 – ISBN 0-8153-4020-6 (pb.)
        1. Salsa (Music)—History and criticism. I. Waxer, Lise.

ML3535.5 .W39 2002
781.64–dc21   2001043113

To the memory of Tito Puente "El Rey"

and to everyone who has ever been swept away
by a night of *descarga* and dancing . . .

and especially to my family,
who had the faith in my being a "salsiologist"
even though our roots are anchored in a different rhythm.

Salsa is not a rhythm,
it's a concept.

—Willie Colón

Contents

PART II: PERSONALIZING SALSA

PART III: RELOCATING SALSA

List of Illustrations

PHOTOGRAPHS

MUSICAL EXAMPLES

Preface

Lise Waxer

This volume emerges from a love affair with salsa that began twelve years ago when I commenced graduate studies in Toronto. I do not come from a Latin American family, but through the experiences accompanying my research, I have become Latina *por adopción*. I am often asked how it is that a Canadian person (of Chinese-Jewish extraction, no less!) comes to be interested in salsa, and I have been forced to reflect on this issue long and hard. As a small child, I grew up listening to my maternal grandparents speak Cantonese and spent weekends between Chinese *dim sum* lunches and my Bubbi's special Jewish feasts. Later, I lived in a middle-class Anglo neighborhood in Toronto that didn't quite feel like somewhere I belonged. In many ways, salsa's diverse, multiracial heritage and complex spread through the world reflects my own disjunct sense of personal identity. It has not been an easy road: learning how to dance, how to decipher and play the complex polyrhythms of Latin music, and how to speak and read Spanish have all presented many obstacles to someone raised in a quiet Toronto neighborhood with training as a classical pianist. It's been worth it, however. Researching salsa has provided an unusual but deeply personal vehicle for me to search out and create my own place in a world that is starting to look as fragmented and fluid as my own background is.

Many people have helped and encouraged me along the way, too many to list here, but I want to thank my first teacher, Memo Acevedo, whose patience and inspiration carried me through the ethnographic research that became my master's thesis, and who first taught me how to play Latin percussion. Other friends and colleagues along the way have also become mentors and guides through salsa's complex history and performance genealogies: Frank Falco, Nicholas Hockin, and Michael Marcuzzi in Toronto; René López, Andy and Jerry González, Roberta Singer, and Willie Colón in New York City; Joe Goldfield, Ron Gotler, and the *Adelante* gang in Urbana; Gerardo Rosales and Juan Carlos Báez in Caracas; Medardo Arias, Gary Domínguez, Jaime Henao, Jaime Camargo Franco, Pablo Solano, Enrique Escobar, Sabina Borja, my sisters from *Magenta,* and many, many others in Cali; Adriana Orejuela, Helio Orovio, Leonardo Acosta, Doris Aguirre, and Los Terry in Havana. I would also like to thank Peter Manuel and Deborah Pacini Hernández for their constant professional encouragement, feedback and support through my years of salsa research.

Situating Salsa was conceived through the aegis and support of my longtime friend and editor of this series, Gage Averill, to whom I send my sincere gratitude for encouraging me to take up this project in the first place and keeping it going when obstacles emerged. But the main vote of *agradecimiento* for this project goes to its contributors, who have generously provided their work and patiently tolerated my quibbles and endless e-mails through these past months. To Marisol, Juan, Frances, Wilson, Shuhei, Steve, Robin, Patria, Chris, Medardo, and Don Tite Curet Alonso—my sincerest thanks. I would also like to acknowledge Chuco Quintero Rivera, Rebeca Mauleón, Edgardo Díaz Díaz, Scott Pérez, and Junko Oba, who were involved in the preparation of this project at earlier stages.

My gratitude goes also to Richard Carlin, senior music editor at Routledge, whose prompt and cheerful leadership throughout the preparation of this book have been deeply appreciated. Thanks as well to former music editor Soo Mee Kwon and her assistant, Gillian Rodger, for their help during the early stages of this project. I would also like to thank Trinity College for the research leave and financial support that ensured the completion of this book.

The production of this volume owes a profound debt to many people who assisted in its realization. I would like to thank Luis Figueroa and Zaira Rivera Casellas for their collaboration in contacting Tite Curet Alonso in Puerto Rico, so that we could include his work here. Many thanks also to Bill Cooley for his detailed work in adjusting the score of "Me Calculaste" for this volume. I would also like to thank Bruce Polin at Descarga Records, who cheerfully answered my questions on record company contacts and other information; the Descarga catalog has become my bible for all things discographical. Thanks also to Victor Gallo and Jose Flores at Fania Records, Izzy Sanabría, Ernesto Aue of Palacio Records, Jean Montiel at Bug Music, and Jim Cassell and Connie of Berkeley Agency for their cooperation in clearing copyrights to reprint material here.

During the early stages of preparing the manuscript, we were all stunned to hear the news that Tito Puente "El Rey" had passed away, on May 31, 2000. He was one of the most important figures in Latin music and an inspiration to performers and audiences around the globe. In his memory we partially dedicate this volume. This volume is also dedicated to all the fans and aficionados who have known the magic of a night of *descarga* and dancing. It is their spirit that has kept me going through these long months of editing.

Finally, I would like to dedicate this volume to my family, the Yips and the Waxers. They have had faith in me since I first stumbled into the world of salsa and began torturing my roommates with fumbling attempts to get a piano *montuno* down. Never have they questioned or criticized my choosing to explore a culture different from my own roots. (Rather, they pulled out stories of Great-Uncle Jack Cho teaching them to mambo in the 1950s!) As I sent home tapes and news clips of my subsequent years of performing with Adelante, Magenta Latin Jazz, and now, Salsafication, they proudly encouraged me to continue forth with my research, contributing books and records to my collection. In this same vein, my husband, Medardo—whose work I am honored to include in this volume—has also provided constant, enthusiastic, and selfless support. I am profoundly grateful for his presence in my life and work, not to mention the many weeks of overtime cooking and doing laundry while I completed this manuscript. My in-laws, the Arias family, have also been extremely generous in their support. To all my kin, this is for you.

Dancer at a party in the UNEAC (Unión de Escritores y Artistas), Havana, Cuba, 1995.

Part 1

LOCATING SALSA

Chapter 1

SITUATING SALSA: LATIN MUSIC AT THE CROSSROADS

Lise Waxer

"*Echale Salsita.*" Put a little sauce on it. When Cuban composer Ignacio Piñeiro wrote this song for his Septeto Nacional in 1933, little did he know that he was setting the precedent for use of a term that would later be synonymous with an internationally popular Latin sound. Salsa, with its roots in the Cuban and Puerto Rican cultural diaspora to New York City, has now grown into a global musical phenomenon with audiences and practitioners ranging from Tokyo to Dakar. Today's salsa market offers Latin dance lessons, several Internet websites, touring dance competitions sponsored by Bacardi rum, and even "salsa cruises" with nightly performances by leading stars.

In Spanish, "salsa" literally means "sauce," with a culinary metaphor that evokes images of a spicy concoction—somewhat mirroring the music's own hybrid origins and infectious appeal. As the authors in this volume discuss, salsa means many things to many people, but a basic part of its attraction has been its ability to make people move together—to dance. Here, everyday troubles are forgotten in the "everynight life" of dancing bodies (Fraser Delgado and Muñoz 1997). The social interaction of salsa dance is mirrored and reinforced by the dynamic exchanges of the musicians themselves. For those of us who find our way into salsa as listeners, following the complex polyrhythmic conversations of salsa performance can be as exhilarating as getting down on the dance floor. For many of its new audiences, salsa is also a gateway to the cultural Other, a fascinating and often exotic world where new selves find liberation from cultural strictures.

Salsa developed in the Latino barrios of New York City during the

3

1960s and '70s. Based largely on Cuban forms of the 1930s, '40s and '50s, salsa also incorporated Puerto Rican elements and influences from North American jazz and rock. Salsa's Cuban and Puerto Rican antecedents were themselves a fusion of African and European elements[1] (see Alén 1984, Echevarría Alvarado 1984, and Dufrasne-González 1994 for more information on these forms). Cuban musicians in the first half of this century frequently used to say "toca con salsa!" (roughly, "hit it!" or "swing it!") when the excitement and energy of the music began to rise. This metaphor was inferred by Ignacio Piñeiro in his famous composition "Échale salsita." Many observers agree that a Venezuelan radio disc jockey, Phidias Danilo Escalona, was among the first to use the term "salsa" to denote Latin dance music in the early 1960s (Rondón 1980:33), although New York publisher Izzy Sanabría claims to have coined the name himself, at the end of the decade (Roberts 1979:187). Certainly, by the early 1970s, salsa had become the standard term of reference throughout Latin America, owing in large part to its use by Fania Records as a commercial label with which to market this music.

Given that the New York community in which salsa developed was strongly Puerto Rican, during the 1960s and '70s salsa became a potent emblem of Puerto Rican identity both for islanders and for those living in the mainland United States (Duany 1984; Padilla 1990), helping underpin nationalist sentiment against the specter of U.S. colonial domination. The use of the ten-stringed Puerto Rican *cuatro,* an icon of island culture, by Willie Colón and the Fania All-Stars during the early 1970s further underscored salsa's Puerto Rican affiliations.[2] The music's own interracial heritage was mirrored by the strong interethnic participation that marked the New York scene, with Jewish and African-American musicians performing in several bands. Jewish pianist Larry Harlow even became an important bandleader and producer in the New York scene. During this same period, salsa music also spread to other parts of Latin America, especially Venezuela, Panama, and Colombia—countries with close geographic and economic ties to the Caribbean. Significantly, salsa's lyrics reflected the experiences of the Latino and Latin American black and mixed-race working class, and—in distinction to its Cuban antecedents—songs mirrored the violence and discontent of the inner city. When salsa's exuberant beat and social message caught on with Latin American leftist intellectuals from the middle and upper-middle classes in the 1970s, salsa music shed its lower-class associations to establish a devoted following not only across national boundaries, but across social ones. By the 1980s, salsa was firmly entrenched as a transnational musical genre, with followers throughout the Americas and also in Europe, Africa, and Japan.

Salsa's complex history and international spread have given rise to much debate about its genesis and legitimacy as a musical category. Cuban specialists and musicians, in particular, have long contested the use of the term, claiming that salsa is nothing more than "Cuban music in new clothes." Marisol Berríos-Miranda and other authors in this volume, however, demonstrate that there are significant stylistic *and* ideological distinctions that mark salsa as a musical style distinct from its Cuban ancestors. Even a casual listening to salsa from the 1960s and '70s (e.g., Eddie Palmieri) and its Cuban antecedents from the 1940s and '50s (e.g., Arsenio Rodríguez) provides empirical grounds for distinguishing between the two. While the rhythms and forms are the same (e.g., *son, guaracha, mambo, cha-cha-chá* and *bolero)*, the stylistic treatment is quite different. Salsa uses more percussion and larger horn sections than its Cuban antecedents.[3] The arrangements are more aggressive, and in the classic *salsa dura* ["hard/heavy" salsa] from the 1960s and '70s, the lyrics refer to a social and cultural milieu different from that of Cuba.

"Salsa" is a term that overlaps significantly with an earlier catchall, "Latin music." The very fluidity of the label "salsa" mirrors that of its predecessor. "Latin music" was a term applied primarily to Cuban and Puerto Rican dance genres in the 1930s, '40s and '50s, although it was occasionally used to denote other Latin American styles such as Argentine *tango* and Brazilian *samba* and *bossa nova*. Similarly, while salsa is generally understood to refer to popular dance styles with a Cuban and Puerto Rican musical base, other Caribbean styles, such as the Dominican *merengue* and Colombian *cumbia* have sometimes—and incorrectly—been thrown into this category, usually by outsiders to these traditions (see, e.g., Manuel 1988:46). As I argue elsewhere, the ambiguity of the term "Latin music" reflects its shifting, transnational character. While the term "Latin" tends to collapse difference in a way that can perpetuate oppressive stereotypes, such as the notion that Latins are all the same, it does point to a notion of Latin popular music as a stylistic complex that cannot be reduced to one specific location (Waxer 1994:140). Latin music and salsa, despite their clear reference to Cuban/Puerto Rican–based styles, have evolved into a musical expression with multiple sites of articulation. Salsa's transcendence of geographic and cultural boundaries has been central to its affective power—its capacity to literally move thousands of people. In a recent essay, Mayra Santos Febres refers to this process as "translocation"— the emergence of a globalized musical community from among its different locales of production and reception (1997).

Despite the fluid and rather slippery usage of the term, "salsa" clearly refers to much more than a specific musical form. Willie Colón notes,

"Salsa is not a rhythm, it's a concept" (1999). Angel Quintero Rivera and Luis Álvarez similarly observe that salsa is a "way of making music" (1990). For this reason, some writers choose to capitalize the word as "Salsa," to emphasize its importance and its distinction from mere "salsa." In this volume, Wilson Valentín (chapter 7), Tite Curet Alonso (chapter 8) and Medardo Arias Satizábal (chapter 11) maintain this emphasis. Our volume does not pretend to resolve the debates concerning salsa's exact origins, or to fix its specific taxonomic location in the terrain of Latin American popular music. Rather, it is concerned with situating salsa as a musical *style*, wherein—as Colón and Quintero and Álvarez suggest—a social and cultural way of looking at the world (concept) is welded to praxis (making) through the creation and reception of musical sound. Style, in other words, becomes intrinsically bound up with larger social values, beliefs, and practices, not only reflecting but actively shaping human experience (Turino 1989; Keil 1985; Feld 1988; Meintjes 1990). Importantly, style and meaning are contingent to local historical processes. We cannot assume that salsa sounds the same or means the same thing everywhere it is played. The diverse and nuanced cases presented by the authors in this book clearly demonstrate that salsa's multiple transnational contexts have given rise to a number of different practices in salsa performance and salsa consumption.

This volume contains recently published and original new research on salsa and salsa-related styles (such as son, boogaloo, Latin jazz, and *timba,* or "Cuban salsa"), in global perspective. Our aim is to enlarge the scope of salsa research, which has concentrated primarily on salsa's Afro-Cuban roots and its New York and Puerto Rican creators. In her landmark study *Listening to Salsa* (1998), Frances Aparicio discusses the need to understand salsa as an emergent musical style whose meaning is being renegotiated by production and consumption in several different parts of the world. Indeed, the chapter in which she analyzes this issue is also titled "Situating Salsa" and serves as a point of departure for this anthology. By including chapters that explore salsa's adoption and localization not only in other Latin American countries (Colombia, Venezuela) and Latino communities in North America, but also in England and Japan, we have attempted to provide a truly international purview of contemporary salsa.

 A central theme of this anthology concerns local-global links in Latin American and Caribbean popular music, exploring the constant circulation of people, ideas, sounds, and musical commodities among salsa's transnational sites. Although the Puerto Rico–New York–Cuba nexus remains a central axis for the creation and commercial production of salsa, the music's strong reception in several other global sites points to a dynamic process of globalization and relocalization that greatly expands salsa's popular significance. Several of these chapters examine the ways in which multinational economic flows and structures of power actually play out and are felt in people's daily lives. As Patria Román-Velásquez points out in her essay on salsa in London (chapter 12), "the local is treated not as self-contained and bounded, but understood in terms of its interaction with global processes." This observation is underscored by Shuhei Hosokawa, who notes "that the global and local cannot be considered as a pair of opposites but rather as an interwoven nexus shaped by the contours of history" (chapter 13).

The collection marks an overdue musicological nod in the direction of Latin American and U.S. Latino cultural studies. Much of the current literature in this field has been concerned with nonmusical expressive forms, such as literature, the plastic arts, and theater (García Canclini 1989, Rowe and Schelling 1991). Even the provocative and influential recent anthology *Everynight Life: Culture and Dance in Latino/a America* (Fraser Delgado and Muñoz 1997) does little to address specific musical concerns, leaving readers with little sense of how salsa—as sound and not only movement—operates in everyday experience and cultural performance. Being a hybrid musical expression, salsa has much to teach us about the dialectic between tradition and modernity in Latin America, and the effects of social diaspora and culture industries in overlapping and expanding contexts. It is also a tremendous laboratory in which to examine the role of musical expression in shaping individual subjectivities and social identities. For example, as Marisol Berríos-Miranda discusses in "Is Salsa a Musical Genre?" (chapter 2), the ways in which salsa represents national identity for Puerto Rican listeners are marked through subtle but essential variations in rhythmic phrasing and ensemble playing that differentiates Puerto Rican salsa from its Cuban antecedents—elements usually overlooked in most writing on salsa. In another case, as I discuss in "Llegó la Salsa" (chapter 10), for Venezuelan and Colombian listeners salsa has marked a cosmopolitan sensibility that ties local performers and audiences to the sphere of transnational culture, becoming a vehicle for them to "be in the world" when barriers of class and race prevent them from accessing elite forms of cosmopolitan culture.

Spurred by increased transport and communications links, mass media, and transnational economic flows, the rapid diffusion and relocalization of salsa points to important cultural processes of our times. Paralleling other styles such as rock and reggae, salsa's transnational popularity clearly illustrates the mechanics of hybridization and globalization that characterize popular culture in the twentieth century. Significantly, salsa has provided an alternative transnational popular style to the hegemony of U.S./British rock music and its association with

U.S. political and economic domination. This has been important not only in the Latin American context but in other parts of the world as well. Our project of "situating salsa" arises from the need to reconsider the complicated and shifting trajectories of one of the most important global popular styles of our time.

GLOBAL MARKETS

Recent scholarship on globalization has questioned classic core-periphery models of international relations and development. Arjun Appadurai notes,

> The new global cultural economy has to be understood as a complex, overlapping, disjunctive order, which cannot any longer be understood in terms of existing center-periphery models (even those that might account for multiple centers and peripheries). . . . The complexity of the current global economy has to do with certain fundamental disjunctures between economy, culture and politics which we have barely begun to theorize. (1990:296)

Certainly, the proliferation of hybrid popular musics on the world landscape during the late twentieth century has blurred any rigid notion that these developments occurred as a direct project of enterprises located in the "Western" or Euro–North American center. A series of essays published as a special edition of *World Music* in 1993 explored this emergent process. The authors call attention to the increasing "transversality" (Erlmann 1993:13) and "polylateral" or "multilateral" (Guilbault 1993b:39, Pacini Hernández 1993:49) flows of contemporary popular music, in diverse ways that shatter any notion of core-periphery movement.

Salsa's rapid spread through Latin America during the 1970s, followed by its adoption in Europe, Japan, and Africa during the 1980s and '90s, has similarly posed the need for considering this genre in terms of multiple sites of production and reception. Though salsa's diffusion to these places does not quite fall into the category of globalization along the lines of McDonald's, MTV, Microsoft, and Michael Jackson, the distinction between "transnational" (cutting across national boundaries) and "global" (truly worldwide) is not always clear in salsa's case. Although salsa's spread to different countries within Latin America might best be classified as transnational, its adoption in Europe, Japan, and West Africa certainly approaches global proportions. Furthermore, the increasing presence of Big Five record companies—especially Sony and BMG—in the salsa industry during the 1990s clearly ties salsa to globalizing forces in the music business, even when salsa is not necessarily promoted with the same emphasis in different world markets. The dozens of salsa-related websites that have emerged on the Internet also speak to increasing globalization along this medium.[4]

Certainly, the burgeoning Latino population in the United States has strongly affected salsa's production and distribution in the multinational music industry since the late 1980s. Keith Negus traces the complex ways in which new "Latin divisions" were established in the major companies—Sony/CBS, EMI, Polygram, BMG, and Warner/WEA—during this period, in an attempt to capture the growing Hispanic market. Ironically, despite the initial presence of salsa as a "domestic" genre in the U.S. market (which includes Puerto Rico), virtually all major companies, with the exception of EMI, farmed their Latin Music divisions out as subsidiaries of their international operations, with the resulting paradox that salsa became an "international" or "foreign" genre within the U.S. market. Even EMI and RMM (which is part of MCA's operations in the United States) were set up as separate divisions segregated along ethnic and language lines within the national market. The lines of communication within these networks are extremely complicated—for example, WEA Latina and Polygram Latina both report to their Latin American divisions, which in turn report to head offices in London. Furthermore, the Latin departments of all these companies maintain production studios in Miami but are controlled by financial offices in New York and Los Angeles (1999:142–45).

Most major salsa artists in the United States, the Caribbean, South America, and Japan—and even some local salsa labels, such as Venezuela's Rodven, picked up by Polygram—are or have been represented by one of the Big Five record companies. The complex and impersonal structure of these enterprises, however, means that the interests of local artists and, often, local audiences are left out of the picture when it comes to production and marketing decisions. As in the early 1980s, when several New York salsa artists began moving out from under the control of Fania Records, artists and producers are now contesting the hegemony of multinational record labels—often as a response to being shut out from access to the major companies in the first place. In the past decade, small independent labels have released numerous productions and compilations of material deemed commercially unviable for mass global markets, often distributed by independent companies such as Descarga Records in New York or local specialty shops. Other international salsa artists whose contracts with the majors terminate for various reasons are also sidestepping the corporatism of the music industry. Colombia's Grupo Niche, for example, represented by Sony throughout the 1990s, released its last album under the self-produced PPM (Productores Profesionales de la Música or Professional Producers of Music) label.[5] Willie Colón, who claims to have been blacklisted in the U.S. Latin market (2000), released his last album on the self-produced Azteca Music label,[6] distributed in Mexico by Polygram LatinoAmérica. More ethnographic research is needed to document these relationships and the effects of the global music industry on salsa performance and production.

Notably, during the late 1980s and early 1990s, salsa played a surprisingly marginal role in the "world beat" boom that spurred the global spread of several other international popular styles. According to Deborah Pacini Hernández, this may be explained partly by subtle yet pervasive anti-Latino racism in the U.S. markets where much of the "world beat" hype was promulgated—particularly against Puerto Ricans and Dominicans, commonly portrayed as drug dealers, pimps, and hot-blooded vixens in the U.S. media (1993b:57). Indeed, in her essay here on salsa clubs in London (Chapter 12), Patria Román-Velásquez notes that a British entrepreneur similarly associated Puerto Ricans with an image of violence and delinquency that he wanted to avoid, preferring instead to cultivate an exotic tropical paradise closer to the stereotype of Miami's Little Havana. On the other hand, Latin American and U.S. Latino sensitivity to U.S. domination may have made artists and promoters reluctant to pursue the "melting pot" of the world beat industry, preferring to maintain a separate identity (Pacini Hernández 1993b: 57). Certainly, as Pacini Hernández notes, several recent currents in Spanish Caribbean music themselves point to internal regional dynamics that play into and off of larger global trends. The rise of Spanish reggae and hip-hop, for instance, while influenced by the worldwide impact of these styles, has developed without top-down domination of multinational record companies.

Currently, there are five principal "schools" or transnational styles of salsa performance: New York, Puerto Rican, Venezuelan, Colombian, and Cuban, with the development of *timba* or "Cuban salsa" in the 1990s. Some observers also add Miami to this list, although—as Christopher Washburne points out in his essay on *salsa romántica* (chapter 5)—the common pool of arrangers and studio musicians used in New York, Miami, and even Puerto Rico has made much contemporary salsa produced in these places sound very similar. Crosscutting these transnational schools is another stylistic matrix that correlates to salsa's historical development. Negus (1999:138–39) characterizes these as: (1) the "old school" (salsa dura, or "hard/heavy salsa"), following the New York, Puerto Rican, and Venezuelan sound of the 1960s and '70s; (2) salsa romántica, a continuation of the *salsa erótica* (sensual salsa) developed in the 1980s; (3) "soulful salsa," incorporating Top 40 pop, rhythm and blues, and soul harmonies and arrangements (e.g., Luis

Enrique, Victor Manuel); and (4) "dance club salsa," which fuses salsa romántica with elements of hop-hop, r&b, and Cuban *timba* (e.g., Marc Anthony, La India).

The history of salsa's Cuban roots and its development in New York and Puerto Rico is well documented in several studies (Blum 1978; Roberts 1979; Rondón 1980; Arias Satizábal 1981; Singer 1982; Duany 1984; Alén 1984; Padilla 1989 and 1990; Gerard 1989; Arteaga 1990; Boggs 1992; Santana 1992; Manuel 1991, 1994, 1995; Quintero Rivera 1998; Washburne 1999). A smaller body of research by Venezuelan and Colombian scholars documents the rise of salsa in those countries (Rondón 1980; Baéz 1989; Arteaga 1990; Ulloa 1992; see also Waxer 1998). Very little work has been published on the rise of Cuban salsa or *timba* in the 1990s, although the strong commercial success of this sound in international markets will no doubt result in a spate of studies in the near future. Robin Moore provides an exploration of salsa and socialism in this volume (chapter 3).

Less understood are the sites outside of Latin America where salsa has also spread. The emergence of Japanese salsa bands in the 1990s sent profound waves through the international salsa scene, especially because these performers subverted Eurocentric stereotypes about what "Oriental" musicians should look and sound like. As Shuhei Hosokawa notes in this volume (chapter 13), the rise of Japanese salsa was marked by a complex negotiation of ethnic and exoticized identities. Notably, however, this development pointed to an important new trend in the globalization of popular music: the adoption of a non-Western style by another non-Western country, without the necessary intervention of North American or European influence. Hosokawa criticizes the ethnocentrism of studies that ignore this trend and offers a detailed analysis of Orquesta de la Luz's success at home and abroad. Current work in progress by Junko Oba suggests an even more nuanced approach to our understanding of salsa's "globalization" in this case, since the shift from regional/transnational audiences to a larger, global public market was precisely what led to the demise and eventual breakup of Orquesta de la Luz:

> A major cause of its poor sales and of the subsequent collapse of the band itself was that the promotional strategies of their new record company [from RMM to BMG], which aimed at capturing a larger global market with Orquesta de la Luz, inevitably de-localized the band and dissociated them from the salsa communities evolved around their music. In hindsight, the failed venture revealed how significantly the previous popularity and international success of Orquesta de la Luz had been grounded on and supported by the skillful local marketing operations designed specifically for the respective local markets in Japan and the Americas.

On another front, Senegalese salsa singers have been recording with Puerto Rican and Cuban musicians in New York, beginning with Laba Sosseh in the early 1980s and intensifying with Pape Seck, Sekouba Diabate, and other artists of the popular group Africando in the 1990s. These pan-Atlantic collaborations mark a new transnational dynamic in salsa's development. Their emergence, in turn, grows from the steady influence of Cuban and salsa recordings in West and Central Africa since the middle of the century (Graham 1988; Collins 1992; Stewart 2000), giving rise to "re-Africanized" Cuban-based styles such as the Zairean *rumba congolaise* and shaping the early sounds of Ghanaian and Nigerian highlife and urban dance band music in Mali and Senegal. Indeed, Africando's founder and producer, Ibrahim Sylla, grew up listening to and collecting imported salsa records in his native Dakar, and the influence of these classic sounds is apparent in the group's performance. Notably, the rise of *salsa africaine,* or African salsa, points not so much to a return of salsa to African soil (Steward 1999:157) but to a complex process of cultural appropriation between two regions of the so-called Third World. As in the case of Japan, this process has emerged without the direct domination of North American or European culture industries, which were focused on rock music. Although I have heard that surplus recordings of Cuban music were allegedly dumped on African markets by U.S.-controlled record companies in the 1930s and '40s,[7] I have not been able to confirm this claim. Certainly, it seems that in the absence of direct international distribution networks for New York labels such as Tico and Alegre in the 1960s, salsa recordings arrived in countries like Senegal through indirect routes—quite possibly through the same process of merchant sailors via which salsa arrived in South America (see Waxer, chapter 10).[8] More research is needed in this area, which remains a fertile but neglected field.

Other regions have given rise to salsa bands and audiences, particularly in areas where Latin Americans from salsa-producing countries have migrated. Virtually every country in Europe has a salsa scene; some of them even have renowned salsa bands. The founding of Conexión Latina in Munich in the early 1980s, for example, emerged from the collaboration between German jazz musicians and Puerto Rican *salseros* stationed on duty at a U.S. Army base in Germany. Their recordings have earned international acclaim. In this volume, Patria Román-Velásquez discusses the "routes and routines" through which English and Latin American entrepreneurs and customers have established a salsa club scene in London (chapter 12). Her findings are similar to research I conducted in my hometown of Toronto, Canada, in the late 1980s (Waxer 1991). Brigido Galvan is conducting current research on more recent developments in salsa and Latin popular music in Canada.

The theme of global markets and the transnational music industry crosscuts several of the essays in this volume. Although, as Oba cautions, it is crucial to distinguish between regional and global levels in the music business, it is certain that the rise of the recording industry and the transnational diffusion of its products through formal and informal channels have been central processes in salsa's development. The production of Latin popular music, furthermore, has often developed in dialectical relation not only to different regional or global markets, but also musical production in other commercial styles. Christopher Washburne, for example, offers an "inside" view of the recording process, noting the ways in which distinctions between the New York and Puerto Rican schools of salsa affected the creation and production of a typical contemporary salsa tune (chapter 5). In another essay, Juan Flores explores the fascinating history of the boogaloo fad in the 1960s, and the ways in which this early form of salsa was informed by trends in African-American popular music (chapter 4). Robin Moore explores the influence that the transnational salsa industry had in revitalizing popular music production by the state-owned Cuban music industry during the 1990s, helping to spur the development of a new commercial style (chapter 3). The commercial success of timba and traditional Cuban music in Europe and North America during the 1990s has had profound ramifications for this socialist country. Not only has it provided a much-needed source of income for the beleaguered nation, it has also obliged the Cuban state to adopt certain mechanisms of the capitalist global music industry.

Despite the strong presence of industry mechanisms at virtually every stage of salsa's history, however, the spread of salsa to different parts of the globe has not necessarily been conducted with its direct administration. Medardo Arias and I (chapters 10 and 11) look at the ways in which sailors served as an informal but vital link in the diffusion of Cuban, Puerto Rican, and salsa recordings to Colombia from the 1940s through the 1960s, before formal networks of record distribution were established in the 1970s. Patria Román-Velásquez (chapter 12) explores the way in which Latin American migration to England also introduced salsa to the country in the 1980s, before industry-controlled channels were consolidated to tap this growing market.

Tied to the notion of global markets is the issue of movement and cultural diaspora, particularly in the case of the Puerto Rico–mainland U.S. migrations that gave rise to salsa in the first place. Ángel Quintero Rivera, for instance, positions salsa as a style rooted in a tradition in which the theme of movement and labor migration have been present since the early twentieth century (1998). He sees many of the topical themes and musical elements articulated in 1970s and 1980s Puerto Rican salsa to be similar to those already expressed in the 1920s Cuban son which is salsa's principal musical predecessor. In this volume, focusing on the career of legendary salsa vocalist Héctor Lavoe, Wilson Valentín explores the concept of "trans-*Boricua*" identity and the affirmation of Puerto Rican migration and subjectivity through music (chapter 7). According to Valentín, the memory of Lavoe (who died in 1993) has become an arena in which cultural identity continues to be negotiated across different geographical and social spaces.

Salsa's transnational diffusion has facilitated a cross-pollination of musical styles, not only with elements of its own Afro-Cuban and Afro-Puerto Rican ancestry, but also with jazz and other Latin American traditions. Steven Loza explores the fusion of Cuban son and jazz in the music of Poncho Sánchez, a successful Chicano percussionist and bandleader (chapter 9). Marisol Berríos-Miranda notes that salsa's localization in different Latin American countries has been marked by the fusion of salsa with national musical styles (chapter 2). In my essay on Venezuelan and Colombian salsa, I briefly touch on some of the fusions between salsa and traditional regional musical genres such as *gaita, joropo, cumbia,* and *currulao* (chapter 10).

Also significant is the way in which salsa's global diffusion has masked a gender ideology that constructs Latin popular culture in terms of male superiority. Women have long been present as dancers and listeners in salsa's transnational diffusion, and during the late 1980s and 1990s, women in several countries (including the United States, Cuba, Colombia, Canada, Japan, and Denmark)[9] have made important contributions as salsa and Latin jazz musicians. Yet, the images promoted by the music industry continue to highlight men over women. In an important extension of her earlier work on salsa and gender (1998), Frances Aparicio here offers a cogent critique of the ways in which women and "feminized salsa" have been consistently subordinated in salsa discourse (chapter 6). Her feminist genealogy of three of salsa's most prominent women performers—Celia Cruz, La Lupe, and La India (all vocalists)—is framed as a step toward understanding how Latino/a cultural politics and transnational identities have been constructed through music.

LOCAL MEANINGS

While a look at salsa's global spread is essential to understanding its significance, focusing on its ability to transcend geographic and cultural boundaries runs the grave risk of depoliticizing the structures of power and ethnic/cultural difference that gave rise to this music in the first place. Aparicio cautions us not to ignore "salsa's value as a historically oppositional expression within the larger tradition of Afro-Caribbean music" (1998:68). In her view, "border crossing" does not automatically assume equality. In his essay "Whose World, What Beat?" Reebee Garafolo similarly observes that the reconfiguration of global political and cultural economies that has led to globalization in popular music has also spawned more complex systems of capitalist oppression and control (1993). In some cases, salsa's history as a countercultural expression made it an ideal voice for people living in similar contexts, such as Panama, Venezuela, or Colombia. In these countries, salsa emerged as an expression of an urban, working-class, black and mixed-race culture in several cities whose histories were similar to that of Cuba and Puerto Rico. In other places, such as Japan and Europe, the political and ethnic elements have been modified in order to make salsa a more "universal" expression—but at the same time, one removed from salsa's roots as a voice for social opposition.

The essays in this volume pay careful attention to salsa's ties to local and regional meanings and structures of power. It is only in local contexts that we begin to understand the ramifications of salsa's spread to different parts of the world. Here, we begin to see the distinct practices that enabled salsa to be used as a vehicle for cultural values in countries as distinct as Puerto Rico, Colombia, and Japan. The strong ethnographic basis of most of the studies contained in this volume further underscores the local meanings and uses of salsa in its diverse transnational sites.

The contributions of Tite Curet Alonso (chapter 8) and Medardo Arias Satizábal (chapter 11) are perhaps the most "local" in their location, since they present very personalized perspectives of the impact of salsa on their own life experiences. Curet Alonso is a prolific composer, journalist, and sociologist (among other careers, including postman), and is one of the most revered composers in salsa today. His vignettes of various artists and producers with whom he has worked offers a unique insider's perspective on the salsa world. Arias Satizábal is a renowned author and poet in Colombia, who won the prestigious Simon Bolívar Award for Journalism in 1982 for his ten-part series on the history of salsa (1981)—a work written parallel to but without knowledge of César Miguel Rondón's acclaimed volume which appeared in Venezuela during this same period (1980). His chapter provides an evocative text recalling a childhood and adolescence growing up to the sounds of Cuban music and salsa in the Colombian Pacific port of Buenaventura.

Marisol Berríos-Miranda (chapter 2) and Wilson Valentín Escobar (chapter 7) also speak from their own subject positions as Puerto Rican scholars, and their exploration of salsa as a simultaneously national and transnational style is unmistakably rooted in their own personal experiences of salsa as an emblem of Puerto Rican identity. Berríos-Miranda criticizes the oft-cited view of salsa as "just Cuban music," analyzing the articulation of musical expression and ideological categories that makes salsa a distinct voice for Puerto Rican cultural sensibilities within the context of colonial subordination. Valentín Escobar, similarly, looks at the ways in which Puerto Rican salsa, while speaking to issues of transnational diaspora and movement, is also rooted in an emergent and constantly negotiated sense of place and cultural roots in the island itself.

Juan Flores, Frances Aparicio, and Patria Román-Velásquez extend this purview to a study of salsa within minority Latino ethnic communities. Flores traces the development of boogaloo as not only an important moment in salsa history, but also an important chapter in black and Latino cultural collaborations mirrored a generation later in the rise of hip-hop culture in New York City (chapter 4). He positions boogaloo as a creative response to cultural and economic circumstances, within the context of minority ethnic struggles in this city. Similarly, Aparicio focuses on salsa in the U.S. Latino/a context, exploring the ways in which competing gender ideologies have intersected with those of race and ethnicity to frame the performance and reception of salsa's three principal female artists: Celia Cruz, La Lupe, and La India (chapter 6). Román-Velásquez, in a different sphere, looks at insider and outsider perceptions of Latin dance clubs, and the role of London's burgeoning Latin dance scene in shaping Latino ethnic identity in England (chapter 12).

In other essays, salsa's local-global links are explored for their impact on local musical practice and meaning. Robin Moore, for example, analyzes Cuban life after the revolution, and the ways in which musicians have responded to local situations (chapter 2). Timba, or "Cuban salsa," while a product of transnational commercial influence, has also acquired local potency for the ways in which it comments upon the return of capitalism and prostitution to the island. In my essay on salsa's adoption in Venezuela and Colombia (chapter 10), I explore salsa as a musical lingua franca for the rapidly expanding, heterogeneous urban environments of Caracas and Cali, where local and regional musical traditions no longer served to express new cultural sensibilities and experiences. In these cities, although Puerto Rico and New York continued to serve as central point of reference for salsa performance, practices of consumption often differed quite radically from their original counterparts—this is especially evident in the rise of the record-centered dance scene and *salsotecas* in Cali. Shuhei Hosokawa presents a similar instance in which salsa served as a vehicle for expressing the rapid changes and disjunctures of contemporary Japanese society, while reaffirming traditional cultural values (chapter 13). Indeed, it is through exact mimicry of New York and Puerto Rican salsa bands that Orquesta de la Luz, Japan's most successful group, has upheld the traditional educational process of *kata* learning. Hosokawa also analyzes the ways in which geographical and cultural distance between Japan and the Americas actually promoted the success of Orquesta de la Luz, in a complex process through which cultural Others were negotiated and embraced through particularly local values on both sides.

Most of the authors represented in this volume approach local-global links through a historical perspective, analyzing salsa's global spread and local meanings in terms of specific historical conjunctures and contexts. This diachronic approach (Quintero Rivera 1998:40) is strongly influenced by the interdisciplinary field of cultural studies. As Quintero Rivera points out, however, a synchronic approach is also necessary for understanding music's impact in actual real-life moments. Such a perspective is represented here in Washburne's examination of the mechanics of a typical *salsa romántica* tune (chapter 5), and Loza's study of two Poncho Sánchez compositions (chapter 9). Berríos-Miranda (chapter 2) also presents a methodical outline of the key elements and musical values that musicians and listeners expect to hear in a "good" salsa performance.

The essays in this volume have been organized along general topical lines that anchor this book's broad look at global markets and local meanings. The essays in the first section, "Locating Salsa," explore salsa as a simultaneously national (i.e., Puerto Rican) and also transnational (pan-Latino) musical style. While my central concern as editor of this volume has been to break away from the Cuba–New York–Puerto Rico focus of most salsa research to date, this is grounded in the philosophy that understanding salsa is fruitless if we forget its initial emergence as a vehicle for Puerto Rican and Nuyorican cultural identity and resistance against U.S. cultural domination. Salsa's initial Puerto Rican creators—Tito Puente, Eddie Palmieri, Willie Colón, Héctor Lavoe, Ismael Rivera, Ray Barretto, Tite Curet Alonso, Papo Lucca, Willie Rosario, and others—remain pivotal icons for contemporary salsa musicians and audiences around the globe. Although salsa's contemporary significance cannot be reduced to Puerto Rico alone, it certainly loses meaning if the dynamics of this fundamental location are ignored.

The second section, "Personalizing Salsa," looks more closely at individual artists and their musical and social impact. Among those profiled in this section are Celia Cruz, La Lupe, La India, Héctor Lavoe, and Poncho Sánchez. Also included are Tite Curet's autobiographical vignettes of

Rafael Cortijo, Cheo Feliciano, Ismael Miranda, and Rubén Blades. The essays in this section outline various ways in which salsa has served as vehicle for expressing social identity at several levels, demarcating categories of race, class, ethnicity, community, gender, and generation. Their biographical orientation casts an important perspective on the complex conjunctures among salsa performance, production, reception, and consumption.

The third section, "Relocating Salsa," provides case studies of salsa's impact in different parts of the world, particularly where these shed light on local-global links at different levels, within and beyond translocal Latin American communities. Though we can certainly perceive what Appadurai refers to as "deterritorialization" (1996) at work in these cases, we also see an equally strong current of relocalization or, as some scholars are starting to put it, "glocalization" of salsa in different sites of the world (Robertson 1995; Kraidy 1996; Swyndegouw 1997). The multiple uses and meanings that salsa has given rise to in diverse places North and South, East and West, are a key part of the reconsideration of salsa's contemporary significance that this volume proposes to address.

Included in the volume are two essays (chapters 5 and 9) that analyze salsa from a more systematic musicological examination of salsa performance and sound structure. These chapters, while certainly accessible for a general reader, are aimed particularly at musicians and specialists—an audience whose interests in musical structure are bypassed in most salsa scholarship.

The articles collected in *Situating Salsa* represent some of the best current scholarship on salsa. Clearly, as we move into a millennium in which Latin Americans and U.S. Latinos are posed to become major figures on the global cultural landscape, salsa's worldwide impact will increase in stature and complexity. This volume will probably raise as many new questions as those we have attempted to answer here. Certainly, we have not been able to address all the issues raised by salsa's current diffusion, and we hope that this volume will help to spur continued research. As salsa continues to reach into new locales in Europe, Africa, Australia, and South America, the significance of its origins as a contestatory Afro-Caribbean style will become increasingly complicated.

Despite the diversity of agendas that have accompanied salsa's adoption in different countries, its overarching nature as a joyful and exuberant musical style seems to be a constant in all its transnational and global contexts. In the introduction to his recent seminal work, *!Salsa, sabor y control!*,[10] Ángel Quintero Rivera says that his objective is to formulate a new approach to sociological studies of Latin America and the Caribbean, one that focuses not on prevalent media images of underdevelopment, hunger, drugs, corruption, dicatorships, and human rights abuses, but rather on *"las contribuciones del Caribe a la alegría en el mundo"* [the contributions of the Caribbean to joy in the world, author's emphasis].

> [This] means not only a thematic innovation, but also a relocation of perspectives. To conceptualize joy also means, necessarily, to speak of sadness, but from the perspective of happiness; to meditate and research and reflect upon those processes that make happiness difficult, and the possible avenues of its future development. *¡Salsa, sabor y control!* trys to broach these complex social processes—communal, national, regional, and global—around one of our great delights. (1998:10)

Quintero Rivera's radical proposition informs the spirit of our project here. Like the beat of the *clave,* or rhythmic time line, that propels salsa's impelling groove, the element underscoring each of these essays is salsa's power to raise voices and move joyful bodies within and across cultural boundaries. Our aim is not only to shed new light on current debates about race and ethnicity, class hierarchy, gender roles, and generational differences, in multiple transnational contexts. Like the legions of fans and aficionados worldwide who know what it is to be carried away by a night of *descarga* and dancing, our own "salsa jam session" aims to convey some of our own passion for salsa's dynamic *afinque* (swing) and *sabor* (essence). I think Ignacio Piñeiro had it right all along. *Échale salsita.*

NOTES

1. Minor vestiges of the extinct Siboney and Taino Indian cultures have also been retained, most notably in the notched scraper known as *güiro,* a percussion instrument made from an elongated gourd.

2. A dearth of research exists on the Puerto Rican *cuatro,* owing in large part to the sensitivity of its nature as an icon of Puerto Rican culture—and hence, nationalism—within the current colonial regime. Attempts to showcase cuatro history by local cultural organizations and even by the Instituto de Cultura Popular have been repeatedly squelched by the government. In this regard, recent work by the Cuatro Project, an independent research consortium, has been especially valuable. See website: www.cuatro-pr.org, and its recently completed documentary film, *Nuestro Cuatro: Los puertorriqueños y sus instrumentos de cuerda, vol. 1,* available in Spanish and English versions.

3. With the exception of some Cuban big bands of the 1940s and '50s such as La Gigante de Benny Moré, the Orquesta Casino de la Playa, and the Orquesta Riverside. These big bands paralleled the New York mambo orchestras of Machito, Tito Puente, and Tito Rodríguez that directly preceded salsa in the New York scene.

4. Salsa-related websites include Latin Music On-line, OasisSalsero, the Willie Colón Web-site and Forum, Descarga Records, San Francisco/Bay Area Salsa and Latin Jazz, Salsa Web, Picadillo, Latin Dance, Der Salsaholic, Hot Salsa (Le Guide de la Salsa), Musica Salsa Forum, Salsa Jam, Salsa Brasil, SalsaJazz, Jazz con Clave, Salsa con Cache, Noti-Salsa, Salsatecas, Bamboleo, Sonero, SalsaNet, Latino, Cadena SalSoul, Dimensíon Latina, Salsa in Finland, Samurai Latino, NYC Salsa, Salsa em

Brasil, Master Timbaleros, Timba Website, Richie Blondet's Montuno Papers, and Nestor Louis's webpage. Most commercial salsa artists also have their own website, as do Fania and RMM Records.
5. Grupo Niche (1999) *A Golpe de Folklore* (PPM 0001).
6. Willie Colón (1999) *Demasiado Corazón* (Azteca Music 2–1719[24]). Colón also spoke about his blacklisting to a small group of students at Trinity College, Hartford, Conn., November 11, 1999.
7. Jay Nash, personal communication, November 1991.
8. Deborah Pacini Hernandez (1993a) describes a parallel process in the other direction, via which records of Afro-pop, South African *mbqanga* (township jive), Zairean *soukous* and Caribbean styles such as *soca* and *zouk* were introduced into the Colombian port of Cartagena in the 1970s and '80s, where they were adopted as an emblem of Afro-Colombian identity in a localized sound known as *champeta* or *terapia*.
9. These include contemporary all-women salsa bands such as Anacaona (Cuba), Son de Azucar (Colombia), and Perfume de Salsa (Denmark), and musicians such as Rebeca Mauleón-Santana (U.S.), Sheila Escovedo (U.S.), Jane Bunnett (Canada), and Nora of Orquesta de la Luz (Japan). During the early to mid-1990s, both Havana and Cali had more than ten *orquestas femeninas* or all-women bands. I analyze the rise of all-women salsa bands in Colombia elsewhere (Waxer 2001).
10. Awarded the 1999 Casa de Las Americas Prize and 2000 Latin American Studies Association Award for Best Book on Latin America.

BIBLIOGRAPHY

Alén, Olavo. 1984. *De lo afrocubano a la salsa: géneros musicales de Cuba*. San Juan: Cubanacán. [Reprinted in English as *From Afro-Cuban Music to Salsa,* with accompanying CD. Berlin: Piranha Records BCD-PIR 1258, 1998.]

Aparicio, Frances R. 1998. *Listening to Salsa: Gender, Latin Popular Music and Puerto Rican Cultures*. Hanover, N. H.: Wesleyan University Press/University of New England Press.

Appadurai, Arjun. 1990. "Disjuncture and Difference in the Global Cultural Economy." In Mike Featherstone, ed., *Global Culture: Nationalism, Globalization and Modernity*. London: Sage, pp. 295–309.

———. 1996. *Modernity at Large: Cultural Dimensions of Globalization*. Minneapolis: University of Minnesota Press.

Arias Satizábal, Medardo. 1981. "Esta es la verdadera historia de la salsa." Printed as an eleven-part series in *El Occidente* newspaper. Winner of the 1982 Premio Simón Bolívar for Journalism.

Arteaga, José. 1990. *La Salsa*. Bogotá: Intermedio Editores. 2nd rev. ed.

Baéz, Juan Carlos. [1985] 1989. *El vínculo es la salsa*. Caracas: Fondo Editorial Tropykos.

Blum, Joseph. 1978. "Problems of Salsa Research." *Ethnomusicology* 22(1):137–49.

Boggs, Vernon, ed. 1992. *Salsiology: Afro-Cuban Music and the Evolution of Salsa in New York City*. Westport, Conn.: Greenwood Press.

Collins, John. 1992. *West African Pop Roots*. Philadelphia: Temple University Press.

Colón, Willie. 1999. Jacket cover to *Demasiado Corazón* (Azteca Music 2–1719[24]).

———. 2000. "The Latin Grammies: Is There no End to the Egotism of the Miami Mafia?" International press release, published simultaneously in English and Spanish by several media.

Duany, Jorge. 1984 . "Popular Music in Puerto Rico: Toward an Anthropology of Salsa." *Latin American Music Review* 5(2):186–207.

Dufrasnes-González, Emanuel. 1994. *Puerto Rico también tiene ¡tambo! Recopilación de artículos sobre la plena y la bomba*. Río Grande: Paracumbé.

Erlmann, Veit. 1993. "The Politics and Aesthetics of Transnational Musics. *World Music* 35 (2): 3–15.

Echevarría Alvarado, Félix. 1984. *La plena: origen, sentido y desarollo en el folklore puertorriqueño*. Santurce: Express.

Feld, Steven. 1988. "Aesthetics as Iconicity of Style, or 'Lift-up-over Sounding': Getting into the Kaluli Groove." *Yearbook for Traditional Music* 20:74–113.

Fraser Delgado, Celeste and José Esteban Muñoz, eds. 1997. *Everynight Life: Culture and Dance in Latin/o America*. Durham, N. C.: Duke University Press.

Garafolo, Reebee. 1993. "Whose World, What Beat: The Transnational Music Industry, Identity, and Cultural Imperialism." *World Music* 35(2):16–32.

García Canclini, Nestor. 1989. *Culturas híbridas: Estrategías para entrar y salir de la modernidad*. Mexico City: Grijalbo.

Gerard, Charley. 1989. *Salsa!: The Rhythm of Latin Music*. Crown Point, Ind.: White Cliffs.

Graham, Ronnie. 1988. *The Da Capo Guide to Contemporary African Music*. New York: Da Capo.

Guilbault, Jocelyne. 1993. "On Redefining the 'Local' through World Music." *World Music* 35(2):33–47.

Keil, Charles. 1985. "People's Music Comparatively: Style and Stereotype, Class and Hegemony." *Dialectical Anthropology* 10:119–30.

Kraidy, Marwan Michael. 1996. "Towards a Semiosphere of Hybrid Identities: A Native Ethnography of Glocalization." Ph.D. dissertation, Ohio University.

Manuel, Peter. 1988. *Popular Musics of the Non-Western World: An Introductory Survey*. New York: Oxford University Press.

———. 1991. "Latin Music in the United States: Salsa and the Mass Media." *Journal of Communication* 4(1):104–16.

———. 1994. "Puerto Rican Music and Cultural Identity: Creative Appropriation of Cuban Sources from Danza to Salsa." *Ethnomusicology* 38(2):249–280.

———. 1995. *Caribbean Currents: Caribbean Music from Rumba to Reggae*. Philadelphia: Temple University Press.

Meintjes, Louise. 1990. "Paul Simon's *Graceland*, South Africa, and the Mediation of Musical Meaning." *Ethnomusicology* 34(1):37–73.

Negus, Keith. 1999. *Music Genres and Corporate Cultures*. London: Routledge.

Oba, Junko. (n.d.). "Making and Selling Japanese Salsa: Orquesta de la Luz and the (Re)imagining of Salsa." Unpublished manuscript.

Pacini Hernández, Deborah. 1993a. "The *picó* phenomenon in Caragena, Colombia." *América Negra* 6:69–115.

———. 1993b. "A View From the South: Spanish Caribbean Perspectives on World Beat." *World Music* 35(2): 48–69.

Padilla, Félix. 1989. "Salsa Music as a Cultural Expression of Latino Consciousness and Unity." *Hispanic Journal of Behavioral Sciences* 2(1):28–45.

———. 1990. "Salsa, Puerto Rican and Latino Music." *Journal of Popular Culture* 24(1):87–104.

Quintero Rivera, Ángel. 1998. *¡Salsa, sabor y control! Sociología de la música "tropical."* Mexico City: Siglo Ventiuno Editores. Reprinted by Casa de Las Americas, Havana.

Quintero Rivera, Ángel, and Luis Manuel Álvarez. 1990. "La libre combinación de las formas musicales en la salsa." *David y Goliat* 57:45–51.

Roberts, John Storm. 1979. *The Latin Tinge: The Impact of Latin American Music on the United States*. New York: Oxford University Press.

Robertson, Roland. 1995. "Glocalization: Time-Space and Homogeneity-Heterogeneity." In Mike Featherstone, Scott Lash, and Roland Robertson, eds., *Global Modernities*. London: Sage, pp. 25–44.

Rondón, Cesar Miguel. 1980. *El libro de la salsa: crónica de la música del caribe urbano.* Caracas, Venequela: Editorial Arte.

Rowe, William, and Vivian Schelling. 1991. *Memory and Modernity: Popular Culture in Latin America.* London: Verso.

Santana, Sergio. 1992. *¿Qué es la salsa?: Buscando la melodía.* Medellín: Ediciones Salsa y Cultura.

Santos Febres, Mayra. 1997. "Salsa as Translocation." In Celeste Fraser Delgado and José Esteban Muñoz, eds., *Everynight Life: Culture and Dance in Latin/o America.* Durham: Duke University Press, pp. 175–88.

Singer, Roberta. 1982. "'My Music Is Who I Am and What I Do': Latin Popular Music and Identity in New York City." Ph.D. dissertation, Indiana University.

Steward, Sue. 1999. *Musica! The Rhythm of Latin America: Salsa, Rumba, Merengue, and More.* San Francisco: Chronicle Books. Published simultaneously in England as *Salsa! Musical Heartbeat of Latin America,* London: Thames and Hudson.

Stewart, Gary. 2000. *Rumba on the River: A History of the Popular Music of the Two Congos.* London: Verso.

Swyndegouw, Erik. 1997. "Neither Global nor Local: 'Glocalization' and the Politics of Scale." In Kevin R. Cox, ed., *Spaces of Globalization: Reasserting the Power of the Local.* New York: Guilford, pp. 137–66.

Turino, Thomas. 1989. "The Coherence of Social Style and Musical Creation among the Aymara of Southern Peru." *Ethnomusicology* 33(1):1–30.

Ulloa, Alejandro. 1992. *La salsa en Cali.* Cali: Ediciones Universidad del Valle.

Washburne, Christopher J. 1999. *Salsa in New York: A Musical Ethnography.* Ph.D. dissertation, Columbia University.

Waxer, Lise. 1991. "Latin Popular Musicians in Toronto: Issues of Ethnicity and Cross-Cultural Integration." Master's thesis, York University.

———. 1994. "Of Mambo Kings and Songs of Love: Dance Music in Havana and New York City from the 1930s-1950s." *Latin American Music Review* 15(2):139–76.

———. 1998. "*Cali Pachanguero:* A Social History of Salsa in a Colombian City." Ph.D. dissertation, University of Illinois at Urbana-Champaign.

———. 2001. "Las Caleñas Son Como Las Flores: All-Women Salsa Bands in Cali, Colombia." *Ethnomusicology* 45(2):228–259.

Chapter 2

IS SALSA A
MUSICAL GENRE?

Marisol Berríos-Miranda

*Salsa is a rhythm, is a reality. . . . That the root is from the
Cuban son, it is true, that the clave is important and one has
to keep it, is true. But salsa is salsa. El Gran Combo plays
salsa. Let's be clear. Eddie Palmieri plays salsa. Ray Barretto
plays salsa. Richie Ray, Joe Cuba play salsa. Machito plays
mambo, plays mambo jazz. Each thing in its place. Machito
does not play salsa. I see it that way because of its harmonic
and rhythmic structures. Cubans cannot play salsa. There is
not a Cuban salsa group, it does not exist.*

Gerardo Rosales

Statements like the one by Venezuelan percussionist Gerardo
Rosales above are musical, social, and political all at the same time.
The very act of asking the question, "Is salsa a musical genre?" is
loaded with these three aspects of the music that from its inception have
been inseparable. Stating that salsa is a musical genre has the political
implication of asserting the independence of the Puerto Rican musician
not as an "appropiator of Cuban styles" but as a genuine creator with
all rights. Puerto Rican musical identity and salsa are inseparable,
because Puerto Ricans in New York made salsa a political movement in
the 1970s. Indeed one could argue that the political dimensions of salsa,
the question of who it belongs to, have drawn attention away from the
kinds of questions about style and sound that are raised by musicologists
in relation to many other genres of music. In this article I will review
some of the ideological implications and controversies raised by the

question, "Is salsa a musical genre?" and then focus more specifically on the way salsa is perceived by musicians and listeners to be musically distinctive.[1]

Compared to salsa, Cuban music had not been so politicized before the Cuban revolution of 1959. From the 1960s to 1980s, approximately, *nueva trova* was the revolutionary music in Cuba. From the 1970s on salsa became a revolutionary music in New York, Puerto Rico, Venezuela, Colombia, and many Latin cities, reaching the peak of its social change manifesto in 1978, with Rubén Blades and Willie Colón's best-selling salsa album *Siembra*. In this era of passionate social messages, the magic salsa kept was that it was always danced to. While salsa during this time became a pan-Latino phenomenon (Blades, for example, is Panamanian), the importance of the Puerto Rican contribution to salsa is recognized by many in Latin America and worldwide (Berríos-Miranda 1997). To many Puerto Ricans this is of utmost importance. However, despite this intense identification with salsa and the association of salsa with the 1970s awakening of Latino cultural identity, some people would deny that there are significant musical differences between salsa and Cuban genres like *guaracha* or *son montuno* that preceded salsa.

One major source of confusion in this argument is the fact that salsa is commonly understood to incorporate a variety of distinct genres. The same people who are quick to identify salsa by its unique musical qualities are also aware that salsa has been a mix of several genres.

> And remember that within salsa there are a quantity of rhythms like the *charanga* and the *pachanga*, that is what we know as salsa, as such. Yes, like the *songo*, the guaracha, the son; there are a quantity of Cuban genres, maybe it is from there [the variety] that the word salsa comes from because is like rice with mango.[2]

Many songs by salsa bands like El Gran Combo, Fania All-Stars, or Oscar D'León are identified in CD and record liner notes with genre names like guaracha, *bomba*, or cha-cha-cha. This explicit recognition by salsa musicians that they are switching between different genres or *ritmos* [rhythms] suggests that salsa might be better described as a style of playing, not a genre unto itself. The debate rests to some extent, then, on how one defines the terms "genre" and "style."

The Webster's Encyclopedic Unabridged Dictionary of the English Language defines "genre" as follows: "a class or category of artistic endeavor having a particular form, content, technique, of the like; the genre of epic poetry; the genre of symphonic music." Webster's defines "style" as follows: "a particular kind, sort, or type, as with reference to form, appearance or character; those components or features of a literary composition that have to do with the form of statement rather than the content of the thought expressed; a particular distinctive, or characteristic mode or form of construction or execution in any art or work."[3] If we say, then, that genre is content, and style is a manner of execution, we might try to answer the question, "Is salsa a genre?" by distinguishing "content" and "execution" in salsa music.

Notwithstanding Webster's definitions, however, many ethnomusicologists have come to believe that musical genres are socially constructed and cannot always be distinguished strictly by criteria of sound (Averill 1997; Dudley 1996; Guilbault 1993; Manuel 1994; Turino 1999). Everyday speech—"a mí me gusta la salsa," "I prefer salsa to merengue," "Do you dance salsa?"—indicates that salsa is commonly considered by musicians and listeners as a genre of music. Therefore, the question I will attempt to answer is whether this designation is motivated by concerns of cultural identity or whether it is grounded in a perception of salsa as musically distinctive, or both. In other words, salsa is a genre because musicians and listeners judge it to be a genre—but to what extent do they make that judgment on the basis of sound? After briefly reviewing the scholarship on salsa, I will turn to the testimony of many salsa musicians and aficionados that I interviewed in Puerto Rico and Venezuela about sound, style, aesthetics, and musical proficiency and skill in salsa. These aspects of the music are, after all, what make salsa what it really is: grooving, exciting, inviting, and extremely challenging. I will argue that, whatever one may think about the politics of labeling, the evidence is clear that salsa is stylistically and sonically distinctive.

SALSA SCHOLARSHIP

The study of salsa music as a scholarly subject in the United States was sparked by Joseph Blum's seminal article "Problems of Salsa Research" published in the journal *Ethnomusicology* in 1978. At the time, Blum challenged ethnomusicologists to investigate the fascinating social, economic, and political aspects of salsa music. During the next two decades the literature on salsa (not all scholarly) grew significantly. This growth in the literature concentrated on the study of salsa in New York and focused primarily on issues of identity and origins of the music. The literature dealing with issues of music and identity recognized a strong union between salsa and Puerto Rican/Nuyorican identity (Cortéz 1976; Singer 1982; Padilla 1989; Cortéz, Falcón, Flores 1986; Den Tandt 1997), but the studies dealing with salsa origins and style stressed Cuban roots (Manuel 1985,1988, 1991, 1994; Boggs 1992; Salazar 1980; Roberts 1975, 1979).[4]

From the mid-1980s to the present the debate on the origins of salsa has been waged not only in scholarship, but also in casual conversations, interviews with musicians, newspaper and magazine articles, and any medium in which salsa is discussed. In order to justify their identification with salsa music, Puerto Ricans have felt a need to prove their contribution. Correspondingly, much debate in the popular press and academia has foregrounded the question of whether salsa is Cuban or Puerto Rican. A Puerto Rican perspective on this question has been presented by Félix M. Padilla in his 1990 article, "Salsa, Puerto Rican and Latino Music," by Catherine Den Tandt, "Caribbean Sounds: Cultural Identity in Puerto Rico" (1997), and by Lisa Sánchez González, "Reclaiming Salsa" (1999). Padilla (1990), who studies salsa lyrics, contends that salsa has been a vehicle for the advancement of Latino consciousness and that salsa is undeniably Puerto Rican music. Den Tandt also follows Padilla's contention that salsa signifies Puerto Rican identity but stresses that salsa is "authentically hybrid and thus Caribbean" (1997:107). Sánchez González rejects that salsa is strictly Afro-Cuban music "resignified" or solely "globalized commercial music." She "reclaims" salsa as "her" Puerto Rican music, a product of working-class people for whom salsa is "meaning and everyday experience" (1999:238–39).

In addition to differences in opinion about salsa's origins, different perspectives on the geography of salsa can be found in English-language and Spanish-language writings. Scholarship in English has primarily focused on the nexus of Cuban and Puerto Rican cultures in New York; this focus downplays the development of salsa music in other parts of the Caribbean and Latin America, and tends to reinforce the view that salsa is a reinterpretation of Cuban music.[5] New York–based studies include Blum's 1978 article, Roberta Singer's 1982 pioneer dissertation, "'My Music Is Who I Am and What I Do': Latin Popular Music and Identity in New York City," Felix Padilla's 1989 "Salsa Music as a Cultural Statement of Latino Conciousness"; Jeremy Marre's 1979 documentary *Salsa: Latin Music in the Cities* (see also Marre and Charleton 1985); Vernon Boggs's 1992 *Salsiology: Afro-Cuban Music and the Evolution of Salsa in New York*; Christopher Washburne's 1998 "Play It *Con Filin!*" The Swing and Statement of Salsa,"[6] and Peter Manuel's several articles in books and journals.[7] Frances Aparicio's (1998) *Listening to Salsa*, an excellent study of salsa, gender, and identity, and Angel Quintero Rivera's *Salsa, Sabor y Control* (1999), are significant exceptions to the emphasis on New York.

Peter Manuel has been one of the most consistent proponents of the Cuban-centered perspective of salsa music. His assertion regarding salsa style is that there is little variation in musical content that differentiates salsa from Cuban genres such as the son and guaracha. I will insist in the course of this article that what might first appear to be slight variations in salsa style, or "nuances," as Manuel prefers to call them, are significant qualitative distinctions. These variations are so important that the style of a salsa piece, although it might be reminiscent of Cuban or Puerto Rican music, is unique to salsa and cannot be easily classified as Cuban or Puerto Rican. While salsa is very significantly based in Cuban dance music, it has evolved into a new species thanks to what at its beginnings might have been considered slight variations on a Cuban model. Keil and Feld note that "'slight variations' become magical, hypnotizing, mesmerizing. They give you deep identification or participatory consciousness" (1994:23)—and I would add that they can become regarded, in time, as the essence of a new music, not "slight" at all but extremely significant.[8]

In the literature on salsa, remarkably little has been written on what constitutes salsa musical style. This is in part because a study of salsa style requires a musical proficiency and musicianship that many salsa scholars lack, particularly those who have approached salsa from a literary or cultural studies perspective. In concentrating on the musical sound and the various ways they are reshaped and re-presented, relative to Cuban music, one discovers a completely different world. This has been my experience. To play and to dance to the music give one an understanding of musical style that has not been well represented in scholarship.

FROM THE OLD *SON* TO THE NEW SALSA

In the 1960s Puerto Rican bandleader Tito Rodríguez updated the Cuban sound,[9] and other Puerto Rican musicians looked to their own country for new ideas to keep the music moving forward. They began mixing Cuban sounds with Puerto Rican genres, and experimenting with the harmonies and brass sonorities of the many New York jazz bands that Puerto Rican musicians had played in since World War I.[10] This experimentation transformed the Cuban son into its new sound, which became known as "salsa." The analogy to a spicy blend of flavors perfectly captured the excitement of the music—a stew of Caribbean rhythms, jazz harmonies, barrio life, and delicious dances cooked to perfection.

Venezuelan salsa historian César Miguel Rondón identifies Eddie Palmieri as one of the pivotal figures in the change from the old Latin sound[11] to what would become salsa:

The Palmierian [Eddie Palmieri] variation [La Perfecta with trombones] would be the one to determine all the later sound of salsa. Eddie arranged them [trombones] in a way that they always sounded sour, with a peculiarly aggressive harshness. Never did they correspond to the conventional functions established by the jazz bands; they, after all, were just a smaller session of only two trombones, and by no means could these [two] reproduce those sonoric buildings that the orchestras did in the "mambo" section. And this difference affected strongly the *melómano*'s ear: the music stopped being ostentatious to become wounded, there was no pomp but violence; the thing was most definitely different. (1980:25)

Eddie Palmieri's brother Charlie remembers what a novel and surprising sound Eddie came up with by integrating trombones into a charanga ensemble, which traditionally consisted of piano, violins, flute, and percussion.

My kid brother, Eddie Palmieri, is a nut. While playing piano with the Tito Rodríguez Band, Eddie decided to leave the financial security of one of the most successful Latin Bands around and formed his own band. The band business is rough enough, but Eddie made it even rougher for himself by going against the tide and instead of organizing a Charanga, the popular sound of the day, he organized what I call a "Trombanga," a band featuring trombones and flute. Novel? . . . yes. A fresh sound? . . . yes. Commercial possibilities? . . . a very big gamble. His gamble paid off though because his Band "La Perfecta" is one of the busiest working bands in New York City. (Charlie Palmieri, liner notes to Eddie Palmieri, *La Perfecta,* 1962)

In addition to changes in instrumentation (and other aspects of style and technique to be discussed later), Puerto Rican musicians from the 1950s onward fused increasingly diverse stylistic elements in their music, both by juxtaposing different pieces, or passages within a piece, and by blending or "syncretizing" different styles and rhythms. Rafael Cortijo and Ismael Rivera, who integrated the Afro–Puerto Rican genres of bomba and *plena* into a Cuban-style *conjunto* format, were perhaps the most pivotal innovators in this regard (Berríos-Miranda 1997, 1999). Other salsa groups, arrangers, and singers that have exploited this technique include El Gran Combo de Puerto Rico, Willie Colón, and Cheo Feliciano. Many of their songs incorporate melodic lines from the Puerto Rican *seis* and *aguinaldo* in the salsa repertoire.[12] These techniques of juxtaposition and syncretism, besides being innovative and just plain fun, enable identification with salsa music in two important ways: by acknowledging different Latin nationalities among their listeners, and by "indigenizing" or giving a local flavor to the salsa played in different countries. Listeners respond strongly to these connections between style and identity, even though the pieces in which they occur may be broadly classified with labels like "salsa" or "guaracha." In many interviews and conversations with Venezuelan musicians, it was clear that they regarded Puerto Rican salsa musicians as pioneers in this expansion of Cuban music to include many different Latin American genres in salsa.

In addition to this recognition of salsa's diversity and inclusiveness, however, Venezuelans also tend to think of salsa in general as a distinctive genre of music that has been created by Puerto Ricans and Nuyoricans. As percussionist Cheo Navarro describes it, this does not in any way negate the Cuban origins of the music.

> You see, this music comes from the displacement of all those people that were brought as slaves and stayed. Then this genre takes off from Cuba with the son, danzón, and then the ensembles. And then the artists who go to New York. But the ones to give this music this other sound were the Nuyoricans and the Puerto Ricans, do you understand? It was not the Mexicans or the Dominicans. I learned with the Nuyoricans. Then with time I learned they had copied it from the Cubans and the Cubans took it to New York and from there comes the relationship of Cubans and Puerto Ricans. But the Puerto Ricans came up with new arrangements and a new musical sound and they are the ones who created that salsa sound.[13]

Salsa musicians and enthusiasts enjoy talking about the music they love, almost as much as listening and dancing to it. Their conversations often center around the qualities that a good salsa musician has to cultivate: creativity, rhythmic virtuosity, mastery of polyrhythm, harmonic maña,[14] concentration, communication. The juice of salsa dialogues lies in the discussion of individual and group styles, and musicians and melómanos[15] derive a great deal of pleasure from talking about aesthetics. What is good salsa, for whom, and why?

RITMO, RHYTHMS, AND FEEL

In 1984 about 6:30 on a Friday evening in Puerto Rico, I had the good fortune to interview Eddie Palmieri, one of the greatest pianists, composers, and arrangers of salsa of all time. After explaining what I was doing and my interest in salsa I asked him what salsa was for him.

> This to me is my entire life, it's like religion, everything, like you want to say it, no? And there are the most complicated rhythmic patterns in the whole world. For thousands and thousands of years that come from Africa, arrive in Cuba, and in Cuba they make a variation, and from there come all these patterns that can never be equaled or extended.[16]

There it was, on my very first musical question, the answer related to the rhythm of the music. The first thing Palmieri wanted me to understand about salsa was that it was based on "the most complicated rhythmic patterns in the whole world."

Musicians often distinguish salsa from other kinds of music by its rhythm. Gerardo Rosales describes the distinctiveness of Puerto Rican/Nuyorican salsa in stylistic terms. This stylistic description and analysis of salsa music is of paramount importance in understanding what is Puerto Rican about salsa.

> In Puerto Rico there are orchestras that lock the rhythm.[17] A locked rhythm is a rhythm *afincao*. Willie Rosario is a guy who locks the rhythm. There nobody is inventing anything. He is not *metiendo palos*[18] where they don't belong, there is nothing extra or less. Willie goes there. He grants certain liberties to the *conguero* in the mambo. But, sincerely, to me what's going on in Puerto Rico is that Willie Rosario locked the rhythm and everybody else has followed that line. In Willie's orchestra everything works to support the singer and the *coro*. The *cascara* is closed (*cerrada*), the *campana* is *cerrada*, the timbal, *cerrado*, everything goes locked, *trancao*, *afincao*.[19]

When Gerardo Rosales refers to salsa as a rhythm it is important to understand that what he means is not one rhythm by itself but rather a composite of rhythms that result from the combination of "fixed rhythms." *Timbalero* Cheo Navarro is more specific in his analysis of what defines salsa rhythm:

> But the richness of the instrument is unique: timbal, conga and bongo . . . this is what identifies salsa; and of course the piano. And you hear a *tumbao* in the piano and it has nothing to do with symphonic music or anything like that, it has to be a delicious *montuno*, understand? A bongo, a *tumbadora* [conga drum], a timbal, it has its autochthonous [native] instruments.[20]

Notice also how Cheo refers to the instrument in singular. When Cheo says "the richness of *the instrument* is unique," I interpret him to mean that it is the quality of the combination of these three instruments that makes the salsa sound, not one instrument or rhythm in particular but the unity of the three playing their interlocking rhythmic patterns (as shown below in fig. 2.2). The almost unvarying rhythmic composite of these instruments all the way throughout the piece creates a distinctive rhythmic feel.[21] He says that when you have these three instruments playing those particular rhythms together it is nothing but salsa. To Cheo and other Venezuelans there is an important qualitative difference between how Cubans and Puerto Ricans play these instruments. Cubans play these instruments individually, "metiendo palos," while Puerto

Ricans and Nuyoricans play these instruments collectively as one, *suena a máquina, camión* (sounds like a machine, like a trailer, i.e., precise).

USES OF THE TERM "RITMO"

In conversations with musicians, the following four definitions/meanings of the term "ritmo" were most common: (a) individual rhythms; (b) genre; (c) the quality of the rhythmic ensemble; and (d) the differentiation of salsa styles associated with the variety of genres included in the salsa repertoire.

Individual Rhythms

Every musician in a salsa band has to master particular rhythmic patterns. Some of these patterns are idiomatic to one instrument, but they must still be understood by everyone in the band because salsa is a polyrhythmic music—that means that the different parts can interlock effectively only when each musician listens to the whole band and plays in the proper relationship to everyone else's parts. The most important individual rhythm in salsa music is the *clave*, played on a pair of wooden sticks by the same name. The clave is a time line that determines the rhythmic patterns and relationships of all the other instruments in the band. The two claves most commonly used in salsa are *son clave* and *rumba clave* (fig. 2.1). The clave rhythmic time line is often discussed in terms of how it relates to the downbeat as established by the melody and the harmony. A song is said to be in "3–2" clave or "2–3" clave, depending on the relationship of the clave pattern to the melodic or harmonic downbeat of a phrase.[22] All the other fixed rhythms (conga, piano, cowbell, etc.) and even the melody must be played in the proper relationship to the clave, so every member of the band has to understand the clave and adhere to it.[23] The example in fig. 2.2 shows the timbales, bongo, and conga parts lined up in their proper relationship to the son clave. The two piano parts (montuno or *guajeo*) show two different possibilities—they would not be played simultaneously. The first piano montuno established the harmonic downbeat on the "2 side" of the clave, creating a piece that is in "2–3" clave. The second piano montuno establishes the harmonic downbeat on the "3 side" of the clave, creating a piece that is in "3–2" clave.

Genre

In the Spanish Caribbean and Latin America the word *ritmo* is often synonymous with "genre" and also with the dance that accompanies that genre. The following quote from Cheo Navarro illustrates the interchangeable use of the terms *ritmo* [rhythm] and *género* [genre].

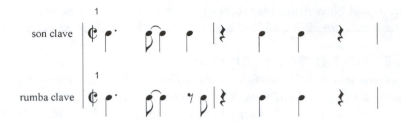

FIGURE 2.1 • *Son clave* and *rumba clave* (in 3-2 clave)

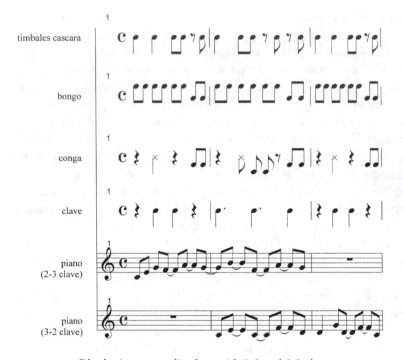

FIGURE 2.2 • Rhythmic patterns lined up with 2-3 and 3-2 clave

Within salsa there are a variety of *rhythms*, the guaracha, the son mon-tuno. What happens nowadays is that the young musicians do not know about the variety of *rhythms*, of *genres*, that are included in salsa. And they are calling everything salsa because they do not know how to distin-guish between the *rhythms*.[24]

Quality of Rhythmic Ensemble
Beyond the mastery of individual parts and their correct relationship to one another, and beyond what can be expressed in musical notation, the

term "ritmo" may refer to the quality of individual rhythms and the overall effect when these interlock. This quality is defined by timing, volume, timbre, and the manner of blending each individual rhythm with the other rhythms played simultaneously. The most talked about aspect of an instrumentalist, particularly a percussionist, is the ability to produce that desired rhythmic quality in these interactions, and musicians and melómanos use many colorful terms and metaphors for the quality of rhythmic interaction in salsa. *Afinque, guataca, trancao, apretao, sólido, pa' lante, mantecoso, camión,* for example, are some ways to describe good-sounding salsa. Of these terms, in Venezuela as well as in Puerto Rico, "afinque" is the most important, meaning everything in the band is "locked" to perfection. Rhythmic thinking is crucial for everyone, because both melodic and percussion instruments are approached like drums. So when musicians complain that the music is not *afincao* it means that if the rhythms are not locked together the music is not happening. The quality of the rhythmic ensemble, which ultimately involves everyone in the ensemble, is of utmost importance.

The following quotation is from one of my most exciting and challenging interviews. I talked for seven hours to Ismael Rivera's son Ismael Rivera Jr. and to one of Rivera Jr.'s best friends, Pedro "Capitol" Clemente, in my sister's house in Puerto Rico. One of the most exciting moments of this interview came about when both began to talk about the music of Ismael's father and the beauty and magic of the ensemble he played in for most of his life, Cortijo y su Combo con Ismael Rivera.

Ismael Jr.: This was the phenomenon of Cortijo y su Combo.

Capitol: In that combo half of the musicians did not read and the other half read very little, very little. Look, Elías tells me that one day he went to substitute for Tito Vélez [the band's arranger and trumpet player], and he thought that there were going to be papers. And when he got there he says, "Oh right, where are the papers?" "What papers, there are no papers here" [replied the whole band]. He said, "And when I heard those musicians and when those musicians counted to start, I said, "Oh man, what interpenetration, *que afinque. . .'"*

Ismael: Ithier did not read, Miguel Cruz did not read, no one in the percussion section read, Cortijo did not read, Ismael did not read. Tito Vélez was the arranger and had some serious musical deficiencies and lack of knowledge, terrible . . . but that didn't matter because those were some musicians with great hearts and a lot of guts. When they played they defined the word "afinque," regardless of their ability to read. That band sounds incredible.[25]

The term "afinque" implies rhythm control, solidity, flexibility, musicianship, virtuosity, awareness, connection, and *buen gusto* [good taste] when performing. When a band is qualified as *afincada,* it is the greatest possible compliment to its musicianship and performance excellence.

Alirio Pérez, one of the most talented pianists in the Caracas scene and former keyboard player for the famous Venezuelan group Guaco, uses a variety of these terms that refer to rhythmic ensemble in his comparison of the internationally known Fania All-Stars, Cuban groups in general, and Guaco:

> The Cubans have some great masters, but aside from Orquesta Aragón, which is a marvel, and the Sonora Matancera that sounds like a group, you listen to these new groups from Cuba and you can hear everything but everything is like too individualistic. You don't hear that solidity like that from Willie Rosario's orchestra that sounds like a machine. The Apollo Sound of Roberto Roena, [likewise]. The Apollo Sound was a totally clean orchestra. It was conga, timbal, and bongo, and nothing else. That [orchestra] didn't even have maracas or güiro. And it was an orchestra where everything sounded in its place and everything *acoplado, afincado.*
>
> This is like what happened to the Fania, which never sounded compact because they were a lot of stars. At the individual level each one trying to shine. On the other hand with Guaco that didn't happen because it was work from a group that was solid. When they got on to play it was just one brick, it was the *gandola*, the *camión*, like we used to call it. Yes, when we were playing like that, we felt that the thing sounded divine, "suena camión" [it sounds solid]. I have a pal in Maracaibo who was a drummer, not with Guaco, he used to say that it was *mantecoso* to mean that it sounded solid. [The only translation I can come up with for *mantecoso* is greasy, buttery, rich.]
>
> To play *apretao, afincao,* requires a lot of concentration and a great ability to listen to all other musicians in the band without going out of clave or of rhythm. The good sense of rhythm and time is mandatory for the band musicians.[26]

When talking about afinque almost everyone had something to say. But percussionist Gerardo Rosales was the most articulate:

MARISOL: Listen, Gerardo, you say *trancao*, I don't understand that term.

GERARDO: Oh, trancao . . . that is a closed rhythm for us.

MARISOL: But what does it mean? That everybody plays the same rhythmic pattern or that his rhythmic pattern is continuously repeated, or what?

GERARDO: That people [musicians] create a foundation. Here, for example, there are orquestras in Puerto Rico that play the rhythm closed. Willie Rosario is an individual who closes the rhythm. It is a rhythm trancao, afincao. There nobody invents anything, understand? Willie Rosario is not putting *palos* [beats] where they don't belong, it doesn't lack nor is there extra, Willie does it just right. So, for us a closed rhythm is what Willie Rosario plays. He allows certain liberties to who is playing the conga in the mambos, at the time of the mambo, they put something there.[27]

As we can see, in salsa music rhythm is extremely important. Rhythm is the driving force. Willie Rosario's "Que siga el afinque" is an excellent example of the "closed" sound—trancao, afincao—that Rosales refers to.[28] In this piece, the percussion parts are consistent and are unembellished except for the breaks.

Ritmo/Genre as a Marker of Regional/National Salsa Styles

Yet another use of the word "ritmo" is the differentiation of a variety of salsa styles that are associated with the rhythms of particular genres, also associated with particular countries, where these rhythms identify the unique salsa style of that particular country. For example, musicians talk about the Colombian rhythm, the Venezuelan rhythm, the Cuban rhythm and so on. This differentiation is based largely on a concept of core defining rhythms for each genre. For example, in Puerto Rico, plena is a genre musically defined by the combination of the basic two interlocking rhythmic patterns played on two framed hand drums. Just the sound of this rhythm is enough for many Latinos to identify the genre as a whole, even without hearing other elements of plena like the vocals and melodic instruments. Another example is the Venezuelan *gaita*, defined by the interlocking rhythmic patterns of three percussion instruments: the *furro* (drum), the *tamborera* (another drum), and the *charrasca* (a scraper). The Venezuelan gaita, like the Puerto Rican *plena*, has many other musical elements, but both genres are commonly identified by their rhythmic cells (fig. 2.3 illustrates the rhythmic cells of plena and gaita). And like these two genres there are many others—the Dominican merengue, the Colombian *cumbia*, the Cuban rumba and cha-cha-chá, and so forth and so on. The following quote from Alirio Pérez is representative of the way salsa musicians perceive the use of different *ritmos* in different styles of salsa.

Remember' what was happening with Guaco when I was not in the group is that they were in search of a group identity. Of course on the side of the gaita conservatives, they got all the bad-mouthing in the world: "you do not play gaita" "you do not play gaita," some people told them. When the thing with the *tamboreras* began, the tamboreras were played at ten thousand miles an hour, but when Guaco records "El Billetero" a little more slowly then it resembles the more salsified thing, then the conga

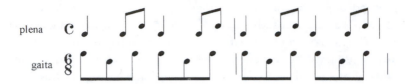

FIGURE 2.3 • Rhythmic cells of *plena* and *gaita*

with true salsa rhythm.[29] And then they add the timbal but then the timbal goes a little more *charangueao*, then there is the mix between tamborera with salsa and with charanga. Besides, there is no furro and the bass is playing a salsa tumbao and the piano is also playing a salsa tumbao as well. *But it is that mix of the sound of the tamboras with the rhythm of the conga in salsa and the rhythm of the timbal in charanga and a drum set that at the moment did not have its sound defined as a rhythm as such, that makes the Guaco sound.*[30] [emphasis mine]

This approach of defining the salsa style of a particular country in terms of a national genre is crucial to the understanding of the association of salsa with national identity. Again, the dialectic process of creation in salsa music depends both on salsa style for defining musical identity, and on musical identity to define salsa style. By using a symbol of the national culture to give a new sound to salsa, Venezuelans feel comfortable now in making salsa their own because they have made it different from the other salsa of other countries.

There are other ways in which a band might access its local musical repositories to give a unique national flavor to the salsa it produces. For example, many of the brass arrangements of El Gran Combo de Puerto Rico include typical phrases of the Puerto Rican seis and aguinaldo. The famous Colombian salsa band Grupo Niche incorporates the cumbia and the *porro* to give its salsa a tinge of its own. And many others in Latin America employ this practice. Thus, what gives salsa styles their unique flavor in different regions is the inclusion of musical elements of particular national repertoires: seis, aguinaldo, bomba, and plena from Puerto Rico, *joropo* and gaita from Venezuela, and cumbia and porro from Colombia. For musicians and fans the ability to distinguish between the different salsa styles is a highly valued knowledge. They feel quite proud to be able to make those fine distinctions.

> I can recognize where a particular style of salsa comes from. If it is from New York, or Puerto Rico, or Cuba or Colombia, just as I hear it I know where it is from. It is something about the phrasing in the singing and arranging and the combination of rhythms.[31]

The word "ritmo" signifies a world of musical meaning that is fundamental to understanding musics from the Caribbean and Latin America. I believe that some of the confusion about salsa's origins and ownership in the academic literature arises from a lack of understanding of the subtleties of this concept and its centrality to the perception of music. Rhythm is the aspect of salsa style that musicians and others are most attentive to and demanding about in their conversations. "Ritmo," in all the senses of the word discussed above, is an important marker of difference and distinctiveness in salsa, so an understanding of rhythm in all these senses is a prerequisite for discernment and criticism—for musicians, listeners, and scholars alike.

OTHER CRITERIA OF EVALUATION

The remainder of this article will be devoted to explaining various aspects of salsa that are important for differentiation of individual, regional, or historic styles and for the criticism and evaluation of salsa. I have chosen to discuss here the following concepts: clave, *fraseo*, *fuerza*, authenticity, use of different genres, breaks, and dance. This is not an exhaustive list, but they are categories that came up frequently in my interviews and conversations with musicians.

Clave

The proper application of the clave concept has been a theme of much debate and disagreement since the bands of the late '60s and '70s began to devise more elaborate arrangements of salsa pieces and more than one way to play the clave (Gerard 1989; Mauleón 1993). Nonetheless, some great percussionists, in my experience, tend to regard the clave as something that should not be applied with inflexible rules. Many of these musicians told me that a lot of great salsa music is *cruza'o* ("crossed," i.e., all rhythms are not properly lined up with the clave), but it still swings and it is still good. Other musicians argue that there are some musical pieces that demand a correct clave but others in which the choice of 3–2 or 2–3 clave is not so crucial. It is also argued by some that these strict laws of clave are used as a simple way to dismiss certain salsa groups without really paying attention to their music.

The concept of clave is sometimes applied, therefore, as a gauge for measuring the rhythmic competence of a band, or perhaps even a weapon by which musicians may question their rivals' competence. Because a band cannot have a harmonic arrangement that demands a 2–3 clave pattern and then play a 3–2 clave pattern throughout the piece, when musicians made this mistake other musicians who knew the correct way of playing the clave would call them *cruza'o*. In some cases whole groups or countries are called into question for their inability to understand and perform clave. Venezuelan salsa musicians, for example, are sensitive to accusations that they do not understand the clave properly. Percussionist Gerardo Rosales states it as follows:

> In the '70s people [in Venezuela] didn't know what a clave was. The first to play clave here were the people from San Agustín who did not understood it very well but could feel it. At that time a lot was recorded out of clave. But toward the end of the '70s and beginnings of the '80s, a conscience about the clave began to develop and groups like Mango by then played everything in clave. And the Trabuco Venezolano played in clave as well. People who had studied. Then the concept of clave began to be spread out to the people and the people began to learn. There was a rumor that the Venezuelan musician was not conscious of the clave. And it was true. In the '70s and '80s they played with the heart, with feeling. And it was also valuable not to know it [the concept of clave] because by not knowing about the clave they dared to do things that, for example, El Gran Combo did not do. Rafael Ithier [the Combo's arranger and pianist] couldn't do it [be out of clave] because he conceived of his arrangements in clave from top to bottom. But here there were some groups who knew nothing about clave, and they recorded incredible records, like Los Dementes. Those were some guys who knew nothing about clave, but they could play incredible. And they were only beginning.
>
> But I understand that the development of the Venezuelan musician in comparison with the Puerto Rican and the Nuyorican musician has been slower. But at the moment when the clave secret was discovered here we opened the pot. Here people began to produce some valuable stuff. Adrenalina Caribe is a group with a very personal sound. There were many orchestras, La Salsa Mayor, La Dimensión Latina, el Grupo Mango, el Grupo La Calle, who didn't record because that has been the disgrace of this country. There have been marvelous groups that have played for two or three years but they break up and don't leave a single recording. [And] the bad fame remained that the Venezuelan musicians had no consciousness of the clave. A lot of people used to say, no, that is a desert, those people know nothing. There were a lot of that type of commentaries from people from New York and Puerto Rico. . . . But with the years that got better.[32]

Those musicians who knew the correct usage of the clave gained a lot of prestige among their peers.

To be able to keep the correct clave throughout a salsa piece requires an absolutely solid understanding, intention, and appreciation of the many rhythmic patterns that are being played at once. Therefore the musicians who can play clave correctly are the best and most in demand. But great musicians have at one time or another lost the clave, and other musicians love to comment about those instances. According to several of my informants, not too many musicians have always played perfect clave. Others shared their mixed feelings about the tyrant clave. Charlie Peñalver, Oscar D'León's timbalero and bongo player, notes the following:[33]

MARISOL: But, do you have that concept of one [the downbeat] like the concept of clave, that even when you are not playing it you have it internalized?

CHARLIE: Sometimes it is very difficult for me. I tell you for example, that the tunes that are in 3 [3–2 clave] become very difficult.[34] [And while he plays the 3–2 clave I sing for him "Las caras lindas."][35]

MARISOL: And why is it so difficult?

CHARLIE: Because sometimes you feel that it changes from 3–2 to 2–3.

MARISOL: Do you know that I get the feeling that the clave changes in that song?

CHARLIE: No, it doesn't change, it is in 3–2 all the time. But the thing is that it is difficult to play in 3 because one has to have one's own tricks, and concentrate so hard that you don't even look to the sides. Concentrate so hard that everybody can break apart but you keep that feel, you play there. Because sometimes the harmony throws you out. What were we saying about "Las caras lindas" of Tite Curet Alonso?— that is in 3.

MARISOL: And how did you learn the clave?

CHARLIE: I remember very vividly that we were at a party and suddenly everybody was playing the clave. And I was hearing the thing, and some were saying that it was like this and others that it was like that. Then I began to do my rhythm, and I felt it right and kept playing it my way.

MARISOL: So that you began to play in clave before knowing the clave?

CHARLIE: Yes, I had a sense of the rhythm.

SHANNON DUDLEY: But it's not only a sense of rhythm but how these rhythms are combined and related?

CHARLIE: Yes, exactly. But something that happens with that Mr. [Ismael] Rivera is that he doesn't have a number that is not in 3 [3–2 clave], and it is something that I don't understand why.

MARISOL: Do you musicians discuss the clave among yourselves?

CHARLIE: Well, I try not to discuss this issue because it all depends on so many things and each one tries to fix it in a particular way in their own mind, understand. So that you have your way and others have their way, and almost everybody plays it [clave] well.

Fraseo and Soneo

The musician most able to express his or her music with total command and control of the rhythm is the most liked, admired, and emulated. This requires not only knowledge of the clave, afinque, and fuerza but the ability to phrase artfully. A case in point is the Puerto Rican singer Ismael Rivera. He is appreciated to the point of veneration because of his ability to *sonear* (improvise lyrics between coros) with extreme rhythmic complexity and master ability to displace the downbeat—reminiscent of jazz vocalist Billie Holiday—and impressive control of the rhymes. The tone of his voice is appreciated as well, but it is mostly his unique fraseo (phrasing) that defines his style. Part of an excerpt from Ismael's soneo in "El Nazareno" (from his 1974 album, *Traigo de todo*) is transcribed in Figure 2.4. Perhaps the most instructive aspect of this transcription is the fact that it cannot capture the rhythmic or melodic subtleties of Ismael's fraseo. Though hard to describe or notate, these subtleties are what distinguish him as a great *sonero*.

Fraseo is mostly associated with the singer but it can also refer to the way any melodic instrumentalist structures melodic lines rhythmically. Fraseo could be defined as the way a sonero connects pitches rhythmically to produce a beautiful rhythmic melody, how many or how few pitches a singer can insert within the beats, the way a singer uses the register, and his or her mastery in fitting in the melody rhythmically. This is what makes a sonero. Although a sonero has much more freedom to display phrasing abilities during the section in which improvisation occurs (the call-and-response section) these abilities are also noted in the verse section of the piece. Although "fraseo" has melodic implications (and melody is inseparable, of course, from rhythm), this word mainly refers to a rhythmic art. It is not necessarily how beautiful the melody is but rather how well the singer uses rhythm to enhance it. When salsa aficionados talk about masters of fraseo, the name of Ismael Rivera stands out above all others. He is referred to as the Sonero Mayor or Master Sonero.[36]

Fuerza and Authenticity

Another important requirement for a salsa band to sound good is what musicians call fuerza, or strength. Fuerza is closely related to afinque, in

Da - le pa - lan - te pa - lan - te pa - lan - te pa - lan - te pa - lan - te con

un e - le - fan - te Ma - e - lo no de - jes que te tum - ben el plan - te

FIGURE 2.4 • Phrase from "El Nazareno," Ismael Rivera (1974)

that to play strong and to sound strong musicians have to play totally in sync with each other. But what musicians mean by fuerza is more than rhythm; it also has to do with instrumentation and the way each performer approaches his instrument. Intonation and timbre are a part of fuerza. For example, Gerardo Rosales feels the strong sound of Eddie Palmieri's La Perfecta had to do with the particular sound of the trombones, which were not totally in tune and did not play totally clean. He calls that sound *rajao*, meaning a little rupture in the well temperedness of the sound of the trombone.

The concept of fuerza may also have connotations of value and authenticity, and is sometimes used to contrast the playing of barrio musicians with musicians having formal training. Many regard the salsa sound of the 1970s as the salsa sound par excellence; and musicians commonly discuss the "fuerza" of this music in terms of not only its sonic qualities but also a variety of social circumstances in the lives of the musicians who made it.

Intonation was one of the most fascinating aspects of salsa aesthetics that I encountered. I was surprised to learn how commonly salsa musicians associated "out-of-tuneness" with salsa authenticity, and how important a point of debate and disagreement this was. For example, Gerardo Rosales claims that salsa is not salsa unless the trombone plays a little bit out of tune.

Then I have formed some groups here with trombones, and they all sound symphonic, and they are excellent musicians. And I tell then, "Brother, split the sound of the trombone because we are playing a Palmieri number." And then they say, "How do you want it, like this, 'prrrrrrrrrrst'?" and make fun of me. And they play and I say, "Men, this is Palmieri's music, not Eddie Santiago." You understand? That is why I think that [some] Puerto Rican groups, for example, the trumpets are very good, but the trombones are too soft. And in recordings the trombones have too many effects, like echo. And they have very little sonic weight. I don't know if it is the arranging style or the recording studio, or the excellent technique of the musicians. Because they have a high technical level, but the trombones have very little strength.[37]

Gerardo's concept of fuerza is incompatible with conservatory musical values of intonation and timbre, or with the modern sounds of *salsa romántica*. (Salsa romántica and salsa erótica are modern salsa styles that many musicians disdain as commercialized and unimaginative.) Charlie Peñalver, on the other hand, is less mistrustful of "sophisticated" technique in salsa, and has played with modern-sounding bands that he thinks have fuerza. He argues that fuerza is not associated exclusively with bands that play in the '70s salsa style.

> MARISOL: One of the things that some musicians comment to me—for example, Gerardo tells me that one of the things that has weakened salsa is the very clean conservatory sound that bands have now, that everything sounds totally tuned and that there is none of the harshness of before— that harshness that gave salsa more strength. That what is happening with salsa romántica is the brass arrangements are a little more elaborated because the percussion is not so strong, there is not so much improvisation, or not at all. Can you comment on this?

> CHARLIE: No, I don't think so. Because not everything has to be out of tune. Because the fact that you have to play a strong note doesn't mean that you have to play it out of tune. I had a very strong experience in Europe that called me into reflection. One time we were playing some *batá* strokes and some *Culo e' puya* chants. And for this we were rehearsing and this friend listened to it. "Yeah, that work is really good, but the voices were out of tune" [commented the friend]. Then I said, "We play it this way because this is the way they play it back home." And he tells me, "Yes, that is the way they play back home, but you are on a stage, and tuning is tuning, and you are a musician." And I had to pick up my face from the floor. I was so ashamed, because he hit me in the right spot. That is the truth. I could be playing music of wherever but tuning is tuning and it has to be clean.

> MARISOL: So for you well-tempered tuning doesn't take away from the sound of the band that plays strong salsa?

> CHARLIE: No. Things have to be tight. And as a matter of fact you have the proof in the tape you have. We are playing *pa'lante* (strong, forward, with momentum) and that sounds really tight. It's good that you listen to it like that without the harmony, so you can see [hear] the parts that are so tight. Because sometimes, with the fun one is having playing, you put some loose hits here and there, but that doesn't necessarily have to happen.[38]

Pure and authentic sound for Gerardo has to do not with a clean, well-tempered sound but with broken sound that is a little out of tune on the part of the trombone. I perceive in Gerardo's tone of voice a longing (*añoranza*) for a more traditional salsa sound, a more "classic salsa sound" as he calls it, the one that produced the original players and the one that gave the stylistic stamp to salsa. But for Charlie salsa does not have to be the same as it was in the 1960s and 1970s. He strongly believes that a well-tempered sound does not necessarily compromise authenticity in salsa. Charlie believes that change is a good thing, and it is precisely the thing that keeps the music alive. Whereas for Gerardo changing the sound of salsa means a loss of fuerza, to Charlie it means development and growth within the salsa idiom.

I gathered from comments of other musicians that older salsa musicians tend to prefer the older *desafinado* (out-of-tune) sound while the younger ones are more accepting of the more polished conservatory sound. It is also important to note that many musicians who like the more polished, well-tempered sound were conservatory-trained, whereas the older ones learned their chops by listening to records and observing live performances.

Importance of Breaks

Rhythmic unison and punch, and a dramatic interruption of the groove creates a heightened sense of excitement for the dancer and listener. Since most breaks involve short and continued rhythmic units separated by very short silences it is very important to have everybody sounding in sync. Younger musicians particularly enjoy this technique because of the energy and drive it generates, as explained by percussionist Charles Peñalver:

> Within the percussion the breaks and other forms of playing create that rich sound, as if the time was suspended for a second and returns to the afinque immediately. . . . The theme gets tight and [he sings the percussion parts more syncopated] the bongo is doing something different [than the rhythms already known], and these are things that musicians invent depending on the melody. . . . And these things didn't happen before [at least in Caracas] this ways of improvising with the percussion, the breaks that before were not done. But now all these things are *returning* and [musicians] do a lot of breaks. That to play a set with Manuel Guerra or Oscar D'León one has to give it all.

As Charlie expressed, breaks give one that sense of the time stopping for one second and then returning with all its force. This is especially challenging if one thinks that all bandleaders count to start a piece. When these breaks happen, the concept of flowing with the music has to be perfectly ingrained in the musicians, for they all have to begin and stop at the same time and in a split second. This is why to play challenging breaks effectively is a measure of a band's musicianship. Eddie Palmieri is one of the greatest masters of the break. He has set new standards with his intricate brass arrangements, with punching, solid breaks that are not only a challenge to the performers but to the listeners and dancers as well. Eddie Palmieri's "Óyelo que te conviene" (from *Unfinished Masterpiece*) is a great example of a series of dramatic breaks. Breaks are a great musical tool for building tension, climax, and release.

Dance

The one link among all aspects of salsa that I have yet to discuss is dance. It is through dancing that people experience salsa as "their" music in the most powerful way. Dancing is the ultimate test of whether or not the music has afinque or fuerza. Venezuelan percussionist Miguel Urbina makes the point very simple: the salsa that people like is the salsa that is good for dancing:

> At the time I listened I was not so conscious of why these orchestras were so much liked. But now that I have more knowledge I think it is because several things that *all [these] orchestras took seriously into consideration, and it was the dancer. The dancer was the most important thing.* So that the dancer could play around the tempo of the [musical] arrangements and manage them with great facility. . . . And, of course, the most important link for the preference for the music was that it had to be good for dancing.[39]

I have observed and noticed myself that the dance styles of Puerto Ricans, Colombians, Cubans, and Venezuelans all vary. For example, while observing people from Cali, Colombia, dance to salsa I noticed a little jump in the way they dance. After observation of the cumbia dance, I realized that the jump comes directly from the way Colombians dance the cumbia, Colombia's national dance. During my stay in Venezuela, I also noticed that people danced differently from the way I, a Puerto Rican, do; but I could not so easily point at the source of the difference as I could with the Colombians. Eventually, after observing Afro-Venezuelan dancers from the Barlovento region I established some similarities in the way Venezuelans dance salsa and the way they dance Afro-Venezuelan music. Dancing parallels music making in the sense that it is localized or domesticated—although there is a common basic step in the salsa dance, there is quite a lot of variety in how people from different nations and regions interpret this step. Both dance and musical interpretation may therefore include markers of a national or local character, which further enable people in different Latin countries to regard this music as their own.

Whether we choose to define salsa as a genre, a rhythm, or a style, it is clear from the many opinions and explanations cited above that salsa is perceived as having unique characteristics that distinguish it from other kinds of music. The terminology of this discourse, shared by musicians and fans all over Latin America, is part of what defines salsa's standing as a category of music unto itself, even as it incorporates regional idioms and undergoes creative innovation. In regard to Puerto Rican cultural identity, Venezuelan opinion would seem to affirm the pride that Puerto Ricans take from their role in the development of salsa. From the Venezuelan point of view Puerto Ricans are regarded not only as disseminators of salsa, but as creators and innovators as well. Rafael Cortijo and Ismael Rivera, Eddie Palmieri, Willie Rosario, and other Puerto Rican musicians are regarded in Venezuela as great musicians and role models. The politics of salsa labeling should not be allowed to overshadow the contributions of these great artists.

Que siga el afinque!

NOTES

The epigraph is taken from comments by Gerardo Rosales in a personal communication, February 5, 1994. All quotes in this essay were originally in Spanish, and all translations are mine.

1. I am indebted to my husband, Shannon Dudley, for his insightful ideas and meticulous editing.
2. Cheo Navarro, personal communication, June 10, 1994.
3. Webster's Encyclopedic Unabridged Dictionary of the English Language (New York: Random House, 1996), p. 797 ("genre"), p. 1890 ("style").
4. Rafael Figueroa (1992) put together a comprehensive bibliographical guide on salsa and related genres. It includes most references on salsa available up to 1992. To my knowledge this is the only bibliography on salsa.
5. The 1990s have spurred a wealth of salsa scholarship, which I believe is a result of the underlying question "Is Salsa Cuban or Puerto Rican?" Although this question may not be the primary focus of the following articles, it is a recurrent thread. Mayra Santos Febres in her article "Salsa as Translocation" proposes that "Puertorricanness is not the dominant signifier in salsa . . . peoplesness is" (1997:179), but it signifies Puerto Rican identity nonetheless. Juan Carlos Quintero Herencia (1997) reinforces the concept of salsa as barrio/people's music. Both base their studies in salsa lyrics and do not include musical analysis.
6. Washburne studies the concept of playing *con filin* relating the need of a deep understanding of salsa music before this *filin* is achieved. He situates himself as an insider because he plays trombone with salsa bands. But as he himself states, even at times when he thought he understood the music to the point to play it with *filin*, the

director of the band demanded a deeper understanding. Washburne includes musical analysis in his essay.

7. Other important articles that also focus on New York and Puerto Rico but that are written in Spanish are José Arteaga Rodríguez's "Salsa y violencia: una aproximación sónoro-histórica" (1988); and Tite Curet Alonso's "Un panorama de la música popular en Puerto Rico a partir de los años 30" (1987). Jorge Duany's "Toward an Anthropology of Salsa" (1984) defines salsa as "the music of the Puerto Rican proletariat." Duany takes the opposite view of Peter Manuel, who insists on the exclusively Cuban origins of the music.

8. It is highly interesting to me that upon the publication of the Human Genome Project scholars discussing it pointed out that humans are 99.9 percent identical, and that only 0.1 percent accounts for all the visible differences among humans. I like to use this information as an analogy to my insistence that minuscule differences in salsa account for the great variety of salsa styles.

9. See "Mango del monte" in *Tito Rodríguez and His Orchestra Back Home in Puerto Rico* (Palladium Records PCD 147).

10. In 1917 jazz bandleader James Reese Europe visited Puerto Rico and recruited several musicians for his newly created U.S. Military Band. Among these were foremost Puerto Rican composer Rafael Hernández and his brother Jesus (see Glasser 1995).

11. The "old Latin sound" refers to the sound of Latin orchestras like Billo's Caracas Boys, the Orquesta of Cesar Concepción, the Sonora Matancera, Orquesta Casino La Playa, and Orquesta Aragón, among others. These orchestras had more weight put into the melodic and harmonic aspects of the songs, while the new salsa sound emphasized the rhythmic aspect. Also these orchestras were much larger than the new salsa bands.

12. Listen, for example, to "Lírica borinqueña" by El Gran Combo (1986), *El Gran Combo de Puerto Rico y su pueblo* (Combo 2048); "Mapeyé" by Cheo Feliciano (1973), *Felicidade* (Vaya Records 23); and "Abuelita" by Willie Colón (1971), *La gran fuga* (Fania 394), to name but a few. Other examples by these artists are included in the discography at the end of this chapter.

Seis is the most Spanish of the Puerto Rican traditional genres. It originated in the central mountains of Puerto Rico, and its often called *jíbaro* music, created by rural people to use for entertainment and dance. There are many types of seises that correspond to choreography, locale, and particular musicians with whom they are associated. It is a song that often uses a *décima* (ten-line) verse which is improvised and is accompanied by the Spanish guitar, the Puerto Rican cuatro, the Indian güiro (gourd), and Afro-Cuban bongos. Through the years *cuatristas* (cuatro players) have produced beautiful melodic phrases that have become repositories in the traditional repertoire often quoted by musicians in a variety of musical contexts (often in salsa music) to evoke Puertorricanness. *Aguinaldo* is a secular religious song accompanied by guitar and cuatro, sung mostly during the Christmas season. Its melodies are also used to evoke Puertorricanness by salsa bands.

13. Personal communication, June 10, 1994.

14. *Maña* refers to craftiness when creating exciting harmonies that work.

15. Melómano is the name by which Venezuelans identify music enthusiasts and salsa experts. The Velázquez Spanish-English Dictionary, 1967 edition, defines it as a person "excessively fond of music." (Mariano Velázquez de la Cadena with Edward Gray and Juan L. Iribas, 1967, A New Pronouncing Dictionary of the Spanish and English Languages, p. 435.)

16. Personal communication, January 13, 1984.

17. When I presented an earlier version of this material (1997), bassist Andy González,

who was present at the time, made the observation that what Gerardo Rosales attributes to Willie Rosario—that is, the locked rhythm, his *afinque*—is in fact the sound that Tito Rodríguez and Machito had produced before him. He insisted that "Mr. Afinque," as Willie Rosario is known popularly, has that sound because he studied it from Tito Rodríguez and Machito. I listened to the three musicians again to better appreciate Andy González's comment, but came to the conclusion that, although there is similarity between the three, Willie's sound is not the same as Tito Rodríguez's or Machito's. The difference consists in the organization of the sound of the conga, bongo, and timbales, which in Tito Rodríguez's orchestra is looser and does not have them playing the same rhythms consistently.

18. *Metiendo palos* refers to the improvisation of accents and rhythms by the percussionist in a piece, usually the conguero, *bongosero*, or *timbalero*. Gerardo Rosales understands this as a salient characteristic of Cuban percussionists and identifies it as a major stylistic difference between Puerto Rican and Cuban percussionists.

19. Personal communication, February 5, 1994.

20. Personal communication, June 10, 1994.

21. For a detailed discussion of this concept of "rhythmic feel," see Dudley 1996.

22. This concept of 3–2 or 2–3 clave was something I never heard growing up in Puerto Rico. My husband, Shannon Dudley, has also observed in his studies of West African drumming with C. K. Ladzepko that the time line is considered to provide a constant beginning and ending of the metric cycle, whereas songs may be conceived to come in at the beginning of the time line or in the middle. By contrast, in some people's conception of salsa, at least, the harmonic/melodic "downbeat" seems to have become the more important point of metrical orientation.

23. Rebeca Mauleón's book is an excellent prescriptive manual for those who want to learn how to play the rhythms and rhythmic variations of the variety of "feels" in the salsa repertoire. She includes the basic rhythms of, for example, the conga, and also full rhythmic scores layering out the rhythms of other instruments (Mauleón 1993).

24. Personal communication, June 10, 1994.

25. Ismael Rivera Jr. and Pedro "Capitol" Clemete, personal communication, October 18, 1993. Listen for example to *Quítate de la vía perico* (Rumba Records 55548, n.d.), *Bienvenido Cortijo y Rivera* (Tico 1140, n.d.), *Baile con Cortijo y su Combo* (Seeco 9130, n.d.), and *Rolando La' Serie—Cortijo—Ismael Rivera: Danger Do Not Trespass* (Rumba 55552, n.d.)

26. Personal communication, July 20, 1994.

27. Personal communication, February 5, 1994. This is an example where musical notation—a transcription—won't help. One has to listen to get it.

28. Willie Rosario (1999), *Back to the Future* (J & N Records JNK 8345).

29. "El Billetero," by Guaco (1997), *32 Grandes éxitos* (Rodven/Pologram 539554).

30. Personal communication, July 20, 1994.

31. Charlie Peñalver, personal communication, May 22, 1994.

32. Personal communication, February 5, 1994.

33. Personal communciation, May 22, 1994.

34. Much of the Latin dance repertoire before the '70s was in 3–2 clave, whereas salsa during the '70s and afterward used 2–3 clave more often. For some musicians who grew up listening to mostly the 2–3 clave pattern, arrangements using the original 3–2 clave pattern are more difficult to play.

35. [Editor's note: "Las Caras Lindas" was written by Tite Curet Alonso (see chapter 8), and made famous by Ismael Rivera on his 1978 album, *Este si es lo mío*.]

36. My mother recalls that in the 1960s the great Cuban singer and *sonero* Benny Moré

visited the island of Puerto Rico and heard Ismael Rivera sing. He was so impressed by Ismael's phrasing virtuosity that he baptized him "el Sonero Mayor," the nickname by which Ismael is known internationally.

37. Personal communication, February 5, 1994.
38. Personal communication, May 22, 1994.
39. Personal communication, June 17, 1994.

BIBLIOGRAPHY

Aparicio, Frances R. 1998. *Listening to Salsa: Gender, Latin Popular Music and Puerto Rican Cultures.* Hanover, N.H.: Wesleyan University Press/University of New England Press.

Arteaga Rodriguez, Jose. 1988. "Salsa y violencia: una aproximación sonoro-histórica." *Revista Musical Puertorriqueña* 4:20–33.

Averill, Gage. 1997. *A Day for the Hunter, a Day for the Prey: Popular Music and Power in Haiti.* Chicago: University of Chicago Press.

Berríos-Miranda, Marisol. 1990. "Salsa: Whose Music Is It?" Paper presented at Society for Ethnomusicology annual meeting, Oakland, California.

———. 1997. "Con Sabor a Puerto Rico: The Influence and Reception of Puerto Rican Salsa in Venezuela." Paper presented at the Rhythms of Culture conference, Ann Arbor, Michigan.

———. 1999. "The Significance of Salsa Music to National and Pan-Latino Identity." Ph.D. dissertation, University of California at Berkeley.

Blum, Joseph. 1978. "Problems of Salsa Research." *Ethnomusicology* 22(1): 137–49.

Boggs, Vernon, ed. 1992. *Salsiology: Afro-Cuban Music and the Evolution of Salsa in New York City.* Westport, Conn.: Greenwood.

Cortez, Felix, Angel Falcón, and Juan Flores. 1976. "The Cultural Expressions of Puerto Ricans in New York: A Theoretical Perspective and Critical Review." *Latin American Perspectives* 10:152–70.

Curet Alonso, Tite. 1987. "Una panorama de la música popular en Puerto Rico a partir de los años 30." *Revista Musical Puertorriqueña* 1:14–19.

Den Tandt, Catherine. 1997. "Caribbean Sounds: Salsa and Cultural Identity in Puerto Rico." *Latin American Postmodernisms*: 103–17.

Duany, Jorge. 1984. "Popular Music in Puerto Rico: Toward an Anthropology of Salsa." *Latin American Music Review* 5(2):186–207.

Dudley, Shannon. 1996. "Judging by the Beat: Calypso vs. Soca." *Ethnomusicology* 40(2):269–98.

Figueroa, Rafael. 1992. *Salsa and Related Genres: A Bibliographic Guide.* Westport, Conn.: Greenwood.

Gerard, Charley. 1989. *Salsa!: The Rhythm of Latin Music.* Crown Point, Ind.: White Cliffs.

Glasser, Ruth. 1995 *My Music Is My Flag: Puerto Rican Musicians and Their New York Communities, 1917–1940.* Berkeley: University of California Press.

Guilbault, Jocelyne. 1993. *Zouk: World Music in the West Indies.* Chicago: University of Chicago Press.

Keil, Charles, and Steven Feld. 1994. *Music Grooves: Essays and Dialogues.* Chicago: University of Chicago Press.

Manuel, Peter. 1985. "The Anticipated Bass in Cuban Popular Music." *Latin American Music Review* 6(2):249–61.

———. 1988. *Popular Music of the Non-Western World: An Introductory Survey.* New York: Oxford University Press.

———. 1991. "Latin Music in the United States: Salsa and the Mass Media." *Journal of Communication* 41: 104–16.

————. 1994. "Puerto Rican Music and Cultural Identity: Creative Appropriation of Cuban Sources from Danza to Salsa." *Ethnomusicology* 38(2):249–80.

Marre, Jeremy. 1979. *Salsa: Latin Music of New York and Puerto Rico*. Harcourt Films, distributed by Shanachie.

Marre, Jeremy and Hannah Charleton. 1985. "Salsa: Latin Pop Music in the Cities." In *Beats of the Heart: Popular Music of the World*. New York: Pantheon, pp. 70–83.

Mauleón, Rebeca. 1993. *Salsa Guidebook for Piano and Ensemble*. Petaluma, Calif.: Sher Music.

Padilla, Félix. 1989. "Salsa Music as a Cultural Expression of Latino Consciousness and Unity." *Hispanic Journal of Behavioral Sciences* 2(1):28–45.

————. 1990. "Salsa, Puerto Rican and Latino Music." *Journal of Popular Culture* 24(1): 87–104.

Quintero Herencia, Juan Carlos. 1997. "Notes toward a Reading of Salsa." In Celeste Fraser Delgado and José Esteban Muñoz, eds., *Everynight Life: Culture and Dance in Latin/o America*. Durham, N.C.: Duke University Press, pp. 189–222.

Quintero Rivera, Ángel. *¡Salsa, sabor y control! Sociología de la música "tropical."* Mexico City: Siglo Ventiuno Editores.

Roberts, John Storm. 1975. *Salsa! The Latin Dimension in Popular Music*. New York: BMI.

————. 1979. *The Latin Tinge: The Impact of Latin American Music in the United States*. New York: Oxford University Press. Reprinted 1991.

Rodriguez, Clara E., Virginia Sanchez-Korrol, and Jose Oscar Alers, eds. 1980. *The Puerto Rican Struggle*. New York: Puerto Rican Migration Research Consortium.

Rondón, César Miguel. 1980. *El libro de la salsa: Crónica de la música del Caribe urbano*. Caracas: Editorial Arte.

Salazar, Max. 1980. "Latin Music: The Perseverance of a Culture." In Clara E. Rodriguez, Virginia Sanchez-Korrol, and José Oscar Alers, eds. *The Puerto Rican Struggle*, pp. 74–81.

Sánchez-González, Lisa. 1999. "Reclaiming Salsa." *Cultural Studies* 13(2):237–50.

Santos Febres, Mayra. 1997. "Salsa as Translocation." In Celeste Fraser Delgado and José Esteban Muñoz, eds. *Everynight Life: Culture and Dance in Latin/o America*. Durham, N.C.: Duke University Press, pp. 175–88.

Singer, Roberta Louise. 1982. "'My Music Is Who I Am and What I Do': Latin Popular Music and Identity in New York City." Ph.D. dissertation, Indiana University.

Turino, Tom. 1999. "Signs of Imagination, Identity, and Experience: A Peircian Semiotic Theory for Music." *Ethnomusicology* 43(2):221–55.

Washburne, Christopher. 1998. "Play It *Con Filin*! The Swing and Expression of Salsa." *Latin American Music Review* 19(2):160–85.

Discography

Colón, Willie. 1971. *La Gran Fuga*. (Fania 394.)

————. 1972. *El Juicio*. (Fania 424.)

————. 1991. *El Malo*. (Fania 337.)

————, and Rubén Blades 1978. *Siembra* (Fania 537.)

Cortijo, Rafael, and Ismael Rivera. n.d. *Quítate de la Via Perico*. (Rumba 55548.)

————. N.d. *Bienvenido Cortijo y Rivera*. (Tico 1140.)

————. N.d. *Baile con Cortijo y su Combo*. (Seeco 9130.)

————. N.d. *Rolando La' Serie-Cortijo—Ismael Rivera: Danger Do Not Trespass*. (Rumba 55552.)

Estefan, Gloria. 1993. *Mi Tierra*. (Sony 53807.)

Feliciano, Cheo. 1973. *Felicidades*. (Vaya Records VS 23.)

El Gran Combo. 1986. *El Gran Combo de Puerto Rico y su Pueblo*. (Combo 2048.)

————. 1992. *30 Aniversario: Bailando con el mundo.* (Combo 2091.)

Grupo Guaco. 1997. *32 Grandes Exitos.* (Rodven/Polygram 539554.)

Palmieri, Eddie. 1962. *La Perfecta.* (Alegre 8170.)

————. 1975. *Unfinished Masterpiece.* (Musical Productions MP-3120.)

Rivera, Ismael y sus Cachimbos. 1974. *Traigo de Todo.* (Tico 1319.)

————. 1978. *Esto Si Es Lo Mío.* (Tico 1428.)

Rodríguez, Tito. 1989 re-release. *Tito Rodríguez and His Orchestra Back Home in Puerto Rico.* (Palladium Records PCD 147.)

Rosario, Willie. 1999. *Back to the Future.* (J &N Records JNK 83435.)

Chapter 3

SALSA AND SOCIALISM: DANCE MUSIC IN CUBA, 1959-99

Robin Moore

The first of this essay's three sections outlines some of the ways that socialist policy has affected Cuban dance music performance since 1959. I discuss early decisions by revolutionary leaders affecting musical activity, a gradual trend toward the politicization of music making in the mid 1960s, changing forms of socialist pedagogy, and I mention a few representative groups of the 1970s and 1980s. The second section considers the musical and extramusical differences between Latino dance music in New York and Havana, and the controversies that the salsa phenomenon has generated within Cuba. The third describes the rapid changes that the Cuban music industry has experienced since the fall of the Soviet Union. After examining the effects of this political crisis on Cuban society, I focus on the decision of government officials to aggressively license Cuban music internationally and to promote increased tourism as a means of expanding the economy, and the impact of these changes on dance musicians. I also document how composers have discussed the realities of present-day Cuba.

Sources for the project include written material from Cuban nationals, the exile community, and academics, as well as interviews. Essays like this one involving history from the socialist period are problematic for various reasons. One is that all books and articles printed within Cuba are issued by government agencies that control their content. It is therefore difficult to evaluate their accuracy or objectivity. A second is that people interviewed on the island are often reluctant to speak openly with researchers about issues that could be construed as critical of the government. A third is that even much of the academic literature about

Cuba from abroad is extremely polarized, either unrealistically support-ive or critical of recent policies, and is often not based upon extended fieldwork in the country. A fourth is that socialism has so fundamentally altered social and cultural life that to provide a thorough background for this analysis would require an extended essay of its own. For all of these reasons, the material presented here should be considered intro-ductory.

SOCIALISM AND THE ARTS: AN OVERVIEW

Cultural production in socialist Cuba is a complicated topic and is diffi-cult to evaluate in general terms. Many wonderful programs have devel-oped in Cuba since 1959 related to filmmaking, publishing, recording, and artistic education that have achieved international acclaim. In gen-eral, the socialist government has been highly supportive of the arts, and Cuba continues to be a country known for exceptional musicians. The gains of the revolution in this sense contrast starkly with heavy-handed campaigns of ideological surveillance during particular periods, censor-ship and, in some cases, the repudiation and/or forced exile of artists.

Whether condoned or condemned, all Cuban artistic expression tends to be subject to stringent regulation by the government. Communist Party members have strong views about what national cul-ture should be and how the country should represent itself through the arts; they constantly examine and redefine the parameters of "national heritage" in accordance with contemporary political discourse. In coun-tries such as Cuba, which centralize control of the mass media and allow only officially sanctioned works to air on radio or television, or to be recorded, such policies have an immediate, real impact on the lives of the population.

Various phases are evident in the development of Cuban cultural policy under socialism (Vélez 1996 II:269). The early to mid-1960s was a time of tremendous exuberance and innovation for most citizens. Freedom of expression was relatively unrestrained, and the government enjoyed the support of an overwhelming majority of intellectuals at home and abroad. The later '60s and the '70s, by contrast, represent a repressive period, giving rise to ideological internment camps, the black-listing of writers critical in any way of party policy, and, in extreme cases, extended imprisonment. The period from 1975 to the present has witnessed a gradual trend toward liberalization, initially under Minister of Culture Armando Hart and later Abel Prieto. Significant restraints on artistic freedom remain, however, both in terms of the kinds of expres-sion supported by the state and their ideological content. Any critique of limitations on musical expression must begin by recognizing constraints imposed on all forms of art and culture, and the extent to which the history of salsa music represents part of a broader pattern.

DANCE MUSIC IN THE EARLY YEARS OF THE REVOLUTION

Socialist leaders stated from their earliest days in power that culture and the arts represented a priority for their leadership. Castro, for instance, stated emphatically in his famous "Words to the Intellectuals" speech that "one of the fundamental aims of the revolution is to develop art and culture, precisely in order that [they] become a true part of the people's heritage and legacy" (Castro 1961:12).[1] Only months after the exile of Batista, he and others began creating new cultural organizations (Chijona 1982:219). They founded the Teatro Nacional (National Theater) on June 12, 1959, which under Argeliers León's guidance became an early venue for the valorization and investigation of traditional music (Leal 1982:234). Moncada revolutionary Haydé Santamaría herself initially took charge of the Casa de las Américas (Americas House) after its creation in July of the same year (Gramatges 1982:133). This institution too developed into an important center for national and international music performance, literary publications, conferences, and the sponsorship of arts festivals. By 1961 a national arts school (ENA) had been established for the training of musicians, dancers, visual artists, and others (Ministerio de Cultura 1982:72, 75). By 1962 the government was sponsoring festivals of popular music on a national scale. The initial event, held in the Teatro Amadeo Roldán and in the Ciudad Deportiva of Havana, is said to have drawn more than thirteen hundred participants, including the dance bands of Benny Moré, Enrique Jorrín, the Septeto Nacional, the Conjunto Chappotín, and the Orquesta Aragón (Urfé 1982:166).[2]

The creation of particular institutions to promote musical activity represents only a small part of larger governmental processes involving the centralization and regulation of virtually all cultural expression. The founding of the National Culture Advisory in January of 1961, and later a Ministry of Culture, demonstrates this overall trend. Both had as an initial goal the fusion of once privately controlled establishments related to the arts into monolithic state enterprises. As early as September of 1960, the government nationalized all radio stations including the influential CMQ, along with three hundred other large businesses including banks, cigar factories, and foreign companies such as Shell, Ford, and RCA Victor (Díaz Ayala 1981:271).

Fundamental political changes during this period quickly began to impact the lives of individual musicians. Foreign travel became more difficult after about 1961 as political relations with the capitalist world worsened. By the mid-1960s, travel abroad was virtually impossible without the express authorization of the government. Copyright and composer royalties were abolished at about the same time, slashing the incomes of high-profile artists and reducing their financial incentive to compose and publish nationally (Díaz Ayala 1981:279). Not until the mid-1970s did party officials reestablish this sort of compensation. The large casinos and cabarets on the island in which many dance bands performed represented, to Castro and his followers, the worst of capitalist excess. As a result, the party outlawed gambling entirely and forced many establishments to shut down as early as October of 1959. These included the Sans Souci and Río Club as well as major hotels known for their casinos, such as the Montmartre and Hotel Nacional. Others like the famous Tropicana as well as cabarets within the Capri and Havana Hilton hotels remained open but under the direct control of the government (Díaz Ayala 1981:268–69). Many smaller cabarets and clubs were allowed to exist as owner-controlled businesses through approximately 1966, at which time the government nationalized all forms of private enterprise.

The government faced a dilemma related to its policy toward the large cabarets. On the one hand, they were for the most part institutions catering to the middle classes and wealthy foreigners. They were often racially segregated, and the entertainment they provided was apolitical in the extreme and viewed as escapist. For all of these reasons, party officials considered them to be undesirable. On the other hand, the Cuban public loved music and dancing, was enamored of its performing artists, and had come to expect television shows, specialized magazines, and other forms of media that featured them. Severe policies that threatened the entire entertainment industry could potentially anger the public and foster a negative image of the revolution. It is perhaps for this reason that officials adopted a somewhat cautious approach to the regulation of dance entertainment in the early years of the revolution.

Well-known dance ensembles performing in Cuba during the early 1960s include *charanga* bands (the Orquesta Aragón, the Orquesta América, Las Estrellas Cubanas, the Orquesta Revé), more traditional *conjunto*-based *son* groups (the newly reformed and state-supported Septeto Nacional directed by Rafael Ortiz, the ensembles of artists like Miguelito Cuní, Félix Chappotín, and *tresero* Niño Rivero), and of course the jazz-influenced *banda gigante* of Benny Moré. In the rarefied political environment of the 1960s, fun-loving dance music continued to receive support and airplay within the state-controlled mass media. Increasingly, however, the directors of radio and television stations called upon performers to openly express their sympathies with socialist issues both through their lyrics and verbally during live performances. It became difficult for a neutral figure unassociated with the Communist Party or with political issues of the moment to remain a viable entertainer.

> The State monopolized all cultural initiatives and became the sole sponsor, promoter, manager, and deployer of [policy], emphasizing and encouraging certain aspects and values of traditional culture while reforming those that were considered to undermine . . . [socialist agendas]. Artists were expected to work in and for the revolution, frequently sacrificing artistic freedom in order to achieve more pressing revolutionary goals. (Vélez 1996 II:68)

Pressures brought to bear by party officials on performers to politicize musical presentations, combined with attempts to standardize performer salaries, led to an early exodus of artists out of the country. This was especially common for major stars who had been highly successful within the capitalist entertainment industry of the 1940s and 1950s. Dance band entertainers who opted for exile in the 1960s include Celia Cruz and the Sonora Matancera, José Antonio Fajardo, Osvaldo Farrés, La Lupe, Ernesto Duarte, and Chocolate Armenteros.[3] Government policy called for the repudiation of musicians choosing to leave and the censure of their songs and professional activities from the media.

The government began to centralize and regulate the musical activity of classical artists beginning in the early 1960s; this process extended to popular performers in 1968 (Robbins 1991: 220). Since that time, most professional musicians have been employees of *empresas* or state agencies. The *plantilla* or staff artists receive a monthly wage in return for a set number of performances every pay period. They are evaluated periodically by regulatory boards and ascribed a rating (hypothetically consisting of six levels, A–F) based on their overall musical proficiency, which in turn determines their salary. As of the early 1990s, monthly salaries varied from approximately $175 to $400 pesos a month (Robbins 1991: 231). More recently, some musicians have begun to work as independent agents once again and to pay taxes to the government, as in capitalist countries.

Prior to 1959, most dance musicians had no direct link to government activities. Since the mid-1960s, the state has largely determined who qualifies to receive a salary as a professional musician, how much he or she will be paid, how often that musician will perform, where, and at which events. For those fortunate enough to receive official recognition, being a musician has many advantages unknown to performers of earlier decades, including a guaranteed right to work, a steady paycheck, and free health and retirement benefits.[4] At the same time, the system also marginalizes many aspiring artists who are unable to receive official recognition. It also influences the types of music they perform and limits the themes and issues they can address lyrically.

In socialist Cuba, music is often used as a means of rewarding those who support revolutionary ideals and endeavors. One of my first experiences at a dance event other than in a tourist hotel, for instance, was in Centro Habana at a government-sponsored *actividad* thrown exclusively for members of a local factory. These individuals had been selected for the relatively high output and quality standards they had maintained as a group over a period of months. Ministry officials in charge of entertainment provided a dance band as well as a meal of rice and fish (not insignificant in 1992 during a period of severe food shortages) and weak beer in wax paper cups. Similarly, music is used to get the public out for important socialist holidays, especially at times when a strong youth presence is desired. Food and music are provided each fall as part of outdoor block parties celebrating the anniversary of the founding of the CDRs,[5] for instance. As David Calzado suggests, Communist Party members may not have the highest opinion of dance music—they generally consider it "low-class" music (*música baja, sin nivel, de la hampa*), crude and vulgar, as well as a *cosa de negros* associated primarily with the AfroCuban community—but nevertheless recognize its utility as a tool to further particular ends.

> Popular Cuban [dance] music has always been a marginal music. What happens is that it has been strongly supported [by the masses]. It has endured because the public wanted it that way. If you want to have an assembly in the Plaza of the Revolution,[6] or a mass rally of the national UJC, well if you don't invite Paulito and his Elite, [Manolín] the Salsa Doctor, the Charanga Habanera, or Los Van Van, or others that I haven't mentioned, no one will attend. That's reality. Our work as musicians has been recognized only because [the government] was obliged to do so.[7]

In general, the period from the 1960s through the early 1980s was not a particularly vibrant one for dance music in Cuba. Various factors impeded its development even after the exodus of major performers, technicians, and industry leaders tapered off around 1967. The constant shuffling and reorganization of musical activity under new agencies and officials, as well as abrupt shifts in government policy, inevitably led to serious disruptions in output. A lack of access to replacement parts from capitalist countries meant that when nationalized equipment became defective it could not easily be repaired. The mass mobilization of workers in an attempt to boost sugar production in 1969–70, known as the *zafra de los diez millones*, resulted in a slump in all artistic production for a time. The onset of the *ofensiva revolucionaria* from the late 1960s through the mid–1970s, the most ideologically oppressive period of the revolution, similarly proved detrimental to creative activity across the board.

Perhaps most important, the government chose for many years to lend its strongest support only to classical music, or pop music with overtly political lyrical content. This led to entirely new sorts of composition: military marches dedicated to the 26th of July or the departure of the Granma,[8] traditional *sones* discussing agrarian reforms of the 1960s, choral works calling for socialist unity, and others.[9] This same tendency eventually led to support of the *nueva trova* movement. Nueva trova artists, originally a marginal group of young players, gained the support of the Communist Party in about 1973. The widespread promotion and eventual popularity of music by Silvio Rodríguez, Pablo Milanés, Pedro Luís Ferrer, and Vicente Feliú, to name only a few, eclipsed other styles for a time.[10]

Groups such as Los Van Van and Irakere represent exceptions to this overall tendency; both formed relatively early and have maintained their popularity for decades. Van Van, which might be considered the "Rolling Stones" of Cuban dance groups given its longevity, was founded in 1969 by bassist Juan Formell (b. 1943). Its name actually derives from slogans seen on TV at that time suggesting (incorrectly) that the country would attain its goal of producing 10 million tons of sugar in a single harvest, that *los diez millones van, señores, van . . .* Formell's group has shown itself to be innovative in a musical sense, adding drum set, trombones, and other horns to a typical charanga format, incorporating recent foreign influences including rap, and developing new rhythms such as *songo*. Lyrically, its compositions are most often lighthearted, though particular pieces like "La Habana no aguanta más" (Havana can't take any more) from the 1980s have addressed contemporary social concerns, in this case related to overcrowding.

Irakere, founded in 1973 by Jesús "Chucho" Valdés (b. 1941), began as an experimental jazz ensemble without official government recognition. This again was at a time in which any foreign music, and especially styles from the United States, did not receive much support from state agencies. In the face of significant obstacles, the band has managed to survive and flourish, creatively blending influences from mainstream jazz, funk, rock, Cuban son, ragtime, Afro-Cuban religious repertories, standard classical repertory, and other sources. Its cadre of amazingly virtuosic musicians (Valdés himself, Arturo Sandoval,

Paquito D'Rivera, percussionist Enrique Plá, collaborations with Leo Brouwer, etc.), its creative and even playful compositions, and its overall excellence have long been recognized internationally. Some of the original members have defected from Cuba—D'Rivera in 1980 and Sandoval in 1990—but new talent of similar caliber continues to join the group. Known for a diverse repertoire, Irakere has consistently included dance music among its styles, achieving commercial popularity early on with "Bacalao con pan" [Codfish and bread] and other songs. Since the 1990s it has produced entire albums of dance music, including *Indestructible* (Valdés 1999).

"SALSA" VERSUS TIMBA

I've put the term "salsa" in quotes here because many authors would question its applicability to the study of music within Cuba. As is commonly known, salsa is a marketing term that developed in New York in the 1960s to denote certain kinds of Cuban-derived dance music. Within Cuba, the term has never been widely used in the press and until perhaps the late 1980s would not have been recognized or understood by a majority of the public. What New Yorkers and most of Latin America refer to as salsa is usually described on the island as son, *timba*, *música bailable*, or perhaps *casino* (the latter term referring primarily to dance). Much of this discrepancy in terminology has to do with the censured nature of the media and the fact that most well-known New York *salseros* received little or no airplay there until recently. The relative isolation of Cuban performers from the bulk of the international market for decades has resulted in the perpetuation of a similar but distinct dance tradition. Its difference derives from the sound of the music itself, from its functions and contexts, and its lyrical and discursively derived meanings.

New York City has been an important center for the innovation of Cuban and other Caribbean musics since at least the 1940s, but its importance increased dramatically in the aftermath of the U.S. trade embargo against Cuba imposed in 1961. The development of salsa music in New York City and its ties to various immigrant communities there are beyond the scope of this essay. I would only emphasize that many of the Latin dance crazes sweeping Europe and the United States prior to 1959—(ballroom) rumba, *cha-cha-cha*, mambo—derived from Cuba itself rather than New York. Breaking economic ties with socialist Cuba created an artistic space in this country among Latinos which paved the way for the preeminence of Fania Records and other U.S.-based enterprises and groups.

Salsa music in New York—considering primarily the "classic" pieces of the 1970s and '80s—is associated with a number of distinct musical characteristics that distinguish it from most dance music in Cuba. Examples include the incorporation of *bomba* and *plena* rhythms in many pieces, as well as rhythms from Colombia and other countries;[11] the use of *güiro* patterns derived from Puerto Rican *seis*; the foregrounding of instruments such as the Puerto Rican *cuatro*; the development of hybrid genres incorporating melodic and rhythmic influences from African-American pop genres such as boogaloo of the 1960s and more recently African-American–style vocal melisma; and a preference for particular timbral/orchestrational blends emphasizing strident percussion and prominent trombone riffs. These significant factors notwithstanding, the essence of the musical style is derived from the Cuban son and specifically the *conjuntos* of the 1940s and '50s. Prominent features derived from this music include the prominence of Cuban percussion instruments (*clave*, *bongó* and *conga* drums, *timbales*, cowbell), characteristic rhythms (e.g., the basic *tumbao* pattern on the conga; *cáscara* rhythms derived ultimately from Cuban rumba; interlocking bell rhythms performed on the timbal and campana; the clave rhythm itself), anticipated bass figures, characteristic piano *montunos* derived from melodies on the *tres*.

More striking than aural differences between Cuban and Nuyorican dance music are the conceptual differences between the two repertories. Salsa in New York became popular during a moment of unprecedented grassroots activism on a national scale. In the context of anti-Vietnam protests, Black Power, the Young Lords movement, and a general politicization of minorities, salsa emerged as a symbol of a new pan-Latino identity. Bombarded with mainstream American commercial culture and living in an environment frequently inhospitable to their traditional musics, Latinos embraced salsa as an assertion of self, a form of resistance. This is the context that led to the development of biting social commentary in the compositions of Willie Colón, Rubén Blades, Eddie Palmieri, and others.

It has also led to at least two distinct trends among artists and producers in more recent years. On the one hand, they continue to aggressively adopt influences from mainstream African-American genres and to experiment with crossover compositions featuring blends of rock, R&B, and rap with salsa. Recent compositions by Dark Latin Groove, Marc Anthony, and La India in both Spanish and English demonstrate these fusions clearly. On the other hand, artists of an earlier generation associated with a more "classic" salsa sound (e.g., Tito Nieves, Tito Rojas) have tended to produce stylistically conservative and at times overly commercialized music linked to the *salsa romántica* movement. One might suggest that these tendencies derive from fundamental problems facing all immigrants. Largely distanced from their cultural roots, they must either adapt themselves to a new environment or attempt to perpetuate older traditions. In either case, the future development of their music will be heavily affected by their adopted surroundings.

The experience of popular musicians within Cuba is quite different. They are not directly threatened by an overarching mainstream Anglo culture. On the contrary, most are unable to travel abroad as much as they'd like and tend to associate external musical influences with an international community they aspire to be part of. For this reason, instruments such as the drum set have become standard fare in most modern Cuban dance bands. At the same time, Cuban pop musicians are part of a strong cultural environment that has not been disrupted through foreign immigration to the island or the constant onslaught of First World media. In addition to performing son-based dance music, they play in *comparsa* ensembles during carnival season, are exposed to and/or involved with African-derived ritual traditions of *Santería* and *Palo Monte*, play in informal rumba events, listen to old and new *trova*, and are frequently members of *abakuá* societies and other groups with distinct and vibrant forms of music. This cultural base is strong enough to absorb foreign elements and "Cubanize" them rather than to be dissipated by them.

Present-day Cuban dance bands tend to have an eclectic sound, drawing widely from international influences (jazz, rock, funk, pop) and a diversity of Cuban folkloric styles. Use of synthesized keyboard sounds is frequent in addition to the acoustic piano. Verbal improvisations, spoken and sung, tend to sound more spontaneous, as if they were invented on the spot rather than pre-planned. Talking to the audience for an extended period over a musical groove is also common. Pianist Elio Villafranca notes that each band has its own arranger who usually writes for only one group over an extended period.[12] In this way, bands strive for a unique sound consisting of characteristic "signature breaks" performed only by them, innovative *montuno* patterns, and other elements (see fig. 3.1). Musicians demonstrate their link to a unique and dynamic cultural environment in a lively variety of ways—by means of ritual *lucumí* exclamations[13] or the incorporation of entire ritual melodies such as the *rezo a Ochún* that begins Ádalberto Alvarez's "¿Qué tú quieres que te den?"[14] (fig. 3.2, Álvarez 1992); constant musical and verbal "riffing" off of national repertory of past decades (e.g., Fellove n.d.; Calzado 1994);[15] references to local people, places, or events; the creation of entirely new rhythms derived from folkloric sources such as the "*ritmo* Dan-Den" (Alfonso 1991); the "quoting" of

FIGURE 3.1 • Piano *montuno* patterns, New York and Cuban styles. The first example is a standard montuno pattern, typical of those played by New York salsa groups. The second example shows a montuno pattern with the same changes representative of present-day dance compositions in Cuba, as heard in Isaac Delgado's rendition of the Pedro Flores song "Obsesión" (1999). Transcriptions courtesy of Elio Villafranca.

FIGURE 3.2 • Traditional devotional chant to the *orisha* Ochún, as incorporated into Adalberto Álvarez's "¿Y qué tú quieres que te den?" (1999). Álvarez is a *santería* initiate and child of Ochún.

FIGURE 3.3 • *Batá* rhythms used in timba. The middle line of this example represents a traditional *iyesá* rhythm for *batá* as played on the large *iyá* drum. This rhythm is imitated in variation on the timbales and floor tom during the José Luis Cortés composition "Santa Palabra" (1992). Listen to the short breaks at 3:24" and 3:35", and the longer section at 6:18". Thanks to Elio Villafranca, Elizabeth Sayre, and Armando Fiol for help with these examples.

distinct Afro-Cuban folkloric traditions on the timbales (fig. 3.3), recognized only by local listeners; and with other playful elisions of music across boundaries of time and genre.

THE SALSA CONTROVERSY

The emergence of commercial salsa music in New York inspired controversy from the beginning, coming only a few years after the onset of the U.S.-imposed economic embargo against Cuba and in the context of CIA assassination attempts against Castro,[16] extreme tensions between Cuban nationals and the exile community, and the height of ideological radicalism among socialist leaders. The remarketing of traditional Cuban genres under the name "salsa" by Fania and other record labels without any clear recognition of the music's origins angered musicians and critics. Many, including Antonio Arcaño, Rafael Lay, and Rosendo Ruiz denounced the term immediately (Acosta 1997:27–28). More than a few suggested that salsa was an "imperialist plot" designed to further marginalize and disenfranchise Cuban artists under socialism.[17]

While probably not as carefully crafted a policy as these criticisms suggest, salsa as an economic phenomenon does raise troubling issues. The combination of an embargo policy prohibiting Cuban artists from performing or marketing their music abroad in many cases, and the simultaneous mass commercialization of the same boycotted music by entrepreneurs in the States seems unethical. Peter Manuel notes, "Since the United States has made a particular effort to isolate Cuba economically, diplomatically, culturally and ideologically, the commercially successful recycling of Cuban music under the 'alienating and mystifying slogan' (Torres 1982) of 'salsa' is seen as especially duplicitous" (1987:170). One might contest this view and suggest instead that the Cuban government created much of the problem for itself by refusing to recognize international copyright agreements as of the early 1960s. This left the legal door open for Jerry Masucci and other entrepreneurs to record songs with little or no compensation to their authors.

Regardless of such arguable complicity, however, the indiscretions of one country do not justify those of another. Companies in the United States have amassed a fortune by brazenly appropriating works by artists banned in the United States because they are Cuban. This has clearly added sting to the salsa debate. Access to the most widespread networks of marketing and distribution has allowed companies like Fania, RMM, and others to dominate the international Latin music trade even when their artists are not the composers of the music they promote. Frequently, producers here print only the letters "D.R." (*derechos reservados* or "copyright reserved") after particular titles as a means of claiming legal rights while avoiding the use of Cuban composers' names and thus allusions to the origin of the music (Díaz Ayala 1981:339). In other cases, the pieces are copyrighted under entirely new names. The José Antonio Méndez composition "Decídete mi amor," for example, is attributed to Edgardo Donato on a recording by Héctor Lavoe (Lavoe/1985) and retitled "Déjala que siga."

It is ironic, given the heated controversy surrounding salsa among critics on the island (especially in the 1970s and '80s), that most Cubans remained oblivious to both the term itself and the artists associated with it for decades. An entire generation of radio listeners grew up without ever hearing the names of groups or artists like El Gran Combo, the Sonora Ponceña, the Fanía All-Stars, or Pete "El Conde" Rodríguez. This was primarily due to a policy of media censorship on the island that suppressed salsa from all capitalist countries (Acosta 1997:28). Such policies, despite their impact on the lives of millions of listeners, have never been formally admitted to or published except perhaps as classified documents for government officials. The informal suppression began in the late 1960s and extended through the early 1980s. Party ideologues even prohibited the term "salsa" from use in the media by deejays or musicologists during this time.[18]

Prohibitions against Latino music from the United States, Puerto Rico, and elsewhere applied not only to the mass media but extended to the use of music in private homes. Radio journalist Cristóbal Sosa remembers that for many years by merely playing an LP of the Miami Sound Machine—whose lead singer Gloria Estefan had open anti-Castro sympathies—one risked denouncement by local CDR members and possible harassment or jailing by tribunals. Similar risks were associated with listening to the music of other artists. "The 'salsa' from New York, that of Eddie and Charlie Palmieri, all that, was considered 'the enemy.'"[19] Music by New York *salseros* never appeared on television and could be obtained only clandestinely through networks of friends willing to make or lend bootleg recordings.

Beginning in the late 1970s, government policy began to move from a position of absolute intolerance toward a more open but confrontative stance vis-à-vis salsa music, and then eventually to a slow reconciliation with some artists. It may be that the strong popularity of salsa abroad at this time actually forced policymakers to reevaluate the importance of dance music on the island and to produce more recordings of it. In the late 1970s, EGREM[20] created a high-profile ensemble known as the "Estrellas de Areíto" or "Areíto Stars," deriving their name from the regional state-owned recording company in Havana. This group, consisting of highly regarded musicians Tata Güines, Rafael Lay, Niño

Rivero, Félix Chappotín, Carlos Embale, Miguelito Cuní, and others, represented a direct response and challenge to the "Fania All-Stars" of Jerry Masucci. It attempted to draw attention away from foreign artists and to underscore again the fact that salsa had roots in Cuba rather than abroad.

Policies of engagement with Cuba advocated by the Carter administration (1977–80) contributed to a gradual thawing of the "cold war" over salsa; this is the same period that saw the reestablishment of consular ties between the two countries for the first time since 1961 and a new allowance for limited cultural exchanges. As a result, CBS Records invited Irakere to record in the United States in 1978 as well as to participate in the Newport and Montreaux jazz festivals. Their recording from that period later won them a Grammy. Politically oriented salsa compositions by Rubén Blades and others sympathetic to socialist issues during the same period also compelled those in charge of Cuban cultural policy to review their long-standing biases against such music.

For the most part, the dance music aired on Cuban television continues to be performed by national rather than international artists. The *Para bailar* show emerged on one of the two national channels in 1979 and soon became popular, and in the mid-1980s the program *Mi salsa* appeared, foregrounding amateur singers. Shows of the early '90s such as *Sabadazo* regularly included live dance music segments. With the onset of economic crisis, popular music of all types has witnessed greater support from the government. This repertory is promoted as never before as means of generating foreign currency. It also motivates more than ever musicians who recognize the attractive options for travel and contacts with foreign entrepreneurs. At present, performing music in tourist venues or abroad offers Cubans a potentially higher standard of living than they could hope to achieve in virtually any other way.

DANCE MUSIC AND SOCIAL CRISIS

Cuba has experienced profound economic changes since 1989. With the collapse of the Soviet Union the island lost subsidies of at least $6 billion per year from East Bloc countries, as well as an additional $1.2 billion in Russian military aid (Frey 1997:3). Without adequate energy supplies or manufactured goods, Cuba's highly dependent agricultural economy suffered an immediate drop of more than 40 percent in domestic GNP in the early 1990s. It has recovered only partially since that time. Blackouts, transportation crises, and shortages of food and basic domestic supplies have all become commonplace. This so-called "special period" will probably not end anytime soon, though conditions have improved somewhat since the mid-1990s. Lacking an industrial base that would allow for economic independence and with little to sell on the international market, Cuba has been transformed overnight from one of the most affluent countries in Latin America to one of the poorest.

Economic crisis has led in turn to the rise of acute social problems. Physical violence has increased in what once was one of the safest of nations. Theft, from individuals and government-owned businesses, is a constant occurrence as Cubans try to survive within a dysfunctional system. Finally, the government's decision to open thousands of new shops offering products only in U.S. dollars has deepened divisions of class and privilege in a society that once prided itself on equality for all. Large numbers of disaffected youth survive by selling stolen goods such as rum or cigars to foreign visitors, through prostitution, or in less controversial ways by competing with the government for tourist dollars. The last ten years has thus given rise to a fundamental crisis of ideology and of values in which the very notion of socialism seems ambiguous and the goals of the nation uncertain.

ECONOMIC CRISIS AND THE ARTS

Within Cuba, economic changes have had many direct effects on the lives of musicians. In a country that experienced chronic shortages of most goods even prior to 1989, equipment for recording, amplification, and transportation, as well as instruments themselves have all but disappeared except for those with strong government sponsorship. As a result, countless promising musicians attempt to secure extended contracts abroad, settling into semipermanent or permanent exile and draining the country of its talent (Acosta 1996). High-profile examples include Gonzalo Rubalcaba, who now spends most of his time in the Dominican Republic; Albita, the singer who defected in the mid-1990s, citing a lack of artistic freedom and problems with radio censorship (Grau 1997); and Alejandro Leyva, former singer for NG la Banda who defected in 1997 after a performance in New York's Lincoln Center.[21] In some cases the government now encourages extended foreign touring as a means of increasing its revenues; legislation presently allows the Ministry of Culture to deduct as much as 50 percent of the earnings of touring groups as a form of taxation. In 1996 alone, more than 3,500 of Cuba's roughly 11,600 state-sponsored musicians performed abroad (Watrous 1997:34).

The licensing of Cuban recordings to foreign contractors has increased dramatically, though individual artists have not necessarily benefited from this change. Government agencies have aggressively promoted foreign sales of music since the early 1990s, recognizing recordings as an important source of income. From a single state-owned company a few years ago, EGREM, the country now has now created countless semiautonomous agencies as well as a host of new video production centers.[22]

Changes of this nature have contributed to the heightened profile of Cuban dance orchestras abroad. Difficult to obtain in the United States until about 1991, Cuban music in a variety of styles is now experiencing a boom in international sales. Titles presently available for purchase include the most recent artists from the island as well as older recordings that have been re-released on CD. Expanded availability over the past decade has contributed to an increased awareness abroad of Cuban music and its significance, past and present. Such interest is manifested not only by the general public, but by major recording artists and entrepreneurs such as David Byrne and Ry Cooder and their promotion of the Cuba Classics CD anthologies, Buena Vista Social Club performers, the Cubanismo ensemble, and others.

The ongoing expansion of the tourist industry heavily impacts the lives of artists today as well. Approximately 1.2 million tourists visited Cuba in 1997 (*CUBAinfo* vol. 10, no. 2, p. 6), lured by new package vacations offers, and their numbers continue to rise. They are welcomed, housed, pampered, and sent on their way again by a host of new state and mixed enterprise agencies. The aggressive promotion of Cuba as a tourist destination represents a radical change from policies of the recent past. Through at least the late 1980s, Cuban citizens were encouraged to avoid contact with visitors from capitalist countries, even to the extent of cutting off communication with their own family members. Tourism's centrality to the economy of today puts the government in the uncomfortable position of changing views long considered fundamental to the perpetuation of revolutionary ideals.

Beginning in the early 1990s, officials effectively divided Havana, Varadero, Santiago, and other major tourist destinations into business areas devoted to commerce in dollars, primarily for foreigners, and other less desirable areas that continued to accept national currency. They determined that many of the best cabarets and dance clubs once open to the general public would be "dollarized" and effectively off-limits to the general public. One unfortunate result of these policies has been the development of a quasi-apartheid music system in which many live concerts today cannot be attended by Cubans themselves. In the newly designed *Palacio de la Salsa* (Salsa Palace), in the tourist ship known as *El Galeón,* in the Café Cantante nightclub of the Hotel Meliá Cohiba, and elsewhere, dance music is heard only by listeners who can afford a hefty cover charge in dollars.

DANCE MUSIC AND CONTEMPORARY SOCIAL COMMENTARY

In the context of economic crisis, popular music has become an important forum for the expression of concerns about the country's future. The greater importance of music as a revenue-generating art form for the state has resulted in new opportunities for individual expression and some reduction in media censorship. Marketability and sales are now the principal factors determining whether a song will be recorded and aired rather than whether its lyrics uphold socialist ideals. As a result, references to crime, anxiety, and criticism of government policy are emerging in many different kinds of music where they could never before be expressed.

The relative freedom now experienced by songwriters to express their views has been matched by a public, largely disillusioned with current politicians, that tends increasingly to read the texts of pop culture as potentially subversive or parodical of official discourse. Adalberto Alvarez's hit "El baile del toca-toca" [The touch-touch dance], for example, was/is understood by many as a veiled reference to the financial "touching" associated with rampant graft, theft of government supplies, and illegal business deals in day-to-day life rather than physical touching. Similarly, "Prepárate para lo que viene" [Prepare yourself for what's coming] by Manolín, "El Médico de la Salsa," is assumed to be a tongue-in-cheek reference to Fidel Castro's autocratic style of leadership instead of the mere boasting of a singer about future exploits.

In reality, two distinct kinds of social critique are fused in the performance of much Cuban popular music today. On a semantic level, lyrics reference the many difficulties confronting the population more directly than was possible in earlier decades. Despair, feelings of insignificance, crime, and a loss of political direction are all common themes; this is especially true in rock music. On the level of sound itself, musicians critique implicitly government policies through their very involvement with dance music, given that for many years it did not receive much recognition or support. They also sometimes challenge pronationalist, exclusionary cultural policies through the incorporation of foreign influences (jazz, rock, funk, rap) that until the mid-1980s were only infrequently heard on the radio.

Themes of rampant consumerism and national anxiety over the lack of basic consumer goods have been incorporated into countless compositions. In the most lyrically sophisticated pieces, references to commercial sales are blended with suggestions that Cuba may be "selling out" ideologically and spiritually with the expansion of the capitalist market. In songs of this nature arranged for dance band, however, the tendency of composers has been to present such themes playfully, with humor. For instance, the Charanga Habanera's 1996 album, *Para que se entere la Habana,* included various controversial pieces such as "El temba" [The rich guy] and "La turística" [The tourist-minded girl]. This album was actually banned in its entirety by the government for a time, in part because of its content and in part because its cover art consists largely of a U.S. hundred-dollar bill.

Los Van Van has recorded similar songs such as "Shopping Maniac" on an album from 1998, *Te pone la cabeza mala.* The traditional theme of a man's suffering for the love of a woman, and for the spending of a woman, gains added significance in the context of the limitations facing most consumers.

CORO: *Se lo gasta todo en el ten-cent, ¡ay de mí!*
Y me tiene la casa llena, que parece *un almacén [coro]*

Besito, besito, todo le parece poco, dice $20, $30, o $100 [coro]
Aunque sé que ya me quiere algo yo *tendré que hacer [coro]*
Y todo lo que se pone, oye, lo compra en el Corte Inglés *[coro]*

En el Corte Inglés. . . , en Yumurí, en Ultra, en 3ra y 70, en 5ta y 42

Oye, sácame la mano del bolsillo, sáca, sáca, sáca, sáca, sácame la mano del bolsillo, ¡que no puedo más!. . .

CHORUS: *She spent it all in the dollar shop, oh my!*
And she's filled my house up with so much stuff it looks like a warehouse [chorus]

A kiss, a kiss, [but] what I give her is never enough, $20, $30, or $100 [chorus]
Though I know she loves me, I still have to do something [chorus]
And all the clothes she wears, hey, she buys them in that pricey English Court shop [chorus]

In dollar stores like English Court, Yumurí, in Ultra, the place at 3rd and 70th, 5th and 42nd

Hey, get that hand out of my pocket, out, out out out, get it out of my pocket
I can't take it anymore!

One other example from the 1990s worthy of mention for its lyrical content is NG La Banda's "Picadillo de soya" or "Soy Hamburger" (Cortés

1994). The song was inspired by a meat substitute distributed across the island for several years when the government had virtually no actual red meat available in butcher shops. *Picadillo de soya* consisted of soy mash mixed together with animal blood and entrails so that it tasted vaguely like meat; in fact, everyone hated it, and officials eventually discontinued its distribution along with that of other nasty items like "goose paste" (*pasta de oca*). Open criticism of the *picadillo* was impossible in the state-controlled media, so Cortés chose instead to praise its virtues in a highly exaggerated manner. By means of this approach, positive discussion of the hated item became a form of parody and muted political protest.

Señoras y señores, lo que les estoy contando es una cosa sabrosa. El picadillo de soya tiene 1, 2, 3, 4, 5, 6 7, 8, 9, 10, 10 puntos sobre la alimentación mundial. En China comen la soya, en Bélgica, en Suiza, en Holanda en Japón comen soya, la McDonald e' de la soya también. ¡Ataca Chicho!

Ladies and gentlemen, what I'm telling you is a great thing. Soy hamburger has 1, 2, 3, 4, 5, 6 7, 8, 9, 10, 10 advantages over most global diets. In China they eat soy meat, in Belgium, in Switzerland, in Holland, in Japan they eat soy, the MacDonald's hamburger is made of soy too.
Play it, Chicho!

Porque la soya es un alimento que tiene a todo el mundo en talla. Las mujeres están sabrosas, unas cinturas terribles, unas piernas que se caen. Yo no sé lo que pasa pero, caballeros, la soya está en ta-, ta, ta-ta, ta-ta, talla, talla, talla, talla, tremenda talla e' lo que tiene la soya, ¡uh!
¡Vale Peruchín!. . . ¿Oyó? ¡Prepárense a comer!

Because soy is a food that is getting the whole world in shape. The women look wonderful, lovely waists, legs that make you fall over. I don't know what's going on, but, man, soy is in good sha-, sha-, sha-sha, sha-sha, shape, shape, shape, shape, great shape is what soy gives you.

OK, Peruchín, hear me? Get ready to eat!

CODA

Dance music in Cuba since 1959 has been implicated in all of the major trends, policies, and repercussions of the socialist experience. Dance musicians have fled into exile, performed in front of tank columns on May Day, volunteered in literacy campaigns, cut sugarcane, and entertained soldiers in Angola. If we consider that *guarachas* by Commander Juan Almeida such as "Dame un traguito" continue to be popular repertoire, we can even say that dance musicians fought alongside Fidel in the Sierra Maestra.

Out of a desire to reeducate citizens and sensitize them to socialist issues, music of all sorts has been subject to regulation by the government. Regulation in some cases has proved highly beneficial to musicians, resulting in free educational opportunities and exchanges and the emergence of performers with amazing technical skill. Conversely, regulation has hindered the careers of some artists. Officials have at times blacklisted those deemed unsympathetic to their cause while supporting others willing to take a clear stand with Castro and the Communist Party. Through monopoly control of the media, the government exerts influence over the lives of musicians, their careers, their access to audiences, and—especially in past years—the content of their art.

By 1968, much of the support for apolitical dance entertainment had disappeared in socialist Cuba. Those interested in studying and/or performing sones struggled within a new cultural reality, one that emphasized close government involvement in the arts, promoted classical music instruction, and demonstrated a preference for performers whose works contained overtly socialist messages. In the late 1970s, leaders began to promote dance music more actively, often as a means of drawing crowds for political events. Since 1989, dance music once again has become the most commonly heard and promoted music on the island. Because of its powerful appeal abroad and its ability to generate revenue, it has prevailed over other styles. Dance musicians now are freer to express themselves than most of the general public and are more engaged with the international community than at any time in the past forty years.

Musicians raised in socialist Cuba have been exposed to Marxist thought, but they are hardly puppets of the authorities. On the contrary, performers in general have suffered as well as benefited from revolutionary change. They must constantly negotiate for freedom of expression and overall autonomy. They compete for equipment, performance space, travel opportunities, and media access in a politically rarefied environment. It is unfortunate that musicians from the island are too often perceived by the exile community as part of a "communist threat," rather than as individual people caught in a complex process and facing difficult decisions. The performances of Cuban dance bands in the United States still generate considerable controversy, and until recently even the airing of their recorded music in Miami resulted in bomb threats phoned in to offending radio stations.[23] One might hope that the growing popularity of Cuban ensembles internationally will result in a greater awareness of the histories and lives of everyone on the island. If commercial incentives have finally led to more favorable attitudes about popular music among Cuban leaders, perhaps the same incentives will result in a more balanced view of socialism from the international community.

NOTES

1. " . . . uno de los propósitos fundamentales de la Revolución es desarrollar el arte y la cultura, precisamente para que el arte y la cultura lleguen a ser un real patrimonio del pueblo."
2. The Urfé article contains a much fuller listing of participating artists.
3. For a more complete listing of the dozens of Cuban artists choosing exile at this time, as well as press and entertainment industry executives, see Díaz Ayala 1981:267.
4. As Paul Ryer notes (personal communication), the typical retirement salary offered to Cubans—80 pesos a month—may have been adequate at one time, but as of the 1990s it is simply too little to live on. This accounts for the many older Cubans one sees today on the street who look thin, ragged, and despondent. Without additional means of support, primarily through the family, surviving on a pension alone is nearly impossible.
5. Comités de Defensa de la Revolución (Committees in Defense of the Revolution). These community-based organizations have existed on virtually every city block of urban areas in the country since the 1960s. They provide many useful services to residents, but also act as antirevolutionary watchdogs, the eyes and ears of the state.
6. This is a huge empty space in central Havana that has traditionally been used for celebrations, speeches, and other activities on the nation's most important holidays. Near its center is a huge marble statue of founding father José Martí; the space is bounded by buildings of equally impressive size including the National Library, the Ministry of Communication, and the Ministry of Defense.
7. Personal communication, interview with David Calzado, October 9, 1996, El Vedado, Havana. "La música popular cubana siempre ha sido una música marginal. Lo que pasa es que se ha impuesto. Se ha impuesto porque la preferencia del público lo ha querido así. Si quieres hacer una convocatoria en la Plaza de la Revolución, o una actividad masiva de la UJC nacional, si no llevas a Paulito, al Médico, a la Charanga, o Los Van Van, o a otros que no mencioné, no va nadie. Esa es una realidad. Ha sido por obligación el reconocimiento al trabajo nuestro."
8. The 26th of July is the date that Fidel Castro and his followers first attempted a direct attack on troops loyal to Fulgencio Batista in Santiago, 1953. Their target was the Moncada army garrison, named after Guillermón Moncada, a hero of the Wars of Independence. Though the event failed, the date of the assault retains symbolic importance to many as the beginning of the socialist revolutionary process. *Granma* is the name of the boat used by Castro and his followers to sail from Mexico to eastern Cuba a few years later and begin their insurrection anew.
9. A fair sampling of this sort of music has been collected on the CD anthology *Música y revolución* (Fernández 1996).
10. For a sample of the sorts of dance music performed in Cuba during the 1970s and 1980s, listen to the Earthworks anthology *¡Sabroso! Havana Hits* (Vanrenen 1989).

This release contains interesting examples of politicized dance music such as "El son de Nicaragua" by the Orquesta Chepín' celebrating the victory of the Sandinistas' and "De Kabinde a Kunene un solo pueblo," a merengue by Los Karache inspired by Cuban involvement in the Angolan civil war.

11. Consider for example the use of *bomba* percussion rhythms on the title track of Ray Barretto's *Ritmo en el corazón* release (Barreto and Cruz 1988) or in Rubén Blades's "Pablo Pueblo" (Blades 1992).

12. Personal communication, interview with Elio Villafranca, June 6, 2000, Philadelphia, Pennsylvania.

13. There are numerous examples of verbal references to *santería* in dance music, but one of the most obvious is the phrase "sía cará" heard during the introduction to NG y la Banda's "Santa Palabra" (Cortés 1994). This is an exclamation used during *limpiezas*, rituals of spiritual cleansing (Villafranca, ibid.).

14. Álvarez is a *santería* initiate and child of Ochún.

15. I'm referring specifically to the Fellove *inspiraciones* in his version of "Decídete mi amor" by José Antonio Méndez [from the 1960s] in which he quotes from at least half a dozen older boleros; and to the song "Mi estrella" by David Calzado filled with Afro-Cuban street slang that makes reference to Donna Summer and Whitney Houston one moment and then quotes the traditional cha-cha-chá "El jamaiquino." Similarly, "La turística" on the same album manages to sound like ultra-modern timba while musically quoting "Tres lindas cubanas" from the 1920s.

16. The CIA's active involvement in assassination attempts against Castro, especially in the 1960s, is well documented. See for instance Oppenheimer 1992:38; Senate 1976:2–6; and Smith 1987:166–75.

17. Personal communication, interview with Leonardo Acosta, September 1, 1996, El Vedado, Havana.

18. Personal communication, interview with Helio Orovio, September 26, 1996, El Vedado, Havana.

19. Personal communication, interview with Cristóbal Sosa (journalist for Radio Habana), October 1, 1996 (El Vedado, Havana).

20. Empresa de Grabaciones y Ediciones Musicales. Initially directed by Medardo Montero, this is the name of the state company that oversees all music recording and distribution in socialist Cuba. It was established in 1962.

21. For more information on Leyva, see *CUBAinfo* vol. 9, no. 10 (July 31, 1997), p. 9.

22. They include: ArtColor, Artex, BIS Music, Caribe Productions, Magic Music, Ojalá, PMR, Pickap, and RTV Commercial.

23. *Cuba News* publications from 1997 are a good source of information on this subject. See, for example, vol. 9, no. 3 (October 2, 1997), p. 11, and vol. 11, no. 12, pp. 8–9.

BIBLIOGRAPHY

Acosta, Leonardo. 1996. "El capítulo que faltaba: unos años después." Unpublished manuscript.

———. 1997. "¿Terminó la polémica sobre la salsa?" *Música cubana*: 26–29. Havana: UNEAC.

Castro, Fidel. 1961. *Palabras a los intelectuales*. Havana: Ediciones del Consejo Nacional de Cultura.

Chijona, Gerardo. 1982. "El cine cubano, hecho cultural de la revolución." In Ministerio de Cultura, ed., *La cultura en Cuba socialista*. Havana: Editorial Arte y Letras, pp. 215–29.

Díaz Ayala, Cristóbal. 1981. *Música cubana del areíto a la nueva trova*. Miami: Ediciones Universal.

Frey, Louis, Jr. 1997. "Report by the Delegation of the U.S. Association of Former
    Members of Congress Visit to Cuba, December 9–14, 1996." Washington, D.C.:
    United States Association of Former Members of Congress.
Gramatges, Harold. 1982. "La música culta." In Ministerio de Cultura, ed., *La cultura
    en Cuba socialista*. Havana: Editorial Letras Cubanas, pp. 124–50.
Grau, Adriane. 1997."Albita mostra que Cuba não é só salsa." *Folha ilustrada,*
    November 15, p. 10.
Leal, Rine. 1982. "Hacia una dramaturgia del socialismo." In Ministerio de Cultura,
    ed., *La cultura en Cuba socialista*. Havana: Editorial Arte y Letras, pp. 230–53.
Manuel, Peter. 1987."Marxism, Nationalism and Popular Music in Revolutionary
    Cuba." *Popular Music* 6(2):161–78.
———. 1991. "Salsa and the Music Industry: Corporate Control or Grassroots
    Expression." In Peter Manuel, ed., *Essays on Cuban Music: North American and
    Cuban Perspectives*. Lanham, Md.: University Press of America, pp. 157–81.
Ministerio de Cultura, ed. 1982. *La cultura en Cuba socialista*. Havana: Editorial Arte y
    Letras.
Oppenheimer, Andrés. 1992. *Castro's Final Hour: The Secret Story behind the Coming
    Downfall of Communist Cuba*. New York: Simon and Schuster.
Orovio, Helio. 1981. *Diccionario de la música cubana: biográfico y técnico*. Havana:
    Editorial Letras Cubanas.
———. 1992. *Diccionario de la música cubana: biográfico y técnico*. 2nd ed. Havana:
    Editorial Letras Cubanas.
Otero, Lisandro, and Francisco Martínez Hinojosa. 1972. *Cultural Policy in Cuba*.
    Paris: UNESCO.
Partido Comunista de Cuba. 1976. *Tesis y resoluciones: primer congreso del partido
    comunista de Cuba*. Havana: Departamento de Orientación Revolucionaria del
    Comité Central del Partido Comunista de Cuba.
———. 1978. *Plataforma programática del Partido Comunista de Cuba: Tesis y resolu-
    ción*. Havana: Editorial de Ciencias Sociales.
Robbins, James. 1991. "Institutions, Incentives, and Evaluations in Cuban Music-
    Making." In Peter Manuel, ed., *Essays on Cuban Music: North American and Cuban
    Perspectives*. Lanham, Md: University Press of America, pp. 215–48.
Smith, Wayne. 1987.*The Closest of Enemies: A Personal and Diplomatic Account of
    U.S.–Cuban Relations since 1957*. New York: W.W. Norton.
Torres, Dora Ileana. 1982. "El fenómeno de la salsa y lo nuestro latinoamericano y
    caribeño." Unpublished manuscript, Havana, CIDMUC.
United States Senate. 1976. "The Investigation of the Assassination of President John F.
    Kennedy: Performance of the Intelligence Agencies." Book 5. Select Committee to
    Study Governmental Operations with respect to Intelligence Activities. Report No.
    94–755 [the Church Report].
Urfé, Odilio. 1982. "La música folklórica, popular y del teatro cubano." In Ministerio
    de Cultura, ed., *La cultura en Cuba socialista*. Havana: Editorial Arte y Letras, pp.
    151–73.
Valladares, Armando. 1986. *Against All Hope*. Trans. Andrew Hurley. New York:
    Ballantine.
Vélez, María Teresa. 1996. "The Trade of an Afrocuban Religious Drummer: Felipe
    García Villamil." 2 vols. Ph.D. dissertation, Wesleyan University.
Verdery, Katherine. 1991a. "Theorizing Socialism: A Prologue to the 'Transition.'"
    American Ethnologist 18(3):419–39.
———. 1991b. *National Ideology under Socialism: Identity and Cultural Politics in
    Ceausescu's Romania*. Berkeley: University of California Press.

Watrous, Peter. 1997. "A Hip-Swaying State-Sponsored Export." *New York Times,* March 23, p. 34.

DISCOGRAPHY

Alfonso, Juan Carlos. 1991. *Si Dan . . . Den. Juan Carlos y su Dan Den.* (Areíto LD-4708.)

Alvarez, Adalberto. 1999. *Adalberto Alvarez y su son.* (POW/Sony PWK 83563.)

Barreto, Ray, and Celia Cruz. 1988.*Ritmo en el corazón.* (Charly 172.)

Blades, Rubén. 1992. *The Best.* (Globo/Sony CDZ-80718.)

Calzado, David. 1994. *Hey, You, Loca! David Calzado & La Charanga Habanera.* Magic Music compact disc C–0011–3. Barcelona, Spain: Cosmopolitan Caribbean Music.

Cortés, José Luís "El Tosco." 1992. *Échale Limón.* (Caribe Productions 9458.)

———. 1993. *Llegó NG, Camará.* (Artex 072.)

Calzado, David. 1994. *Hey, You, Loca! David Calzado & Le Charanga Habanera.* Magic Music compact disc C–0011–3. Barcelona, Spain: Cosmopolitan Caribbean Music.

Delgado, Isaac. 1999.*La primera noche.* (RMM 82272.)

Fellove, Francisco. N.d. *Fellove: Conjunto Habana.* (Areíto LD-3803.)

Fernández, José Loyola, et al. 1996. *Música y revolución.* (Producciones UNEAC, EGREM 0206.)

Formell, Juan. 1997. *Te pone la cabeza mala.* (Metro Blue 7243–8–21307–2–7.)

Lavoe, Héctor. 1985. Revento. (Fania 634.)

Valdés, Jesús "Chucho." 1999. *Indestructible.* (POW/Sony PWK 83558.)

Vanrenen et al. 1989. *¡Sabroso! Havana Hits.* (Earthworks/Caroline Carol 2411–2.)

Chapter 4

"CHA-CHA WITH A BACKBEAT": SONGS AND STORIES OF LATIN BOOGALOO

Juan Flores

The following essay originally appeared in the journal Black Renaissance *(1999) and is a shortened version of a chapter in Juan Flores's book* From Bomba to Hip-Hop: Puerto Rican Culture and Latino Identity *(2000).*

"Let's just try it out, Sonny. If it doesn't work, I'll buy you a double." Jimmy Sabater remembers the night he kept coaxing his bandleader, Joe Cuba, to play a new number he had in mind. It was 1966 at the Palm Gardens Ballroom in midtown Manhattan, and the house was packed. "It was a black dance," Jimmy recalls, "*de morenos, morenos americanos de Harlem* and stuff, you know, they had black dances one night a week there and at some of the other spots. So that night we were playing selections from our new album *We Must Be Doing Something Right* that had just come out, the one with "El Pito" on it, you know, "I'll never go back to Georgia, never go back . . . " The place was packed, but when we were playing all those mambos and cha chas, nobody was dancing. So at the end of the first set, I went over to Joe Cuba and said, look, Sonny (that's his nickname), I have an idea for a tune that I think might get them up. And Joe says, no, no, no, we got to keep on playing the charts from the new album. Then toward the end of the second set, I went on begging him, and said, look, if I'm wrong, we'll stop and I'll buy you a double. So finally he said o.k., and I went over to the piano and told Nick Jimenez, play this. . . . Before I even got back to the timbal, the people were out on the floor, going 'bi-bi, hah! bi-bi, hah!' I mean mobbed!" As Joe Cuba himself recalls, "Suddenly the audience began to dance side-to-side like a wave-type dance, and began to chant 'she-free, she-free,' sort of like an African tribal chant and dance."[1]

The new tune by the Joe Cuba Sextet was "Bang Bang." Within weeks it was recorded and released as a single, which soon hit the national Billboard charts and stayed there for ten weeks, one of the few Latin recordings ever to reach that level of commercial success. It even outdid "El Pito," which the year before had also made the charts, and the album on which "Bang Bang" appeared, *Wanted: Dead or Alive,* was a huge hit as well. It was the heyday of Latin boogaloo, and Joe Cuba's band was at the height of its popularity. Nineteen sixty-six was also the year that saw the closing of the legendary Palladium Ballroom, an event marking the definitive end of the great mambo era in Latin music, which had been waning since the beginning of the decade. And, looking ahead to developments to come, it was some four years later at that very same Palm Gardens venue, by then called the Cheetah Club, that the Fania All-Stars were filmed in performance in the making of the movie *Nuestra Cosa* (Our Latin Thing) which is sometimes regarded as the inauguration of salsa. Between the mambo and salsa, in the brief period spanning the years 1966–1968, the boogaloo was all the rage in the New York Latin community and beyond. It was both a bridge and a break, for with all the continuities and influences in terms of musical style, the boogaloo diverged from the prevailing models of Latin music in significant ways.

Jimmy Sabater's story about the making of "Bang Bang" helps explain the social function of boogaloo, while the song itself is characteristic of its style and musical qualities. As neighbors and co-workers, African Americans and Puerto Ricans in New York had been partying together for many years. For decades they had been frequenting the same clubs, with black and Latin bands often sharing the billing. Since the musical revolution of the late 1940s, when musical giants like Mario Bauzá, Machito, and Dizzie Gillespie joined forces in the creation of Cubop or Latin jazz, the two traditions had come into even closer contact than ever, with the strains of Afro-Cuban *guaguancó, son,* and *guaracha* interlacing and energizing the complex harmonic figures of big band and bebop experimentations. For African Americans, that same midcentury mambo and Cubop period corresponded to the years of rhythm and blues, from the jump blues of Louis Jordan to the shouters and hollerers and street-corner doo-woppers of the 1950s. Scores of American popular tunes of those years bore titles, lyrics, or musical gimmicks suggestive of the mambo or cha-cha, while many young Puerto Ricans joined their African-American and Italian partners in harmonizing the echo chamber strains of doo-wop love songs and novelty numbers (see Boggs 1992a and 1993a; and Fileti 1995).

With all the close sharing of musical space and tastes, however, there were differences and distances. African-American audiences generally appreciated and enjoyed Latin musical styles, yet those who fully understood the intricacies of Afro-Cuban rhythms and came to master the challenging dance movements remained the exception rather than the rule. Most black Americans, after listening admiringly to a set of mambos and boleros, will long for their familiar blues and r&b sounds, and by the mid-1960s, it was of course soul music. Popular Latin bands thus found themselves creating a musical common ground by introducing the trappings of black American culture into their performances and thus getting the black audiences involved and onto the dance floor. "Bang Bang" by the Joe Cuba Sextet, and Latin boogaloo music in general, was intended to constitute this meeting place between Puerto Ricans and blacks, and by extension, between Latin music and the musical culture of the United States.

"Bang Bang" begins with a short piano vamp, which is then immediately joined by loud, group hand clapping and a few voices shouting excitedly but unintelligibly, and then by a large crowd chanting in unison, "bi-bi, hah! bi-bi, hah!" The chant is repeated four times, increasing each time in intensity and accompanied throughout by the repeated piano lick, hand clapping, and shouting, which is then supplemented by Jimmy Sabater on *timbales*, all the while building up to the resounding chorus "bang, bang!" This refrain phrase is introduced by the solo vocal, then repeated over and over by the group chorus while the solo, none other than the legendary Cheo Feliciano, goes off onto a kind of skat *soneo* or ad-lib, blurting out random phrases, mostly in Spanish, very much in the improvisational style of the *son montuno*. This lead vocal interacts with the choral "bang, bang" and with the bongo bells (played, it turns out, by Manny Oquendo), and throughout the song resounds in indirect and playful dialogue with another solo voice line, in English, carried by Willie Torres, mostly exhorting the crowd and the band with slang phrases like "come git it," "sock it to me," "hanky panky," and the like. Somewhere in the middle of the four-minute recording is the line, "Cornbread, hog maw, and chitlins," repeated several times and then teased out with Spanish comments like *comiendo cuchifrito* and *lechón, lechón!* The last half of the song involves three or four false endings, as over and over the irresistible rowdy clamor is rekindled by the same piano vamp, with the solo vocal exchanges taking on a more and more gossipy and jocular tone.

Though some changes were obviously required for the studio recording of the tune, "Bang Bang" remains very much a party. Like the other popular songs of boogaloo, such as Héctor Rivera's "At the Party," Peter Rodríguez's "I Like It Like That," and Johnny Colón's "Boogaloo Blues," it reenacts a bawdy happening at the peak of its emotional and sexual energy, with instrumentals and vocals playing in full and wild association with the crowd. Joe Cuba recalls, thinking mainly of "Bang Bang," that "when I recorded in those days I always left a big boom mike overhanging above all the musicians to put in a little live effect." The musical texture of the song is a patchwork of noises, emotive outbursts, cries of glee, short musical phrases, and the recurring, abiding counterpoint of the crowd chorus and the leitmotiv piano lick. The lyrics, though of no consistent narrative or dramatic significance, nevertheless do have a meaning, which is the interplay of black and Latin festivity and culture, the playful mingling of African-American phrases and cultural symbols with those from Puerto Rican daily life. Musically this same message is carried across with the collage-like mixing of familiar trappings from mambo and r&b styles. The perspective is clearly that of the Latino, and Latin music is the main defining sound of the piece; but the traditional features and structuring principles of the Afro-Cuban model are consistently overridden by their conjoining with qualities from the r&b and soul traditions. The overall effect of the recording is one of collective celebration, gleeful partying where boundaries are set not so much by national and ethnic affiliation, or even language or formalized dance movements, but by participation in that special moment of inclusive ceremony.

As "Bang Bang" illustrates, the defining theme and musical feature of boogaloo is precisely this intercultural togetherness, the solidarity engendered by living and loving in unison beyond obvious differences. Its emergence coincided with the historical moment of the civil rights movement and the coming-of-age of the first generation of Puerto Rican youth born and raised in New York City. Latin music expert and producer René López calls boogaloo "the first Nuyorican music," and a consensus has gathered in concurrence with that description. It is the sound that accompanied the teenage years of the Young Lords and of the Nuyorican poets in the later 1960s; Piri Thomas's groundbreaking novel *Down These Mean Streets* was published in 1967. Like those experiences, it attests to the guiding, exemplary role of African-American culture and politics for that generation of Puerto Ricans growing up in New York. "Bang Bang" is an explosion of excitement arising from that cultural conjunction, the linking of Puerto Rican backgrounds with the African-American influences so prevalent in all aspects of social life, including of course their music and dance.

PRELUDES IN BOOGALOO

Latin boogaloo burst onto the scene in 1966, the year that saw the recording not only of "Bang Bang" but of the other best-known boogaloo tunes as well. Johnny Colón's "Boogaloo Blues," Pete Rodríguez's "I Like It Like That," Héctor Rivera's "At the Party" all hit the record stores in 1966–67 and made overnight stars of many of the young musicians in El Barrio and in the clubs throughout the New York area. Much to the concern, and even hardship, of the established bandleaders from the 1950s and early 1960s, it was the young boogaloo musicians who seemed to come out of nowhere and were suddenly getting top billings, selling the most records, and getting the hottest requests for airplay. The standbys, on the other hand, notably Tito Puente and Charlie Palmieri, suddenly found themselves in dire straits. As Joe Cuba recalls, with boogaloo, his band, which had been around for more than ten years by then, was catapulted into the national and international spotlight; now it was sharing shows and touring with big-time performers like the Supremes, the Temptations, Marvin Gaye, James Brown, and the Drifters, and traveling widely. It had a long and successful run at the Flamboyán Hotel in Puerto Rico, where boogaloo caught on like wildfire. The most popular band in Puerto Rico in those years, El Gran Combo, brought out an album with six of the twelve cuts listed as boogaloos, and it included the immensely popular "Gran Combo's Boogaloo." The fever then held on for another year or two, longer than most of the dance crazes of those years, and even the disdainful holdouts among the more sophisticated musicians, like Eddie Palmieri and Tito Puente, came around to recording their own boogaloos. It was a time when, as many of the musicians attest, you could not *not* play boogaloo and expect to draw crowds and get recording contracts.

Jimmy Sabater got that piano lick which served as the fuse for "Bang Bang" from a tune by Richie Ray. "Bang Bang," for all its symbolic interest in responding directly to African-American tastes and for all its commercial success, was not the first boogaloo tune, nor did it even mention the word in its lyrics. Who was the first one to use the term, or to start making Latin music explicitly called boogaloo? Several musicians involved at the time point in the direction of Ricardo Ray, whose two albums *Se Soltó—On the Loose* and *Jala Jala y Boogaloo* drew immediate attention when they came out on Alegre in 1966 and 1967. Evidently, when Pete Rodríguez, Johnny Colón, and other boogaloo bands were introducing their new sides under that designation, Richie Ray had already made the term and associated musical styles familiar to dance and listening audiences. Discussions of origins always stir up debate and dissension, but if Richie Ray wasn't in fact the first he is certainly responsible for giving music called boogaloo a certain standard of fascination and quality, which little of what followed was able to live up to.

But the roots of boogaloo run deeper than its presumed founding act, even if it is of the accomplishment shown by Richie Ray and his group, with its creative mingling of jazz and rock flavors into a range of traditional Cuban styles, all in the name of boogaloo. Indeed, without using the word, "Bang Bang" and "El Pito" are closer to the core of what boogaloo is about, musically and socially, than anything in the Richie Ray and Bobby Cruz repertoire of those years. The bawdiness, the strong presence of funk and soul music, the abrupt break with some tradition-bound conventions of Latin style, all figure centrally in most boogaloo, and point more clearly to the musical influences that set the stage for that brief yet dramatic transition in Latin music of the mid-1960s period. After all, Jimmy Sabater got the inspiration for "El Pito," which in 1965 might well have preceded the songs on Richie Ray's *Se Soltó* album, not from Ray's piano but from basic motives of "Manteca." Jimmy was thinking of Machito and Dizzy Gillespie and their historic recording of the tune that became the cornerstone of Latin and jazz fusion. Even the words of "El Pito," "I'll never go back to Georgia," were spoken by Dizzy at the beginning of the "Manteca" recording, and constitute a phrase that Jimmy associates more than any other with African-American experience and expression. What appealed to him most for the purposes of "El Pito" was the perfect fit between the rhythm of that spoken phrase and the cadence of Latin musical phrasing: "Never go back to Georgia, never go back." It was all this, Jimmy comments, "and none of us had ever been to Georgia."

Puerto Rican musicians during the boogaloo era, whether newcomers or those with years of experience, were all formed during the illustrious mambo period of the 1950s. All of them, even those who venture furthest into non-Latin musical fields, acknowledge their indebtedness to the "Big Three" and speak with awe and unqualified gratitude of the crowning achievements of the Machito, Tito Rodríguez, and Tito Puente orchestras, especially in their unforgettable home at the Palladium. Mambo, guaguancó, *son guajira, cha-cha-chá,* guaracha, *bolero,* all performed at the peak of their potential, constituted the music that nourished and inspired Latin musicians during the 1950s and throughout the 1960s and beyond. Both major crazes of that decade—the charanga-pachanga fever of the first half and the boogaloo of the second—arose and faded in the afterglow of the Palladium years.

But the new generation of Latinos emerging in the 1960s, including the musicians then in their teens and twenties, was reared on another musical culture as well. While surrounded by a full range of Latin styles at home, on the radio, and on family and neighborhood occasions, many young Puerto Ricans in the 1950s and early 1960s were listening to and singing doo-wop and other rhythm and blues and rock and roll sounds. While the "older" musicians associated with boogaloo, those then in their thirties, had earlier performed with or in association with the bands of the mambo era, the younger ones typically recall that their favorite music when growing up, "our music," had been r&b and other forms of African-American popular song, especially doo-wop. Influential boogaloo composers and performers like Tony Pabón of the Pete Rodríguez band, Johnny Colón and his vocalist Tito Ramos, and Tony Rojas, Bobby Marín, King Nando and countless others were members or sometimes founders of doo-wop groups even before they connected, or reconnected, with Latin music. Bobby Marín speaks authoritatively of the Puerto Ricans involved in some of the major doo-wop acts, beginning with the three who formed the Teenagers with Frankie Lymon, and who evidently composed some of his biggest hits. For King Nando, the Drifters was his favorite group after he arrived from Puerto Rico in the 1950s, and for Jimmy Sabater it was the Harptones, though his all-time "king," of course, was Nat King Cole.

Two musical languages thus coexisted in the world of the boogaloo musician, that of his cultural and family heritage and that of life among peers in the streets and at school. The challenge was how to bring these two worlds together and create a new language of their own. King Nando tells of how as a teenager raised on doo-wop and early rock and roll he once went to the Palladium and heard Tito Rodríguez play "Mama Güela." "From then on," he recalls of this moment in 1961, "I Latinized all my r&b arrangements" (Salazar 1992:244). The musical career of Johnny Colón, whose band gained fame with its 1967 recording of "Boogaloo Blues," began when he formed and sang with the East Harlem doo-wop group The Sunsets. For Colón, boogaloo was above all "a kind of bridge, a way for the young, r&b-reared Latino musicians and fans to link back with their musical heritage." This musical linkage took many forms, and only some of it was called boogaloo; the boogaloo repertoire actually ranges along a continuum from basically Latin sounds and rhythms with the trappings of African-American styles on one end, to what are r&b, funk and soul songs with a touch of Latin percussion, instrumentals, Spanish-language lyrics or inflections. The only proviso for it to be part of the world of boogaloo is that both musical idioms be present, and that both the Latino and the African-American publics find something of their own to relate to.

Though foreshadowed by it, the cross-cultural fusions characteristic of the boogaloo period differed in significant ways from those of Cubop and Latin jazz of the previous generation. For one thing, the Latin musicians of the boogaloo period had both traditions, the Latin and the African American, active in their experience from the beginning of their musical efforts, while with few exceptions there was in the 1940s and 1950s still a divide between Latin and African-American musicians in terms of background familiarity. Furthermore, boogaloo involved the mixing of Afro-Cuban style with the vernacular, blues and gospel-based currents of African-American music, the r&b and soul sounds that saturated the airwaves and broadly popular settings of the 1960s period, and sold to broad markets not even approximated by any jazz offerings. It was the dance and party music of the wide American and international public that the boogaloo fusion took as the most direct partner of the popular Latin sounds, such that aside from the most immediate connection to African-American styles, boogaloo involved the engagement of Latin Caribbean music with the pop music market to a degree unprecedented in previous periods. Salsa personality Izzy Sanabria considers Latin boogaloo "the greatest potential that we had to really cross over in terms of music" (Boggs 1992c:191).

While mambo and doo-wop thus form the dual heritage from the 1950s that went into the making of boogaloo, there are more immediate precursors, from the early 1960s, that anticipate many of the features of Latin boogaloo, and help us to understand in a broader context the fad that was to hold sway in the Latin music field later in the decade. That context may be thought of as New York Latin music of the 1960s, the period prior to the advent of salsa, in chronological terms, or in musical terms as Latin soul, the whole range of Latin–African-American fusions of which boogaloo is a part. Before boogaloo hit the scene, for example, there was Latin music in English, connecting to soul and funk rhythms and sounds (as well as jazz), based on improvised conversation or party noise, and with sales capable of cracking the national charts. In songs like Willie Torres's "To Be with You," Ray Barretto's "El Watusi," Mongo Santamaría's "Watermelon Man," and Eddie Palmieri's "Azúcar," all recorded in the early 1960s, many of the identifying ingredients of Latin boogaloo are already present, and at a level of musical achievement seldom surpassed during the boogaloo years. They were, along with Tito Puente's "Oye Como Va," the most popular Latin recordings of those years, and all involved an inflection of Latin traditions in the direction of African-American r&b and soul sounds. They are among the "classics" of Latin soul (excepting perhaps Puente's, where the association is based more on Santana's Latin rock cover version of 1969), and thus prefigure in varied ways the whole gesture of boogaloo.

"To Be with You" has been called the "all-time classic Latin soul ballad," and there are few New York Latinos around in the early 1960s who would dispute that judgment (Salazar 1992:241). What may appear surprising is that such a stature is accorded a song entirely in English, and evidencing far more "soul" than "Latin." It was written in the early 1950s by Willie Torres and Nick Jiménez, a team responsible for composing some of the first pieces of Latin dance music in English, starting with a version of "I've Got You under My Skin" in cha-cha tempo, and the very popular "Mambo of the Times" (Salazar 1992:240). Torres, reflecting on those early crossovers, feels there was a need for English lyrics not only in order to reach non-Latino audiences, but among the New York Latinos of the day as well. "You have to remember," says Torres, whose musical career extends back to the early 1940s, "that most of us were Nuyoricans, born here, bred here. Machito and them, they were like the anchor, but as it kept going, most of the kids, their Spanish was limited, like mine. I spoke Spanish at home because I had no choice. But as far as having a great knowledge of it, I didn't. So I got with Joe," he continues, referring to bandleader Joe Cuba, and he might have added Nick Jiménez, Jimmy Sabater, Cheo Feliciano, and the others. "He was of my era, too. So we said, let's do this in English, and it worked out." It is thus clear that long before the boogaloo era, as exemplified by the early years of the Joe Cuba Sextet, there was already a major bilingual and English-dominant Latin music community in New York.

Torres never got to record "To Be with You" with the Joe Cuba band, though he sang it to countless hotel and club audiences through the 1950s, beginning with a memorable debut at the Stardust Ballroom in 1953. Torres even recorded the tune on the *Manicero* album of the Alegre All-Stars, where producer Al Santiago labeled it a "bolero gas." But Torres had left the Joe Cuba group in 1956, and so it was Jimmy Sabater, the lead English vocalist of the band at the time, who came to immortalize the song in the 1962 single recording. Its inclusion in the 1967 *Steppin' Out* album draws the song into association with boogaloo, with which it has mainly its penchant for English lyrics in common. But it is, no doubt, Latin soul, of the Nat King Cole with a slight Latin accent variety. The "Latin" musical accents of this r&b love ballad are also muted, with bolero tempo and bongo slaps playing off against the vocal harmonies and crescendos that carry the romantic feeling of the song. As tailored as the sound is to an American ballroom setting, Torres is quick to recall that "To Be with You" is actually an interpretation of an old bolero, "Nunca (No Te Engañé)" that he himself often sang in Spanish as "Estar Contigo."

Willie Torres did get to be "El Watusi," though. "You remember that song 'El Watusi'?" he asks, "Well, you're looking at him. For real,

I'm the other voice. Not the deep one that does most of the talking, but the other one, *el watusi* himself, the one he's talking about, and to. Ray Barretto, who did the tune, got me to be the other voice, to just grunt a few words in response to the deep one, the one who's talking about el watusi as the biggest and baddest in all of Havana: 'Caballero, allí acaba de entrar el watusi. Ese mulato que mide siete pies y pesa 169 libras . . . El hombre más guapo de La Habana.' That was Wito Cortwright, the Cuban who used to be second voice and *güiro* player in Arsenio Rodríguez's band. We were the voices. And so I am el watusi."

Few beyond Willie Torres's own circle would know that he was the voice of the fearsome neighborhood tough guy, but Ray Barretto's 1962 recording went on to hit the Top 20 on the U.S. pop charts in 1963, peaking at number 3 in May of that year. It thus became the first recording by a Latin band to reach that milestone, and stands to this day as the greatest commercial success, still unsurpassed in Barretto's long and varied career. "El Watusi" was originally the B-side novelty number intended to accompany the more accomplished "Charanga Moderna" as part of the raging charanga-pachanga craze in New York Latin music. But it was "El Watusi," that odd, charanga-flavored sample of braggadocio in tough-talking Cuban street Spanish that caught on and set the stage for the boogaloo phenomenon in other ways. Here it is obviously not the bilingual or English lyrics, nor the admixture of r&b sounds, though there can be no doubt that there were many African Americans among its fans. In this case it is the spontaneous, conversational nature of the voices and the general rowdy crowd atmosphere that anticipates songs like "El Pito," "Bang Bang," "At the Party" and others in the boogaloo mode. The hand clapping, which accompanies the unchanging bass beat throughout the tune, becomes an earmark of Latin boogaloo, as does in many cases the free and open song structure. "Lyrics?" Willie Torres recalls, laughing, "we made it all up as we went along."

But the fluke hit "El Watusi" prefigured the boogaloo craze in other ways as well, an association that was furthured with the popular recording by Willie Rosario, "Watusi Boogaloo," from 1968. Its commercial success itself, a tune by a Latin band hitting the charts, was proof that it was possible to play around with Latin sounds and have a hit. But there were other reasons for the appeal of this zany Spanish rap with the charanga flute, beyond its musical novelty, which also point to a commonality with boogaloo. For the Watusi was also one of the most popular dances in the same year as the release of Barretto's recording, especially after the release of the smash hit "Wah Watusi" by the Orlons, which was high on the charts for thirteen weeks, peaking at number 5, in the previous year. The dance craze itself was introduced by The Vibrations with its 1961 hit "The

Watusi," which in turn is based on the similar tune "Let's Go, Let's Go, Let's Go," by Hank Ballard and the Midnighters, the group, incidentally, which sang the original version of "The Twist" in 1959, a year before Chubby Checker's historic cover version. The word "watusi," then, along with its sundry undefined connotations and connection to a well-known dance move, was in the air when "El Watusi" came out, such that Barretto's recording, in a musical language totally unrelated to the American watusi, rode the wave of that catchy familiarity of the moment.

Clearly, Latin boogaloo was similarly implicated in the prevailing dance crazes and pop categories in its time a few years later. Though there is no certainty as to its place of origin—Chicago and New York being the main contenders—it is established that the boogaloo was "the most successful new dance of 1965–66," the very years of the emergence of Latin boogaloo, quickly overshadowing the Jerk, the Twine, and the Monkey of the previous season (see Pruter 1991:204). The first of the many boogaloo records, according to this version, was "Boo-Ga-Loo" by the Chicago dance/comedy/singing duo Tom and Jerrio, who got the idea from seeing the dance done at a record hop. "The record, released on ABC, was a huge, million-selling hit for the pair in April 1965." A slew of boogaloo recordings then followed, including the Flamingos's "Boogaloo Party," many of which became moderate hits on the soul and funk markets. Another account of black boogaloo, less oriented toward city of origin and pop charts and more toward musical force, identifies as the quintessential sound that of classic soul tunes like "Mustang Sally" and "In the Midnight Hour," both of which were made popular by Wilson Pickett. It was Pickett, too, who recorded the huge 1967 hit "Funky Broadway." Whether boogaloo is defined by these recordings, some more memorable than others, or the peculiar dance move, which "had a totally new look compared to previous dances, and its popularity crossed over to whites" (Pruter 1991: 204) it is clear that boogaloo was the foremost name for funky soul music at that moment in its history, and that Latin boogaloo took its name and direct crossover impulse from that immediate source. Though closer musically to its African-American namesake than was "El Watusi," the same process of mass popularity through association occurs, on a far more influential scale, with Latin boogaloo.

But neither "To Be with You" nor "El Watusi" exemplified or foreshadowed the main musical quality of Latin boogaloo, which is the fusion of Afro-Cuban rhythms with those of funk. That accomplishment is most directly attributable to Mongo Santamaría and Willie Bobo, and most familiar to general audiences in another chart-setting hit of the times, Mongo's "Watermelon Man," listed nationally in August 1963.

Some would even consider "Watermelon Man," written by Herbie Hancock, to be "the original boogaloo," but here the reference is specifically musical. For beyond the ad-libbed, conversational atmosphere in the vocals, a few grunts, animal sounds, and exhortations, Mongo's tune has the sound, the rhythmic feel of the Latin-funk fusion, most notably in the percussive backbeat on the timbales and other mostly Afro-Cuban elements of the rhythm section. While the moaning brass sound is more in the Latin jazz idiom for which Mongo is famous, the rhythmic texture of the piece is closer to that of r&b, and it is the pronounced backbeat that anticipates the signature effect of Latin boogaloo.

Though it was Mongo's recording of "Watermelon Man" that drew the broad attention to this musical possibility, there were other musicians who shared this early Latin-funk field with him and who personified more directly the Puerto Rican–black American rhythmic fusion. One was obviously Willie Bobo, the black Puerto Rican born William Correa in Spanish Harlem who had been Mongo's protégé since the late 1940s. "I was his interpreter," he said of his relation to the great Cuban drummer Mongo, and "in return he showed me the different shades of sounds the drum is capable of producing" (Salazar 1992:241). In tunes like the significantly titled "Fried Neck Bones and Some Home Fries," Bobo stands squarely at the crossroads of Afro-Cuban and African-American cultures, with a particularly sharp nose for funk. At the other side of the Latin-black divide is Pucho, the African-American Henry Lee Brown from Harlem who formed the Latin Soul Brothers, famous, among other things, for its recording "Boogaloo on Broadway" of 1967. It is Pucho, in fact, who remembers Willie Bobo circulating among the musicians sniffing for funk. Pucho recalls that his band was, along with Mongo's and Willie Bobo's, one of the top three Latin-funk acts in the years before boogaloo, his own group serving as the training ground for the other two, which surpassed his in prominence. He was one of various African Americans from Harlem who mastered timbales, according to the recollection of Benny Bonilla, the *timbalero* for the Pete Rodríguez band. During the mid-1960s Pucho would typically make Latin boogaloos by taking known soul hits of the time (he mentions "Mustang Sally" and "In the Midnight Hour," among others) and "put Latin rhythms to them." And it was Pucho, the deft timbalero for the all-black American Latin Soul Brothers, who coined his own catchphrase for the music of Latin boogaloo—"cha-cha with a backbeat."

Ironically, the Latin musician who stood most prominently at the threshold of boogaloo was the one who held it in the most utter disdain. For it was Eddie Palmieri, who to this day regards boogaloo as the most tragic retrogression in New York Latin music, whose bold creativity brought Latin music into the 1960s and opened the eyes and ears of the musicians of the boogaloo era to what Latin music could be like for their own generation. The admiration for him among musicians associated with Latin boogaloo is unanimous. Palmieri's La Perfecta, with five excellent albums since 1962, was the hottest Latin band around by the mid-1960s when boogaloo hit the scene. He had top billings every-where, and with Manny Oquendo on timbales, Barry Rogers and Jose Rodríguez on the trademark trombones, and Palmieri's ingenious arrangements, he set the standard for sheer musicianship and audience appeal, among Latins and audiences of many other nationalities. In fact, in another foreboding of boogaloo's social appeal, Palmieri had a huge, enthusiastic following among African Americans.

The origin of one of Palmieri's biggest hits of those salad years, "Azúcar," directly prefigures the making of vintage boogaloo songs like "Bang Bang" and "I Like It Like That." "'Eddie, play some sugar for us,' Blacks would yell at him time and again. 'Sugar' was the word they invoked whenever they wanted a fiery up-tempo Palmieri tune. Palmieri wrote 'Azúcar' (Sugar For You) and it attracted an even larger number of Blacks to his dances" (Salazar 1992:242). This is but one example of Palmieri fashioning the qualities of Latin music in response to an African-American dance public, just as the Joe Cuba, Richie Ray, Pete Rodríguez, and other groups were to do in the subsequent boogaloo phase.

Though a proto-boogaloo model in this sense, however, and pre-ceding them in popularity by only a few years, Palmieri has never had a kind word for anything related to boogaloo. He scorned the amateur-ishness, the banality, and especially the retreat from serious and creative adaptations of Afro-Cuban models being developed in those years after the blockade of Cuban music following the 1959 revolution. "It was like Latin bubblegum," Palmieri recalls. "'Bang Bang,' what's that? It's like something you find in a Frosted Flakes box. And half the musicians did-n't even know what side of the instruments to play out of." Aside from his musical judgment, which was shared by many, including many of those associated with boogaloo, Palmieri was of course thinking of the disastrous impact the boogaloo craze had on the established musicians, such as his brother Charlie and of course Tito Puente, Machito, and even Tito Rodríguez. The top billings and frequent bookings they had grown accustomed to were suddenly in jeopardy, and their recordings vastly outsold; ominous changes were afoot in the Latin recording and broadcast fields. Though he accepts the recognition, Palmieri considers himself among the victims of boogaloo rather than a benefactor, and of course would resist being considered the model of any kind for what was for him the boogaloo "epidemic."

"¿Qué qué, Eddie Palmieri, boogaloo?" Such is the first line of "¡Ay Qué Rico!," a boogaloo by Eddie Palmieri. The voice is Cheo Feliciano, on bass is the legendary "Cachao" López doing a shing-a-ling, on a recording from 1968, when the boogaloo fever was already beginning to subside. The final irony of the Eddie Palmieri–boogaloo story is that it was Palmieri, the staunchest antagonist of everything boogaloo, who composed and led what is arguably the best boogaloo recording of them all. "¡Ay Qué Rico!" is bawdy, festive, conversational, and has all the trappings of Latin boogaloo sounds. Its special attraction in the booga- loo repertoire is that its playful irony seems to be directed at itself — as if it is saying, "You want boogaloo, here's boogaloo!"—and of course its consistent musical excellence. That and another number on Palmieri's important *Champagne* album of 1968, "The African Twist," show Palmieri fully in the spirit of Latin funk. Another play with pop styles, "The African Twist," was written and sung by an African-American woman, Cynthia Ellis, in a Motown-reminiscent style. In these tunes it is clear that Palmieri was not spending his time berating boogaloo, but taking it to another level.

HARD-CORE BOOGALOO: "I LIKE IT LIKE THAT" AND "BOOGALOO BLUES"

"Eddie Palmieri was the headliner," recalls Benny Bonilla, the timbalero for Pete Rodríguez y Su Conjunto. "They needed a cheap band to open up for him, so they heard about us. So the booking agents, I remember it was two West Indian guys, came to hear us at one of our gigs, and they liked us. So they asked us for a short recording to help promote the dance on the radio. We looked at each other and said, 'Recording? We ain't got no recording.' And they said, 'No problem, we'll book a stu- dio, just do a short spot, one minute, and we'll use that.'" Pete Rodríguez and his band members started groping around for something to play and couldn't come up with anything. Then Bonilla remembers that Tony Pabón, the group's trumpeter, vocalist and composer, said, "Let's try this." He taught Pete how to do that piano vamp, and started ad-libbing: "Uh, ah, I like it like that." The spot was played on the radio and, according to Benny, "the phone at the station started ringing off the hook."

"I Like It Like That" was recorded in 1966, in a full studio session for Alegre, and the Pete Rodríguez orchestra became an overnight sen- sation in El Barrio and around the city. The group had been around awhile, since the end of the 1950s, but mostly as openers, a backup band with low billings beneath all the major attractions: Machito, Tito Puente, Tito Rodríguez, El Gran Combo, Johnny Pacheco, Orquesta Broadway. They even played on the closing nights of the Palladium, all of which featured the likes of Eddie Palmieri, Vicentico Valdéz, and Orquesta Broadway. "We didn't have the best band," Benny Bonilla admits. "We had no training or anything. We were out there to have fun." Unlike the Joe Cuba Sextet or even Richie Ray, the other possible initiators of Latin boogaloo, the Pete Rodríguez band had not established itself before the advent of boogaloo. The group's recognition began and ended with the boogaloo craze, making them, of all the major groups, the boogaloo band par excellence (Carp 1996:14–15). And "I Like It Like That," by far their greatest hit and known to the world through cover versions, movie sound tracks, and Burger King commercials, might well be considered the quintessential song of Latin boogaloo.

Sex, drugs, and rock and roll. Latin boogaloo thrived during the years of the 1960s counterculture, the heyday of flower power, hippies, psychedelic drugs and sexual liberation. Young people were listening to the Beatles, the Rolling Stones, and Jimi Hendrix as they milled in their publicized "be-ins." "Boogaloo Blues," the only major hit of Latin boogaloo to use the word boogaloo in its title, touched on many of these chords of appeal to the youth culture of the times and its market. The song is an acid trip, an orgasm, a loud party, a brooding reverie, a taunt and seduction, all to a fusion of bluesy jazz piano, r&b vocalizing, and outbursts of *montunos* and Latin rhythms. Like most other boogaloo tunes, it is a seemingly disheveled patchwork of musical modes and tempos, the only structuring principle being the repeated movement from slow, hand-clapping, and bass beginnings to a buildup and climax of energy, and then a restart and new buildup. Yet, as representative as it is taken to be of Latin boogaloo as a phenomenon, "Boogaloo Blues" is in some ways idiosyncratic among the best-known recordings of the genre, in part because here the lyrics tell a story.

Tito Puente said the song sounded like a Coca-Cola commercial. The judgment of "El Rey" may be harsh, and must have been discouraging to Johnny Colón and his youthful band members. But there can be no doubt that the song is to a significant degree a fabrication of the recording industry. Despite the creativity and sincerity of the musicians, who did want to put out a new kind of sound in tune with their times, the intervention of experienced record producers and radio disk jockeys proved decisive in the construction of the song, and in its immediate popularity.

"GYPSY WOMAN": THE SINGULAR JOE BATAAN

The boogaloo fever and marketing potential, while bringing important and timely innovations to Latin music of the day, spawned a whole crop of new musicians and groups, all responding to the opportunity to combine their two musical heritages, Latin and African American. Some were adept and experienced musicians and composers who managed to record sizable hits, like Héctor Rivera with his "At the Party." Rivera provided a range of bands, including Joe Cuba's and Eddie Palmieri's, with many of their compositions and arrangements, and "At the Party" was on the Billboard charts for eight weeks in 1966–67, peaking at number 26. Though he brought in seasoned musicians for the recording, notably Cachao on bass and Jimmy Sabater on timbales, and though he boasts using an African-American singer, Ray Pollard, for the r&b vocals, "At the Party" has a derivative effect when heard today, not quite matching the freshness and playfulness of "Bang Bang," resonating too closely with Sabater's other big seller, "Yeah, Yeah," and lacking the infectious hook-line refrain and shifting tempos of "I Like It Like That." Rivera himself never liked or used the term boogaloo, and he is surely right in claiming far more interests and accomplishments than are implied in it. But given the influence of commercially motivated tastemakers in stamping performers and their acts, he is known to posterity primarily by that one tune, and by his association with the boogaloo period.

But the rash of Latin boogaloo bands consisted mostly of newcomers, young singers and novice instrumentalists who jumped on the bandwagon and, for better or worse, made their musical start and left their mark. Singers like Joey Pastrana and Ralfie Pagán, for example, enjoyed immense popularity in El Barrio at the time, and are remembered fondly for their soulful ballads infused with Latin rhythms and lyrics that typically trailed off into or were interspersed with Spanish. King Nando (Fernando Rivera), the guitarist and singer from El Barrio famous for his shing-a-lings, captivated audiences in the summer of 1967 with his composition "Fortuna," a slow, grinding number inspired by memories of his native Puerto Rico. The Lebrón Brothers, a family-based group from Brooklyn, were another creation of George Goldner's boogaloo hit-making machine, though before being named (by Goldner) they had minor hits on their own with tunes like "Tall Tales" and "Funky Blues." Yet they were also casualties of the same process, and like so many of the other youthful acts of the time, they remember the experience with a note of bitterness. Speaking of Goldner and their best-known album, the group's spokesman, Ángel Lebrón, comments, "When we recorded *Psychedelic Goes Latin*, we didn't get paid for it.

Despite the propaganda that was printed then, the boogaloo bandlead-ers were the hottest bands at the time. The boogaloo era came to an end when we threatened to rebel against the package deals" (Salazar 1992:245–46). Beyond these examples, young musicians with evident potential and genuine popularity, there were other groups who appear to have been made for the occasion, bearing bubblegum-sounding names like the Latin-aires and even the La-Teens. But this gimmicky nomenclature can be deceiving, as a forgotten group like the Latin Souls produced some impressive a capella songs, and there is no telling how many of the selections of the Hi Latin Boogaloos, organized by Gil Suárez, might have survived oblivion were it not for the vagaries and interested selectiveness of the commercial gatekeepers. The Coquets, two African-American woman singers who did backup for Joey Pastrana, might also have made a contribution to the repertoire of Latin soul vocalizing.

But of all of these upstarts from the boogaloo era, the one who stands apart and who has enjoyed a long though difficult career since is surely Joe Bataan. His first recording, "Gypsy Woman," was an imme-diate and lasting hit among black and Puerto Rican audiences when it was released in 1967, the midst of the Latin boogaloo era. Yet neither that song, a Latinized cover of Curtis Mayfield's huge 1961 hit with the Impressions, nor any of his many other compositions, are considered boogaloo, nor has he ever wanted them to be. "I don't like the word, never did," Bataan comments. "In fact I hate it. I consider it insulting and always have. My own music, and most of what's called boogaloo, is for me Latin soul." He sometimes refers to it as "La-So" for short, and after salsa set in, he takes credit for coining the term "salsoul," which was then popularized as the name of a briefly successful record label.

Though raised in El Barrio and a well-known figure in the street gangs there during the late 1950s and early '60s, Bataan was not of Puerto Rican ethnic parentage. "My father was Filipino and my mother was African American, and my culture is Puerto Rican," as he explains it. His childhood associates were as much African American as Puerto Ricans, and his music, which he undertook after spending years in prison, has tended to have greater appeal among blacks and whites than among strictly Latino audiences. If the music of the Latin boogaloo period made up a continuum from Latin to r&b, Bataan's is clearly on the black side of the spectrum. But he has always been an extremely eclectic composer and performer, drawing ideas and experiments from a wide range of sources. And far more explicitly than any of the young barrio musicians of the time, he was inspired in his creations by his own experience and from life in the streets. Even a reluctant admirer like bassist Andy González, who has little regard for the music itself, had to admit that "if you want to know what was going on in the streets, listen to the songs of Joe Bataan" (Luciano 1971:53).

Bataan's life in music is a story of survival and determination, and provides further insight into the machinations of the industry. "Music was my salvation," he says. "At 15 I began a five-year sentence at Coxsackie. One day after a guard's lecture shook me up I decided I was going to learn a skill and stay out of prison. . . . Through trial and error I learned to play the piano. I imitated Eddie Palmieri's style, he was my man. . . . In 1965 I organized a band and [promoter] Federico Pagani got us steady gigs" (Salazar 1992:244). The band consisted of very young kids from the neighborhood, with little or no musical experience. When his singing of "Gypsy Woman" caused an enthusiastic response from the audience, he continues, "Pagani referred me to Goldner. After I sang 'Gypsy Woman' for him, he told me in a polite way, 'It's great, but let someone else sing it. You do not have a masculine voice.'" Bataan was furious, offended perhaps more in his masculinity than his musicianship, and was determined to get even. "I signed a contract with [famed deejay] Dick 'Ricardo' Sugar, who in turn introduced me to Jerry Masucci of Fania after he heard me sing at the Boricua Theater. I signed with Fania and recorded 'Gypsy Woman' in 1967" (244).

Bataan explains the popularity of his music, created as it was with so little professional training or support, to be the public's identification with his realistic themes taken from everyday life in society, and not just the parties and good times. Well-known early tunes like "What Good Is a Castle," "Poor Boy" and "Ordinary Guy," he says, "were bestsellers because I was singing about me, my life, my experiences. . . . Mr. Goldner once told me that my songs were sad. Suddenly I realized it was true. There never was much happiness in my life. I rarely used the word love. Many people identified with my songs because they also experienced the same pain, day after day" (244). Even his first hit "Gypsy Woman," an upbeat dance tune overtly about admiring love for an exoticized woman, is also tinged with a tone of sadness, partly due to Bataan's own unpretentious, "ordinary guy" voice with its characteristic flattening at the end of each line. Without being gloomy or morose, his songs do not typically revel in the kind of ecstasy and enthusiasm notable in most songs identified with Latin boogaloo. They seem like the sounds left after the party is over, or coming from outside the party looking in. Their effect is not to dampen the festive atmosphere—thousands of young people have partied to his music over the years—but they tend to remind the revelers of the hard, cold world around them in everyday life. Their musical simplicity and apparent lack of sophistication are thus deceptive, and in no way negate the emotional depth and homespun creativity of his fusions of black and Latin cultural idioms. Joe Bataan stands as the social conscience, and with his contributions to the formation of later styles like disco and rap, the continuation of Latin boogaloo as a cultural impulse of the 1960s.

BYE-BYE BOOGALOO

"The Boogaloo didn't die out. It was killed off by envious old band-leaders, a few dance promoters and a popular Latin disc jockey." By 1969, just three years after its explosive entry onto the New York music scene, Latin boogaloo was gone, and most musicians involved, young and older, agree with King Nando's explanation of its rapid demise. "We were the hottest bands and we drew the crowds. But we were never given top billing or top dollar. The Boogaloo bandleaders were forced to accept 'package deals' which had us hopping all over town . . . one hour here, one hour there . . . for small change. When word got out we were going to unite and no longer accept the package deals, our records were no longer played over the radio. The Boogaloo era was over and so were the careers of most of the Boogaloo bandleaders" (Salazar 1992:245).

Not everyone bemoaned its passing in equal measure, of course, or view it in such conspiratorial terms. The boogaloo was after all just another dance fad on the American pop scene, and thus destined to a fleeting life span and instant oblivion. Latin boogaloo was more than that, as it marked an important intervention in the history of Latin music as well, and served as an expression of Puerto Rican and African-American cultures in those pivotal years of their experience in New York. But in the name of boogaloo, rather than the broader Latin soul concept, the style was doomed to fade, as a new generation of young Latinos come to seek out something that they, too, can call their own. The "next big thing" for Latin music in New York went by the name of "salsa."

"Boogaloo was eclipsed? Yeah, I guess so. And you know, thank God, in a way." Willie Torres, the veteran vocalist and composer in whose career boogaloo was just a phase, was relieved when the fever subsided, though he qualifies his judgment when he recalls the sheer fun they had playing music in those years. "Un vacilón," he says, "it was a goof." He himself didn't go on past boogaloo, leaving the music business in 1970 to take a job driving a bus with the MTA. But he is comforted to think that the proven musicians, abruptly sidelined by the boogaloo craze, did have a chance to come back and prove their longevity. "Sure, a lot of promising young talent got blocked, but look at Cheo Feliciano, Eddie Palmieri, Tito Puente, Ray Barretto, Larry

Harlow . . . They and a lot of other greats survived the craze and went on to greater heights than ever." For Willie Torres, the main responsibility for the eclipse of boogaloo in the name of salsa, aside from the musicians themselves, was Fania Records. Though the category "salsa" did not come into currency until 1972, it was Fania that shook New York Latin music loose of the boogaloo and went on to define the sound of the 1970s to world audiences.

Boogaloo, Shing-a-ling, *jala jala*—none of that was part of the package, nor was the fusion with r&b or the street origins of the music. The boogaloo musicians were not named to the Fania All-Stars, and none were present on that historic night at the Cheetah when "Our Latin Thing" was filmed. Not that Fania has been consistent in excising these sounds, having been the first to record Joe Bataan, Willie Colón, and other initiates. Its invaluable 1983 anthology "60's Gold," which includes many of the boogaloo classics, is evidence that it was anything but conspiratorial in its marketing strategy. But Izzy Sanabría, sometimes called "Mr. Salsa" for his role as master of ceremonies and publisher of *Latin New York* magazine, points to Fania in drawing the relationship between musical tastes and potential economic gain. "What destroyed it," he says of Latin boogaloo, "was a movement by Fania. And what happened was, Puente and the others, who were not with Fania at the time, put down the Latin Boogaloo because the kids were off clave. I mean eventually Puente recorded the Boogaloo. But you see, they were not on clave. They were not perfectly syncopated. But they were singing English lyrics. And this music became extremely popular. . . . So this was eventually eased out, in order to return to the more typical, correctly played music, supposedly. They were critical of all these kids. I mean Tito Puente used to describe Willie Colon as a kiddie band. Which it was" (Boggs 1992c:191).

Because of the broad visibility achieved by salsa in the intervening years, the musician most widely (though mistakenly) associated with the inner-city, streetwise spirit of boogaloo is surely Willie Colón. Born in 1950, Colón was perhaps too young in the boogaloo days to participate, and never recorded any boogaloos, either in name or in musical style.[2] But his first album, *El Malo*, came out in 1967, during the height of boogaloo, and achieved great success. Though the musicianship of the "kiddie band" was widely scorned by knowing musicians, that and subsequent releases featured album covers establishing his identity as a "bad" street tough. Of course Ray Barretto's 1967 album *Acid* was also a major hit of that year, which, along with his all-time 1961 hit "El Watusi," made him another Fania stalwart bearing a continuity with the boogaloo era. As is Larry Harlow, along with Johnny Pacheco, perhaps

the musical mastermind behind Fania, who dabbled—unsuccessfully—
with boogaloo during those years. But it is Willie Colón, along with his
vocalist, Héctor Lavoe, whom many of the boogaloo musicians remember from the streets, that, justifiably or not, represents the bridge
between the boogaloo era and the advent of salsa. As part of the Fania
stable, he then went on to become "more and more of a force in this
business," as Sanabria concludes, much to the "amazement" of Tito
Puente.

But the "movement by Fania," its effort to establish a certain range
of identifiable stylistic possibilities for its "salsa" concept, was more
intent on change than continuity, at least with the immediate past. The
emphasis would be on "roots," continued recovery and reworking of
Afro-Cuban traditions in their varied combinations with jazz. English
lyrics were out, as was any strong trace of r&b or funk. The rich legacies of Arsenio Rodríguez, Orquesta Aragón, Machito, Arcanio, and the
whole *guaguancó-son*-mambo tradition took precedence over any
experimentation with American pop styles. Even traditional Puerto
Rican music, though always secondary to the Cuban, served as a source,
as in the *danzas, aguinaldos, seises,* and *plenas* in a few of the landmark
albums by Eddie Palmieri and Willie Colón from the "salsa" period.
Explicit musical references to the African roots of the music were typically via Cuba and the Caribbean, even in stereotypical terms as in one
of Colón's biggest hits, "Ché Ché Colé."[3] The African-American connection with the New York Latino community receded in prominence,
at least in terms of vernacular musical styles. Willie Colón even raises
the all-Spanish lyrics to a matter of principle, saying, "The language was
all we have left. Why should we give in on that one?"[4] It is a point that
is perhaps easier to insist on when you can count on the likes of a Tite
Curet Alonso, the prolific Puerto Rican songwriter who composed many
of Colón's most memorable lyrics.

"The Boogaloo might have been killed off," notes Latin music historian
Max Salazar, "but Latin Soul lived on" (1992:247). With a broader
understanding of the musical and social experience called boogaloo, or
salsa for that matter, and disengaging it from those commercially created
categories, it becomes possible to see the continuity and coherence of the
Latin–African American musical fusion in clearer historical perspective.
Many of the musicians themselves preferred the idea of Latin soul all
along, even during the peak of boogaloo's popularity, and the term may
be seen to embrace musical styles both prior and subsequent to the rise
and fall of boogaloo, perhaps even including much of what has been
called salsa. With the help of his guiding concept of "Afro-American

Latinized rhythms," Salazar is able to identify an entire lineage of musical follow-through on the impulse of boogaloo, an inventory that includes not only direct holdovers from the era like Louie Ramírez, Bobby Marín and his Latin Chords, and Chico Mendoza, but unexpected standbys like Johnny Pacheco, Mongo Santamaría, and the Fania All-Stars, along with non-Caribbean Latinos like Santana and Jorge Dalto.

Dislodged from the power of Fania's formative influence, the term salsa itself can be thought of in more expansive and inclusive terms, and as is necessary a full twenty-five years after its "founding," can also be conceived in its various stages and tendencies. Maybe, as Tito Ramos suggests, boogaloo should be considered part of what he calls *salsa clásica* (as against the *salsa monga,* "lame salsa," of more recent years) and its repertoire a significant inclusion among the "oldies" of the genre. Certainly the music radio programming in Puerto Rico and other parts of Latin America present it in that way, as do some of the recent anthologies of Latin music from the 1960s and '70s. The sounds of Pete Rodríguez, Joe Cuba, and Richie Ray are still adored in countries like Colombia and Venezuela, and there no sharp distinction is made between those old favorites and what is called salsa.

In retrospect, perhaps it is true, as is claimed by some commentators, that the most important influence that Latin boogaloo exerted was not on Latin music but on black American music. John Storm Roberts describes Latin boogaloo as "one of the single most important factors in moving black rhythm sections from a basic four-to-the-bar concept to tumbao-like bass and increasingly Latin percussive patterns" (1979:169). That may be the case, but of course that impact started well before boogaloo, and it should be no reason to understate the change which that eclipsed era brought to Latin music, even if mainly by negative example. Growing out of a time of "strong Puerto Rican identification with Black politics and culture," cultural critic George Lipsitz has it, Latin boogaloo "led organically to a reconsideration of 'Cuban' musical styles . . . as, in fact, *Afro*-Cuban and . . . a general reawakening of the African elements within Puerto Rican culture. Condemned by traditionalists as a betrayal of the community, Latin Bugalú instead showed that the community's identity had always been formed in relation to that of other groups in the U.S.A." (1994:80). Whatever musical elements of boogaloo might have been left behind, the social context of which it was an expression, the historical raison d'etre of Latin soul, has only deepened through the years.

A Latin boogaloo revival? Many of the musicians speak of a rekindled interest on the part of the present generation, and the huge success of Tito Nieves's 1997 *I Like It Like That* album, which also contains still another cover of "Bang Bang," is an obvious indication. They also point to the enthusiasm of fans in Puerto Rico, Latin America, Western Europe, and Japan. In England it is now classified, along with kindred styles, as "Latin acid" or "acid jazz," and much is included under that umbrella, from re-releases of Héctor Rivera's and Mongo Santamaría's old material to the work of Pucho and other African-American musicians in the Latin groove. *The Latin Vogue, Nu Yorica: Culture Clash in New York City* and *¡Sabroso! The Afro-Latin Groove* are some of the compilations of recent years, and all of them include Latin boogaloo classics and related and more recent material. The Relic label has even issued a collection titled *Vaya!!! R&B Groups Go Latin*, which features twenty tunes by doo-wop and r&b groups from the 1950s who mixed in mambo and other Latin rhythms, starting with the Crows' "Gee" and the Harptones' "Mambo Boogie" in 1954.

But a renewal of the spirit of boogaloo in our time, and a recuperation of some of the musical experiments seemingly left by the wayside, will need to be forward looking and not just nostalgic. With the emergence of hip-hop in the late 1970s and '80s, another common space was forged for joint African-American and Latino musical expression, and again it was black and Puerto Rican youths from New York City who created and laid first claim to that new terrain. As with boogaloo, it is the African-American dimension that appears most visible, but the Latino contribution can also be established (Flores 2000, chapter 7). Commercially successful acts like Mellow Man Ace and Cypress Hill introduced such fusions of rap and Latin sounds in the early 1990s, as have rappers in Puerto Rico and the Dominican Republic. Current salsa stars like La India and Marc Anthony were reared on rap and house and got their starts there, while salsa musicians as far-ranging as Manny Oquendo's Libre, El Gran Combo, and Tito Rojas have turned to rap techniques and collaborations to diversify their repertoire. Salsa in English, a long-standing crossover goal, is attempted with increasing frequency, though until now with minimal musical success. Surely it is in the context of such experiments, as the adjacent and kindred black and Latino cultures continue to intermingle, that the spirit of Latin boogaloo may live on in the years ahead. Jimmy Sabater, the all-time master of "cha-cha with a backbeat," has that spirit in mind when he says, "Boogaloo? Boogaloo for me was basically an early form of rap."

NOTES

Acknowledgments. I thank the following music historians and others knowledgeable about aspects of the boogaloo experience: David Carp, René López, Bob Moll, John Storm Roberts, Max Salazar, Harry Sepúlveda, Henry Medina, Richie Bonilla, Sonia

Marín, Miriam Jiménez Román, John Sánchez, and David Maysonet. Max Salazar in particular provided many key insights and opened many doors for me as I got started on the project, and his richly informative article "Latinized Afro-American Rhythms" (1992) served as the basis of the present essay. Finally, I wish to thank my friend and colleague, the late Vernon W. Boggs, who first got me into the Latin r&b groove ten years ago, before his tragic and untimely death.

1. Unless referenced in the endnotes, all citations are from personal interviews and conversations conducted in June and July 1998 with the following musicians: Joe Bataan, Benny Bonilla, Johnny Colón, Joe Cuba, Andy González, Pucho Harris, Bobby Marín, Richard Marín, Eddie Palmieri, Tito Ramos, Richie Ray, Fernando Rivera (King Nando), Héctor Rivera, Tony Rojas, Jimmy Sabater, Pete Terrace, and Willie Torres. I thank all of them for their time and generosity.

2. [Editor's note: Actually, Colón's first album, *El Malo* (1967), was made during the height of the boogaloo era and features two tunes listed as boogaloos: "Willie Baby" and "Skinny Papa."]

3. On the stereotyping in "Ché ché colé," see Garabis 1998:111–14.

4. Says Colón, "I feel that until things really change for Latinos in this country, they should really hold on to Spanish and not assimilate. . . . This is the only thing that they've got left. They don't have much, so I think they should hold on to the language rather than always use English lyrics" (Boggs 1993b).

BIBLIOGRAPHY

Boggs, Vernon. 1992a. "Rhythm 'n' Blues, American Pop and Salsa: Musical Transculturation." *Latin Beat* 2(1): 16–19.

———. 1992b. "Visions and Views of a Salsa Promoter, Izzy "Mr. Salsa" Sanabria: Popularizing Music." In Vernon Boggs, ed., *Salsiology: Afro-Cuban Music and the Evolution of Salsa in New York City.* Westport, CT: Greenwood, pp. 187–93.

———. 1993a. "Behind the Harptones and Mambo Boogie (1954)." *Latin Beat* 2(10):32–35.

———. 1993b. "Willie 'El Trombonista' Colón" (interview)." *Latin Beat* 2(10):11.

———. ed. 1992c. *Salsiology: Afro-Cuban Music and the Evolution of Salsa in New York City.* Westport, Conn: Greenwood.

Carp, David. 1996. "Pucho and His Latin Soul Brothers." *Descarga Newsletter* 27:14–15.

Fileti, Don. 1995. Liner notes to *Vaya! R & B Groups Go Latin* (Verve).

Flores, Juan. 2000. *From Bomba to Hip-Hop: Puerto Rican Culture and Latino Identity.* New York: Columbia University Press.

Garabis, Juan Otero. 1998. *Naciones rítmicas: La construcción nacionales en la música popular y la literatura del Caribe hispano.* Ph.D. dissertation, Harvard University.

Lipsitz, George. 1994. *Dangerous Crossroads: Popular Music, Postmodernism and the Poetics of Place.* London: Verso.

Luciano, Felipe. 1971. "The Song of Joe Bataan." *New York*, October 25, pp. 50–53.

Pruter, Robert. 1991. *Chicago Soul.* Urbana: University of Illinois Press.

Roberts, John Storm. [1979] 1991. *The Latin Tinge: The Impact of Latin American Music in the United States.* New York: Oxford University Press.

Salazar, Max. 1992. "Afro-American Latinized Rhythms." In Vernon Boggs, ed., *Salsiology: Afro-Cuban Music and the Evolution of Salsa in New York City.* Westport, Conn.: Greenwood Press, pp. 237–248.

Thomas, Piri. 1967. *Down These Mean Streets.* New York: Knopf.

SELECT DISCOGRAPHY

Alegre All-Stars. 1963. *Vol. 2: El Manicero.* (Alegre 8340.)

Barretto, Ray. 1963. *Charanga Moderna.* (Tico 1087.)

———. 1967. *Acid.* (Fania 346.)

Bataan, Joe. 1970. *Riot!* (Fania 354.)

———. 1971. *Poor Boy.* (Fania 371.)

Bobo, Willie. 1966. *Spanish Grease / Uno, Dos, Tres.* (Verve/Poly 521 664–2.) Reissued 1994.

Colón, Johnny. 1967. *Boogaloo Blues.* (Cotique 1004.)

Colón, Willie. 1967. *El Malo.* (Fania 337.)

———. 1972. *Cosa Nuestra.* (Fania 384.)

Cuba, Joe. 1965. *We Must Be Doing Something Right.* (Tico 1133.)

———. 1966. *Bang! Bang! Push, Push, Push.* (Tico 1146.)

———. 1967. *Steppin' Out.*

El Gran Combo. N.d. *Boogaloos Con El Gran Combo.* (Gema 3044). Reissued 1994.

Kenner, Chris. N.d. *I Like It Like That.* (COL 5166.)

Lebrón Brothers. 1971. *Psychedelic Goes Latin.* (Cotique 1008.)

Nieves, Tito. 1997. *I Like It Like That.* (RMM 82066.)

Palmieri, Eddie. 1965. *Azúcar Pa' Ti (Sugar For You.)* (Tico 1122.)

———. 1968. *Champagne.* (Tico 1165.)

Ray, Ricardo "Richie," and Bobby Cruz. 1966. *Se Soltó.* (Alegre 8500.)

———. 1967. *Jala Jala y Boogaloo.* (Alegre 8570.)

———. 1969. *The Best of Ricardo Ray and Bobby Cruz.* (Alegre 8760.)

Rivera, Hector. 1966. *At the Party.* (Barry 101.)

Rodríguez, Pete. 1966. *Latin Boogaloo.* (Alegre 8520.)

———. 1967. *I Like It Like That (A Mí Me Gusta Así).* (Alegre 8550.)

———. 1967. *Oh That's Nice! Ay, Que Bueno!* (Alegre 8520.)

———. 1968. *Hot & Wild: Yo Vengo Soltando.* (Alegre 8650.)

Rodríguez, Tito. n.d. *Live at the Palladium.* (WS Latino 4167.)

Santamaría, Mongo. 1963. *Watermelon Man!* (Battle 6120.)

Various artists. 1990. *The Latin Vogue.* (Charly 229.)

———. 1995. *Vaya!!! R&B Groups Go Latin.* (Verve.)

———. 1996. *Nu Yorica: Culture Clash in New York City.* (Soul Jazz Music SJR 29.)

———. N.d. *Sabroso! The Afro-Latin Groove.* (Rhino R2–75209.)

Chapter 5

SALSA ROMÁNTICA: AN ANALYSIS OF STYLE

Christopher Washburne

Leonard Meyer writes, "A musical style is a finite array of interdependent melodic and rhythmic, harmonic, timbral, textual, and formal relationships and processes. When these are internalized as learned habits, listeners including performers and composers are able to perceive and understand a composition in the style as an intricate network of implicative relationships, or to experience the work as a complex of felt probabilities" (1967:116). Interpreting style in Meyer's sense, salsa of the late 1980s and early 1990s incorporated significant stylistic changes that differentiate it from the salsa of the 1970s and early 1980s. The processes that brought on those stylistic changes were complex and dynamic, including both musical (music structure) and extramusical (contextual) factors. The following discussion explores elements of salsa's sound structure by examining performance practices associated with the composing, arranging, and recording of the predominant style of the late 1980s and 1990s, known as *salsa romántica*. In particular, an analysis of the construction and production of a salsa romántica arrangement, "Me Calculaste," will be conducted to provide insight into the salsa scene of the 1990s.[1] The scope of the following discussion is too limited to serve as a comprehensive study. Instead, the goal is to serve as an introduction to how the sound structure of salsa romántica differs from other styles, the influences it incorporates, and how musicians and producers make the recorded product. A brief history will help contextualize some of the factors that prompted the stylistic changes in salsa's sound structure.

HISTORICAL BACKGROUND

In the early 1980s, the salsa recording and performance scene entered a lull brought on by several factors. Declining record sales and dwindling performance opportunities were caused in part by the breakup of New York–based Fania Records. Beginning in the late 1960s and continuing throughout the 1970s, Fania held a monopoly on all aspects of the salsa industry, including recording contracts, concert promotion, and radio airplay. Competition was quickly and at times fiercely squelched by Fania. This prevented other recording and production companies from establishing the type of business infrastructure needed to fill the void after Fania left the scene. In addition, the merengue craze that accompanied the influx of Dominican immigrants to New York and Puerto Rico and the rise in popularity of North American urban dance styles among Latino youth contributed to salsa's decline in popularity.

In response to the stagnation of the scene, during the 1980s two closely aligned styles of salsa emerged: namely, New York and Puerto Rican. Proponents of both styles were concerned with rejuvenating the salsa scene and providing a marketable product. Taking note of the popularity of rock and pop music among Latino youth both in New York and Puerto Rico, salsa producers turned to pop music for direction and influence. New York–based producer Louie Ramírez is credited with the introduction of the new salsa sound. In 1982 and 1983 he produced two recordings for K-Tel Records known as *Noches Calientes* (Caiman 2888 and 2889) that featured four young salsa singers (José Alberto, Tito Allen, Johnny Rivera, and Ray de la Paz) singing well-known *boleros* and Latin *baladas* arranged with a laid-back salsa dance beat. Ramírez's productions toned down the "hot" or hard-driving sound that dominated the recordings made by Fania Records, known as *salsa dura* or hard salsa; they had a milder, more tranquil sound, and slick, highly polished, pop-influenced studio productions replaced the looser and grittier recordings of earlier days. Tempos were slower, percussion and brass parts were executed in comparatively subdued fashion, and vocals were sung in a smooth, crooning style. The lyrics centered on topics of love, replacing the politically charged lyrics of Rubén Blades, Héctor Lavoe, and the like. This new stylistic approach reached out beyond New York City, appealing to middle-class Latinos in the United States and other countries in Latin America and the Caribbean. In addition, this new approach to salsa deemphasized images of *barrio* life and reduced the call for Latino unity, hence aligning itself with the sociopolitical environment of the Reagan era in the United States, in which political activism and global awareness were largely pacified. The commercial success of Ramírez's productions changed the direction that New York and Puerto Rican salsa producers and arrangers would take for the next fifteen years.

The emergence of the new sound in New York was further boosted by the founding in 1987 of the RMM (Ralph Mercado Music) Record company by Ralph Mercado, a concert promoter and entrepreneur. He employed Sergio George as producer and arranger in charge of A&R (Artists and Repertoire). The company's initial success with the 1989 production for singer Tito Nieves, *The Classic* (Sony 80707), propelled Mercado and George to a dominant position in the New York salsa scene. By the early 1990s, RMM Records had effectively filled the void left by the closing of Fania Records and was the largest and most influential Latin music record company and concert promoter in the salsa business. The company's prominence and commercial strength contributed to the success and dominance of George's style of New York salsa. Like Ramírez's, George's arrangements featured a mild, pop-oriented salsa style that used slick studio production techniques.[2] At the same time, productions from Puerto Rico by producer/arrangers Julio Ceasar Delgado, Humberto Ramírez, Cuto Soto, and Ramón Sánchez emerged. These featured even more subdued performances than George's, with a mellow vocal quality, a smooth brass sound, and restrained percussion parts, on highly polished and perfected recordings. They also incorporated richer harmonies and more contrapuntal writing than did their New York counterparts. Along with the change in arranging and producing styles came a new generation of singers in both New York and Puerto Rico.

Borrowing from pop music, an artist's visual and sexual image became increasingly more important than his or her musical talent. Young, predominantly white or light-skinned pretty boy and girl singers with sex appeal were sought by RMM and other record companies. Many middle-aged singers prominent in the 1970s and early 1980s found themselves without recording contracts. The new generation of singers included Luis Enrique, Eddie Santiago, Lalo Rodríguez, and Frankie Ruíz. These singers were featured as bandleaders singing songs of love and romance. Their new style was labeled with interchangeable names (*salsa sensual*, *salsa erótica*, salsa romántica, or, more pejoratively, *salsa monga* [limp salsa]), which reflected the content of song lyrics as well as new marketing images used by the artists.

THE SCORE

This arrangement of "Me Calculaste" was selected for analysis for several reasons.[3] First, I was hired to record the trombone tracks and consequently witnessed much of the recording process. Second, the arranger, Ricky González, views this arrangement as embodying many of the standard conventions in salsa romántica's performance practice.[4] In other words, it is a typical arrangement. In addition, Danny Rojo, with his boyish good looks and sex appeal and smooth vocal quality (i.e., less of a nasal or harsh quality that was so prominent in salsa dura), is representative of a typical salsa romántica singer/bandleader. Third, the song's moderate commercial success verifies its acceptability to consumers. During the first year of its release it continually received radio airplay on New York and Puerto Rican Latin music stations and it was often included on deejay play lists in New York salsa clubs. Fourth, this recording is sonically representative of an emically acceptable product. It was recorded at Skylight Studios, located in Belleville, New Jersey. Throughout the 1990s Skylight was the studio with the highest volume of salsa productions in the New York City area.

The score (Appendix 1) is a copy of the original used during the production of the recording. González, who also produced the recording, worked from this score as the musicians read from individually extracted parts. Most salsa instrumentalists have had formal musical training, either studying at a conservatory or with private instructors. As a result, the reliance on written parts is standard. Notating salsa with four beats per measure in cut time has become the established practice. The cut time signature best represents how salsa musicians rhythmically approach each measure. Musicians will most often tap two beats to the bar, beats one and three, while simultaneously maintaining the subdivision pulses within themselves to guide them through quarter, eighth, and sixteenth note figures. The clave rhythm must be felt concurrently (I have observed bassist Johnny Torres tapping his foot on beats one and three while simultaneously chewing gum to the clave beat). To ensure that the proper clave configuration is maintained throughout the arrangement, a "2/3" notation can be found at each percussion change denoting which clave measure is to be played first (e.g., m.5, m.9, m.25 et al.). [5]

The formal structure of the arrangement of "Me Calculaste" conforms to today's salsa conventions, which are originally derived from the structure of Cuban *son*. This bipartite form features a songlike section, followed by an extended *montuno* section. The basic song structure of this arrangement is as follows:

I. Song:	Instrumental Introduction
	Verse/Refrain
	Instrumental Interlude
	Verse/Refrain
	Instrumental Interlude and Vocal Interlude
I. Montuno:	Montuno
	Mambo

Montuno
Moña
Montuno
Coda

An instrumental introduction is followed by the main body of the tune (verses and refrains). Interspersed are brief instrumental interludes serving to accentuate the text and melody and transitional material between specific sections. This is followed by the montuno, a vamping section that incorporates a repeating harmonic progression and features a call-and-response exchange between the lead vocalist and *coro* (chorus) singers. Montuno sections are typically two, four, or eight measures in length; "Me Calculaste" contains an eight-measure montuno. Notice that in the montuno section, measures 89 through 96, chord changes, without specified pitches or rhythms, serve as the bass and piano parts. The actual montuno patterns and degree of variation employed within them are left to the discretion of the musicians during the montuno sections.

The montuno section is first interrupted by an instrumental section known as the *mambo*. The mambo is derived from the instrumental genre and popular dance craze of the 1950s known by the same name. Providing a brief respite for the singers, the mambo features the horn section playing flashy melodic figures and it often incorporates rhythmic breaks played homophonically by the entire group. Measures 113 and 121 provide examples. After a return to the montuno, a second interruption is made by another instrumental section known as the *moña*. Historically, moñas have been spontaneously improvised instrumental riff figures played by the horns over the harmonic progression of the montuno that provide an additional vocal rest. However, recent trends among arrangers, including the employment of more harmonically complex montuno sections and an interest in taking greater control of all aspects in their arrangements, have led to the precomposition of moñas becoming standard practice. Finally, there is once again a return of the montuno section before the coda (the closing instrumental section).

In other salsa arrangements minimal formal variations are occasionally employed, such as the omission of the moña section, the inclusion of an instrumental solo, or a fade-out vamping section used in place of a coda. However, most salsa arrangements adhere to the standard formal structure outlined above.

ANALYSIS

Drawing from the tradition of Cuban *son,* the harmonic structure of salsa typically favors a single tonal center, using primarily unaltered diatonic chords (i.e., I, ii7, iii7, IV, V7, vi7, and vii°) with particular emphasis on the I, IV, and V7 chords. Often movement between tonic and dominant, or among tonic, subdominant, and dominant, will be the only harmonic movement used throughout an arrangement. In "Me Calculaste," González observes traditional practices by maintaining a single tonal center in the main body, montuno, moña, and coda sections centering around D major. However, the influence of jazz and popular musics on today's salsa arranging style is also evident in his abundant use of the ii7–V7 chord progression, tritone substitutions, inverted chords, and use of the upper chordal extensions and alterations within the D major tonal center (i.e., 9ths, 13ths, flat 5ths, flat 9ths, augmented 5ths, and suspended 4th chords). González's decision to use standard lead sheet chord symbols borrowed from popular and jazz musics points to this influence as well.

The harmonic structure of montunos is generally a simplified derivation from the chordal structure established in the main body. González follows conventional practice in constructing his montuno section by combining the harmonic movement found in the A section (m. 17–24), where he uses the chords in measures 17, 18, 21, and 24, with the last four measures of section G (m. 85–m. 88), the instrumental interlude. In this way the montuno remains harmonically homogeneous with the main body. At the same time, the montuno's chord progression (m. 89–m. 96) is rooted in traditional salsa montuno practice by remaining within one key and emphasizing the I, IV, and V chords.

The mambo often serves as an occasion for the arranger to introduce new material. In this case, notice the brief harmonic shift to B-flat major in measures 98 through 105, a key relatively distant from what has come before.[6] By contrast, note the close relationship of the harmonic progression employed in the moña (m. 128–m. 135) with the chords found in the montuno. This close harmonic relationship is a reflection of the traditional practice in which moñas were improvised over the montuno's harmonic structure. The coda conveys a sense of closure to the arrangement by bringing back fragments of previous material. Harmonically this is accomplished by returning to the chordal movement reminiscent of the harmony found in the introduction. In measures 1 through 3 the harmony moves from a DM7 chord to a C major triad over D bass note. The C/D chord functions as a D7sus chord that leads to the subdominant GM7 chord in measure 4. In measures 137 through 138, similar harmonic movement is incorporated. The coda begins with DM7 chord followed by CM7 chord. Sharing most of the same notes as the C major triad over D from the introduction, the CM7 chord also shares the same function by leading to the GM7 chord in measure 139.

Derived from Cuban popular music performance practices, salsa creates a unique vertical alignment within the harmonic structure. The bass *tumbao* pattern anticipates harmonic change that is notated on the downbeat by one quarter note, with its attack on beat four of the preceding measure. It is then most often tied over to the following measure, avoiding an attack on the downbeat. Examples of this can be seen throughout the score (e.g., m. 5–m. 6, 9–m. 10, et al.). Peter Manuel writes that this "anticipated bass" is "perhaps the single most distinctive feature in Afro-Cuban popular music" (1985:249).[7] In addition, piano *guajeos,* sometimes called *montunos*, the repeating rhythmic figures played by pianists that outline the harmonic structure, tend to alternate every other measure between anticipating the harmonic change one eighth note before the downbeat and supporting the harmonic change on the downbeat. This alternating pattern coincides with the clave rhythm, where the downbeat attack occurs in the two stroke measure and the anticipated bar occurs just before the downbeat of the three stroke measure. One example is found in measures 134 and 135. Present notational practice misleadingly depicts the harmonic change from Emin7 to A9sus4 in measure 13 and 135 as coinciding with the downbeat in measure 135. Although not notated, the bass actually attacks an "A" on beat four of measure 134, implying the harmonic change to A9sus4 one beat earlier. The clave measure in measure 135 is the three-stroke measure and consequently the piano attacks the A9sus4 chord on the last eighth note of measure 134. This results in a degree of momentary harmonic tension. The tension is accentuated further by the woodwind and brass section attacking an Emin7 chord on the last eighth note of measure 134 and not resolving to the A9sus4 until the second eighth note of measure 135. This type of harmonic tension between the bass and piano is present in most measures in salsa unless otherwise notated. Further, the bass tumbao pattern, with its anticipated tie into the third beat of each measure, also anticipates harmonic changes that are notated on the third beat (see m. 12 and m. 14 as examples). Depending on the pianist's guajeo pattern, this can also displace the harmonic change between piano and bass parts by one eighth note.

The harmonic tension and release within each measure of music contributes to a "driving motion" within the salsa groove, propelling the music forward. This continual harmonic tension creates what Manuel describes as "a desire for the corresponding harmony of the next bar. At the same time, the weak stressing of the downbeat, when it does arrive, undermines its potentially cadential effect, such that the rhythm in effect 'rides over' the downbeat. . . . The deliberate avoidance of the downbeat also lends to the rhythm a unique flow and momentum which make it ideal for the supple and fluid salsa dance style" (1985:255). The basic salsa dance foot movements do indeed correspond to this by often initiating steps on beats two and four and tending to deemphasize downbeats.

TEXT AND MELODIC ANALYSIS: TRANSCRIPTION OF TEXT STRUCTURE

Love and romance are topics typical of today's salsa romántica and the themes of "Me Calculaste" are no exception. A transcription and translation of the text, coros, and *soneos* follows. The Spanish text from the main body of the song, verses and refrains, appears as Rojo submitted it in written form. The boldface notations,[8] the transcribed soneos and coros, and the indented English translation are my additions.

Instrumental Introduction

A. Y la pasión nos tocó en esa noche de amor
> *The passion touched us in that night of love*

Tan sólo eramos dos
> *We were only two*

Tratando de arreglar el mundo
> *Trying to change the world*

Y nos invadió el sentimiento hasta lo más profundo
> *And the most profound emotions invaded us*

B. Más no pude descifrar tu primera mirada
> *I could not decipher your first look*

Y a plena oscuridad rompimos el celofán
> *And at full darkness we broke through the cellophane*

Nuestros labios se hincharon de tanto besar
> *Our lips swelled from so many kisses*

Nuestras almas rodaron por un canal
> *Our souls ran through the same channel*

C. (Refrain) Sentía que te estremecías
> *I felt you tremble*

Llegar a tí yo no sabia
> *I never knew how to come to you*

Pero me calculaste y te adelantaste
> *But you figured me out and got ahead of me*

Y este episodio iniciaste
> *And this episode you initiated*

D. (Refrain continued) Llevas en tu pecho la cruda esperanza
> *You carry in your heart the raw hope*

El valor de lanzarte
> *The courage of going for it*

La dicha de amarte
> *The bliss of loving you*

Más yo en aquel momento no supe encontrate
> *However, in that moment I did not know how to find you*

E. **Instrumental Interlude**

F. Así llegaste a mí, con tanta sed de amor
> *In this way you arrived to me, with a great thirst of love*

Como un regalo de Dios
> *Like a gift of God*

Te tuve en aquel rincón
> *I had you in that special place in my soul*

El reloj no funcionaba, el tiempo no pasaba
> *The clock was not working, the time did not pass*

Los besos colmaban aquella ocasión
> *The kisses filled the occasion*

B'. Nunca pude imaginar aquella noche
> *I could never imagine that night*

Bajo las estrellas
> *Below the stars*

Jamás el sueño llegó
> *The dream never arrived*

Mi corazón palpitó de una manera feroz
> *My heart beat in a furious manner*

Tus palabras cambiában el curso de mi voz
> *Your words changed the course of my voice*

C. (Refrain) (Repeated as before)

D'. (Refrain cont.) (Repeated as before with an additional)

Más yo en aquel momento no supe encontrate
> *However, in that moment I did not know how to find you*

G. **Instrumental Interlude**

Coro 1: Sentía que te estremecías
> *I felt you tremble*

Llegar a tí yo no sabía
> *I never knew how to come to you*

Pero me calculaste
> *But you figured me out*

Soneo 1: Como una calculadora decifraste mi demora
> *Like a calculator, you deciphered my hesitation*

Coro 1: (Repeated)

Soneo 2: Con la dicha de amarte pero que tonto fui que no supe encontrate

	With the bliss of loving you but I was so dumb I did not know how to find you
Coro 1:	(Repeated)
Soneo 3:	Llevas en tu pecho la cruda esperanza, el valor de lanzarte
	You carry in your heart the raw hope, the courage of going for it
Mambo	
Soneo 4:	Quería andar por tu cuerpo, mi timidez me frenaba
	I wanted to caress your body, but my shyness stopped me
Coro 2b:	Pero me calculaste
Soneo 5:	Que pronto te diste cuenta como mi corazón palpitaba
	How soon you noticed how my heart was beating
Coro 2a:	Sentía que te estremecías
Soneo 6:	Y me calculaste desde la primera vez
	And you figured me out from that first look
Coro 2b:	(Repeated)
Soneo 7:	En lo que cerré mis ojos cuando los abrí te encontré
	I closed my eyes, then when I opened them I met you
Coro 2a:	(Repeated)
Soneo 8:	Llegar a tí yo no sabía
	I never knew how to come to you
Coro 2b:	(Repeated)
Soneo 9:	Tuviste el valor de iniciar este amor y me calculaste
	You had the courage to initiate this love and you figured me out
Moña	
Coro 1:	(Repeated)
Soneo 10:	Tu ataque de amor que pronto llegó me sorprendió
	The suddenness of your attack of love surprised me
Coro1:	(Repeated)
Soneo 11:	Pero, me calculaste más yo en aquel momento no supe encontrate
	But you figured me out and in that moment I did not know how to find you
Coda	

Salsa lyricists have considerable freedom in their poetic choices (i.e., rhyme schemes and topic construction). As songwriter Lino Iglesias states, "There is no standard format that we use in salsa. For me, and I think it is the same with many other composers, my choices have to do with the feeling, the emotion of the song. Sometimes I use rhymes, sometimes nothing rhymes in the lyrics. Sometimes I write in stanzas, sometimes not. Every song is different."[9] Surveying the compositions of Rojo reveals that he writes in a similar fashion where each song has its own unique poetic construction. For instance, in "Me Calculaste" note the lack of a repetitive rhyme and syllabic schematic throughout, and also the variation between four- (sections A, B, C, D, D') and five-line stanzas (sections F and B').

González and Rojo use recurring melodic material and text repetition to create cohesion within the arrangement. The formal structure of the main body is inherently repetitive with an AA'BC form that is repeated (notated as ABCD and repetition as FBCD in the score). One example of recurring material is the melodic figures and their accompanying percussive effects (i.e. the finger snaps) in measures 1 through 7. They appropriately return in the instrumental interlude (E section) in measures 51 through 57 to serve the same introductory transitional role that leads to the return of the verse melody.

Rojo's use of the final line of text from the main body, "más yo en aquel momento no supe encontrate," demonstrates how text repetition is employed. As the first occurrence of text repetition, the repeated words stand out, alerting the listener to their significance. In this case, they signal the end of the main body and the start of the montuno. This text and melodic line are brought back in Rojo's final soneo (11), "pero, me calculaste más yo en aquel momento no supe encontrate" in combination with the title lyrics. Once again this line of text serves to denote a sectional change, from montuno to coda. The addition of the title lyrics contributes to the line's punctuating effect.

The coro is extracted from the repeated C section (refrain) and serves as the "hook" for the song. The lead vocal melody found in the refrain is used for all three lines of coro text. The first two lines "sentía que te estremecías, llegar a tí yo no sabía" are sung in unison, and the third, "pero me calculaste," is sung in three-voice harmony. The harmony split serves to emphasize the significance of the title words. Typically two different coros, long and shorter versions, will be used in an arrangement allowing for varying soneo space and harmony. In line with conventional practice, "Me Calculaste" employs two versions of the coro. The first is notated as Coro 1 and includes the three extracted lines from the refrain. The second version uses only two of the original three lines and splits them into two separate coros, notated as Coro 2a and 2b. The soneos accompanying Coro 1, which is five measures in length, are sung over the last three measures of the montuno. Coros 2a and 2b are one measure in length and are placed in the first and fifth measures of the montuno respectively. In turn, the soneos are placed in the second through fourth and sixth through eighth measures of the

FIGURE 5.1 • Rojo *coro* and *soneo*.

montuno allowing for harmonic diversity. Changes of the coro (Coro 1 to Coros 2a and 2b and then back to Coro 1) occur only after the instrumental mambo and moña sections. These instrumental sections serve to buffer the switch between coros.

The soneos found in this arrangement derive in three distinct ways from textual and melodic materials from the verses and refrains. In the first type, found in soneos 3, 8, and 11, text is extracted verbatim. In each of these cases melodic and rhythmic similarities to the verse and refrain remain; however, the divergent harmonic structure of the montuno and/or personal artistic preference often causes note changes and/or phrasing adjustments. In the example below (fig. 5.1), two comparative transcriptions demonstrate how changes and adjustments are executed. The upper staff contains a transcription of the vocal melody used for the text "llegar a tí yo no sabía" as it appears in the refrain (C) and in Coro 1. The lower staff is the vocal melody of soneo 8. In this case Rojo's pitch choices and melodic contour differ while his rhythm remains fundamentally the same. In the second type, partial repetitions of text serve as departure points for new material to be introduced. In soneo 2, the refrain texts "la dicha de amarte" and "que no supe encontrate" are combined with the new lyrics "pero que tonto fui." The additional text adds further commentary, from the sonero's perspective, on the ideas set forth in the refrain. Soneos 6 and 9 are constructed in a similar fashion. The third type of soneo creates new text, expounding upon ideas previously put forth. Examples include soneos 1, 4, 5, 7, and 10. By remaining with the same theme, these three types of soneo construction provide a thematically coherent performance.

THE ARRANGER'S NOTES

Composer Rojo provided arranger González with a tape containing the text, melody, a simplified harmonic structure, and preliminary ideas concerning the arrangement (i.e., number of soneos and coros between sections, and melodic suggestions for the instrumental accompaniment). González then proceeded to formally design the arrangement by reharmonizing the overall structure, composing the instrumental sections (introduction, interludes, mambo, moña, and coda) and orchestrating the accompaniment parts during the vocal sections. According to González these arranging decisions are based not only on musical considerations but on commercial ones. One aim of the arranger is to provide a product that will achieve commercial success. It must be in line with consumer expectations, but also stand out in some way. González comments, "I try to write simple but interesting melodies that will be, in some way, memorable."[10] In "Me Calculaste" the repetitiveness of the title lyric both in the refrain and coros is well suited for this purpose.

According to González, arranging decisions begin with melodic and textual considerations. "I start with the melody and text to determine the overall feel of the composition, either laid back or with a lot of energy. Then I decide where energy level changes are going to take place. Energy change is important. A tune that is always laid back and never moves anywhere is boring. Similarly, if it is always at a high energy level, it is boring. You change the energy level by the use of different instrumentation and orchestrational techniques."[11]

The treatment of percussion in the arrangement of "Me Calculaste" is illustrative of how instrumentation can provide shifts in energy level in salsa performance. González categorized the range of standard salsa percussion options from the following combinations, ranging from low to high energy:

1. timbale drums (*paila*), bongos, congas, and small hand percussion (maracas, güiro, and/or clave);
2. timbale bells, bongos, congas, and small hand percussion;
3. timbale bells, *campana* cowbell, congas, and small hand percussion.

Furthermore, any one of these options can be combined with additional drums, such as a snare and kick drum, and/or other percussion effects, such as chimes and cymbals. Other rhythms, such as *bomba, plena, rumba,* funk, hip-hop, and so on, can be mixed with the standard percussion parts as well.

González relies on the standard salsa percussion patterns, notated in the example below (fig. 5.2), for the rhythmic foundation of the arrangement. The congas, timbales, bongos, and maracas, for the most part, play throughout the piece. Alternatives to the standard salsa percussion patterns occur in several places. In measures 1 through 4 and 51 through 53 (notated as *efectos* [effects] in the score) finger snaps are heard on beats 2 and 4. Wind chimes (notated as "opt. effects") are used in measure 17. Cymbal effects are also included. The first (notated by the word "cup," referring to where the cymbal should be struck—the innermost

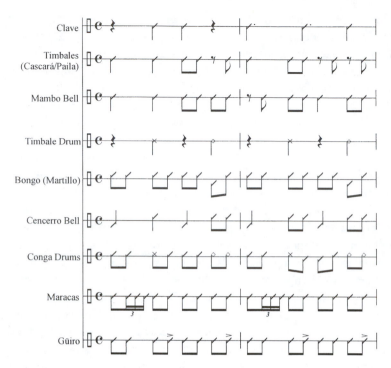

<small>FIGURE 5.2 • Salsa percussion.</small>

elevated region that emits a semipitched dry ring) is employed in measures 8, 15–23, and 71–72. The "ride cymbal" notation in measure 141 instructs the *timbalero* to cease playing the timbale bell and begin playing a similar rhythmic pattern on the outer edge of the cymbal, creating a wash of sound that rhythmically accents the timbale bell pattern. Another option that is explored is the absence of all percussion except the güiro in measures 114 through 121 resulting in a substantial drop in dynamics and energy level. This in turn effectively accentuates the energy jump when the full percussion returns in measure 122.

Throughout the first fifty measures, González orchestrates a gradual build in energy levels, crescendoing as the song progresses through the first two verse and refrain stanzas.[12] The arrangement begins with the quiescent combination of maracas, finger snaps, and sparse cymbal attacks (m. 1–m. 4). A concerted rhythmic break in measure 4 introduces the first elevated energy level with the congas, bongos, timbale bell, and maracas playing together for the next four measures (m. 5–m. 8). A decrease of intensity occurs when the timbalero switches from timbale bell to paila (drum shell) in measure 9 through 16. This slight decrease serves a transitional function leading from the elevated energy level of measures 5 through 8 to the substantial energy drop that accompanies the entrance of the lead vocalist at A, in measure 17. In measures 17 through 24, with the exception of sporadic cymbal and clave attacks, the percussion remains tacit. Synthesizer, guitar, and bass accompany this change while the piano and winds are tacit as well. In measure 25, the start of the second verse stanza (or B section), González employs his first energy level combination of timbale drums (paila), bongos, congas, and maracas as the energy level increases. To enhance the effect, the piano replaces the synthesizer at the start of the B section playing loose accompanying figures. The trombones are reintroduced as well, playing middle registered unison lines. At this point in the recording I was instructed by González to play with a soft dynamic and a mellow, vibratoless timbre. The crescendo in measures 32 through 34, executed by all four wind instruments playing harmonized figures, leads to the heightened energy level of the refrain (section C). The simultaneous gradual pitch buildup that extends to the upper registers of the trumpet and first trombone, along with the full open timbre employed by the brass, intensifies the effect of the crescendo. At letter C (m. 35) the percussion switches to González's second energy level with timbale bells, bongos, congas, and maracas. The piano begins playing a guajeo pattern, providing rhythmic drive that also contributes to the heightened energy level. All four horns continue playing harmonized accompaniment figures throughout both refrain sections (C and D). The crescendo in intensity peaks in measures 45 through 48 of section D. At this point the percussion changes to González's third energy level with timbale bells, campana, congas, and maracas while the horns crescendo in measures 45 and 46. A return to the paila and bongos in measure 49 serves to gently decrease the energy level in order to smoothly return to the introductory material found in the instrumental interlude (section E) beginning in measure 51.

Within the first 50 measures, González uses changes in the percussion accompaniment along with orchestrational adjustments to employ the entire gamut of energy intensity, from laid back to hard driving. As a seasoned arranger, González knows how to manipulate the orchestrational and instrumental choices for the desired effect. His constant orchestrational shifting of instruments creates a dynamic presentation that provides direction and motion in the music.

THE INFLUENCE OF NORTH AMERICAN POPULAR MUSIC

North American popular music has had a large impact on salsa performance practice. In addition to the previously discussed influence on the harmonic structure, its effects on the arrangement of "Me Calculaste" are evident in several other ways. In the first four bars of the moña, measures 128 to 131, a snare drum backbeat accompanied by a kick drum is integrated into the salsa groove. González attributes the incorporation of this North American groove to Sergio George's arrangements. González remarked, "Sergio was the first to put the snare and kick back into salsa since the boogaloo days. His addition opened the door for us to experiment."[13]

This rhythmic and instrumental addition is coupled with a musical quote, played by the trombones in the moña at measure 128 and 129, from the refrain of George Harrison's composition "Here Comes the Sun." This familiar melody is played verbatim in measures 128. Measure 129 repeats the melodic figure with a slight rhythmic variation in order to conform to the 2–3 clave. The quote of this Beatles tune, accompanied by the backbeat groove, provides a contemporary popular music feel to the passage.

Further popular music influence can be heard in the woodwind and brass writing and the coro harmonization. González claims that his woodwind and brass writing style is strongly influenced by the horn sections of the groups Chicago and Earth, Wind, and Fire. During the recording I was instructed to play like James Pankow, trombonist for the rock group Chicago, on certain passages. González's voicings and timbral choices are often reminiscent of these groups, and his abundant use of slides, glisses, falls, and bends attests to their influence. Measures 8, 9, 13, 46, 50, 78, 88, 98, 102, 107, 108, 110, 111, 121, 131, 138, 139, and 142 incorporate examples of these types of embellishments. The vocal harmonies and the way they are performed on the last line of the coro are reminiscent of the performance style of the group Take Six, another influence that González acknowledges.

The slick and highly polished studio production borrows heavily from popular music production techniques. Such techniques include creating the final product by overdubbing and layering each instrumental and vocal part individually; incorporating synthesizers for timbral and ambience enhancement; using advanced digital technology to provide reverberation and ambience; and the use of digital computer editing tools to manipulate pitch and temporal discrepancies.

These production changes were influenced by the preference of Sergio George and many Puerto Rican producers for pop music practices. These practices differed from the established recording techniques used by Fania Records, where musicians who regularly performed with the bands recorded the band's albums. After the late 1980s, it was rare that band members participated in the recording. With virtually the same group of musicians and arrangers in each locale backing every new singer/bandleader, diversity in sound among recordings was limited. The small number of recording musicians and arrangers limited variation in stylistic possibilities, and this resulted in a standardization of style for both New York and Puerto Rican salsa. With only two production centers and two groups of studio musicians, a listener's ability to distinguish New York productions from Puerto Rican ones was enhanced. Often one studio musician's personal style of playing or one arranger's writing preferences, appearing on numerous recordings, could quickly become a common stylistic practice. Newer recording techniques, borrowed from polished pop recordings, eventually led to the practice of recording one musician at a time, overdubbing each individual part. This removed the traditional recording context wherein musicians could spontaneously interact with one another, simulating live performance, a common practice in Fania productions. In the view of some, this led to the deadening of the recorded medium's performance quality.[14] In the Rojo session González employed studio musicians, none of whom had performed previously with Rojo, and each part was recorded separately.

THE PUERTO RICAN INFLUENCE

Puerto Rican productions during the 1990s favored a higher level of studio perfectionism and a more refined, mellower timbre than the New York ones. For a complex of social and economic reasons, including issues of authenticity, identity politics, and the like, in the 1990s Puerto Rican productions became a standard.[15] During that period RMM started to record and produce many of its productions in Puerto Rico, causing great financial loss for musicians, arrangers, and producers based in New York. This forced New York arrangers and musicians to learn and adapt to the Puerto Rican style of recording. For instance, salsa brass playing has historically favored a loud, full-bodied sound, owing in part to the necessity of horn players to project their sounds over large rhythm sections without sufficient electronic amplification. Not only did this serve the utilitarian need of being heard over loud percussion and amplified piano and bass parts—the fiery tones were in line with the "hot" aesthetics associated with the salsa of the 1970s and early 1980s. Comparatively, Puerto Rican salsa musicians, many of whom have been classically trained, prefer to play with a softer, more refined sound. As the Puerto Rican influence gained strength in the 1990s, timbral changes in the brass sound began to take place in New York salsa.

During the Rojo session, González attempted to counteract this trend, preferring to record with musicians he regularly performed with in the New York area. The record company wanted a Puerto Rican sound for the Rojo production. Consequently, several Puerto Rican arrangers were hired to contribute arrangements, and the mixing session was scheduled to be completed in Puerto Rico. González claimed that it was only after some difficult negotiation, with promises that he could provide the sound they desired, that he received permission to record in New York. He stressed the importance of playing with the Puerto Rican trombone sound (i.e., mellow and refined) and also emphasized that the production needed to be of the highest quality. "They are going to hear this in Puerto Rico. It has got to be good."[16] The two trombone parts that I would normally record in eight hours took a grueling twenty-three hours. Each phrase was played several times and then polished so that the attack, sustain, and release of every note were executed to perfection. Upon his return from Puerto Rico he exclaimed, "We did it. They could not believe that this production was recorded in New York with New York musicians."[17] The Puerto Rican influence on the Rojo production is most pronounced in the cleanly executed instrumental parts and the mellow brass timbres and subdued percussion playing (with the exception of the heightened energy sections previously discussed). After achieving the refined quality of the Rojo production, González acquired numerous contracts for arranging and producing from Puerto Rican bands.

STYLE AND PRACTICE IN SALSA ROMÁNTICA

Throughout the 1980s and 1990s the salsa style has been transforming, reflecting cultural factors taking place within the salsa scene. These changes have been precipitated by a complex of factors, including the dynamically interdependent relationship between the New York and Puerto Rican salsa scenes, economic pressures such as the drive to sell records and RMM record company's monopoly on the salsa recording and concert promoting industry, the influence of popular music forms, immigration patterns in New York City and in Puerto Rico, the cultural and linguistic Americanization of Latino youth in New York City, and attempts to reestablish or reaffirm the cultural roots of salsa. The diverse and dynamic nature of those processes involved in stylistic change demonstrates that style encompasses more than Meyer's definition allows. The cultural factors so integral in determining the "complex of felt probabilities" and means with which participants negotiate and explore the stylistic possibilities must be included in the definition as well. As Steven Feld writes,

> Style is more than the statistical core reflection of the place or time, or
> patterned choices made within constraints. It is the very human resources

that are enacted to constitute the reality of social life in sound. Style is itself the accomplishment, the crystallization of personal and social participation; it is the way the performance and engagement endows humanly meaningful shape upon sonic form. Style is an emergence, the means by which newly creative knowledge is developed from playful, rote, or ordinary participatory experience. Style is the way an internalization and naturalization of felt thoughts and thought feelings guide experience. (1988:107)

The effects of cultural factors on the music resulted in the emergence of a new "salsa aesthetic" and a new salsa style that changed from the preferred "hot" and hard-driving sound of the 1970s and early 1980s to a milder, more subdued sound that dominated salsa of the late 1980s to mid-1990s.

The differentiating features of salsa romántica are highly polished and slick studio productions, smooth vocal quality, a controlled and refined brass sound, subdued percussion playing, the predominance of song texts featuring romantic themes, and often pretty-boy crooners as bandleaders. "Me Calculaste" embodies many of salsa romántica's arranging and performance practices by adhering to conventional formal structures and providing an acceptable product as judged by salsa insiders. Insider acceptance is achieved by incorporating elements that meet listener/consumer expectations and at the same time provide something of interest. González achieves this by balancing traditional salsa practices with the influence of jazz and newer popular music practices, and by arranging a cohesive and energetic dynamic arrangement. Cohesion is accomplished through the use of recurring textual, melodic, harmonic, and rhythmic material. The energy shifts are produced by the manipulation of orchestrational devices and through instrumentation changes. The polished production techniques, the blending of popular music influences, and the love topic of the text firmly root "Me Calculaste" in the salsa romántica style.

NOTES

1. "Me Calculaste" was composed and performed by Danny Rojo and arranged by Ricky González. It was recorded and released in 1996 on Rojo's debut recording *Regálame Tu Amor* (Mas Music MM10062).
2. Such techniques include digital editing, digital reverberation, and other effects, as well as overdubbing. [Editor's note: These techniques create a warm, intimate effect that underscores the romantic appeal of this style.]
3. The author is gratefully indebted to Ricky González and Danny Rojo for donating this score and their insightful perspectives, which greatly assisted in the following analysis.
4. Personal communication, 1996.
5. Clave is a rhythmic concept found in a variety of Latin American musical styles.

Within the salsa context, clave is a negotiated multilayered symbol that embodies ethnicity, issues of identity, and serves as a gauge for judging authenticity. In Spanish, the word literally means key, clef, code, or keystone. *Claves* are two wooden sticks hit together to produce a high, piercing sound. In Latin music terminology the word "clave" refers not only to these instruments but also to specific rhythmic patterns associated with them and the underlying rules that govern these patterns. All musical and dance components in salsa performance are governed by the clave rhythm.

In performance the clave may be overtly stated by someone playing the claves (sticks), or implied by the other instrumental parts without the actual playing of the sticks or clave block. Competent salsa musicians develop a "clave sense," which is a variety of what Waterman (1952) labels a "metronome sense," whereby a subjective pulse serving as an ordering principle is felt by the participants in a musical event. Each participant must maintain this clave sense throughout a performance for the proper (i.e., acceptable to insiders) execution of the music. As Steve Cornelius writes, the clave pattern is two measures in length "in which each measure is diametrically opposed. The two measures are not at odds, but rather, they are balanced opposites like positive and negative, expansive and contractive, or the poles of a magnet. As the full pattern is repeated, an alteration from one polarity to the other takes place creating pulse and rhythmic drive" (1992:15–16). If adhered to in a competent fashion, the clave provides the swing in salsa. In a salsa composition, adherence to certain rhythmic placement criteria ensures the piece to be "in clave." Ignoring those criteria will produce rhythmic passages that clash with the clave framework; such passages are said to be "crossed" or *cruzao* (from the word *cruzado*).

The phrasing of the melody determines which measure of the clave will be played first (e.g., where the accented rhythms of melody occur). This is referred to as either 2–3 or 3–2, meaning either the measure with the three-strokes is played first with the two-stroke measure following, or, the two-stroke measure is played first followed by the three-stroke measure. Once a song begins, the clave does not change its measure order (e.g., a 3–2–2–3 clave sequence is rare and considered inappropriate by today's salsa performers). Its function, similar to that of bell patterns found in West African musical traditions, is to provide a rhythmic formula that serves as the foundation for the performance.

6. Downward modulation by a major third was an uncommon harmonic shift before salsa romántica, although it has existed in Western classical music for many years. The advent of the *romántica* style introduced a more elaborate harmonic vocabulary that became one of the new style's distinguishing features.

7. See Manuel (1985) for a historical discussion exploring the roots of this phenomenon.

8. Boldface letters coincide with notations placed in the score by the arranger.

9. Personal communication, 1997.

10. Personal communication, 1996.

11. Personal communication, 1996.

12. The arrangement was recorded with a click track and maintains the same beats per minute (bpm) throughout. Live performance often relies on bpm manipulation to enhance energy-level shifts. The use of the click track forces the arranger to rely on other means. Although not used for this recording, González has since used programmable click tracks that progressively speed up throughout a recorded track to help simulate a live performance feel. "With the new programmable click people think that we recorded live. They don't believe that it is a click when I tell them" (personal communication, 1998).

13. Personal communication, 1996.
14. See Peter Manuel 1991 and 1995 for further comment and criticism of the new recording techniques used in salsa productions.
15. The scope of this article is too limited to explore the complexities of this shift from a New York–centered aesthetics to a Puerto Rican one. Refer to Washburne 1999 for an in-depth discussion of these issues.
16. Personal communication, 1994.
17. Personal communication, 1995.

BIBLIOGRAPHY

Cornelius, Steve, and John Amira. 1992. *The Music of Santería: Traditional Rhythms of the Batá Drums*. Crown Point, Ind.: White Cliffs Media.

Feld, Steven. 1988. "Aesthetics as Iconicity of Style, or 'Lift-up-over Sounding': Getting into the Kaluli Groove." *Yearbook for Traditional Music* 20:74–113.

Manuel, Peter. 1985."The Anticipated Bass in Cuban Popular Music." *Latin American Music Review* 6(2): 249–60.

———. 1991. "Latin Music in the United States: Salsa and the Mass Media." *Journal of Communication* 41(1):104–16.

———. 1995. *Caribbean Currents: Caribbean Music from Rumba to Reggae*. Philadelphia: Temple University Press.

Mauleón, Rebeca. 1993. *Salsa Guidebook for Piano and Ensemble*. Petaluma, Calif.: Sher Music.

Meyer, Leonard. 1967. *Music, the Arts, and Ideas*. Chicago: University of Chicago Press.

Washburne, Christopher. 1998. "Play It *Con Filin*: The Expression and Swing of Salsa." *Latin American Music Review* 19(2): 160–85.

———. 1999. "Salsa in New York: A Musical Ethnography." Ph.D. dissertation. Columbia University.

Waterman, Richard. 1952. "African Influence on the Music of Americas." In Sol Tax, ed., *Acculturation in the Americas*. Vol. 2. Chicago: University of Chicago, pp. 207–21.

Appendix to Chapter 5

SCORE OF "ME CALCULASTE"

ME CALCULASTE

Composed by : Danny Rojo
Arranged by: Ricky Gonzalez

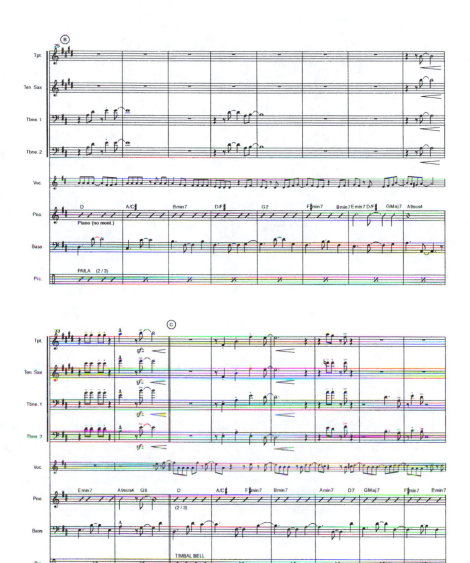

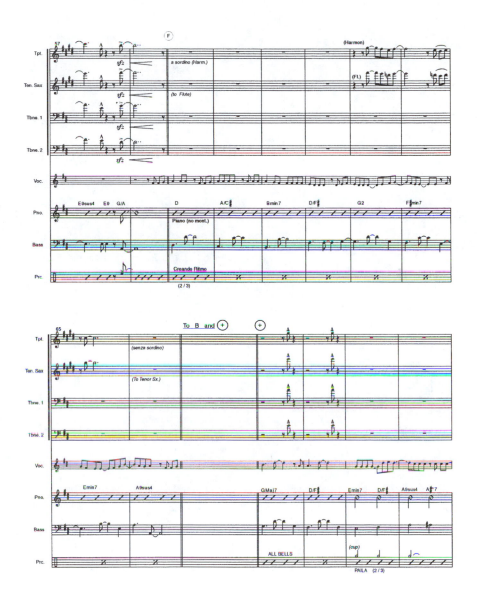

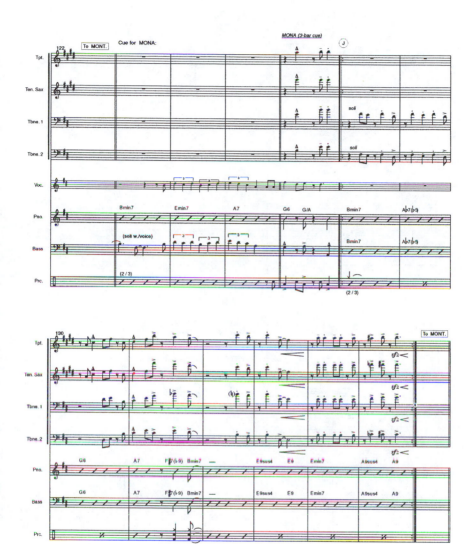

Part 2

PERSONALIZING SALSA

Chapter 6

LA LUPE, LA INDIA, AND CELIA: TOWARD A FEMINIST GENEALOGY OF SALSA MUSIC

Frances R. Aparicio

Soy la dueña del sabor...

> La Lupe, *"Yo soy como soy"*

Eliding the conceptualization of gender as a social construct, scholarship on Latino/a popular music continues to ignore female participation in the salsa musical industry and focuses only on male musicians, producers, and interpreters, naturalizing the unmarked masculine privilege underlying the selection of their objects of study. This gender ideology is less clearly at work, yet equally embedded, in the politics of citation as well as in the logic behind academic and cultural events on popular music, for which female scholars are invited "to take care of the gender thing."[1] I do not question the need—which still looms large—to study and unearth the participation of women in the Latin music industry, a task that necessitates further collaborative work and that, indeed, fuels my own approaches to music scholarship. This area deserves our serious scholarly analysis precisely because it has been neglected by masculinist writings on popular music. Yet the logic that defines gender exclusively as "women" leaves masculinity—as a gendered ideology and social construct—untouched by analysis. It also relegates women to an exceptional category in the musical industry, as if their presence and participation were the *exclusive* result of a feminist politics of inclusion on the part of scholars.

This essay argues that gender *and women* are central to our understanding of the negotiations of a Latino/a cultural politics through music and to the construction of transnational identities. First, it examines the gendering of salsa music as a historically shifting process integrally linked to the cultural politics of Latino/a identity articulated through music. For instance, the associations that tie *salsa romántica* (romantic salsa)—as a particular category or subgenre within Salsa—to women interpreters and to sentimental discourse is not altogether unconnected to the discursive and ideological subordination of this particular salsa style. Despite its disavowal on the part of traditional *salseros*, the voices and musical productions of Latinas in the 1990s have been an integral part of the cultural politics of salsa music. Although the musical interpretations and productions of women such as La India, Corinne, Brenda K. Starr, Lisette Meléndez, and the Dominican Yolanda la Duke have been mediated by male producers and musicians, particularly Sergio George, Little Louie Vega, Ralph Mercado, the late Tito Puente,[2] and Eddie Palmieri, these women have been central to the development of a new salsa during the 1990s that is transculturated by mostly African-American musical structures: hip-hop, r&b, gospel, jazz, and soul. The new salsa of the 1990s proposes a generational construction of Latino/a identity in the United States that disidentifies from classic salsa of the 1970s.

Careful and attentive listening to these women's recordings also reveals a discourse on issues of female authority and influence—a feminist genealogy—of salsa music, as Foucauldian countermemory, that elucidates how gender and female agency cannot be divorced from the larger analysis of the construction of Latino/a transnationalism and cultural politics through music. My reading of women's songs and performances/performativity will suggest that their contributions and discourses are central to our understanding of the debates about the origins and authorship of salsa and of the role of music as a site of resistance. Furthermore, this study implies that women's ideologies are diverse, complex, and conflictive. Lumping all women together under the category of "gender" inevitably homogenizes women as subaltern subjects, something that women of color have long critiqued in the Anglo feminist movement. Unfortunately, male-authored Latino scholarship on popular music continues this process of reification.

GENDERING SALSA AND ERASING WOMEN

Celia Cruz, the Queen of Salsa and the only woman featured in the British documentary titled *Salsa: Latin Pop Music in the Cities*, commented that the absence of women in the Latin music industry, and in salsa music in particular, was due to the fact that women were not trained in popular music and that women dared not improvise—*sonear*—on stage (Marre and Charlton 1985). Indeed, despite the strong historical tradition of Latin women as singers and interpreters of romantic ballads, very few women, with the exception of Celia Cruz, have been associated with the development of salsa and with the music industry that produces it. This has been the result of various factors: the cultural traditions of Latin American families that prohibited young women from inhabiting the male-dominated, public spaces of music making; the lack of music education programs that included training in Latin popular music; women's lack of access to training in popular music, which has taken place mostly through all-male networks in production; and the discursive constructions of salsa music as a masculine cultural space.

This does not mean that women have not been historical agents in the development of Afro-Caribbean music, but that musical historiography has rendered them invisible. In the lyrics of boleros, which inform the gender ideologies of salsa songs, the central role of the Latina woman has been mostly as the object of male desire, as unrequited love; women abandon men, so they are constructed as physical absence and emotional distance, as ungrateful beings who cannot love the men who sing to their desire (Aparicio 1998). Thus, when the musical history of the Caribbean recognizes woman, it does so exclusively in her role as singer of boleros, that is, it contains her within the sentimental discourse in which patriarchal society also inscribes her. In the 1990s, women have broken through the sexist boundaries of the music industry, and Celia's words are no longer valid. Nonetheless, it is not a coincidence that salsa romántica has been equally associated with women's voices and concomitantly rendered as depoliticized. Gender dynamics in salsa music foreground how issues of female authority and authorship, and the representation or lack thereof of women in musical historiography, are related to the ways in which particular musical subgenres or forms are gendered and judged.

The predominant current discourse around salsa music is the highly gendered differentiation between *salsa dura* (hard salsa) and *salsa monga* (limp salsa). This binary refers to the difference in sounds, styles, and content represented by the salsa of the 1970s and its continuation in the 1990s, and the emergence of salsa romántica since the 1980s with its particular arrangements and sonority that have been deemed as homogenized, depoliticized, and ultimately, feminized (Manuel 1991). While the development of salsa romántica, its various articulations, and its shifting historical and cultural meanings still need to be systematically studied, here I want to focus on the relationship of these discursive constructs/binaries to the representation of women's work in the music industry.

What Paul Gilroy has observed regarding African-American rap is equally applicable to the construction, through music, of a Latino masculinity during the 1970s:

> Gender is the modality in which race is lived. An amplified and exaggerated masculinity has become the boastful centrepiece of a culture of compensation that self-consciously salves the misery of the disempowered and subordinated. This masculinity and its relational feminine counterpart become special symbols of the difference that race makes. They are lived and naturalised in the distinct patterns of family life on which the reproduction of racial identities supposedly relies. These gender identities come to exemplify the immutable cultural differences that apparently arise from absolute ethnic difference. To question them and their constitution of racial subjectivity is at once to be ungendered and to place oneself outside the racial kin group. (1993:85)

This statement foregrounds the ways in which gendering—such as the construction of a hypermasculinity through sound and song—is a central tactic in the negotiations of power between racialized subjectivities and dominant institutions. Thus, salsa dura refers to the self-construction of masculinity through sound, style, and words that emerged during the 1970s in the context of the political economy of the Puerto Rican barrios in New York City. The titles of important recordings—such as Willie Colón's *El malo, Lo mato, El crimen paga* and Ray Barretto's *Indestructible*—inscribe a collective, violent male subjectivity that is clearly articulated in opposition to and in resistance to the forms of colonization and social oppression that dispossessed Puerto Rican men in the diaspora from their social, cultural, and economic agency.

Like the Nuyorican poets of the time, the salsa singers established an oppositional voice as an alternative to what we can call the political "feminization" that they were experiencing collectively. As César Miguel Rondón observes but does not fully explain, the constructions of this Latino masculinity were inscribed also in the Fania film *Nuestra cosa latina* (Our Latin Thing) and in the lyrics of *guapería* or male delinquency that populate the songs of Rubén Blades and Willie Colón (Rondón 81:64). In the film, one of the closing scenes in which young Latinos set up an explosive should not be read literally, but rather interpreted as a symbolic discourse that visually suggests the radical critiques that this music articulated at the time. Marginality was not only imposed from above, but also tactically constituted a liminal space from which to construct an oppositional social discourse from below. At this time, then, this subjectivity, constructed in both literature and music, implies a high degree of anxiety and expressions of violence against women, who are defined as traitors and *bandoleras* (gold diggers). This motif is still prevalent today, although in more subtle ways. If in the 1970s men accused women of being gold diggers, traitors, and treacherous—women could not be trusted—today we still hear echoes of those very same images in the songs of Marc Anthony and Ricky Martin ("Living la Vida Loca"), yet in articulations that are mediated by much more androgynous performances and mediated sounds and arrangements that make it appear less masculinist or *machista*.

The emergence of salsa romántica during the 1980s stands in sharp contrast to the masculine discourse that accompanied the cultural nationalism of the 1970s. However, this type of feminization of salsa was not originally conceived of by singers or composers, but rather by the music industry itself. Interested in creating a wider audience, producers and sponsors weakened and neutralized the political, social, and cultural reaffirmation of salsa music by plugging the romantic ballads into radio play (Manuel 1991) and by integrating the ballad into the arrangements and content of salsa songs. Lyrics shifted from predominantly collective, decolonizing reaffirmations of the community to a repertoire of romantic ballads that articulated individual, heterosexual subjectivities.[3] In fact, Willie Colón refers to the salsa of the '80s as the "mass production" of salsa through which Miami "undermined and revamped" "the agenda and criteria for Salsa recordings" (1999). Salsa romántica is, undoubtedly, the reflection of a shift in the geopolitical location of the music industry that illustrates the struggles for power between the Cuban industry in Miami—the Estefans—and the New York labels as they vie with each other to become the center for the production of Latin music. *Salseros* like Willie Colón and Jerry González oppose the musical trends produced by RMM which, in fact, "has controlled most of the contemporary salsa market during the 1990s and is certainly aligned with the anti-leftist stance of Miami's Cuban producers."[4] While Latino musical production does not necessarily reflect an opposition between New York and Miami, the ideological and aesthetic oppositions between traditional NY salseros and salsa romántica is partly informed by these shifts in the spaces of production.

The strong sounds of the brass instruments that characterized historically the New York style have remained in the New York–based salsa romántica. Yet these are now mediated by the classical lyricism of violins and by the sonorous effects of the synthesizer, which situates salsa romántica closer to pop than to *salsa clásica* (classic salsa) or salsa dura. Moreover, interpreters such as Gilberto Santa Rosa, whose fame has been established as a singer of salsa romántica, have strategically sung salsa in high art venues, such as the Centro de Bellas Artes in San Juan, Puerto Rico, and with the Orquesta Sinfónica of Puerto Rico and of

Venezuela.[5] The ensuing social and cultural meanings of salsa, then, shift from a working-class, black/mulatto, male oppositionality that is indexed by strong sounds of drumming and percussion and that exhorts a dialogic relationship with its audience, to a music that is meant to attract passive, middle-class audiences in concert-hall settings and that is not perceived as socially threatening or as chaotic, disturbing "noise."[6] Salsa romántica is deemed salsa monga (limp salsa) because of the resignified social, race, and class meanings that it has produced.

In addition to the shifts marked by the industry, style, and sound, gender also lies at the very heart of these discursive binaries and debates. When we define salsa romántica as "feminized" and "flaccid" or when we refer to salsa dura we are invoking the very hypermasculinity of the 1970s as the central criterion by which to evaluate and judge all other arrangements and trends in salsa. The salsa dura versus salsa monga binary (illustrated in Jimmy Bosch's 1999 album, *Salsa Dura*) perpetuates a sexist discourse that has been questioned by feminists: the opposition between political agency and affective, sentimental discourse. Although there are male singers of salsa romántica—Marc Anthony, Tito Nieves, Frankie Ruiz, and Gilberto Santa Rosa among them, and male listeners, female salsa singers continue to be dismissed as unimportant because they are exclusively identified with the affective issues of the heterosexual couple, thus eliding the contributions that they have made to a Latino/a cultural politics through their musical repertoires and performances. For instance, Willie Colón has defined the content of the 1980s as "refried ballads" that "are provocative only in a sexual manner, rarely in a sensual or truly romantic way" (1999). While here he may be making reference to the *salsa erótica* (erotic salsa) of Eddie Santiago, for instance, it is fascinating how the shift from New York to the Cuban-dominated musical industry in Miami signals for him not only the cooptation of the salsa of the '70s but a form of trivialization of what he considers the "truly romantic way," ironically a reference to his own productions of salsa romántica, which I have analyzed elsewhere (Aparicio 1998). This differentiation privileges the male-dominated productions of a discourse on heterosexual love that has been prevalent since the '70s and erases the liberatory possibilities that *salsa erótica* briefly represented in the public performance of sexuality within the Latino ethos. Willie Colón also considers salsa romántica a threat to the musical authority and knowledge of the *salseros*, one indexed by its hybridity: "Even if they never know what the hell it was, they can come and add their innovative r&b, Hip Hop or whatever chops it" (1999). These arguments, which are shared by many other "traditional" salseros from New York, are not unfounded and, in fact, reveal the mechanisms by which mainstreaming and cooptation have occurred in salsa music. However, it is essential to tease out the discursive connections between homogenization and depoliticization, on the one hand, and feminization, on the other. The defense of "good" salsa and of the musical authority and expertise of the New York salseros is inextricably bound to gender differentiations.

Yet salsa romántica, despite its dominant, capitalist-authored origins, has circulated in different ideological planes and has assumed a diversity of expressions and articulations. In other words, this salsa cannot be categorized only as a hegemonic cultural text, but rather needs to be considered in its social circulation and in the role it has played during the 1990s. As Lise Waxer observes in her study of salsa music in Cali, Colombia, the existence of salsa romántica helped to galvanize the development of all-women bands in this urban center so important to the history of salsa music. By producing an audience of women listeners who were interpellated by the romantic discourse of heterosexual love, salsa romántica created the potential audience and market that would allow all-female bands to flourish (1998:327). In the United States, the new hybrid salsa that has emerged in the 1990s—what some have problematically called "tropical pop" (McLane 1996)—is a significant phenomenon that reveals and articulates a new generational identity for U.S. Latinos. It also suggests the possibility that salsa romántica is being appropriated and put to use in diverse symbolic ways.

THE NEW SALSA(ERAS)

The new salsa of the 1990s has been mainly attributed to two male producers: Little Louie Vega and Sergio George (McLane 1996). The project of transculturating salsa with hip-hop rhythms, reggae, r&b, soul, and other musical styles, has resulted in a level of intermusicality (Monson 1994) that is not totally new, but rather consistent with the intertextual and intermusical history of Afro-Caribbean popular music and salsa music. Yet this hybridization takes on different meanings at this particular historical time and place, the diaspora and the new millennium. Critics and musicians who demonize the new salsa of the 1990s or who conflate it with the homogenizing effects of the '80s may have forgotten that traditional salsa itself is historically a fusion and hybrid musical form, bringing together Afro-Cuban and Puerto Rican music, African-American jazz, and rock music elements. Yet, to use Mark Slobin's term (1993:61–82), perhaps the difference lies in the fact that while salsa has been an "intercultural" musical style that fuses musical forms from various subaltern, colonized Third World cultures—the diasporic interculture—the new salsa is being mediated by, and listened through, a homogenized formulaic sound, exemplified in the use of the synthesizer, that seemingly inserts it into the pop category. Thus, the rejection of this hybrid salsa by traditional salseros and audiences may be explained by its double location as salsa romántica and U.S. pop sonority. But is it even justifiable to reify the new salsa as an instance of how "Latin music goes pop," as mainstream journalism has done?[8] To conflate the new salsa interpreters such as La India and Marc Anthony with the pop performances of a Ricky Martin and a Jennifer López is to ignore the cultural politics and historical identities that are being produced through the musical hybridity of the 1990s.

The entry of women singers into the salsa industry during the 1990s has been defined as a "crossover" by the mainstream press. Yet La India, Brenda K. Starr, Corrine, and Lisette Meléndez all sang dance music, house, and hip-hop in English before interpreting salsa music in Spanish. If anything, the shift from English to Spanish lyrics, which is not totally evident in any of their musical recordings, reveals the inverse of crossover. Marc Anthony and Huey Dunbar from DLG, also exemplify this bicultural positionality. Because the collective effect of these musical productions has blurred the boundaries between salsa and U.S. pop music and, most significant, has also adapted salsa to the younger generation's own hybrid multiracial musical tastes and identities, traditional salseros perceive it as suspect, as another form of mainstreaming or dominant appropriation of Afro-Caribbean salsa productions. Yet the fact is that the new salsa is a musical articulation of a new generational *latinidad* (Latin identity) that transcends the cultural nationalism of the 1970s and that makes "all things Latin suddenly seem cool" within the new social and cultural locations that are accessible to them in the U.S. public space (Larmer et al. 1991:50).

Marc Anthony's comment regarding the erroneous label of "crossover" used by journalists and music critics is helpful here: "Crossover's just a label. What I really did was go back to my roots. What is this place called Puerto Rico that I have these feelings for? What is it about this land, our people, our history?" When he unraveled those puzzles, he decided that he "was raised too Americanized. I realized that there was a whole other different set of color on my palette of life."[9] La India has also explained this move as a homecoming based on generational differentiation and individuation fueled by her "Americanization": "I grew up with salsa, but I didn't want to sing it then because I was here in America, and I wanted to be Americanized." This "musical-cultural homecoming" is an interesting historical move that allows the younger generation of Latinos to embrace the music that they had rejected for years as the traditional music of their parents.

Because it is not traditional salsa, but salsa with a difference, transculturated by other urban musical styles such as hip-hop, r&b, dance, and house, and mediated by pop, this musical space allows young U.S. Latino/as to reaffirm their own national identities and simultaneously to move across cultural, racial, musical, and linguistic boundaries. This is particularly significant for a Latina such as Brenda K. Starr, who is Jewish-Boricua, and whose own interracial identity would not have necessarily fit within the nationalist/masculinist paradigms of salsa dura/clásica.

This generational difference—between the generations called Generation ñ and Generation Mex—emerges out of a diverse set of factors: sociologically speaking, the demographic changes among Latino/a populations within the United States has fostered new processes of identity formation that transcend a fixed national identification (Oboler 1995). Thus, second- and third-generation Latinos do identify themselves as Latinos rather than as Mexicans or Puerto Ricans, as their parents still do (Flores-González 1999:18–21). This suggests not only that national boundaries are being dismantled for and by a number of younger Latinos, but also that intercultural and interracial identities will also be foregrounded in these hybrid forms of cultural expressions. Music, then, articulates a new "fusion" that allows individuals to negotiate among the various identities that conform them. Demographic changes also indicate that young Latino/as are increasing in numbers. This implies that individuals will feel less intimidated than their parents to reassert and perform their cultural identities in the public space, for, although numbers do not automatically translate into power, large numbers have legitimated Latino/as as consumers and as a particular audience and market (Negus 1999). As Rudy Acuña observes, "Past generations have always assimilated. This time around, there are enough of them to say, 'We aren't going to make it your society. We want to make it on our own terms'" (Leland and Chambers 1999:53).

Yet, it is also very significant that young Latinos, as integrated (not assimilated) as they are to dominant institutions and Anglo mainstream society—and they have had much more access than their immigrant parents precisely because of affirmative action laws—feel empowered to enact their bicultural latinidad in the public space. They are "rediscovering their roots," as Marc Anthony and La India have exemplified, "doing things that immigrants wanted to get away from" (Leland and Chambers 1999:54). This has been possible not only because of the large numbers, which in certain ways protects them from being marginalized, but also because of the educational experiences that many of them have had (although only 9 percent of Latinos hold a bachelor's degree). The efforts of the Chicano movement, the Nuyorican cultural nationalism, the Young Lords, and all other organizations that have struggled and continue to struggle for the rights and representation of Latinos in education, citizenship, civil rights, health, and other dominant institutions, find concrete evidence in these new, generational public enactments of Latino/a identities that are informed by the knowledge production, teaching, and empowerment that ensued from the 1970s. As Jaime Cortez explains, "We *know* we came from a rich history and culture, and we want to celebrate that" (Leland and Chambers 1999: 54; my emphasis).[10] Indeed, the convergence of salsa with U.S. pop does not necessarily suggest that these Latina/o singers are assimilated and sold out but, indeed, that as a result of the 1970s, they are integrated into the United States in ways that the earlier generations were not. Rather than demonizing the new salsa, salseros should celebrate it as evidence of the impact of their own efforts as cultural workers. What is ironic is that what may be considered "U.S. pop" is historically the amalgam of black musical forms mediated by the homogenizing forces of the music industry.

By examining the intermusical, intertextual, and transcultural aspects of selected cuts from La India, Brenda K. Starr, and Corrine, we can understand how women *salseras* centrally contribute to this particular Latino/a cultural politics in the 1990s. Because musical productions are a collective result of multiple levels of decision making, from composing to arrangements, editing, sound mixing, singing styles and improvisation to publicity and promotions, it would be unproductive to separate issues of female agency from the cultural politics articulated in the songs. Thus, gender politics are embedded in cultural politics as much as issues of national identity, tradition and innovation, race, class, and ethnicity, and generational differences. Brenda K. Starr's salsified version of "I Still Believe" (1998), later popularized by Mariah Carey as a pop ballad, constitutes a public reclaiming of this song. Starr's reinterpretation in salsa style cannot be explained as her piggybacking on traditional salsa, but rather as a rearticulation, in a mixture of English and Spanish, that returns it, linguistically and musically, to the cultural space from which it originally emerged. If the process of popularizing a song—making it pop—has meant diluting or "de-racinating" its original locus of emergence, its cultural authority, then we can consider Starr's salsified version of "I Still Believe" an act of oppositional reclaiming away from mainstream pop.

Likewise, Corrine's inclusion of Madonna's earlier popular hit, "La isla bonita" (1999), in its arrangement by Wyclef Jean, constitutes a remixing of a song that originally articulated the dominant gaze of, and desire for, an eroticized Latino/a culture that stands as a utopian escape from the tenets of U.S. society: "all the nature wild and free," again echoed recently by Ricky Martin's "La vida loca." Wyclef Jean's arrangement begins with hip-hop, then moves on to salsa rhythms and a *montuno* part, and returns to a hip-hop style in its ending. This remix allows Corrine to put her experience with freestyle to good use. Through the hybridity of salsa and hip-hop, she symbolically returns the songs to the voices, rhythms, and sounds of the cultural communities who were silenced and stereotyped in Madonna's composition. The use of Spanish in the rap sections is politically significant, partly because its content is a reassertion of Latin culture in the aggressively masculine voice of Wyclef Jean, who reminds listeners about the subaltern status of Latinos who are alienated but also *aliados* (allied). The practice among many new salseros and salseras of including two versions of the same cut allows not only for a more diversified potential audience, but also for foregrounding the fluidity of styles and the hybridization of culture. The Spanish version of "La isla bonita" by Corrine stands in sharp contrast to the dominant text by Madonna, where Latin subjects are only objects of desire, not subjects or agents of culture. This type of new salsa counters, indeed, the eroticized use of Spanish that has permeated mainstream rap in the 1990s and is particularly obvious in Will Smith's "Bienvenidos a Miami" and Dru Hill's "How Deep Is Your love?"

While freestyle and remixing may be characteristic of the 1990s hybrid, interracial, and intercultural lives of youth of color in our urban centers, and transnational/interracial also in the ways in which African-American musicians are relocating their own personal and musical identities, rewritings of dominant musical texts are not new. La Lupe, the well-known Cuban interpreter, the Queen of Latin Soul, recorded in 1971 *They Call Me La Lupe,* a collection of international songs that were remade and reinflected with various Afro-Caribbean rhythms under the arrangements and conducting of Cuban trumpet player and arranger Arturo Chico O'Farrill. Among these songs is "America" from *West Side Story,* arranged as a Brazilian samba by O'Farrill. La Lupe turns this song upside down, singing in Spanish about the experience of the Cuban exiles and transforming the image of the Latino as a recent migrant or *ave de paso* to one of a permanent presence in the North ("no nos movemos de América" [we are staying in America]. By foregrounding the Cuban resistance to assimilate and the way that humor allows for emotional survival in conditions of cultural displacement, La Lupe and O'Farrill contest the well-known dominant stereotypes that *West Side Story* ingrained in the minds of a mainstream audience and that still permeates the U.S. popular imaginary (Sandoval 1999). According to the liner notes of this collection, the French "Dominique" becomes a merengue in honor of the Dominican Republic; the Mexican ballad "El preso número nueve," a *son huapango*, is sung as a slow rock; the Peruvian *vals* "Que nadie sepa mi sufrir," as a Venezuelan *joropo*; the Spanish *pasodoble* "El cascabel"—also known as a Mexican song—as a Cuban *guaguancó*; and the U.S. song "Take It Easy" as a cha-cha rock "sung in English as only La Lupe doesn't know how."[11]

These transnational arrangements transculturate national musics by the very act of displacing and replacing their lyrics in different nationally and culturally informed rhythms. Yet the transformations are also textual and ideological, as La Lupe adds, deletes, and recontextualizes these songs to speak to her own subjectivity as a woman in a male-dominated industry as well as a Cuban exile in the United States. In addition, by blurring the national boundaries of music, La Lupe and O'Farrill propose a larger, diasporic and transnational paradigm through which to define Afro-Caribbean and Latin music, a paradigm that had been already evident in O'Farrill's own latinizing influences on African-American jazz during the 1950s (Díaz Ayala 1981; Orovio 1981). To be sure, while the transculturation behind the new salsa of the 1990s speaks to a new generational, historical experience, La Lupe's performances of these remusicalized national songs remind us that intermusicality and intertextuality are, indeed, the historical basis for popular music. La Lupe herself transgressed numerous boundaries in her musical career, and it is not a coincidence that she has become an important, foundational figure in the musical production of the new salseras.

A FEMINIST GENEALOGY OR THE MANY VOICES OF EXPERIENCE?

The musical productions of women such as Linda Caballero, born in the Bronx and professionally known as La India, have had a central role in the transnational cultural politics of salsa music. La India has constructed a transnational and interracial, diasporic space analogous to the "Black Atlantic" (Gilroy 1993) through her own hybrid salsa, but also through the establishment of a feminist genealogy of salsa music. By "feminist genealogy" I refer to the process of unearthing, historicizing, and inscribing the agency of women in the cultural politics of Latino/Caribbean popular music, thus serving as a discourse of counter-memory (Foucault 1977) that contests the masculinist historiography of popular music. Yet while the Foucauldian genealogy refuses to search for origins, which liberates it from any particular form of teleology or even ultimate genesis or authority, this "feminist genealogy" seems to provide a foundational gesture that is needed precisely to contest the male-dominant musical historiography.

Genealogies, as Joseph Roach writes, foreground collective memory and orature as an alternative discourse to the reifying, text-based concept of history (1995). Likewise, performance as "restored behavior"—and the genealogical impulse to trace the erased voices and bodies behind cultural performances and their official representations—are helpful, critical tools by which to analyze the ways in which La India contests the erasure of women in the history of salsa. While Roach uses the term "genealogies of performance" to reclaim the silences behind the history of performances, I examine genealogy within the performance itself.

For Judith Butler genealogy calls to question "the category of women" as "the subject of feminism" (1990:5), thus providing a critique of the "heterosexual matrix" that lends stability and coherence to the category of women but unwittingly regulates and reifies gender relations, as my opening observations indicated. Thus, a "feminist genealogy" in the context of the salseras of the 1990s will also destabilize the very binaries of the feminine and masculine, particularly through the selection of La Lupe as a foundational figure for the younger salseras, including La India. By selecting the Afro-Cuban singer La Lupe and memorializing her through intertextual references, and by reproducing her radical performativity of the 1950s and early 1960s, which has been itself embraced and appropriated by Latino/a queer audiences and performers (Muñoz 1999), La India calls into question the essentialist and reified notions of what is feminine and what is masculine. This is quite significant within the gendered ideologies of Latin American societies, which are rearticulated in the music.

La India is not alone in her feminist recuperative project. Others include Yolanda Duke's *Nostalgias de La Lupe*, in which the Dominican *salsera* uncannily imitates the excesses and vocal styles of La Lupe.[12] The CD anthology titled *Holding Up Half the Sky: Voices of Latin Women* (Shanachie 1998) represents perhaps the most complete recovery project up to now. This CD traces the history of women singers in Latin America and within the United States. It identifies Lydia Mendoza as Selena's antecedent, and María Teresa Vera as "the great grandmother of all Latin women singers today." If, on the one hand, this anthology project is structured on the concept of linear influences, La India's song "La voz de la experiencia" suggests a much more dialogic, contradictory, and complex view of female musical production. Behind the paradigm of generational influences, one finds references to a female and feminist dialogism that recognizes multiple and conflicting presences of Caribbean women behind the development of salsa.

The only book-length history of salsa music, written by the Venezuelan journalist César Miguel Rondón, foregrounded the role of

La Lupe in two of her principal contributions: as a figure of transition between the big-band sound and the strident aesthetics of the barrio, and as a singer who interprets the compositions of the Puerto Rican composer Tite Curet Alonso and who "would offer the irreverent, disorderly, and malicious touch to Tito Puente's orchestra, a style that was already necessary in that new music" (Rondón 1980:46). In other words, La Lupe served to ground the new, urban style of the barrio—precisely the style that has mediated the aggressive masculinity of the 1970s—and to open the path to Tito Puente's orchestra and to Curet Alonso's compositions. While Rondón recognizes La Lupe's talent as a singer of boleros (1980:153), his tendency is to define her contributions as singer and performative artist as a vehicle for the development of the male figures of *la farándula* (celebrity circuit). This relational and derivative value afforded to women is thus questioned by La India.

The musical production of La India is characterized by its diversity and generic hybridity, by its experimentations with style, by its manipulations of the voice, and by songs that clearly articulate a strong, feminist ideology. In 1992, her album, significantly titled *Llegó la India (via Eddie Palmieri)* represents her first incursion into salsa in Spanish after having interpreted hip-hop and house and dance music. This shift does not suggest that La India would abandon those earlier styles, nor that she would stop singing in English; rather, it reveals a cultural politics that embraces not one particular style, but a variety of them, hybridizing and transforming them in the process as well as creating a much more varied listening audience.

La India is known not only for her strong feminist songs (such as "Dicen que soy," "Ese hombre," "La mayor venganza") but also for a singular performative presence that echoes the excesses of La Lupe. Her improvisations as a *sonera* include very difficult rhythmic shifts, a nasal style of singing, growls and screams that evoke an androgynous style rather than a soft, melodious tone. These performative elements indeed transgress the homogenizing and feminized aspects of salsa romántica, breaking listeners' expectations based on those standardized formulae and indeed "masculinizing" herself. Such transgressive elements are definitely traceable to La Lupe, whom José Esteban Muñoz defines as "the supreme figure in the history of *chusmería*." Chusmería is a concept that Muñoz appropriates from the discursive repertoire of the Caribbean bourgeoisie. Originally, somebody *chusma* was a person of working-class origins whose style, clothing, speech, and bodily performance did not agree with the expected regulated styles of the upper-class upbringing. Muñoz rewrites the class-inflected term in order to examine the poetics and politics of performance artists such as Carmelita Tropicana, who likewise has been inspired by the transgressive excesses of La Lupe. According to Muñoz, Carmelita Tropicana disidentifies herself from the negative and racist values that the dominant, bourgeois society has imposed on the working class. Her performance in *Chicas 2000* rearticulates this hegemonic discourse and proposes a "transformative politics" in its rewriting:

> Carmelita turns to La Lupe for the purposes of establishing a Latina self who is not lessened by restrictive codes of conduct. Santa La Lupe serves as a beacon; through her model and her shining example, an identity that has been spoiled is newly reinhabited and recomposed as a site of possibility and transformation. Chusmería is *puro teatro* or pure performance. This pure performance salvages something that has been disparaged and rendered abject. (Muñoz 1999:193)

The performative excesses of La India, such as smoking a cigar, transgress the class and gender codes of conduct imposed on women in public. As Gus Puleo observes in his chronicle about La India's concert in Carnegie Hall, that image is not only androgynous and transgressively masculine, but it also "evokes a sense of promise and possibility, a vision of freedom. Feminist in the sense that she dares to transgress sexist boundaries. With a cigar in her mouth, she reclaims the female body as a site of power and hope" (1997:225). This image, which appeared as the publicity poster outside Carnegie Hall, also subverts class hegemony, for smoking a cigar rearticulates not only the role of women in *santería*, but is also a defiance of proper female behavior in public. Interestingly enough, after the Clinton-Lewinsky affair, the phallic signifier of the cigar has taken on new layers of signification related to sexuality, the desire for the cultural Other (Monica is Salvadorean-American), and the commercialization of the woman's body (in Miami, cigars began to sell as Monica cigars). If we think of "performance" as "restored behavior" (Schechner 1985; Roach 1995), then the paradox of La India restoring La Lupe's behavior "resides in the phenomenon of repetition itself: no action or sequence of actions may be performed exactly the same way twice; they must be reinvented or recreated at each appearance. In this improvisatory behavioral space, memory reveals itself as imagination" (Roach 1995:46). Like Latina performance artists, the new salseras of the 1990s can reimagine themselves through the memory of La Lupe, the abject singer of her time, and appropriate old signifiers, including their own bodies, remaking them into spaces of potential freedom.

But the presence of La Lupe as a subtext to La India is found not only in these transgressive performative styles, but also in the intertextuality and intermusicality of her songs (Monson 1994). "La voz de la experiencia" (The voice of experience), composed by La India as an homage to Celia Cruz, is a major text in establishing this feminist genealogy of salsa. It locates the female influence in La India's work and it dismantles the male mediation previously inscribed in her first album (via Eddie Palmieri) and in her commercial and personal relationship to her ex-husband and producer, Little Louie Vega. However, her current contract with Ralph Mercado belies any possibility of total autonomy for La India. One has to consider the multiple levels of decision making in the process of musical productions—from composers, arrangers, and technicians, to singers, producers, and marketing—to realize that La India is not necessarily in total control of her musical productions. Yet a cursory look at the credits in her CDs reveals that she has selected many more compositions by women than were recorded in the 1970s and 1980s. She has also composed a couple of cuts. Thus, the feminist discourse in "La voz de la experiencia" is not necessarily a direct proof or reflection of feminist autonomy in music, but rather a symbolic discourse that recovers women's invisibility in history.

The last recording by La India, *Sola* (1999), is a direct homage to La Lupe. In it she sings two of La Lupe's most famous boleros—"Qué te pedí" and "Si vuelves tú"—and also recognizes La Lupe's influence in her work:

> Seven years of admiration of La Lupe, the most eccentric singer of the Caribbean, created in me the desire and the inspiration to bring this homage to this great singer. I would like to dedicate this production to her and to her fans and to those who follow me today. (liner notes)

This statement renders ironic the title *Sola* (Alone), which is based on the eponymous song included twice in the recording. "Sola" appears both in a salsa arrangement and as a ballad, in which the strong brass instrumentation of the first is replaced by a soft ballad accompanied by a guitar, violins, and a female backup chorus. Yet both versions express a woman's apology to her man for having cheated on him. While she blames her transgression on her being lonely and alone, the adjective "sola" can also be read metacritically. La India rejects the previous male mediations in her work and now reaffirms her independence from male authority through this adjective. However, her homage to La Lupe suggests that her independence has been possible through her identification with and through the feminist genealogy that she builds in relationship to La Lupe, Celia Cruz, and earlier female figures. In other words, she can be "alone," that is, musically independent, only by unearthing her musical antecedents and models, particularly La Lupe. It is almost as if La India ironically suggests a homosocial context from which to understand her own musical production, one that is exclusively female and feminist and that contests the masculinist historiography of salsa.[13]

Yet "La voz de la experiencia" reveals a much more complex relationship between La India and her musical antecedents La Lupe and Celia. This song is meaningful in various ways. First, it breaks with the tradition of the male-female duet, which has also been quite popular in Latin pop music and in the interpretation of romantic ballads. The song proposes, instead, a tradition of salseras in the world of Latin popular music. By identifying Celia Cruz as the Queen of Salsa, and La India, her disciple and admirer, as the Princess, Ralph Mercado, their producer, could very well have considered that this song and the video would serve as great publicity for the globalization of his two most important female stars. Indeed, the introductory lyrics define Celia as Cuban music and La India as the embodiment of Puerto Rican music. The national associations immediately take on global implications, as the chorus dialogizes the national with the phrases of presentation to the world: "De Cuba para el mundo, Celia Cruz! and "De Puerto Rico para el mundo, India!" But this duet represents much more than a commercial enterprise. It is a feminist foundational text because it constitutes one of the first musical expressions that recognizes different generations of *salseras*, that establishes a historical continuity, and that suggests itself as a paradigm that traces the participation, legacies, influences, and continuity of women singers, many of whom have imitated and rewritten each other's songs.

At the surface structure, La India expresses her gratitude to Celia for having served as a role model, and Celia responds as "the voice of experience," offering advice to her and to the women listeners. Celia advises La India to maintain her autonomy and a degree of control over her musical productions, something that has characterized Celia's musical career according to her (Fernández 1996). The chorus reaffirms this female autonomy with the refrain: "Yo soy como soy," which is a repetition of lyrics from one of La Lupe's famous songs: "Yo soy como soy/no como nadie quiere" (I am how I am/not the way others want me to be) (Tito Puente and La Lupe, 1965). This phrase articulates the feminist resistance of these singers, who have faced the homogenizing pressures of the musical and entertainment industry and have refused to yield to the Eurocentric beauty criteria. La Lupe, Celia Cruz, and La India have not capitulated to those dominant beauty values as mulatta, black, and Latina singers. It is interesting that rather than refashioning their bodies and physical features, their bodies are performative through their dress and the transgressive excesses of the body, features that definitely oppose the industry at the same time that they produce the necessary desire to create an audience and a following.

The epithets of *reina* (queen) and *princesa* (princess), very typical in the world of popular music, are reaffirmed by Celia Cruz throughout the song. However, these hierarchies are implicitly and ironically questioned in the very act of the performance, since Celia Cruz is singing La India's original song. In other words, the advice and the voice of experience, the content itself, emerges not from the most legendary singer, Celia, but as an artistic, literary, and musical creation of the disciple, of the admirer, and of the Puerto Rican, La India. It is also quite significant that the subtextual presence of La Lupe, as minimal as it may be, destabilizes the central foundational role in salsa that Celia reaffirms for herself as the Queen.[14]

Two Cuban singers, Celia and La Lupe, with two opposite destinies and career paths and lifestyles, with very different personalities, social positionings and audiences, and ideologies in terms of the construction of their artistic personae, both coincide in New York City in the early 1960s. They are both Cuban exiles, and they are embraced and welcomed as artists by a mostly Puerto Rican community of listeners, a reception that illustrates the inter-latino spaces created by popular music as a symbolic discourse. Yet La Lupe died in oblivion in the early 1990s, while Celia has become a living legend, a singer who has spanned half a century singing to audiences in her native Cuba, in Mexico, Latin America, the United States, and internationally. Thus, Celia's official visibility as the Queen of Salsa is subtly dismantled by the evocation of La Lupe through La India's strategic selection of the refrain.

Another significant irony or double-voiced discourse in this performance is the subversive presence, or subtexts, of santería that reveal themselves in performance and in the text. Common to much Afro-Caribbean secular music, this song makes references to Yemayá and to "la negra Tomasa nos bendice" and "mar y candela," which are snippets of santería ideologies and beliefs. This religious affiliation becomes readable in the performance of this song at a concert by Elvis Crespo, La India, and Celia Cruz in San Francisco on February 27, 1999 (fig. 6.1).[15] While Celia and La India perform "La voz de la experiencia" La India kneels in front of Celia, and calls her *mi madrina* (my godmother). Although Celia Cruz has publicly denied her participation in santería, the point here is not whether either has been initiated in santería or not, but the importance, although veiled, of the discourse and faith in the *orishás* that La India and Celia share. The affiliations to santería also inform La India's reading of La Lupe, who herself assumed a stage persona based on santería (1969). Indeed, when La India dressed as a *santera* on stage, "muchos asociaron su excentricidad con la personalidad de la desaparecida La Lupe" (many associated her eccentricity with the disappeared La

FIGURE 6.1 • Celia Cruz embraces La India in concert, San Francisco, February 27, 1999. Photo by Elisabeth Jusino. Courtesy of Isabel Vélez.

Lupe) (Torres Torres 1999). This santería discourse, then, dismantles the more "official" discourse about individual effort, hard work, and professionalism that Celia vocalizes in "La voz de la experiencia." Thus, the text here is constantly being ironized, and rendered much more complex, by the intertextual and performative aspects of this duet.

This speaks to the ways in which "the elimination or the abjection of the third party" (Roach 1995:53), in this case La Lupe and santería, which appear in veiled and subversive ways yet are nonetheless evoked, constitute a central part of the negotiations of a Latino/a cultural politics. What Joseph Roach calls "surrogation" (53–54) is evident here, although not exactly as he identifies it in his analysis of funerals. While santería "disappears" into "white speech" and is replaced by the textual articulations of the American Dream in the voice of Celia, it is simultaneously invoked by La India's recovery of santería discourse and bodily gestures. In addition, the unofficial presence of La Lupe within the intertext of the musical refrain foregrounds the liminality of women's place in salsa, but also questions Celia's exclusivity as the "voice of experience."

Yet the politics of this feminist genealogy cannot be explained only in terms of gender. On the one hand, these genealogical discourses are recuperative and foundational as well as they are deconstructive. Rather than essence, writes Foucault, genealogies find dissension (1977:142). The subversive nature of La Lupe's utterance in a song that is officially an homage to Celia has to do with the multiple, dialogic strands of female influences that La India, perhaps, wants to foreground. But it is also a commentary about the nationalist-informed debates on the authorship, origins, and authenticity of salsa. Cubans have insisted that salsa music was a commodity created by the Anglo music industry at a time when Cuban musicians could not participate in its development, and that it is basically Cuban rhythms and music recycled and packaged for international distribution. Puerto Ricans, on the other hand, argue that salsa music is not just Cuban music, but a musical style that was born in New York in the 1960s at a time when second-generation Puerto Rican musicians looked for new paradigms that would express the reality of being a minority in the United States. It is also a musical style that has synthesized diverse local musical traditions and has become the urban music of Latin America. These debates still continue among scholars, some musicians, and also listeners. They foreground the strong articulations between popular music and national identity, particularly among subaltern communities that have experienced and suffered colonial dispossessions throughout history, at a time when transnationalism and globalization tend to erase said tensions.

In this context, then, "La voz de la experiencia" is a significant text because it brings together Cuban and Puerto Rican musical traditions, sounds, rhythms, and styles. The song begins with *batá* drumming—based on religious African chants and rhythms—that establish the foundational role of popular religions (santería) in the development of Afro-Caribbean music, then suddenly shifts to the brass instruments, a rupture that signals the historical continuity and divergence between traditional religious music and the urban, secular functions of salsa. The song moves on to Celia's and La India's dialogue—accompanied by arrangements more akin to salsa romántica—and concludes with an invocation to Yemayá, the Yoruba goddess of the sea and an icon of female power. The coexistence of Cuban and Puerto Rican musical markers throughout the song—the references to the various national musical forms, to the echoes of *música jíbara* juxtaposed to references to Yemayá, *rumba*, and *guaguancó*—propose a definition of salsa that transcends the nationalisms embedded in these debates. The subversive presence of La Lupe in the song with regard to Celia takes on another meaning in this context. While Celia has publicly insisted that salsa is Cuban music, La Lupe was one of the few Cuban singers who identified salsa as Puerto Rican.[16] Thus, La India's echoes of La Lupe in this song also destabilize

Celia's Cuban-centric perspective on salsa. The feminist discourse of La India and Celia exhibits this tension between the definitions of salsa as derived from the Cuban son, and a view of salsa as a compendium and amalgam of various interpreters, composers, arrangers, and voices from the Caribbean, Latin America, and the diaspora.

La India and Celia Cruz, two singers with very different musical styles, also differ in political ideologies: the Queen of Salsa sings from her recalcitrant position as a Cuban exile, the Princess from her hybrid subjectivity as a Puerto Rican born in the Bronx. But they both sing together La India's composition that celebrates and honors the participation of women in the development of salsa and Latino music. This is perhaps an illustration of "transborder feminisms," as Sonia Saldívar-Hull proposes in her own work about Chicana writers and Mexicana women (1999). Yet the solidarity is never totally achieved, as "La voz de la experiencia" suggests. While this song memorializes La Lupe, honors Celia Cruz, and establishes La India as a singer in her own right, the ironies behind this triad of female singers cannot be overlooked. They speak to the fact that La India is well aware of Celia Cruz's official status as La Reina, yet she also subverts and questions these hierarchies imposed by the industry and by Celia herself. Three Afro-Caribbean women, three Latina minorities in the United States, three voices who develop their singing careers in the United States. Yet despite the foundational gestures of this feminist genealogy, La India also recognizes and foregrounds the struggles of power and the differences among women that foreclose any homogenizing category of "woman." La India provides her listeners with a complex negotiation between the official recognition of Celia Cruz as the Queen of Salsa, and the fact that this title has been established, in part, as a result of La Lupe's invisibility in the history of popular music. La India's homage to Celia is a subversive recovery of La Lupe's radical performances, excesses whose ultimate meanings were perhaps not understood in her own time.

Leonardo Padura Fuentes, a Cuban ethnomusicologist, has written that salsa music in the 1960s and 1970s was a "new aesthetic" that "came to fill a cultural vacuum in all of the popular dance music of the Caribbean and of a great part of Latin America" (1997:19). It proposed a "consciousness" to music itself. Likewise, we could argue that the feminist discourse of La India and of the salseras in the 1990s, although not as systematically overt as in classic salsa, offers a particular consciousness about, in this case, women's invisibility in the history of popular music. Yet this discourse is not just about women. The genealogy in La India's musical performance and text negotiates the articulation between music and national identity, mediating Cuban and Puerto Rican contributions to salsa music and reaffirming the historical role of salsa as a site of oppositionality. Yet this position is articulated in more nuanced ways in the 1990s, particularly through "surrogations" and "recovered behaviors" that allow these women to sing/speak to diverse ideological listeners at the same time. By tracing the multiple, contradictory, and conflictive levels of textuality, musicality, and performance in women's new salsa of the 1990s, we can trace its continuities with the classic salsa of the 1970s as well as understand its historically based and gendered divergences.

NOTES

1. Two exceptions in scholarship are Wilson Valentín Escobar's essay in this volume (see chapter 7), which analyzes the constructions of masculinity in the music of Héctor Lavoe and in early salsa music in New York City, and Peter Manuel's incursion into the gender politics of Caribbean music and issues of reception. In "Gender Politics in Caribbean Popular Music: Consumer Perspectives and Academic Interpretation," Manuel argues that while gender has "inspired some of the most insightful and lively scholarly literature on popular music in the last decade," these analyses have been limited to the reading of song lyrics and have not examined audience response and listening practices (1998). He then offers his own interpretation of the responses of more than two hundred of his students to issues of gender in various Caribbean musical forms. Ironically, most of Manuel's assertions about how students read "gender" and the contradictions and disidentifications behind reception have been discussed already in those gender analyses that he critiqued.

2. As I write this essay I am saddened by the news today, June 1, 2000, of the death of the King of Latin music, Tito Puente, on May 31.

3. Aware of the risk of oversimplifying here, let me clarify that boleros and romantic ballads were always a central part of the musical repertoire of salseros during the late '60s and '70s, and they continue to play a significant role throughout the '70s and '80s. The shift is in frequency and in the strategic replacement on the part of the industry of salsa dura with the romantic ballads of, for example, Julio Iglesias (cf. Manuel 1991). See Keith Negus (1999) for a lucid discussion of the ways in which salsa romántica has been reified by Peter Manuel and others. Negus not only contests the gendering that underlines this binary, but also describes the various strands of hybrid salsa that has been produced since the 1980s.

4. I want to thank Lise Waxer for this information on Ralph Mercado Productions. She clarified that RMM's headquarters are in New York, but does most of its productions in Miami, thus belying a fixed opposition between these two cities. However, the opposition that I refer to here comes from the musicians themselves, not necessarily the producers, and it is targeted precisely at the ideologies and trends established by RMM.

5. Gilberto Santa Rosa's *Salsa Sinfónica* is a live recording of his 1998 concert at the most important high-arts theater in Caracas, Venezuela, the Teatro Teresa Carreño. At the concert, he thanks the people of Venezuela for "dejarme entrar a su casa y a su teatro más importante, pero sobre todo a su corazón." [allowing me to enter your home and your most important theater, but mostly your heart].

6. The shifts in instrumentation exemplified in the *salsa sinfónica* of Santa Rosa, or in the pop romantic ballads of a Julio Iglesias, and in other samples of salsa romántica productions, suggest that percussion, drumming, and the brass sounds index social oppositionality, partly because of the polyrhythmia and partly because of the social

meanings of volume/sound. The addition of violins, flutes, and more so-called melodic instruments index a more acceptable aesthetics related to class and social identities.

7. In her lucid article "Doubleness and Jazz Improvisation: Irony, Parody, and Ethnomusicology," Ingrid Monson proposes the distinction between "intermusicality" and "intertextuality" to refer to the analysis of subtexts and intertexts at the level of sound versus the song lyrics and content. My use of these terms is consonant with Monson's proposal.

8. *Time* magazine cover (March 24, 1999) and coverage of Ricky Martin and other Latino/a figures in the so-called musical Latin boom of the 1990s conflate Martin, López, and others with the new salsa style that has come out of New York. The musical productions of La India and Marc Anthony, for instance, need to be differentiated from those of Martin and López based on the musical arrangements, instrumentation, and relationship to the U.S. musical industry.

9. Marc Anthony has been one of the most outspoken Latino/a public figures in the music industry who has rejected the label of "crossover." He refutes this in the CBS production hosted by John Quiñones on the Latin boom, as well as in the *Newsweek* features about Latino America: "Anthony, 30, bristles over a recent magazine article that featured jalapeño peppers beside his picture. "Jalapeños are Mexican. I've never eaten one in my life." "This whole 'crossover wave' thing really displaces me," he says. "Like I'm coming in and invading America with my music. I was born and raised in New York, man" (Leland and Chambers 1999:55).

10. My contention with this article is that the integration of young Latinos is not sufficiently explained and historically contextualized. Some or most of the individuals profiled in the article on Generation ñ and Generation Mex are either graduates from major universities with Latino studies programs (Milton Rodríguez finished at University of Michigan and enrolled in my course on Spanish for Latinos, among other Latino studies courses) or are graduate students in Latino studies (Rod Hernández). The impact of ethnic studies programs in the cultural empowerment of this generation is elided, and, thus, the concomitant awareness that affirmative action policies have made both the programs, the faculty, and the students, possible.

11. I want to thank Russell Rodríguez, from Stanford University, for his help in identifying the correct musical structures contained in this album. Liner notes are not always dependable, yet what is significant here is the fact that some of these songs have circulated in various countries as different musical genres, thus eluding the possibility of defining them as a musical form unique to a specific country or nationality.

12. Duke's own musical career has mirrored La Lupe, particularly in her mentoring by Tito Puente. Puente foregrounded and introduced La Duke as part of his own performances, although at times his descriptions of her were framed through sexist remarks about her body. La Duke's own stage name also mirrors the Afro-Cuban singer through the assonantal rhyme pattern. My own assessment of the CD is that it has its musical problems (being out of tune), yet it is also another instance of the "recovered behavior" of La Lupe by a younger generation of Latina performers.

13. The cover of *Sola* is itself worthy of analysis. La India appears in attire that conforms to the Hollywood image of Native Americans. Enacting her stage name through and on her body, this attire may symbolically constitute a number of potential ideological stances, foremost of which could be a visual reaffirmation of her own U.S. racialized identity as Other and of the historical and political analogies between Puerto Rican colonized subjects and the territorial, cultural, and linguistic dispossessions suffered by Native Americans. This meaning locates her as a U.S. ethnic and racial minority. On the other hand, La India's name—as a racial signifier—

suggests in the context of Caribbean racial politics the tendency of the revitalized Taíno movement to displace the recognition of blackness as a fundamental cultural element in the Hispanic Caribbean or the practice of using "indio," as in the Dominican Republic, to displace black identity, which is accorded to Haitians. This transnational and Caribbean meaning would pose more complex contradictions, although both of them illustrate the racial and cultural fluidity with which performers such as La India can interpellate various constituencies across racial, cultural, social, linguistic, and gender lines.

14. The epithet "Queen of Salsa" in relation to Celia Cruz is questioned by César Miguel Rondón (1980:140). Concluding his remarks about Celia's genial contributions to salsa, he writes: "Para la salsa ella fue un regalo, un personaje que venía de la vieja guaracha y que supo prolongar el mismo espíritu en la turbulencia de los nuevos tiempos. Decir que ella fue lo mejor de la salsa, es decir una mentira. Celia, tan sólo, es la mejor guarachera que se ha conocido, antes y quizás después de la salsa. Pero no es la salsa, porque Celia, simplemente, supone otra cosa muy distinta." [She was a gift to salsa, a protagonist who came from the old guaracha and who knew how to prolong the same spirit in the turbulent midst of the new times. To say that she was the best of salsa, is to lie. Celia, if anything, is the best guaracha interpreter that the world has known, before and perhaps after salsa. But she is not salsa, for Celia, simply, is about another, very different thing.]

15. The concert was sponsored by El Mensajero, San Francisco's leading Latino newspaper. I want to thank Isabel Vélez, Program in the History of Consciousness, University of California at Santa Cruz, for this reference and for generously sharing her photos with me. Also my appreciation to Elizabeth Jusino who took the pictures during the performance.

16. La Lupe's own statements regarding the affiliation of salsa to Puerto Rico throughout her songs attest to this recognition. Moreover, her strong collaborations with Tito Puente, her album in honor of Rafael Hernández, and the performance of many Puerto Rican favorites established her as an important figure for Puerto Rican audiences, to the extent that even today many Boricuas believe that La Lupe was Puerto Rican.

BIBLIOGRAPHY

Aparicio, Frances R. 1988. *Listening to Salsa: Gender, Latin Popular Music, and Puerto Rican Cultures*. Hanover, N.H.: Wesleyan University Press/University of New England Press.

Butler, Judith. 1990. *Gender Trouble: Feminism and the Subversion of Identity*. New York: Routledge.

Colón, Willie. 1999. Willie Colón on-line Forum (November 26), *http://forums.delphi.com/wacco/messages/?msg=1333.84*.

Díaz Ayala, Cristóbal. 1981. *Música cubana del areyto a la Nueva Trova*. San Juan, Puerto Rico: Editorial Cubanacán.

Fernández, Raúl. 1996. Interview with Celia Cruz, Hollywood, California, September 15. Jazz oral history project, Smithsonian Institution.

Flores-González, Nilda. 1999. "The Racialization of Latinos: The Meaning of Latino Identity for the Second Generation." *Latino Studies Journal* 10(3):3–31.

Foucault, Michel. 1977. *Language, Countermemory, Practice: Selected Essays and Interviews by Michel Foucault*. Ed. Donald F. Bouchard. Ithaca, N.Y.: Cornell University Press.

Fuentes, Leonardo Padura. 1997. *Los rostros de la salsa*. Havana: Ediciones Unión.

Gilroy, Paul. 1993. *The Black Atlantic: Modernity and Double Consciousness*. Cambridge, Mass.: Harvard University Press.

Larmer, Brook et al. 1999. "Latino America." *Newsweek,* July 12, pp. 48–51.
Leland, John, and Veronica Chambers. 1999. "Generation ñ." *Newsweek,* July 12, pp. 53–58.
Manuel, Peter. 1991. "Latin Music in the United States: Salsa and the Mass Media." *Journal of Communication* 41(1):104–16.
———. 1998. "Gender Politics in Caribbean Popular Music: Consumer Perspectives and Academic Interpretation." *Popular Music and Society* 22(2):11–29.
Marre, Jeremy and Hannah Charleton. 1985. "Salsa: Latin Pop Music in the Cities." In *Beats of the Heart: Popular Music of the World.* New York: Pantheon, pp. 70–83.
McLane, Daisanne. 1996. "Salsa for the High-Tops Generation." *The New York Times* (August 11), pp. 26, 29.
Monson, Ingrid. 1994. *Saying Something: Jazz Improvisation and Interaction.* Chicago: University of Chicago Press.
Muñoz, José Esteban, 1999. *Disidentifications: Queers of Color and the Performance of Politics.* Minneapolis: University of Minnesota Press.
Negus, Keith. 1999. *Music Genres and Corporate Cultures.* London: Routledge.
Oboler, Suzanne. 1995. *Ethnic Labels, Latino Lives: Identity and the Politics of (Re)presentation in the United States.* Minneapolis: University of Minnesota Press.
Orovio, Helio. 1981. *Diccionario de la música cubana.* Havana: Editorial Letras Cubanas.
Puleo, Augusto. 1997. "Una verdadera crónica del Norte: Una noche con La India." In Celeste Fraser Delgado and José Esteban Muñoz, eds., *Everynight Life: Culture and Dance in Latin/o America.* Durham, N.C.: Duke University Press, pp. 223–38.
Roach, Joseph. 1995. "Culture and Performance in the Circum-Atlantic World." In Andrew Parker and Eve Kosofky Sedgwick, eds., *Performativity and Performance.* New York: Routledge, pp. 45–63.
Rondón, César Miguel. 1980. *El libro de la salsa: crónica de la música del caribe urbano.* Caracas: Editorial Arte.
Saldívar-Hull, Sonia. 1999. "Women Hollering Transfronteriza Feminisms." *Cultural Studies* 13(2):251–62.
Sandoval, Alberto. 1999. "A Puerto Rican Reading of the America of 'West Side Story.'" Chapter 2 in *José, Can You See? Latinos On and Off Broadway.* Madison: University of Wisconsin Press.
Schechner, Richard. 1985. *Between Theater and Anthropology.* Philadelphia: University of Pennsylvania Press.
Slobin, Mark. 1993. *Subcultural Sounds: Micromusics of the West.* Hanover, N.H.: Wesleyan University Press/University Press of New England.
Torres y Torres, Jaime. 1999. "Canta a La Lupe." *El nuevo día,* August 11, p. 104.
Waxer, Lise. 1998. "*Cali Pachanguero:* A Social History of Salsa in a Colombian City." Ph.D. dissertation, University of Illinois at Urbana-Champaign.

DISCOGRAPHY

Barretto, Ray. 1973. *Indestructible.* (Fania 456.)
Bosch, Jimmy. 1999. *Salsa Dura.* (Ryko 1007.)
Colón, Willie. 1967. *El Malo.* (Fania 337.)
———. 1972. *Crime Pays.* (Fania 406.)
———. 1973. *Lo Mató.* (Fania 444.)
Corrine. 1999. *Un poco más.* (RMM 82261.)
Duke, Yolanda. 1992. *Nostalgias de La Lupe.* (RMM 80978.)
India, La. 1992. *Llegó la India (via Eddie Palmieri).* (Soho Reocrds 80864.)
———. 1997. *Sobre el fuego.* (RMM 82157.)
———. 1999. *Sola* (RMM 0282840232.)

Lupe, La. 1966. *They Call Me La Lupe.* (Tico 1144.)

————. 1969. *La Lupe es la reina/La Lupe the Queen.* (Tico 1192.)

Puente, Tito, and La Lupe. 1965. *Tú y yo/You 'n' me.* (Tico 1125.)

Santa Rosa, Gilberto. 1998. *Salsa Sinfónica: En Vivo Teatro Teresa Carreño Caracas.* (Sony 82913.)

Starr, Brenda K. 1998. *No lo voy a olvidar.* (Plátano Records 2022.)

Various artists. 1998. *Holding Up Half the Sky: Voices of Latin Women.* (Shanachie 66014.)

Chapter 7

EL HOMBRE QUE RESPIRA DEBAJO DEL AGUA: TRANS-*BORICUA* MEMORIES, IDENTITIES, AND NATIONALISMS PERFORMED THROUGH THE DEATH OF HÉCTOR LAVOE

Wilson A. Valentín Escobar

Se te olvidó decir que yo soy el hombre que respira debajo del agua.

Héctor "Lavoe" Pérez

Si yo me muero mañana / mañana por la mañana /
No quiero que nadie llore / no quiero que digan nada.

Héctor "Lavoe" Pérez

Pulling you this way and that, mimesis plays this trick of dancing between the very same and the very different. An impossible but necessary, indeed an everyday affair, mimesis registers both sameness and difference, of being like, and of being Other. Creating stability from this instability is no small task, yet all identity formation is engaged in this habitually bracing activity in which the issue is not so much staying the same, but maintaining sameness through alterity.

Michael Taussig, Mimesis and Alterity

On Tuesday afternoon, June 29, 1993, one of Salsa music's greatest *soneros* (improvisational singers), Héctor Juan Pérez, commonly known as Héctor Lavoe, passed away at St. Clare's hospital in New York City. Lavoe died of a heart attack, bringing to an end his struggle with AIDs. His passing marked a turning point in the world of Salsa music as well as in the transnational Puerto Rican and Latino communities in the United States, Puerto Rico, and Latin

America.[1] Thousands of Lavoe's admirers in Puerto Rico, the Dominican Republic, Venezuela, Colómbia, Perú, Panama, New York City, Chicago, and other urban and national hubs conducted vigils in his name. Throughout New York City, the songs and sounds of Héctor Lavoe's music emanated from people's homes, car stereos, and boom boxes, blurring the boundaries between public and private cultures.[2] The popular "La Mega" FM radio station in New York City played Lavoe's music all week long, motivating his followers and admirers to sing and dance, almost in unisonlike fashion, in the streets of "la Gran Manzana" (the Big Apple).

Nancy Rodríguez, disc jockey for Pacifica Radio station WBAI in New York City, aired a three-hour musical tribute to Héctor Lavoe soon after his death, remembering him in interviews with various Salsa music artists who discussed his musical career and personal life as well as his impact, contributions, and historical significance to Salsa music. Shortly after his death, T-shirts with imprints of Héctor Lavoe's face wrapped up in a Puerto Rican flag were produced and sold, and they soon became one of the hottest-selling items that summer. Musicians and Salsa singers, as they performed live in concert halls, street fairs, and Salsa clubs paid homage to Héctor Lavoe by declaring that "el cantante de los cantantes todavía vive con nosotros" (the singer of singers continues to live with us).

Eight years after his death, Héctor Lavoe continues to be a cultural hero who has been memorialized through various cultural forms including urban street murals, theatrical productions, poetry recitals, clothing bearing his image, commemorative Salsa concerts throughout Latin America, the Caribbean, and the United States, and re-releases of his musical recordings. In addition, he is embodied in some of Salsa's contemporary singers, such as Marc Anthony, Van Lester, and Domingo Quiñonez. These simulations of "restored behaviors" may represent a symbolic form and link to the past of musical lineage and history that entails respect for elders, predecessors and ancestors, and are grounded in a spiritual, historical, and musical repertoire or tradition that transcends temporal and spatial conditions (Roach 1996). This active process of *memorializing* Lavoe through various styles, forms, and practices is the catalyst that guides my analysis. I argue that the circuitous mimetic and altered practices of Héctor Lavoe signify trans-Boricua communal imaginations. Lavoe's Salsa music and performances help to construct national and diasporic imaginations.[3] In memorializing Héctor Lavoe, Puerto Ricans in the diaspora—in this case "Diaspo-Ricans" (Pagán 1997)—articulate and affirm their identities and nationness in the social and geographical locations that Homi Bhabha describes as the "ambivalent margin(s) of the nation-space" (1990:4). In this "in-betweenness" of transnational identities and cultural productions, Héctor Lavoe's music creates a feeling of national belonging that transgresses geographical boundaries.

The *style* and *forms* that these performances embody—be they oral history, song, dance, mural art, or ritual ceremonies—articulate the complexity of enacting translocal narratives of identity and memory. Analyzing Héctor Lavoe's burial ceremony allows us to witness the encoded memories and nationalisms embodied in this collective ritual. Lavoe's death and the ensuing struggle over his corpse and burial illuminate the ways in which identity is still very much contingent on place. Yet, Lavoe acts as a floating trans-Boricua who traverses disparate geographical locales, while also engaging multiple discourses regarding Puerto Rican nationalisms, identities, and historical agency. In the process, Lavoe has become a "performed effigy" of diaspo-Rican alterity, trans-Boricua memories and cultural histories, and a metonymic symbol of Latinidad (Roach 1996). A "performed effigy," as described by Joseph Roach, is the organized activity that substitutes social and cultural vacancies "created by the absence of the original [figure, providing] communities with a method of perpetuating themselves through specifically nominated mediums or surrogates" channeled via a "set of actions that hold open a place in memory into which many different people may step according to circumstances and occasions" (1996:36). Surrogation is a rite of passage that sacrificial effigies come to represent. For Puerto Ricans living within and outside of Puerto Rico, Lavoe's corpse transforms into a trans-Boricua effigy that embodies and interpolates overlapping nationalist and diasporic narratives, enacting a surrogate process constituted by diasporicity, transnationalism, and collective memory.

Deceased cultural heroes like Lavoe are reincorporated into overlapping and competing narratives of the nation. Different contexts create various meanings for cultural texts; similarly, popular and manufactured memories and commemorative practices or ceremonies construct local meanings of deceased cultural heroes like Lavoe (García Canclini 1993). Oral histories and media institutions generate both collective memory and manufactured memory, which travel across multiple social locations and contribute to the formation of a larger public memory. In the case of Lavoe, these histories and meanings are in constant flux, articulated distinctly by members of various generations and across numerous geographical spaces. The fluid meanings encoded in commemorative practices can then be described as *memoria resemanticizada* (resemanticized memory), a reformulation of diverse meanings produced and attached to particular individuals and events across temporal and spatial boundaries. Whether Lavoe is imagined as an "unchanging, incorruptible," authentic Puerto Rican *jíbaro*, or as a diaspo-Rican *sonero* claiming New York City as his new home, these positions exemplify how local communities exercise their historical agency and come to constitute a trans-Boricua/transmigratory imaginary.[4] These shared memories not only transcend the dual and Manichean polarities between the geographical sites of Puerto Rico and New York but also emphasize the diasporicity that embodies cultural practices between both translocales and how each shapes the Other (Flores 1996; Basch, Schiller, and Blanc 1994). Transmigrant imaginations incorporate diasporic narratives into the traditional inscriptions of the nation, entangling and deterritorializing bounded historiographies that encompass the various embodied forms, practices, and "collective mentalities" that migrate across national and diaspora communities produced *through* Lavoe and that also reconstitute him before and after his death.[5] The collective mentalities that reenact and re-present Lavoe are more than simple reappearances; they are mimetic reinventions rooted in translocal community rituals and performances (Roach 1996; Taussig 1993). Although resemanticized constructions of Lavoe inscribe varying memories, identities, and narratives surrounding his life and death, they also demonstrate the vibrancy of translocal Puerto Rican communities. In the act of resemanticization, Lavoe is then crowned a surrogate successor of tradition and difference, evoking diasporic alterity and national sameness.

"EL HOMBRE QUE RESPIRA DEBAJO DEL AGUA"/THE MAN WHO BREATHES UNDER WATER

Héctor Lavoe was born Héctor Juan Pérez in Ponce, Puerto Rico, on September 30, 1946, to Panchita and Luís Pérez. He grew up listening and studying the music of Puerto Rico's most famous folklore and popular musicians and singers, such as Ramito, Chuito el de Bayamón, Odilio González, and Daniel Santos. He also admired and was influenced by Salsa, *bomba,* and *plena* singers Cheo Feliciano and Ismael Rivera. In 1960, Lavoe dropped out of school and began singing for local bands in Ponce. Against his father's wishes he left for New York City in 1963, when he was seventeen years old, and soon was singing with several bands, such as the New Yorkers, Kako and His All-Stars, and the Tito Puente Orchestra. Soon thereafter, the promoter Franquis christened Héctor with the nickname "Lavoe," which meant "La Voz" (The Voice).[6] Shortly thereafter, Héctor met the South Bronx–born Willie Colón, a young emerging musician who had begun his Salsa career with the support of the late Al Santiago, the former owner, founder, and producer of Alegre Records, one of the first labels to record New York-based Salsa music. Santiago helped Colón and Lavoe record their first album.

That album, titled *El Malo,* was recorded in 1967, the same year Lavoe joined Colón's band. Critics and musicians argued that it lacked the "superior" musicianship and arrangement complexity found in the music performed by more established musicians, such as Tito Puente, Tito Rodríguez, and Charlie and Eddie Palmieri (Rondón 1980). Nonetheless, the album was a great success, in part because its emphasis on Salsa and boogaloo spoke to a younger generation of Puerto Ricans born and raised in New York City, and also signified the Nuyorican culture and identity of the time.[7] The music was distinguished by its brash, urban, or "street" barrio sound and philosophy that departed from the Cuban-influenced musical arrangements performed in ballroom settings.

This New York sound—shaped by racial, gender, social, cultural, economic, migratory, and political ideologies and processes, with its distinct instrumentation, phrasing, and arrangements—highlights local agency in reconstructing innovative techniques within and across musical traditions (Álvarez 1992; Aparicio 1998; Leymarie 1994; Negus 1999; Quintero Rivera 1989, 1998; Quintero Rivera and Álvarez 1990; Rondón 1980). For example, the New York trombone and *trombanga* (trombones played with violins in a *charanga* format) sound performed by Ray Barretto, Willie Colón, Manny Oquendo and Libre (formerly Conjunto Libre), Eddie and Charlie Palmieri, and Efrain "Mon" Rivera heavily emphasized trombone instrumentation and arrangements. The "singing trombone" assumed a leading role while other brass, wind, string, and percussive instruments became supportive instruments. The new leading role of the singing trombone changed in relation to how other instruments were arranged and performed within other music scenes.

Another character to this New York Salsa sound was the philosophical attitude that musicians brought to its construction. Their willingness to experiment with tradition often created eagerness to modify musical paradigms. In this process, the new tradition that emerged—in varying degrees—was a reformulation and resemanticization of musical texts and boundaries. New York–based musicians were less ethnocentric than their Cuban counterparts in their willingness to mix other folkloric and musical traditions into the creation of Salsa. Many Salsa arrangements incorporated the heterogeneous urban spatial economy of the city, reflecting and articulating the transnational consciousness of many musicians and consumers. Though bands from Havana or New York may share similar orchestrations, the particular instruments emphasized and the phrasing used in a recorded or live performance register the aural distinctions that develop within a musical scene and tradition. In addition to reformulated instrumentation and experimentation, faster "3–2" and "2–3" clave patterns were also developed, reflecting the pace of the city.[8] This free mixing of jazz, rhythm and blues, Cuban music, and Puerto Rican folkloric styles such as *bomba, plena,* and the *seis* is testament to the artistic renaissance and philosophical approach of the time, collectively contributing to the artistic distinctions found in the musical styles (including Latin jazz) created in New York.[9] Yet despite the innovation involved, the brash New York sound was often deemed a product of unskilled musicianship.

Described as "untrained" musicians because their training had taken place outside classical musical conservatories, Colón, Lavoe, and many of their contemporaries were portrayed as musicians who functioned "por el oido y no por el conservatorio" (performing by ear and not by their conservatory training) (Rondón 1980:50). They further flaunted this unpolished image of themselves through the bad-boy barrio construction represented in the title track song of *El Malo,* (The Bad One). In this song Willie Colón and Héctor Lavoe express their social marginality and "Macho Ca-ma-chismo" through the strident trombone arrangements and the following lyrical commentary:

Quien se llama El Malo	Who is called the Bad One
No hay discusión	There is no discussion
El Malo de aquí soy yo	The Bad One here is me
Porque tengo corazón.	Because I have heart.

The trombone arrangements punctuated Lavoe's *jíbaro* (rural) twang as well as the young *salseros*' barrio philosophy.

Lavoe and Colón, along with Eddie and Charlie Palmieri, Ray Barretto, Joe Cuba, Johnny Colón, Ricardo Ray, Bobby Cruz, and others, created the distinctive Nuyorican sound of Salsa in their 1960s and 1970s Fania label recordings (Rondón 1980). In addition to *El Malo,* Colón and Lavoe recorded a number of other popular albums, including *The Hustler* (1968), *Guisando/Doing a Job* (1969), *La Gran Fuga/The Big Break* (1971), *Crime Pays* (1972), *Cosa Nuestra* (1972), *Asalto Navideño* Volumes 1 (1971) and 2 (1973), *El Juicio* (1972), *Lo Mató* (1973), and *The Good, the Bad, and the Ugly* (1975). They released some of Salsa's most popular songs on these albums, including "Soñando despierto," "Piraña," "Aguanile," "La Murga," "Esta Navidad," "No me llores más," "Hacha y machete," "Todo tiene su final," "Guisando," "No me den candela," "Ché Ché Colé," "El Malo," "Juana Peña," and "Te conozco." Lavoe and Colón became a "tag team" known as *Los Malotes de la Salsa*—the bad boys of Salsa.

Interestingly, the success of this "bad boy" image may have influenced rap artists to adopt similar images from the late 1970s to the current period. More important to this essay, Colón and Lavoe's album covers were in intertextual dialogue with cinematic representations of New York City organized crime. Prime examples include the album covers for *Guisando/Doing a Job*, *Crime Pays*, *The Good, the Bad, the Ugly*, and *Cosa Nuestra*. In the latter (fig. 7.1), Colón reverses the syntactical order of Nuestra Cosa to Cosa Nuestra, mnemonically similar to the slogan "Cosa Nostra," the Mafia. The album cover amusingly mimics the urban myth that organized crime kills its enemies near the Fulton Fish Market on the South Side of the Manhattan Island waterfront (hence the phrase "swimming with the fishes"). Additionally, Colón may be suggesting that Salsa, as "Our [Latin] Thing," refers to both the Fania-sponsored documentary on the history of Salsa in New York City and a musical genre distinct from the Cuban *son*. On the foreground of the album cover, Willie Colón is wearing a black suit and blue shirt. He holds a black Fedora hat with his right hand while it rests on his chest as if in a farewell gesture; his other arm props up what appears to be a black leather trombone carrying case doubling as a rifle case (the trombone is his weapon). With a cigar dangling from his lips, which incidentally repeats the phallic image of the trombone/rifle case, Colón gazes upon a corpse wrapped in a brown blanket. In the background his figure straddles the Brooklyn Bridge on the right and the Manhattan Bridge on the left.[10]

The "bad boy" album covers cannot be dismissed simply as examples of youthful indiscretions; rather they are heavily laden with class and gender symbolism. The album covers signify other masculine-driven representations of national mythologies and identities such as the Wild West (*Guisando/Doing a Job* and *The Good, the Bad, the Ugly*), urban street gangs (*Asalto Navideño* Volumes 1 and 2; *La Grán Fuga*), organized crime (*Crime Pays*), and ethnic rivalry (*Cosa Nuestra*). In the course of these self-representations, Lavoe and Colón draw on these mythical constructions to recast the personal and the collective. Album covers become more than textual self-representations but are also self-reflexive metaperformances of diasporic identities and musical style. Lavoe and Colón actively refashion what it means "to be a Puerto Rican," complicating the "culture of poverty" and "criminal" depictions of Puerto Rican culture (while carefully playing with and exaggerating them), consequently subverting traditonal discourses surrounding urban life in the diaspora.[11] Contrary to adopting a stereotypical "rags-to-riches" (im)migrant narrative, Lavoe performs a variety of urban and ethnic roles and begins to refashion his own identity. The association with

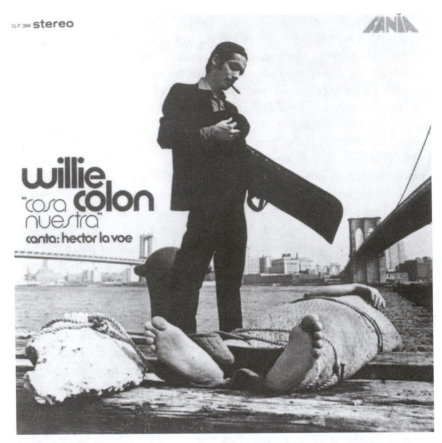

FIGURE 7.1 • Willie Colón and Héctor Lavoe, *Cosa Nuestra* (1972). Photo by Izzy Sanabría. Courtesy of Fania Records.

Colón further bestows a diaspo-Rican identity to Lavoe, who undergoes a transformation of doubly signifying island and diaspora translocality, rural jíbaro, and urban Nuyorican. The triangulation is further completed by virtue of Lavoe's birthplace, upbringing and jíbaro aesthetics, which confers authenticity to the New York–born Colón. Together, Willie Colón and Héctor Lavoe represent the translocal spaces of the Puerto Rican transnation, while also signifying modern and postmodern moments of identity formation. Overall, it may seem that binary oppositions of identity are at work in these albums, but they are entangled, nonlinear, and postmodern (re)presentations of trans-Boricua imaginations.

In 1974, Willie Colón left the band to pursue other paths within Salsa music, but he continued to produce many of the albums Héctor Lavoe recorded with Fania Records. With the original band members now in Lavoe's band, they released successful recordings, such as *La Voz* (1975), *The Good, The Bad and the Ugly* (1975), *De ti Depende* (1976), *Comedia* (1978), *Héctor's Gold* (1980), *Revento* (1985), *¡Que Sentimiento!* (1981), *El Sabio* (1980), *Strikes Back* (1987), *Recordando a Felipe Pirela* (1979), and the *Master and the Protégé* (1993).[12] In 1988, Lavoe was nominated for a Grammy Award for his album *Strikes Back*, a nomination many feel belatedly recognized the talent of one of Salsa's best soneros. Some of the popular songs that emerged from these albums were "Hacha y machete," "El periodico de ayer," "Mi gente," "Comedia," "El todopoderoso," "Songorocosongo," "De tí depende," and "Rompe saragüey." Many followers often note that Héctor's improvisational skills were the best in the Salsa music scene. In some cases, during a live performance, he would improvise a theme with the audience participation for an estimated time of fifteen minutes—a mark of his improvisational skills as a sonero. Although success continued after Willie Colón's departure, Lavoe juggled many personal tragedies that overwhelmed him both personally and professionally.

TRANSMIGRATORY IMAGINATION

Transnational imaginations operate in Lavoe's declaration that "I am the man who breathes under water" (Yo soy el hombre que respira debajo del agua). This declaration is more than light banter exchanged between Johnny Pacheco and Lavoe during a 1975 performance published in the *Live at Yankee Stadium* album.[13] Rather, it serves as a prophetic commentary and takes on metaphoric dimensions for Lavoe's life and death. These transatlantic connections fuel a transmigratory imagination between Puerto Rico, Latin America, its diaspora, and other U.S.-based Latino communities.

Many of Lavoe's friends, fellow musicians, Salsa music promoters, and music journalists have described his life as plagued by adversity. In 1988 Lavoe attempted suicide by jumping out of a ninth-floor room at the Regency hotel in San Juan, Puerto Rico, breaking both his legs, one hip, and several ribs, causing massive internal bleeding. This attempted suicide was a response to distress that overcame his personal life. His seventeen-year-old son was accidentally shot and killed. Shortly thereafter, Héctor's mother-in-law was brutally murdered in Puerto Rico, and a mysterious fire destroyed his home in Queens, leaving four relatives dead. Lavoe also frequently battled drug addiction, which damaged his professional life. His addiction often made him late to performances and regularly aroused the anger of promoters and club owners. His tardy appearances were so common that Lavoe deflected his lateness onto audience members and fans, jokingly communicating through song and statements that they had arrived too early for the performance. Yet, if his tardiness created any animosity it surely dissipated at the news of his death on June 29, 1993. Lavoe's fans remember the urban *jíbaro salsero* as a cultural hero, although at times they forget that he died of an AIDS-related complication. In the process, he became a tragic figure and a crowned martyr of the trans-Boricua and Latino communities. Lavoe's request to be buried next to his son in St. Raymond's Cemetery in the Bronx was honored, and he was interred on July 2, 1993.

For two days, thousands of people from New York's Latino communities, particularly Puerto Ricans, paid homage to Héctor Lavoe by offering their condolences at the Frank E. Campbell Funeral Home at Eighty-first Street and Madison Avenue. Throngs of people lined up to see Lavoe's body, and the crowds circled an entire New York City block up to and around Fifth Avenue and Eighty-second Street. Annually, Puerto Ricans congregate in this area of Manhattan to celebrate the Puerto Rican Day Parade in early June. On this occasion, however, citizens whose public cultural expressions are often relegated to working-class, "ethnic" neighborhoods appropriated this heavily policed Upper East Side space by singing and dancing to Lavoe's music. With Lavoe's voice and Colón's strident trombone blaring from boom boxes and car stereos, subaltern bodies and cultural practices disrupted the sanctioned schedule that allowed them to occupy this space for only two days in June. The occasion of Lavoe's death allowed Puerto Ricans and other Latinos to rupture the spatial and temporal dichotomies that govern their annual parade festivity as well as the everyday expression of public culture.[14]

The appropriation of this affluent New York City neighborhood takes on particular significance given the ambivalent social and political location of diaspo-Ricans "in-between" two nation spaces.[15] In both the island and the mainland United States, the social location of the diaspora lies within a colonial dilemma in which institutional recognition of Puerto Rican is not sanctioned or even superficially recognized. This social liminality may help to explain the public cultural expressions of Puerto Ricans during the burial and funeral procession. The lacuna between social cultural practices and public culture can provide insight to an understanding of public culture as described by Arjun Appadurai and Carol A. Breckenridge. Public culture is distinct from sanctioned national culture. It encompasses a "zone of cultural debate" serving as "an arena where *other* types, forms and domains of culture are encountering, interrogating and contesting each other in new and unexpected ways" (1988:6, emphasis added). In between "national culture," which is a contested mode defined by the nation-state, and commercial culture, public culture is "directed to audiences without regard to the limits of . . . locality or social category" (6). In the public gathering and public performances of Salsa music and dance around the Frank E. Campbell Funeral Home, admirers of Héctor Lavoe and his music mediated this space and de-centered the practices of a homogenized and purified geography and soundscape, putting forth a new site for Latino culture. Despite police surveillance, the power to occupy this geographical space with subaltern diasporic bodies and with the once-outlawed West African clave rhythms piercing the aural Upper East Side soundscape informs us of the nexus of space, culture, and power. Moreover, it addresses the importance of occupying and redefining restricted territories marked by elite and privileged communities. This shift and public occupancy of the aural and physical "contact zones" continued at Héctor Lavoe's funeral procession and burial (Pratt 1991).

The funeral mass was held at St. Cecilia's Catholic Church on 106th Street in El Barrio. As Héctor Lavoe's body was being taken out of the church and into the hearse, hundreds of his followers outside began shouting, "¡Que Viva Héctor Lavoe! ¡Héctor Lavoe Vive! ¡Tú eres eterno! ¡Se fue pero se queda!" (Héctor Lavoe lives! You are eternal! He left but remains with us!). Others clapped and sang the plena song, "¡Que bonita bandera, que bonita bandera, la bandera puertorriqueña!" (What a beautiful flag, What a beautiful flag, the flag of Puerto Rico!), referring not only to Lavoe's Puerto Rican nationality, but also claiming him as a cultural hero of Puerto Rico (see fig. 7.2). Fans continued to perform *plena* music and interwove Salsa music throughout the funeral procession. The public performance around the hearse and throughout the procession between the church and the cemetery demonstrate the resemanticized practices of plena and Salsa enacted during the funeral as well as the liminal social position of the diaspo-Rican community. For example, various sectors of the crowd performed and sang plena music with Spanglish lyrics while other groups performed Salsa music. At times, the soundscape became indistinguishable because both musical styles were being performed simultaneously. Marching, dancing, walking and singing through the noisy urban streets between El Barrio in Manhattan and St. Raymond's Cemetery in the Bronx, *pleneros* and salseros used microphones and speakers to help carry their voices within this urban metropolis. Salsa music in the diaspora serves a similar social function to the plena, bomba and seis in Puerto Rico (Jorge Perez 1991; Quintero Rivera 1989). Plena and Salsa were performed interchangeably during the ceremony illuminating the fluid movement between both musical styles in memorializing Lavoe.

The funeral procession to St. Raymond's Cemetery lasted six hours.

FIGURE 7.2 • Héctor Lavoe's funeral procession, July 2, 1993. Courtesy of *El Nuevo Día*.

During this time the crowd and those following the *caminata* (procession) played, sang, and danced to Héctor Lavoe's music. At the cemetery, many climbed on top of mausoleums and continued to sing plena music in tribute to him during the final benediction and hours after the lowering of the coffin into the grave. One plena song, sung by those present at the cemetery, canonized Héctor as a plenero and national hero by placing him among a community of Puerto Rican pleneros:

Túmbale a Cortijo	Pay homage to Rafael Cortijo,
Túmbale a Ismael	Pay homage to Ismael Rivera,
Túmbale a Lavoe	Pay homage to Héctor Lavoe
Como le gustaba a él.	The way Héctor liked it.[16]

And:

Fuego al cañon, fuego al cañon,	Fire the cannon, fire the cannon,
Así se respeta a Héctor Lavoe	This is how we must respect Héctor Lavoe

This acclamation and reclamation can be viewed and interpreted in a number of different ways. It not only recognizes the historical significance that Lavoe has on Puerto Rican music, but also elevates him into the male pantheon of pleneros: Mon Rivera, Rafael Cortijo, and Ismael Rivera.[17] Canonizing Héctor Lavoe into this male pantheon reinforces a masculine hegemony in plena music while also accenting the gendered construction of public culture and how masculinity constructs collective memory and national celebrations. Implicit in this action is a fundamental understanding of plena music as the national music of Puerto Rico. Recognized as one of the national Afro–Puerto Rican musics of Puerto Rico (along with the bomba), plena's origins derive from freed black Puerto Rican slaves and English-speaking slaves who once worked and lived on the sugar plantations along the southern and southeastern coasts of Puerto Rico and on other Caribbean Islands. The musical birthplace derives from a working-class neighborhood in Ponce known as La Joya del Castillo (the Jewel of the Castle).[18] Black families from the English-speaking Caribbean islands of St. Kitts, Nevis, Barbados, and Jamaica arrived and settled into this southern coastal city, interacting with local Ponceños and workers during the turn of the century. Among these new arrivals was the Barbadian couple Catherine George and John Clark, who often performed in the streets of La Joya del Castillo, singing the English refrain "Play Ana" or "Play Now," translated by local Ponceños into plena. Played by a variety of instruments, including *panderetas* (a tambourine-like instrument), *güiro* or *güícharro* (a dried and hallowed gourd), *marímbula* (a wooden box), the Puerto Rican *cuatro* (a guitar-like instrument with five pairs of strings), and an accordion, the plena often recites in four-line verses daily events, gossip, tragedies, and national and international news, helping to explain its reference as the "public's newspaper." With an understanding of plena's racial history, we can better understand how Lavoe—a "white" Ponceño—is *racialized* into this black Puerto Rican musical tradition as he is canonized and remembered in the process.

This public reclamation of Héctor Lavoe as *plenero* can be read as an attempt to reclaim and remember him as an "authentic" and "true" Puerto Rican and Ponceño. Working on the established premise that *plena* is the authentic music of Ponce and Puerto Rico, in this performance it may serve as a means of *authenticating* Héctor Lavoe through this musical tradition, creating a reversion back to homeland references. Lavoe was not a plenero but a salsero popularly recognized by many as "el cantante de la Salsa" (the singer of Salsa music) and "el cantante de los cantantes" (the singer of singers) (Rondón 1980). In the process of being memorialized, Lavoe, unlike Ismael Rivera, who was mainly a performer of plena music, crosses genres from Salsa into plena. This crossing highlights the agency exercised by diasporized accounts of memory and commemoration and the role that collective memory and racial ideology have in reconstructing meaning and historical events and figures.[19] Besides historical reconstruction, this crossing may be also be attributed to the arrangements that constitute Salsa music in New York City. Because Salsa is not a rhythm, but a "way of making music," encompassing various genre elements, including plena, the reconstruction of Lavoe as plenero may also be rooted in the way he incorporated plena music and lyrics into his live Salsa performances. Overall, the fluidity of historical meanings demonstrates how collective memory functions to mitigate racial and class boundaries while also claiming them.

This process directs us to examine the agency exercised in the social imaginary articulated through performance. Memory and performance coalesce to become an "organized field of social practices" on the one hand, and a "form of [negotiated] . . . sites of agency and globally defined fields of possibility" on the other (Appadurai 1993:274). Agency is exerted in the commemorative musical performance of Lavoe while also negotiating the floating transnational significance he draws from overlapping and connected communities across disparate locations on one hand, while also negotiating the difference between everyday life and structural processes on the other. Embedded in this crossing of genres is a crossing of racial and class positions, fronting a unified community while also erasing and diluting racially coded distinctions.

In Puerto Rico, the "Plaza de Salsa," also referred to as "La Plaza de los Salseros" (the Salsa Musicians' Plaza) is the central location where deceased Salsa and plena musicians are memorialized through large funeral processions and celebrations. At Héctor Lavoe's funeral, the surrogate embodiments of La Plaza de los Salseros become the El Barrio neighborhood in Manhattan and St. Raymond's Cemetery in the Bronx. Close resemblance of the Lavoe funeral to those celebrated at the plaza informs us of the flexibility of a cultural repertoire to create an impression of reversion linked to a lineage of homeland practices. The ancestral connection to history and spiritual reverence to the deceased is operating in this celebration. Joseph Roach reminds us that the voices of the dead continue to be heard in the bodies and practices of the living (1996:xiii). The public performance style of the funeral and burial in New York City was not simply reversive practices referencing an Afro-Caribbean and indigenous tradition, but a celebration that articulated complicated qualities of diversion.[20] This performance and ceremony exemplifies the transnational identity of Lavoe—as both Nuyorican and Ponceño—and the continued hybridity of plena musical history and its contributors beginning with, for example, Joselino "Bumbún" Oppenheimer (Flores 1993). The acclamation of Héctor Lavoe as a plenero recognizes the impact that a diaspo-Rican singer can have on a national Puerto Rican musical tradition, symbolizing the impact of transmigrancy upon Island cultural expressions.

Immediately after his death, a number of articles were published on the life and impact of Héctor Lavoe on Salsa music and Nuyorican history. One letter published in the Puerto Rican newspaper *El Nuevo Día* continued to enforce the authenticity argument. The letter petitions the government of Puerto Rico to excavate the bodies of Héctor Lavoe and his son, Héctor Jr., from St. Raymond's Cemetery and to bury them in Puerto Rico. The logic, as articulated in the letter, is that "it is obvious that el coquí cannot rest in a land outside Borinquen [Puerto Rico]" (Valle and Méndez 1993).[21] Yet a month earlier, Héctor's daughter Priscilla, who lives in Puerto Rico, made a public acknowledgment in the same newspaper responding to the island community's demand to have Héctor buried there. She notes: "Comprendemos que el pueblo de Puerto Rico desearía que sepultaramos a Héctor en Ponce, pero la voluntad de él fue otra. En noviembre pasado (1992) yo lo visité y me dijo que en cualquier momento esperaba fallecer y que quería que lo enterraran con [el hijo in el Bronx]" (We understand that the Puerto Rican community desires to have Héctor buried in Puerto Rico, but his wish was different. Last November (1992), I visited him and he told me that should he ever die, that he wanted to be buried with his son in the Bronx) (Torres Torres 1993:25).

The letter published in *El Nuevo Día* reinscribes traditional borders and notions of what constitutes a nation. Implicit in the writer's nationalism is the linkage between land, identity, and memory. From the writer's perspective, geographical borders and "biological bonds of solidarity" supersede the deterritorialized transnational community of the Puerto Rican diaspora (Basch, Schiller, and Blanc 1994:269). In this case, the land where diasporas reside is perceived as less authentic. Implicit in the writer's letter is a perception that national identities should be confined within a specific geographic location. Ironically, this admirer fails to recognize the transnationality of some of Puerto Rico's national heroes and intellectuals, such as Eugenio María de Hostos and José Luis Gonzalez (to name a few), who are buried outside the geographical borders of Puerto Rico. Héctor's buried body in the Bronx can also be interpreted not simply as a body outside its "home" but as a metaphor of the transnational character of the Puerto Rican community. Being buried in the Bronx outside the borders of Puerto Rico sustains the national myth of a tragic hero dying in the belly of the beast. The insistence to return his body accents how space, geography, and land are ingredients essential to traditional constructions of nationalism while also expanding current discussions of the nation via the diaspora.

DOUBLENESS AND RESIGNIFICATION

One of Héctor's most popular songs, "Mi gente" [My people] written by Johnny Pacheco, a bandleader, flutist, and co-producer of Fania Records, is considered by some respondents interviewed for this project as the "Nuyorican national anthem." The transformation of this Salsa song into an anthem allows listeners to remember the death of Héctor Lavoe and his music as well as memorialize him as a transnational representative of the nation. "Mi gente" addresses the listeners as belonging to Héctor Lavoe, and him to them. Lavoe is positioned as the spokesperson and signifier of the translocal nation. Again, as in the male pantheon of *plena* music, a *jíbaro* Ponceño becomes the chosen transnational representative. Lavoe is diasporized by his listening audience in New York City and nationalized by the community of listeners in Puerto Rico. This practice acknowledges how the song articulates diasporic and national identity(ies) and experiences of Puerto Ricans and other Latinos/as.

The collective emotional affinity that emerges when listening to the song "Mi gente" evokes, as some respondents noted, a connectedness to the larger community of Salsa listeners and other Puerto Ricans. Similar to Alessandro Portelli's critique of the relationship between memory, orality, industrial folk music, and labor among the working class in Italy, this song "lives in the memory of an emotion" (1991:187). The collective and historical experiences shared by many listeners simultaneously reinforce a shared emotion of solidarity (Portelli 1991:174). In this case, the collective experiences of the diaspora serve as the source for its writing and presentation, and for how it is remembered and encoded in the song and memory of its listeners. This shared agency of resignifying "Mi gente" to the status of an anthem demonstrates the discursivity and malleability of popular culture and music, where time, memory, and locality change the meaning of the song. Although the lyrics have remained the same since its inception, the meanings attached to them by a collective body of listeners have changed during the course of Lavoe's musical career, and more dramatically, after his death across different spaces. This diaspo-Rican national anthem extends the anthems of Puerto Rico as well as provides a distinctive and fluid lineage to the nation. Interestingly, how the anthem becomes resignified to represent both the diaspora and the island-nation is further testament to Lavoe's reconstruction as a floating signifier of national sameness and diasporic alterity.

It comes as no surprise then that live concerts performed by the Fania All-Stars in Puerto Rico, Venezuela, Colombia, and other Latin American countries, and within various locations in the United States include a performance of Lavoe's song "Mi gente." However, the song is now inverted to "Que canten su gente" (Let his people sing), referring here to Héctor's people/community (Fania All-Stars 1995 and 1997). The audience, identified as Héctor's community, sings in unison to the emotionally charged lyrics, creating a shared memory and emotion of the late sonero. What is more important, "mi gente" and its derivative, "su gente," interpellate the imaginary relationships of individuals, which constitute them to imagined transnational communities (Althusser 1971). The song helps to construct and position these "imaginary relationships" to a transnational community, synthesizing collective memories, transnationalisms, and identities across multiple spaces.

Héctor is also remembered by some not just as a Nuyorican, but also as a jíbaro from the city of Ponce whose singing style embodied Puerto Rico and New York simultaneously. His voice is described as having both a Nuyorican "brashness" as well as a Puerto Rican jíbaro (country) sound.[22] Close friend Willie Colón articulates this simultaneity in an interview with Pacifica Radio's Nancy Rodríguez: "Although Héctor was born in Ponce, he became a symbol of the New York Salsa sound during the 1960s and 70s" (Colón 1996). Ray Barretto, bandleader, *conguero*, and fellow member of the Fania All-Stars with Héctor Lavoe and Willie Colón, describes the doubleness of Lavoe in this way: "What made Lavoe a little different from the little guys was that he was closer to the jíbaro thing from Puerto Rico and that's what made him different. That's what people loved about him. He [also] projected that *barrio* quality and that was his strength" (Barretto 1993). Rubén Blades articulates it best when reflecting upon the significance, singing style, and doubleness of Héctor Lavoe: "[Héctor's singing style], delivery, and the things that he said were more street [streetwise] than what my tastes at the time could understand. It was a very New York slang style, a more N[u]yorican approach. Héctor's strength was his power in terms of inventing things. He would invent things that reflected upon life in New York and also a dose of *jíbarito* [country], of Puerto Rican in him. *Héctor's gift was his New York brash, in your face style with that pristine crystal clear voice that he had. Héctor's style was more a mixture of emigrant Boricua and N[u]yorican*" (Blades 1993, my emphasis).

Embodying both Puerto Rican and New York identities and musical styles simultaneously alludes to the complexities that constitute the diasporality of his musical performances and identities. Héctor's orality and singing style became transmigratory with his movement to New York City. Rather than just seeing his Nuyorican brashness as an additive layer disconnected from his "jíbaro-ness," I argue that both identities equally shaped and constituted who he was, as well as what and how he sang and performed. Rather than just seeing a Puerto Rican jíbaro singing *in* New York, *Héctor became a Nuyorican who transformed his identity from Héctor Pérez to Héctor Lavoe in New York City.* This transformation and doubleness that embodied and shaped his music and identity speak to the process of diasporality that form, reformulate, and recategorize genres and identities (Bhabha 1996). The mobility of music and identities in diasporas fragment the ways the past and present are narrated and imagined (Hall 1990). Because music, according to Mark Slobin, resides at the margins of "the person and the people . . . it presents a crucial point of articulation in viewing diasporic life" (1994:244). The doubleness of jíbaro and Nuyorican, the singing of and being shaped by multiple social and cultural factors within New York and Puerto Rico, presents Lavoe as an intercessor of diasporic processes that are constantly converging, "producing and reproducing . . . through transformation and difference" (Hall 1990:235). In the case of Lavoe, his voice and singing style not only embody his doubleness, but also represent and mirror the social experiences that Héctor shared with other diaspo-Ricans.

The emphasis on his linguistic sound is coupled with Héctor Lavoe's ability to improvise and "think on his feet," telling stories and ideas to the clave meter of Salsa music. The ability to "improvisar" (improvise) in "el espíritu de la clave" (the clave spirit) is what distinguishes skillful from inexperienced Salsa singers (Alvarez 1992:35).[24] Many people I interviewed for this project, as well as other sources, stressed Héctor's talent for improvisation. Their focus on his voice and sound speaks to the importance that orality plays in codifying diasporic and homeland linguistic traditions and identities. This movement from the page to the performance emphasizes Héctor's skill in mediating and resemanticizing the written lyric.[25] Lavoe's ability to free himself from scripts and prewritten codes is further evidence of the multiple transnational significations at work in his life and art.

To speak about the intersecting "authentic" and transnational identities and musical style of Héctor Lavoe is to acknowledge how much diaspo-Rican cultures have equally become a part of Puerto Rico. This transmigratory perspective shifts the colonialist binary model of Puerto Rico as the center of culture and the diaspora as the "natural imitators" of that authentic culture. This shift emphasizes the fluid and scattered processes that shape diasporic transmigratory cultures. Through Lavoe's music, life, and death, Puerto Ricans on the island are capable of vicariously acquiring a transient diaspora viewpoint while simultaneously differentiating themselves from this liminal location and condition. Diasporality rather than "ethnicity" reshifts our attention to how the larger social constructions and processes of power—imperialism, coloniality, circular migration, and race, to name just a few—are intricately entwined with identity formation and musical construction. Moreover, diasporality denaturalizes "authentic" perceptions of cultural origins and the one-way process that obliterates historical and cultural processes.

When Puerto Ricans and other Latinos gathered to pay homage to Héctor Lavoe across the various barrios of the diaspora, Puerto Rico, and Latin America, they articulated shared memories, feelings, and identities. These multiple sites converged through the transnational imaginations embodied in surrogate mediums of performance and collective memory. The burial of Héctor Lavoe's body at St. Raymond's Cemetery and the ensuing controversy over its return to Puerto Rico still exemplify the importance of locality for nationalist and diasporic discourses. In the transnational circuit of resemanticized memories, Lavoe's corpse is not confined to its Bronx location, but becomes an effigy that performs overlapping and competing discourses of trans-Boricua memories, cultural histories, and diaspo-Rican alterity. The polysemy of meanings and memories that encode community agency create Lavoe as a sacrificial effigy for a historical rite of passage. However, this rite of passage is not limited to him; other figures and cultural heroes, such as Frankie Ruiz, Guadalupe Victoria Yoli (La Lupe), and Tito Puente, may come to shed light on other dimensions of diasporicity, collective memory, and transnationalism. In doing so, they may engage and further complicate the constructed rites of passage that encode communal formations and historical recollection. Thus, a closer examination of other cultural heroes may continue to illustrate how resementacized meanings and memories develop across distinct social and geographical spaces. On June 29, 1993, Lavoe's last breath of life brought together distinct and translocal communities bonded by their collective memory and transnational imaginations of his legacy and music. "El hombre que respira debajo del agua" was not buried, noted the famous Puerto Rican singer Cheo Feliciano, but was "sembrado" (sowed and scattered).[25]

NOTES

Acknowledgments. While I was conducting this research and writing this essay, many friends, colleagues, professors, and relatives offered their assistance. First, I thank Professors Frances R. Aparicio, Susan Douglas, Travis Jackson, Richard Cándida Smith, Betty L. Bell, and June Howard for reading earlier drafts of this essay. I especially want to thank Graciela Hernández for her insightful readings and diligent editing. Friends and colleagues at the University of Michigan who reviewed earlier drafts include Adrian Burgos Jr., Alexandra M. Stern, María Elena Cépeda, Mérida Rúa, and the members of both La Colectiva and Latinos in the Industrial Age reading groups. I am deeply indebted to Lise Waxer for her theoretical and editorial review of an earlier draft of this essay. Many thanks to Eddie Valentín and Luis Vázquez for sharing their musical knowledge and record collections. Others who agreed to be interviewed and/or assisted me include Ramón Rodríguez, Luis

Bauzó (both from the Harbor Center for the Performing Arts in New York City), Richie Pérez, Larry Harlow ("El Judio Maravilloso"), Madélena Fontáñez, and Mario Ruíz. The library and research staff at El Centro de Estudios Puertorriqueños, Hunter College, CUNY, particularly Roberto Rodríguez, Juan Flores, Blanca Vázquez, and Pedro Rivera, welcomed me as a graduate student researcher during the summer of 1996 and shared their time, resources, and knowledge. A special acknowledgment to filmmaker Leon Gast for allowing me to review his video footage on Héctor Lavoe. Finally, the the Office of the Provost (especially Dr. Lester Monts), Office of Academic and Multicultural Initiatives, the Office of the Vice President for Research, Rackham School of Graduate Studies, and the Program in American Culture, all at the University of Michigan, Ann Arbor, provided financial resources that made this project possible. Dedico este ensayo a mi familia, especialmente a mi mamá Felicita Escobar Valentín (1938–1999). Like all intellectual projects, this work is collectively influenced but individually written; any errors and shortcomings are obviously my own.

1. The use of the term *Salsa* here is a deliberate marker to distinguish it from the Cuban *son*. Rather than place "quotation marks" around the word Salsa—which is often done by some academic scholars to describe it as a euphemism for Cuban music—I purposefully capitalize the first letter to prescribe it as a cultural arts expression that emerged in New York City during the 1960s and '70s. Salsa, in other words, is not simply "refashioned Cuban musical rhythms" but rather "a way of making music" (Quintero Rivera and Alvarez 1990). For an insightful discussion on the distinction between Salsa and the Cuban son, see Alvarez 1992; Aparicio 1998; Berríos-Miranda 1997; Quintero Rivera 1998; Quintero Rivera and Alvarez 1990; Negus 1999; and Rondón 1980. For a "culture-of-poverty" perspective on Salsa and the Puerto Rican community(ies), refer to the work by Peter Manuel, most particularly, his controversial essay "Puerto Rican Music and Cultural Identity" (1994).

2. For a discussion on public culture, see Appadurai and Breckenridge 1988.

3. For a comprehensive analysis of diaspora as a process, social location, and discourse, see Gilroy 1997; Lavie and Swedenburg 1996; Clifford 1994; Young 1995; and Stuart Hall (1990, 1995, 1996).

4. *Jíbaro* means different things to different people and can be employed to describe various sectors of the Puerto Rican population. Important in this essay is the constant flux the term signifies. The term often refers to an agricultural peasant living and working in Puerto Rico. It also refers to behavior and cultural practices that are often aligned with agricultural workers. The term is often used in a derogatory manner, referring to "hick" or "backward" while also symbolizing "native purity." *Jíbaro* usually connotes a racially white, male, "pure"/static, and native idea of Puerto Rican authenticity. Crucial to this essay is how *jíbaro* constructions are now enacted by diaspo-Ricans through popular culture. As a consequence, many island-based Puerto Ricans view U.S.-based Puerto Rican cultural expressions as "hick" because they often embody static and nostalgic depictions of the nation. In other words, the "hick" is not simply residing in Puerto Rico, but is now part of the diaspora and its social and cultural practices. To complicate this further, "intra-diaspo-Rican authenticity" discourses parallel the *jíbaro* discourse between the island and the United States. This discourse arises among the translocal Puerto Rican communities residing in California, Connecticut, Florida, Illinois, Massachusetts, New York, Pennsylvania, and other U.S. states. Because of the mass migration of Puerto Ricans to New York during the first half of the twentieth century, Nuyoricans often construct themselves—and are constructed—as the "authentic" diaspo-Rican, while Puerto Ricans residing in other U.S. cities are perceived as "inauthentic." Oftentimes, Puerto Ricans in the U.S. may also consider their island counterparts as

"backward hicks" unable to realize the (im)migrant narrative. For a discussion on the authenticity debate between Puerto Ricans in the diaspora, see Rúa 2000. For detailed and insightful historical analyses of the *jíbaro* as a discursive and historical figure and process, see Scarano 1996 and Guerra 1998.

5. For a fuller review of "collective mentalities," see Patrick Hutton's work on Philippe Ariès (1993).

6. I'm unsure of the correct spelling of Lavoe's promoter "Franquis." According to Al Santiago and Johnny Pacheco, "Franquis" gave Héctor the nickname "Lavoe" because of his excellent voice and singing style. This information is included in the live radio broadcast produced by Nancy Rodríguez and aired by WBAI Pacifica radio station in New York City (1996).

7. For a discussion on boogaloo music, see the Vernon Boggs interview with Johnny Colón in his book *Salsiology: Afro-Cuban Music and the Evolution of Salsa in New York City* (1992:261–83). Also see Juan Flores, *From Bomba to Hip Hop: Puerto Rican Culture and Latino Identity* (2000).

8. For a discussion of clave, please refer to Gerard and Sheller 1989.

9. For a great overview regarding New York and Puerto Rican Salsa, see Vázquez 1999.

10. This masculine image of Salsa continues today but in "kinder" and "gentler" terms. Contemporary examples include "El Caballero de la Salsa" (the gentleman of Salsa) which is used in reference to the Puerto Rican singer Gilberto Santa Rosa while "El Gallo de la Salsa" (the rooster of Salsa) refers to Tito Rojas. Other examples of current gendered terms are *Salsa dura* and *Salsa monga*. The former is used to describe a Salsa sound that is commonly attributed to the music performed during the 1960s and 70s in New York City while the latter derisively describes Salsa arrangements that contain little or no brass and percussive sounds and/or improvisational swing. *Salsa dura* and *Salsa monga* may draw on masculine/sexual discourses that connote binary interpretations of gender: femininity vs. masculinity / "active" vs. "passive." These remarks are speculative and deserve further attention. To date, the most complete analysis concerning gender, Puerto Rican identity, and Salsa is Aparicio 1998. For a discussion of *Salsa dura* and *Salsa monga* see Washburne 1999.

11. Lewis 1966 and Chavez 1991 best illustrate the culture of poverty perspectives that shaped both public policy and public discourses regarding Puerto Ricans.

12. For a complete discography, refer to the two-CD Héctor Lavoe collection (1993). It is important to note that Héctor's last recorded album was originally recorded in 1986 but was completed in 1993. Fania Records commissioned the Salsa singer Van Lester to complete several songs and complete tracks on the album. Several tracks have Héctor Lavoe singing alone, while on other tracks Van Lester sings alone. On some tracks, Lavoe's and Lester's vocals are mixed together.

13. Fania All-Stars (1975). According to César Miguel Rondón, the actual recording occurred during a live performance in the Clemente Coliseum in San Juan, Puerto Rico (1980:101).

14. Significantly, the Frank E. Campbell Funeral Home is one block east of the Metropolitan Museum of Art, an institution that regulates and legitimizes public knowledge of national and marginal cultures.

15. As reported in the 1990 Census (Tract 142 in New York County, which corresponds to Seventy-seventh through Eighty-fourth Streets and from Park Avenue through Fifth Avenue), the racial and economic composition of the neighborhood surrounding the Frank E. Campbell Funeral Home helps to further describe the signification of Puerto Ricans and other Latinos in this community during the wake. The median household income was $108,898, which is even higher if you take extra-household income to include the median family income, which was $150,001. In other words, this is a very affluent neighborhood. The median real estate value for owner-occu-

pied homes was $500,001 while the racial makeup of householders was 1,557 whites compared to only 33 Hispanics (blacks, Asians or Pacific Islanders, and American Indians were not reported to own a home). Finally, the renters in this area were 1,308 whites and 19 Asians or Pacific Islanders and 9 Hispanics (no blacks or American Indians), the majority (462) paying a monthly rental of $1,000 or more.

16. This refrain is also a praise of great valor.

17. Interestingly, Lavoe is, thus far, the only "white" Puertorriqueño in this pantheon of pleneros.

18. For a more detailed and thorough discussion on the Puerto Rican plena, refer to Dufrasne González 1994, Echeverria Alvarado 1984, Flores 1993, and Glasser 1995.

19. For an excellent discussion on collective memory and historical reconstruction, see Portelli 1991.

20. For a discussion of reversion and diversion within diaspora communities, see Glissant 1989.

21. A coquí is an amphibious organism native only to the ecosystem of Puerto Rico and is unable to survive outside of the island. The coquí is then considered to be truly "Puerto Rican." It is common to hear people compare their Puerto Rican identity to a coquí, linking their identity to the native amphibious organism. This helps to explain the discourse and the underlying logic employed in the editorial.

22. Personal communication, interviews with Madalena Fontañez, July 2, 1996; Richie Pérez, July 8, 1996; and Mario Ruiz, June 27, 1996.

23. Personal communication, interviews with Richie Pérez, July 8, 1996, and with Mario Ruíz, June 27, 1996.

24. Many contemporary critics note the difference between a *sonero* and a singer of Salsa music. The former follows in the tradition of a singer's ability to improvise and "rhyme a story" spontaneously during a live performance. A Salsa singer may have a pleasant voice and adequate singing skills, but is not thought to have the ability to improvise and "rhyme a story" while performing before a live audience. At the time of this writing, examples of popular *soneros* would be Ismael Rivera, Gilberto Santa Rosa, Jose "Cheo" Feliciano, Domingo Quiñones, Victor Manuel, and Cano Estremera; on the other hand, Salsa singers who are not regarded as soneros would be Marc Anthony, Brenda K. Starr, and La India (Linda Caballero). It is obvious that most Salsa singers are male and are inheritors (and maintain their domination as transmitters and guardians) of an oral tradition. Interestingly, this suggests how masculinity and gender constitute the underlying criterion for soneros and Salsa singing styles.

25. For a discussion on the act of transcribing from the written text to the oral performance see Edwards and Sienkewics 1990: 37.

26. This observation was first articulated by Cheo Feliciano and aired by a Spanish-language radio station in New York City. The exact station that aired this is unknown.

BIBLIOGRAPHY

Althusser, Louis. 1971. *Lenin and Philosophy and Other Essays*. Translated by Ben Brewster. New York: Monthly Review Press.

Alvarez, Luis Manuel. 1992. "La presencia negra en la música puertorriqueña." In Lydia Milagros González, ed., *La tercera raíz: presencia africana en Puerto Rico*. San Juan: Centro de Estudios de la Realidad Puertorriqueña (CEREP)–Instituto de Cultura Puertorriqueña (ICP), pp. 29–41.

Anderson, Benedict. 1991. *Imagined Communities: Reflections on the Origin and Spread of Nationalism*. 2d ed. New York: Verso.

Aparicio, Frances R. 1998. *Listening to Salsa: Gender, Latin Popular Music, and Puerto Rican Cultures*. Hanover, N. H.: Wesleyan University Press, 1998.

Appadurai, Arjun and Carol Breckenridge. 1988. "Why Public Culture? *Public Culture Bulletin 1/1* (Fall):5–9.

Baker, Houston A., Jr., Manthia Diawara, and Ruth H. Lindenborg, eds. 1996. *Black Cultural Studies: A Reader.* Chicago: University of Chicago Press.

Barretto, Ray. 1993. Interview by Nancy Rodríguez. *Ritmo y Aché Radio Program.* Pacifica Radio, September 8.

Basch, Linda, Nina Glick Schiller, and Cristina Szanton Blanc, eds. 1994. *Nations Unbound: Transnational Projects, Postcolonial Predicaments, and Deterritorialized Nation-States.* Langhorne, Pa: Gordon and Breach.

Berríos-Miranda, Marisol. 1997. "Con Sabor a Puerto Rico: The Reception and Influence of Puerto Rican Salsa in Venezuela." Paper presented at *The Rhythms of Culture: Dancing to Las Américas An International Research Conference on Popular Musics in Latin[o] America,* March 21–22 at the University of Michigan, Ann Arbor.

———. 1998. "Salsa: Whose Music Is It?" (revised). Paper presented at the American Studies Association Annual Conference, *American Studies and the Question of Empire: Histories, Cultures, and Practices,* November 19–22, Seattle, Washington.

Bhabha, Homi K. 1990a. "Introduction: Narrating the Nation." In Homi K. Bhabha, ed., *Nation and Narration.* New York: Routledge, pp. 1–7.

———., ed. 1990b. *Nation and Narration.* New York: Routledge.

———. 1996. "Culture's In-Between." In Stuart Hall and Paul Du Gay, eds., *Questions of Identity.* Thousand Oaks, Calif.: Sage, pp. 53–60.

Blades, Rubén. 1993. Interview by Alfredo Alvarado. *New York Latino: Music, the Arts, and More* 6:17, 24.

Boggs, Vernon W., ed. 1992. *Salsiology: Afro-Cuban Music and the Evolution of Salsa in New York City.* Westport, Conn.: Greenwood.

Brennan, Timothy. 1990. "The National Longing for Form." In Homi Bhabha, ed., *Nation and Narration.* New York: Routledge, pp. 44–70.

Centro de Estudios de la Realidad Puertorriqueña (CEREP). 1992. *La tercera raíz: presencia africana en Puerto Rico.* San Juan: Centro de Estudios de la Realidad Puertorriqueña.

Chatterjee, Partha. 1993. *The Nation and Its Fragments: Colonial and Postcolonial Histories.* Princeton, N. J.: Princeton University Press.

Chavez, Linda. 1991. *Out of El Barrio: Toward a New Politics of Hispanic Assimilation.* New York: Basic Books.

Clifford, James. 1994. "Diasporas." *Cultural Anthropology* 9(3):302–38.

Colón, Willie. 1993. "Héctor Lavoe." *Claridad,* July 9–15, p. 30.

———. 1996. Interview by Nancy Rodríguez. *Ritmo y Aché Radio Program.* Pacifica Radio, September 8.

Díaz-Quiñonez, Arcadio. 1993. *La Memoria Rota.* Río Piedras, Puerto Rico: Ediciones Huracán.

Dufrasne González, J. Emanuel. 1994. *Puerto Rico también tiene !tambo! Recopilación de artículos sobre la plena y la bomba.* Río Grande, Puerto Rico: Paracumbé.

Echeverria Alvarado, Félix. 1984. *La plena: origen, sentido y desarrollo en el folklore puertorriqueño.* Santurce, Puerto Rico: Express.

Edwards, Viv, and Thomas J. Sienkewics. 1990. *Oral Cultures Past and Present: Rappin' and Homer.* Oxford: Basil Blackwell.

Finnegan, Ruth. 1989. *Hidden Musicians: Music-Making in an English Town.* Cambridge: Cambridge University Press.

Flores, Juan. 1993. *Divided Borders: Essays on Puerto Rican Identity.* Houston, Texas: Arte Público Press.

———. 1996. "Broken English Memories." *Modern Language Quarterly* 57(2): 381–95.

————. 2000. *From Bomba to Hip Hop: Puerto Rican Culture and Latino Identity.* New York: Columbia University Press.

García Canclini, Néstor. 1992. "Cultural Reconversion." In George Yúdice, Jean Franco, and Juan Flores, eds. *On Edge: The Crisis of Contemporary Latin Amerian Culture.* Minneapolis: University of Minnesota Press, pp. 29–43.

————. 1993. *Transforming Modernity: Popular Culture in México.* Austin: University of Texas Press.

Gerard, Charley, and Marty Sheller. 1989. *Salsa: The Rhythm of Latin Music.* Crown Point, Ind.: White Cliffs.

Gilroy, Paul. 1997. "Diaspora and the Detours of Identity." In Kathryn Woodward, ed., *Identity and Difference: Culture, Media, and Identities.* Thousand Oaks, Calif.: Sage, pp. 299–343.

Glasser, Ruth. 1995. *My Music Is My Flag: Puerto Rican Musicians and Their New York Communities, 1917–1940.* Berkeley: University of California Press.

Glissant, Edouard. 1989. *Caribbean Discourse: Selected Essays.* Charlottesville: University Press of Virginia.

Guerra, Lillian 1998. *Popular Expression and National Identity in Puerto Rico: The Struggle for Self, Community, and Nation.* Gainesville: University Press of Florida.

Hall, Stuart. 1990. "Cultural Identity and Diaspora." In Jonathon Rutherford, ed., *Identity: Community, Culture, Difference.* London: Lawrence and Wishart, pp. 222–37.

————. 1995. "Negotiating Caribbean Identities," *New Left Review* 209:3–14.

————. 1996. "New Ethnicities." In Houston A. Baker Jr., Manthia Diawara, and Ruth H. Lindenborg, eds., *Black Cultural Studies: A Reader.* Chicago: University of Chicago Press, pp. 163–72.

Hall, Stuart, and Kuan-Hsing Chen. 1996. "The Formation of a Diasporic Intellectual." In David Morley and Kuan-Hsing Chen, eds., *Stuart Hall: Critical Dialogues in Cultural Studies.* New York: Routledge, pp. 484–503.

Hutton, Patrick H. 1993. *History as an Art of Memory.* Hanover, N. H.: University Press of New England.

Laó, Augustín. 1997. "Islands at the Crossroads: Puerto Ricaness Traveling between the Translocal Nation and the Global City." In Frances Negrón-Muntaner and Ramón Grosfoguel, eds., *Puerto Rican Jam: Essays on Culture and Politics.* Minneapolis: University of Minnesota Press, pp. 169–88.

Lavie, Smadar, and Ted Swedenburg. 1996. "Introduction: Displacement, Diaspora, and Geographies of Identity." In *Displacement, Diaspora, and Geographies of Identity.* Durham, N. C.: Duke University Press.

Lewis, Oscar. 1966. *La Vida: A Puerto Rican Family in the Culture of Poverty—San Juan and New York.* New York: Random House.

Leymarie, Isabelle. 1994. "Salsa and Migration." In Carlos Antonio Torre, Hugo Rodríguez Vecchini, and William Burgos, eds., *The Commuter Nation: Perspectives on Puerto Rican Migration,* edited by Río Piedras: Editorial de la Universidad de Puerto Rico.

Manuel, Peter. 1994 "Puerto Rican Music and Cultural Identity: Creative Appropriation of Cuban Sources from Danza to Salsa." *Ethnomusicology* 38(2):249–80.

McClintock, Anne. 1996. "No Longer in a Future Heaven: Nationalism, Gender, and Race." In Geoff Eley and Ronald Grigor Suny, eds., *Becoming National: A Reader.* New York: Oxford University Press, pp. 260–84.

Morley, David, and Kuan-Hsing Chen, eds. 1996. *Stuart Hall: Critical Dialogues in Cultural Studies.* New York: Routledge.

Negus, Keith. 1999. *Music Genres and Corporate Cultures.* New York: Routledge.

Pagán, Adam. 1997. "Indestructible: The Young Lords Party and the Cultural Politics of

Music in the Construction of Diaspo-Rican Identity." Paper presented at *The Rhythms of Culture: Dancing to Las Américas An International Research Conference on Popular Musics in Latin[o] America*, March 21–22 at the University of Michigan, Ann Arbor.

Pérez, Jorge. 1991. "La plena puertorriqueña: de la expresion popular a la comercialización musical." *Centro de Estudios Puertorriqueños Boletin* 3(2):51–55.

———. 1996?

Portelli, Alessandro. 1991. *The Death of Luigi Trastulli, and Other Stories: Form and Meaning in Oral History*. Albany: State University of New York Press.

Pratt, Mary Louise. 1991. "Arts of the Contact Zone." *Profession* (New York Modern Language Association) 91:33–40.

Quintero Rivera, Angel. 1989. "Music Social Classes, and the National Question in Puerto Rico." Working Paper 178, Woodrow Wilson International Center for Scholars, Washington, D.C.

———. 1998. *!Salsa,! sabor y control sociología de la música tropical*. Mexico: Siglo Veintiuno Editores.

Quintero Rivera, Angel, and Luis Manuel Álvarez. 1990. "Libre combinación de las formas musicales en la salsa!" *David and Goliath* 57 (October): 45–51.

Roach, Joseph. 1995. "Culture and Performance in the Circum-Atlantic World." In Andrew Parker and Eve Kosofsky Sedgwick, eds., *Performativity and Performance*. New York: Routledge, pp. 45–63.

———. 1996. *Cities of the Dead: Circum-Atlantic Performance*. New York: Columbia University Press.

Rodríguez Julia, Edgardo. 1991. *El entierro de Cortijo*. San Juan: Ediciones Huracán.

Rodríguez, Nancy. 1996. *Ritmo y Aché Radio Program Special on Héctor Lavoe*. Pacifica Radio, September 8.

Rondón, César Miguel. 1980. *El libro de la salsa: cronica de la música del caribe urbano*. Caracas, Venezuela: Editorial Arte.

Rúa, Mérida. 2000. "Porto-Mexes and Mexi-Ricans: Inter-Latino Perspectives on Language and Cultural Identity." Paper presented at the *Shades of a New Era: Pushing Intellectual Boundaries in Theory and Practice Conference*, February 11–12 at the University of Michigan, Ann Arbor.

Ruíz, Geraldo. 1995. *Selena, The Last Song*. New York: El Diario Books/Latin Communications Group.

Scarano, Francisco. 1996. "The Jíbaro Masquerade and the Subaltern Politics of Creole Identity Formation in Puerto Rico, 1745–1823." *American Historical Review* 101: 1398–1431.

Slobin, Mark. 1994. "Music in the Diaspora: The View from Euro-America." *Diaspora* 3(3): 243–51.

Taussig, Michael. 1993. *Mimesis and Alterity: A Particular History of the Senses*. New York: Routledge.

Torres Torres, Jaime. 1993. "Desconsuelo a Héctor Lavoe." *El Nuevo Dia,* July 2, p. 25.

Valle, Antonio del Carta, and Carlos Méndez. 1993. "Felicitaciones por el Program Sobre Héctor Lavoe." *El Nuevo Dia*, July 29, p. 125.

Vázquez, Luis A. 1999. "Salsa as Discourse, Salsa as Practice." Unpublished manuscript.

Washburne, Christopher J. 1999. "Salsa in New York: A Musical Ethnography." Ph.D. dissertation, Columbia University.

Woodward, Kathryn, ed. 1997. *Identity and Difference: Culture, Media, and Identities*. Thousand Oaks, Calif.: Sage.

Young, Robert J. C. 1995. *Colonial Desire: Hybridity in Theory, Culture, and Race*. New York: Routledge.

DISCOGRAPHY

Colón, Willie. 1967. *El Malo*. (Fania 337.)

———. 1968. *The Hustler*. (Fania 347.)

———. 1969. *Guisando/Doing a Job*. (Fania 370.)

———. 1971. *Asalto Navideño*. (Fania 399.)

———. 1972. *Cosa Nuestra*. (Fania 384.)

———. 1972. *Crime Pays*. (Fania 406.)

———. 1972. *El Juicio*. (Fania 424.)

———. 1973a. LoMató. (Fania 444.)

———. 1973b. *Asalto Navideño—Volume 2*. (Fania 449.)

———. 1975. *The Good, The Bad, The Ugly*. (Fania 484.)

———. 1976. *La Gran Fuga*. (Fania 394.)

Fania All-Stars. 1975. *Live at Yankee Stadium (Volume 1)*. (Fania 476.)

———. 1978. *Live*. (Fania 684.)

———. 1995. *Live in Puerto Rico, June 1994*. (Video, Fania 684.)

———. 1997. *Viva Colombia: En Concierto*. (Latina 225.)

Lavoe, Héctor. 1975. *The Good, the Bad and the Ugly*. (Fania 484.)

———. 1975. *La Voz*. (Fania 461.)

———. 1976. *De Ti Depende [It's Up to You]*. (Fania 492.)

———. 1978. *Comedia*. (Fania 522.)

———. 1979. *Recordando a Felipe Pirela*. (Fania 545.)

———. 1980. *El Sabio*. (Fania 558.)

———. 1980. *Hector's Gold*. (Fania 574.)

———. 1981. *¡Que Sentimiento!* (Fania 598.)

———. 1985. *Revento*. (Fania 634.)

———. 1987. *Strikes Back*. (Fania 647.)

———. 1993. *Héctor Lavoe: The Fania Legends of Salsa. Volume 1*. (Fania JM 700.)

———. 1993. *The Master and the Protégé*. (Fania 674.)

———. 1994. *Héctor Lavoe. The Fania Legends of Salsa. Volume 2*. (Fania 701.)

Chapter 8

MEMOIRS OF A
LIFE IN SALSA

Catalino "Tite" Curet Alonso
Translated by Lise Waxer

T*ite Curet Alonso is one of the most important composers in salsa history, having penned landmark songs for nearly every famous salsa performer of the 1960s, '70s, and '80s. His hits include "Anacaona," "Las caras lindas," "La Tirana" "Pueblo latino," "Plantación adentro," "La Oportunidad," and many, many more. Curet's compositions are characterized not only by tuneful melodies, poetic lyricism, and catchy refrains, but also incisive social commentary and a strong critique of injustice, oppression, and neocolonialism. Along with singer-songwriter Rubén Blades (profiled below), he is one of the leading proponents of "salsa with a social message."*

A lifelong resident of Puerto Rico, Tite Curet was born and raised in the salsero neighborhoods of Barrio Obrero and Santurce in San Juan. While a close friend to many stars, (including famous vocalist Ismael "Maelo" Rivera, fig. 2.1), he has never lost his touch with the people and can often be seen conversing with friends and acquaintances in the streets of San Juan. In addition to his career as a composer, he is also a journalist, sociologist, and a former postman. The recipient of two honorary doctorates and numerous accolades, Tite Curet Alonso is revered by musicians and aficionados as the elder statesman of salsa. The following five autobiographical vignettes are taken from his book La Vida Misma (1985). Together, they constitute an important insider's perspective on the salsa world. In these pages, Tite Curet recounts his personal memoirs of musicians, producers, and also his own experiences as a salsa composer. We are grateful and honored to be able to include a translated version of these chronicles here.

FIGURE 8.1 • Tite Curet Alonso (right) with Ismael Rivera "El Sonero Mayor" in Loiza, Puerto Rico, during the first Fiesta de Loiza, early 1970s. Courtesy of Tite Curet Alonso.

PANCHO CRISTAL

Pancho Cristal was the record producer who launched Tite Curet on his path as a successful salsa composer in the 1960s. Cristal worked for Tico Records, an important New York salsa label that produced albums by such renowned bandleaders as conga players Ray Barretto and Mongo Santamaría, and pianists Eddie and Charlie Palmieri. In the following memoir, Curet outlines his encounter with Cristal, who served as liaison between the composer and popular vocalist Guadalupe "La Lupe" Yoli. La Lupe recorded three songs by Tite Curet that not only became her sig-

nature tunes, but made him famous and entered the repertoire of Latin popular music as widely loved classics: "La Tirana," "Carcajada final," and "Puro teatro" (the last of which was used in the soundtrack to Pedro Almodovar's film Woman on the Verge of a Nervous Breakdown*). In this vignette, Curet also mentions other important salsa bandleaders of the 1960s:* timbalero *and* pachanga *pioneer Joey Quijano, who recorded one of Curet's very first songs, and the well-known percussionist and "Mambo King" Tito Puente, who performed with La Lupe during the period that Curet wrote his famous tunes for her.*

I don't know what direction his life has taken. This business is like that. It takes us from one place to another without our realizing it at times. The first time I heard his name was in 1965. Back then he was producer of Tico Records, in the Latin music branch. Under his wing, individuals such as Ray Barretto, Tito Puente, Mongo Santamaría, and La Lupe became famous, along with other stars in Latin dance and romantic music of the day.

The name "Pancho Cristal" was the last word in prestige and authority. To know him and be his friend were the same thing. Something spontaneous. He needed a local promoter, and I, who knew the scene by memory, lent my services. Furthermore, to be perfectly honest, I needed to earn a few extra dollars to bolster a lifestyle that was, at the time, devoted to one spree after another. That was all.

The big things came later. My career as a composer had already burst open with a *son* titled "Efectivamente" [Effectively], recorded by Joey Quijano and his Combo Cachana. The year was 1965, when Raffy Torres and I produced the radio show *Ritmo Rendezvous* [Rhythm rendevous] on Station W, broadcast from the neighborhood of Hato Rey, Puerto Rico.

The singer La Lupe kindled my urge to write, for her dramatic and shocking style. I liked her. When I heard her sing "El Amo" [The master] my decision was already made, and Pancho Cristal helped to get my bolero "La Tirana" [The female tyrant] to her. The tune was a hit that brought me five hundred dollars. It felt glorious when my name was mentioned along with those of "La Yiyiyi"[1] and Tito Puente, who was arranger and accompanist for the sensational singer. Later, through Pancho Cristal's connections once again, La Lupe accepted another two tunes of mine, "Puro teatro" [Pure theater] and "Carcajada final" [Last laugh]. Two more hits!

"The Pancho Cristal Connection" was a trampoline for me. Just what I needed. The author, the promoter, the artist, and a person full of faith who believed in me—Pancho Cristal, nicknamed for a brand of Cuban beer, *Cristal*. His real name: Morris Pelman.

After he left Tico Records and then moved on from a record shop he later had on New York's Tenth Avenue, I never saw him again. They say that once retired from the world of business, he moved to the city of Miami, Florida.

They say. I'm not clear what happened when he retired. I do know that I, grateful, will always have a high place of honor for him in my memory, very high. He was my open door, the piston and valve necessary to launch my career in an extremely difficult and competitive field: musical composition.

I have enjoyed public applause in many places. Plaques, eulogies, diplomas, cultural, legislative, and mayor's awards, triumphs in song festivals celebrated in various countries. All a pleasure!

Here, in secret, at the bottom of my being I give a standing ovation to that superb gentleman who gave me his hand without thinking twice, placing me on the road to triumph: PANCHO CRISTAL.

Like that, all with capital letters that, for me, he deserves!

THE LETTER THAT CORTIJO WON'T BE ABLE TO READ

Bandleader and percussionist Rafael Cortijo was one of the most important innovators in Puerto Rican popular music of the mid-twentieth century. During the 1950s, he adapted the traditional rhythms of Afro–Puerto Rican bomba *and* plena *to the dynamic format of an eight-member ensemble that featured Cuban percussion, trumpets, saxophones, piano, bass—and the inimitable lead vocals of Ismael "Maelo" Rivera. Founded in 1954, the group of Cortijo and his combo inaugurated a new era in Latin popular music, breaking away from the large, staid dance bands of the 1940s to introduce a more energetic presentation marked by driving rhythms, catchy refrains and horn choruses, and infectious dance routines by the front line of vocalists. Cortijo's bomba and plena recordings were enormously popular not only in Puerto Rico, but also Colombia and Venezuela. The band lasted until 1962, when Cortijo and Maelo suffered problems with the law owing to marijuana possession. The rest of the band, under the leadership of pianist Rafael Ithier, regrouped under the name El Gran Combo de Puerto Rico, which continued Cortijo's legacy to become Puerto Rico's most stalwart salsa orchestra.*

The following memoir was written as a letter to Cortijo shortly after the percussionist's death in 1984. Tite Curet recounts his close personal friendship with Cortijo, candidly recalling the experiences they shared together. Of note is his commentary on the hard times Cortijo faced after the disbanding of his first combo in the 1960s, when the music industry turned its back on him. The letter opens with reference to the incredible public outpouring at the maestro's funeral—in Puerto Rico, the death of a famous musician becomes an occasion not only for mourning, but for exuberant celebration and music making in homage to the memory of the beloved artist.

Rest in peace, friend, now you don't need anything, not even to breathe. Your death has caused such grief that the public poured out their hearts to you. Santurce [Cortijo's neighborhood] knew how to say "see you later," with *panderetas,* drums, dance bands and singers gathered together, pumping out *plenas* and *bombas* at full steam. It looked like one of those massive fiestas, full of people. You knew how to penetrate to the very heart of the populace, since [forming your combo in] 1954. There you remained openly, like a manifesto, without obstacles or restrictions. There was a multitude that spilled out into the streets to remember you and cry tears of love, to the strains and rhythms of your captivating music.

At one time you put the name of Santurce and Puerto Rico high up in the world, very high up. And the people repaid you with a spectacular funeral as moving as the end of a global war. Or the beginning of a true peace.

Now that you aren't here it's good to know that I shared your struggles through the moments of triumph and hardship, from close up and afar. You were that unselfish friend who put his wallet at my service during my worst times of alcoholism. And when he saw me without a single cent put his dollars in my hand, "so that you can go shopping for your kids." Favors that I felt were never repaid even by all my attempts to reciprocate, not even with the music that I later wrote, with pleasure, for the combo. . . . From close up, from afar, it was most remarkable to be your friend and your brother, in life and in music.

That time with "Pa' los Caseríos" [For the small towns] and the awards that the CRUV conferred on us on television, in full color . . . we looked like a pair of black princes both crowned as kings. The truth is, we brought down the house.

I always viewed your career, filled with trophies, plaques, awards and emblems, without a trace of envy, as one does when truly grounded in the fundamentals of friendship. You planted a tremendous seed of music and sentiment when you raised the so-called music of the streets to the valued position it occupies today. Before your red-hot combo, any musician who lived well had to belong to one of the big orchestras. With your triumph, you brought them honey and pastries [easy times]. You broke that monopoly and superiority.

You put expensive clothes on our everyday music, luxurious garments of fine cloth . . . records, radio, television, movies, sacred exports. This innovative task falls only to the creators, it does not matter if they later have to confront, as in the case of some heroes, people's indifference. In the long run, that which shines, shines. The mediocre, while it may shine, will tarnish and remain stuck in its given time and place. Such is life and so it will be.

In difficult times I suffered a lot for you and with you. When your two children Timber and Zoila arrived in this world, you were already fifty years old. And after reaching a half-century, such things worry anyone, for obvious reasons of love.

It was then that the owners of the music business turned their backs on you, promoting those who reaped from you instead.[2] It seems that they were waiting, slyly, for the moment that this would most hurt and maim you. I remember you, roaming the streets in a struggle to tough this out. And also your words, "It's now that I've got two children that I feel happy, but worried about not being able to offer them comfort and all the other things they need . . ."

The only thing you needed was work, to settle your new situation as a father. I knew it. Just as you had been charitable to extremes, even to the point of being cleaned out on numerous occasions, you never liked asking for a handout. I saw how they closed doors to you, ruining whatever business you launched.

I was shocked to find out, and forgive me for telling this, how they tried to make someone kill you. And how death's emissary, before your largesse and sincerity, repented from doing so. There are just some men too great and beloved to be eliminated like that, by a paid pistol shot. And there are little guys who grow a bit larger by motivating their conscience to not pull a trigger for a few dollars.

After your passing I looked in a book that was published about Puerto Rican musicians. They barely dedicated a few lines to you. All of it parsimoniously expressed, almost as if by fluke. But it doesn't matter. I know that in the heart of your people you wrote an encyclopedia of affection, music, and rhythm. The people showed it on October 6. Your career was glorious. Your life overturned sadness, converting it into happiness and color. You were a total winner. You established a new era for our music and our musicians. Everyone knows that and now nobody can argue that or take that away from you.

Rest in peace now . . . Be calm, my friend and brother. Where you are now, you don't need anything . . . Not even to breathe . . . !

CHEO FELICIANO IN THE CENTER FOR FINE ARTS, BY HIS OWN RIGHT
(Chronicle dedicated to Fernando Sterling and Luis Máquina)
Vocalist José "Cheo" Feliciano is a long-standing veteran of the salsa

scene, most commonly associated with the famous Fania All-Stars. He launched his performance career in the mid-1960s with the sextet of boogaloo pioneer Joe Cuba (see Flores, chapter 4), recording such hits as "Bang Bang," "El Pito," and his signature tune, "El Ratón." Feliciano struggled with drug addiction and was jailed for narcotics possession in the late 1960s, but upon his release launched a solo career. His association and friendship with Tite Curet is legendary among salsa aficionados—in this memoir Curet alludes to the constant stream of advice he gave his friend concerning the singer's delivery and style. Many of Feliciano's most renowned tunes were composed by Curet, including "Anacaona" (a song with strong anticolonialist undercurrents), "Nabori," "Salomé," and several others. In 1973, Curet composed an entire album's worth of songs for Feliciano during a downslide in the singer's career and personal life. The recording, prophetically titled With a Little Help from My Friend, *was released by Fania Records and received much critical acclaim. Curet refers to this project below.*

This chronicle originally appeared as a newspaper column about Feliciano's appearance at the Centro de Bellas Artes (Fine Arts Center) in San Juan in the mid-1980s, a period when popular artists began breaking through barriers of race and class to appear in venues formerly reserved for elite culture. Indeed, during the early 1990s a considerable debate was raised by the proposal, later scuttled, to rename the Centro de Bellas Artes after Rafael Cortijo. Curet positions Feliciano's performance in this theater as a legitimization of the artist's long and turbulent career as one of salsa's most popular vocalists.

The singer Cheo Feliciano and I met each other in New York City on 110th Street, almost at the corner of Madison Avenue. That is, in El Barrio [Spanish Harlem]. It was during his time as vocalist with the Joe Cuba Sextet, when the *salseros* of the time crowded about to see him *sonear* [improvise] and the ladies sighed to hear him sing boleros in a smooth and infectious manner that inspired romance.

Right there on that marvelous corner of the city, I unloaded my first critique on him. "Cheo, brother, when you are *soneando* [singing improvisations] you stray too much from the main theme, so you should really think much harder about that . . ."

A very special and long-lasting friendship grew from this point forward. My advice rained on him each time we met in Puerto Rico or in the metropolis. A mutual friend who introduced Cheo and I, Nandy Sterling, had already given the lead. . . . "Cheo, there's a friend of mine in Puerto Rico who thinks highly of you and has great things planned for you."

These so-called "great things" had to wait their turn. The man flung himself down the negative side of life. Many people turned their backs on him. They saw him in a bad light, wandering through the neighborhood streets of Santurce, destitute. Our friendship remained the same. A meeting with him meant a bear hug, and then that gesture of "What do you need?". . . .

When he decided to get himself together I silently applauded him. . . . Knowing he was on the road to recovery and beginning to prepare projects for him was one and the same thing. Jerry Masucci, the director of Fania Records, saw me with the hefty stack of papers called the Cheo Feliciano Project, and in his fractured Spanish merely commented: "Yes, but you're in charge of him, you deal with Cheo . . ." Honey over pastry. The project waited another couple of years more . . . And physically and mentally detoxified, the man set out on a sure path . . .

Then came those hits with "Anacaona," "Pa' que afinquen," "Mi triste problema," "Franqueza cruel," "Este es el guaguancó" . . . And into his hands, fortune. He seemed like a child handling a new toy. One called fame.

Mexico, Chile, Holland, Panama, Venezuela, England, Argentina, Peru, Colombia, Japan, United States, Dominican Republic, Africa, France, where he sang in the Miden Festival of Cannes, and in the world-famous Olympic Theater of Paris . . . The crowds adored him and from afar I tasted the satisfaction of having won my bet on the "underdog."

Meanwhile, in Puerto Rico the singer led a family life, the easy life that he had not enjoyed for some time. In his leisure time he devoted himself (among other things) to gardening and planting vegetables, despite my jokes that consisted of calling him "the Jackie Robinson of agriculture, the first black farmer of the modern era." And dozens of similar compliments. To be sure, he was happy, and to an extent I was happy for myself too. Jerry Masucci's requirement that I take charge of him was followed to the letter. And to that of the music . . .

Then came a stretch of total idleness. During this lapse he hardly recorded any albums, and those that he did make were not hits. He went back to cloistered meetings with that irritable big brother of his. New warnings and shakings by the neck . . . "Life changes, you have to get involved in something else, kid."

When he went back to the recording studios a string of successes returned to him: "Los entierros pobres," "Estampa marina," "Juan Albañil," "Trizas," and a hell of an accomplished bolero written by José Nogueras titled "Amada mía," considered to be the master work of sentimental song. . . .

Our friend Cheo is already big. He's a grandfather. And he continues to be as outstanding as a certain whiskey.

He has completed twenty-five years in lyric song. A quarter century pleasing the public and offering his warmth as an exquisite singer. They are going to celebrate all this through a concert, a sort of double bill, this Friday in the Festival Salon of the Center for Fine Arts. Something that he as much as his public deserves.

There I will be in the audience, whether it goes ahead or not. And although we won't be able to see each other, for obvious reasons, in the prevailing semidarkness, he will be aware of my presence, which will be like the best wish for everything to go well. A wish that they applaud him deliriously. Because you all cannot imagine how much I love him and esteem him, this accomplice of my career as a composer and other things. This Cheo Feliciano, tremendous partner.

ISMAEL MIRANDA: A WELL-OFF *SONERO*

Ismael Miranda is another famous vocalist of classic 1970s salsa, who, like Cheo Feliciano, has long been associated with the Fania All-Stars. He launched his career at the age of seventeen, earning him the sobriquet "El Niño Bonito de la Salsa" [salsa's pretty boy]. Through the early 1970s, Miranda was lead vocalist with the salsa band of pianist Larry Harlow (Harlow was also a chief producer for Fania Records), before going solo in the middle of the decade. Although born in Puerto Rico, Miranda grew up in New York City and did not speak fluent Spanish— which Curet advised him to learn to do before attempting a solo career. In contrast to salsa artists who have struggled with substance abuse and personal finances, Miranda has enjoyed great stability thanks to his sharp nose for business investments.

The following memoir outlines Curet's relationship with Miranda, touching on the singer's early years and subsequent path to stardom. During the late 1960s, Miranda was a friend and contemporary of another rising salsa vocalist, the legendary Héctor Lavoe (see Valentín, chapter 7). Curet recounts how the fledgling singers pursued their idol Ismael Rivera, the famed singer who fronted Cortijo and his combo in the 1950s and was an important influence for salsa in the 1960s and 70s (see Berríos-Miranda, chapter 2). As he did for many salsa vocalists, Curet penned some of Miranda's most popular hits, including "La Oportunidad" and "Galera tres."

The man himself told me the story, in a bar located in the now not very luxurious sector of Miramar. He drank a beer, and me, that ever-present soda![3]

"I pursued Ismael Rivera there in New York. Same as my friend Héctor Lavoe, who shared an apartment with me. We both wanted to be *soneros* [singers] no matter what, and we were really surprised that a star like Ismael Rivera would let two eager novices share the stage with him. We liked the attitude he had." He and I imagined how the next day went, with them telling their friends in the barrio: "Last night we sang with Ismael Rivera. He's our buddy and said we sounded great."

Life, the *son,* the *guaracha,* followed as usual. Ismael Miranda was signed to the Larry Harlow orchestra, then known for the style of *son montuno* that Harlow had learned in Havana watching dance sets by the *conjunto* of Arsenio Rodríguez, the most important cultivator of that style.[4] The so-called "Amazing Blindman" owing to his skill playing the *tres* [Cuban guitar]. With reason!

The truth is that Ismael belted out some incredible high notes when singing boleros, and his vocal timbre seemed to have been invented for those *montunos* with four-line choruses. Stupendous! And since he was a good dancer and well-groomed fellow, in time he was nicknamed "The Pretty Boy of Salsa."

The Latino dance crowd—thirsty for new idols and now completely recovered from the postwar slump—gave great importance to singers, so like everyone else he wanted to set out on his own path, with a band of his own. It was logical.

My advice for him was quick. I recommended that he take some extra time before launching himself as a soloist. "A year," was the sentence. "You have to learn how to speak correctly, or the best possible, in Spanish. You're still saying a lot of words and terms very poorly, not the way they should be. Take it easy and then we'll see. I'll be standing by you."

After a year was over he called me. He was speaking Spanish "by the book." With an enormous desire and spirit to triumph. He also expressed his concerns about living in Puerto Rico. In beloved *Puertorro!* Here, with his people. After all, he was no more than a little country boy from Aguada[5] trying to make his fortune.

"Now you're on. This very week tell Masucci [director of Fania Records] that I will send a tune made to your wishes." And it arrived just in time to record it. Titled: "La Oportunidad" [The Opportunity]. It ended up being his first big hit as a soloist. "At long last it's come. Now my time has come for sure. And this time I'm not letting it pass. My opportunity has come." Remember, *salseros?* That was tremendous!

From that point on everything was honey over pastry, whether it was bolero or *guaracha* and *son montuno,* that kid was an ace in the hole. His personal manner through all this did not vary. He would dine in a luxury restaurant just the same as when he went to the beachfront in Piñones to eat a pair of *alcapurrias*[6] with gusto. In terms of alcohol, he never was a habitual drinker. He hardly drank more than a glass of whiskey.

In his triumphant career he always was an interpreter who, although he knew how to compose and had some solid original hits, never turned his back on me. He kept asking me for work continuously. A thousand thanks! There was a moment, however, that was a top hit for both. It concerned "Galera tres" [Ward three]. It came at a moment when there were many uprisings in the jails and prisons. A female colleague in journalism studies told me that the song was a best-seller in Peru and other countries. At that time, another university colleague of mine from back in the 1940s, a tremendous *mulatta* woman and lawyer named Irba Cruz de Batista, was director of the Department of Correctional Services. She was receiving strong and harsh criticisms. After all, the situation in the penal system hasn't changed much, despite the sermons of the distinguished lady and professional Doña Trina Padilla.

Let's come back to Ismael Miranda. If there was something to admire in him, it was his good instinct for business. First he was a tire dealer, then property sales, then urban development, restaurants, and an office building in the Golden Mile, the banking zone. He's made! It's well known than he has millions of dollars. May San Pedro bless every one of them!

We know that he doesn't need to sing for a living, since he invested well in his future. He had enough vision so that now, in his adult life, he can live at ease. Even so, singing tugs at him. And he returns to the stage with the same charm as always. To earn applause on all continents.

A good artist never retires. We see this in the case of [Cuban] singer Olga Guillot, and this tells us why. There is Ismael Miranda on the scene once again, ready to sing with all the *sabor* that salsa requires and awaits from one of its grand maestros.

RUBÉN BLADES

Rubén Blades is the most renowned singer-songwriter of 1970s and '80s salsa, and one of salsa's most political artists. A native of Panama, Blades studied law as a young man and eventually earned a doctorate in law from Harvard University. Moving to New York in the early 1970s, he worked as an errand boy for Fania Records before launching his singing career in 1974 with the band of conga player Ray Barretto. In 1976, he moved to the band of legendary trombonist and composer Willie Colón, replacing Colón's former vocalist Héctor Lavoe. Colón and Blades recorded some of the most important salsa albums of the late

1970s, including Metiendo Mano *and* Siembra, *which pointed strong criticism at capitalism, social prejudice, and injustice. Included in these albums was Tite Curet Alonso's anticolonialist "Plantación adentro."*

Blades stands alongside Curet as author of some of salsa's most socially conscious repertoire. The hard-hitting commentary of Blades's songs, modeled on the Latin American protest genre of nueva canción, *attracted thousands of new listeners to salsa in the late 1970s, particularly leftists, intellectuals, and university students. Blades left Colón in 1980 to record and perform with a band of his own, continuing to produce acclaimed albums while branching out as an actor in Hollywood films. He returned to politics after receiving his law degree in 1985, and ran as a presidential candidate in the 1994 Panamanian national elections. In the following chronicle, originally published in two parts, Curet recognizes Blades as a friend and kindred spirit, referring to several of his hit songs and also discussing Blades's involvement in politics. Notably, Curet acknowledges Blades's "salsa with a social message" as an important contribution that smoothed out the rough, barrio-oriented edge of salsa prior to that time and got listeners thinking more profoundly about broad social issues of the day.*

It was at the corner of Ashford and Magdalena Avenues, in the middle of Condado district.[7] There it was, although I don't remember the date anymore. The hour, yes, it was night, under the stars and out in the open, one of those hours that are good for getting into a long conversation which leads to a firm friendship. Rubén Blades has been that, a good friend made initially through our connection to Caribbean music, and then consolidated by the support of friendship itself.

His dreams of triumph shone through in his gaze. First he had to complete his law studies in Panama, his native country, in order to venture forth and unleash the flood of inspiration that trembled inside him. His path was already laid out. He knew where he was going.

The animated chat continued on that corner. Both of us practically immobile alongside the relentless horns of cars locked in a traffic jam. They proved his streetwise philosophy that "corners are the same everywhere."

Brazil and its music drew both of us. We talked about "over there" as if we had found ourselves on the sidewalks of Copacabana or on the streets of Ipanema next to the hexagonal Bar Veloso, where the poet Vinicius de Moraes and the composer Antonio Carlos Jobim, watching the exquisite girl Eloísa Helena pass by, wrote the famous bossa nova titled "Chica de Ipanema," which became popular worldwide.

Neither one of us even imagined that in time he was going to record my samba, "La palabra adiós," and the hymnlike *guaracha* "Plantación adentro," based on an Amazon theme. It was, well, a happy encounter, seasoned with comments about how much good he could do for Caribbean music, bestowing it with work that both of us, hopeful, catalogued as "high thought."

As we nonchalantly agreed, the learning exchange that night was on both sides, both of us pinned down at Magdalena and Ashford, a corner like any other, because after all, "corners are the same everywhere," although the surroundings change.

One resounding triumph after another. Salsa music and its many thousands of worshipers have come to accept the singer Rubén Blades without limits. Salsa with a social message has produced a string of hits, and also smoothed out the genre a little, making young people think about the issues of the moment, of the everyday path.

"Pedro Navaja," "Chica plástica," "El Cantante," "Cipriano Armenteros," "El Tiburón," Ligia Elena," "El Camaleón," the work *El solar de los aburridos* and a world more of tunes from his pen and in his melodious voice—all of them didactic and proclaiming his name as a singer-songwriter, perhaps the best of them all in the salsa business.

Nobody doubts his talent at producing hits now. The public adores him, it follows him and pursues him from one place to another. On many occasions he has had to resort to protection from police or security guards, since he is valuable property. Sometimes human affection, when en masse, can hurt the person who is admired. He has even made it to Hollywood films. Now he's quite international.

From that position as errand boy in the offices of Fania Records he went, without guide ropes, climbing the slope to fame, a steep trajectory that costs much hard work and much dreaming. Yes, the slope, the slope.

I understand him very well. The same here in this capital city of San Juan as over there in the city of New York; however many times we've met he's been the same. He hasn't changed a bit. We share opinions about each other's new projects, shaking hands and ideas whether we have time or not, given that his life has left him with few spare moments because of obligations and more obligations. He has traveled so much of late that he seems like a minister of external affairs. I don't know how he managed to take the time out to complete his law studies and graduate with a doctoral degree in law from prestigious Harvard University, but he hasn't let go of the music, the backbone of his life, the field where he conquered the public's love.

Within him stirred another social force. Politics! Some people do not tire of affirming that he wants to be president of Panama, thus entering the public life of the homeland that he has lived far away from for obvious reasons, but that he has never stopped thinking about. And for his native isthmus, he wants the best.

"It's not that I want to be president, unless the position comes from the mandate of the people. Yes, I would like to form part of the government that settles many things that are not going well over there for the people on the bottom."

"Really?"

"Yes, but I'm no magician. It would have to be operating a group of leaders, people willing to struggle for the common good. Alone I couldn't do it, you know."

We were conversing this time in his dressing room at the Poliedro Stadium in Caracas. Backstage, we could hear ovations from the restless public, eager to see and hear him sing on the wide stage with his group Los Seis del Solar, tonight augmented by wind instruments.[8] He left for the stage then, escorted by security guards.

I stayed far back, observing his triumph. Every bit a great artist! Suddenly I thought about the labyrinths of Latin American politics, where vendettas rule. And where to this day there's always been an inflamed rivalry that usually doesn't hold back, attacking, injuring, and even fatally eliminating the opposition. May God keep you, Rubén! God keep you!

EDITOR'S NOTES

1. "La Yiyiyi" was a nickname for La Lupe, owing to the yelps she often emitted in performance. See Aparicio, chapter 6 this volume.
2. A possible reference to El Gran Combo, which capitalized on the sound it had developed with Cortijo's band to successfully launch itself in the early 1960s.
3. An allusion to Curet's own victory over alcoholism.
4. In 1957, while still a teenager, Harlow left his native New York to live, travel and study music in Cuba for a few months. He spent much of his time attending performances and hanging out with the famous *conjunto* (ensemble) of Arsenio Rodríguez, a pioneer who revolutionized the Cuban *son* in the late 1930s by adding a conga drum, piano, bass, and more trumpets to the traditional instrumentation, and concentrating on heavy, slow grooves known as *son montuno*.
5. Miranda's birthplace.
6. A typical Puerto Rican snack made of fried mashed plantain mixed with different types of meat.
7. An upscale neighborhood and tourist zone in San Juan, Puerto Rico.
8. Blades's group Seis del Solar was a small combo that featured synthesizers instead of horns; for the concert Curet refers to, additional wind instruments had been added to the ensemble.

Chapter 9

PONCHO SÁNCHEZ, LATIN JAZZ, AND THE CUBAN *SON*: A STYLISTIC AND SOCIAL ANALYSIS

Steven Loza

Within the past twenty years, Poncho Sánchez has emerged as one of the major stylists and leaders in the cross-genre known as Latin jazz (fig. 9.1). Since the innovations of Machito, Mario Bauzá, Dizzy Gillespie, and Chano Pozo in the 1940s, this style has blended, in dynamic fashion, essential elements of Afro-Cuban music and jazz. Sánchez, a Mexican American from Los Angeles, California, has maintained this progressive, stylistic blend while at the same time continuing with a traditional Cuban base of interpretation and performance practice. Previous to performing and recording with his own ensemble, he spent more than seven years as the *conguero* for Cal Tjader (till the latter's death in 1982), one of the major constituents of Latin jazz. After various nominations, he was awarded a Grammy Award for his 1999 CD *Latin Soul*.

In this article I will present a general account of the historical and stylistic aspects of the Cuban *son*, followed by stylistic (i.e., musical, poetic, and other structural) analyses of two examples from the recorded repertoire of Sánchez incorporating the form. The analysis presented is based on primary, original fieldwork that I conducted, including professional work with Poncho Sánchez. In addition to examining the traditional format of Sánchez's use of son in Latin jazz, I conclude with some deliberation of the converse use of the jazz idiom in Latin jazz.

One of my principal goals in this study is to reiterate the importance of what has been referred to as the "juncture" of musical and social analysis.[1] Through the musical analyses presented here, we can detect some of the elements of change in the compositions and arrangements

FIGURE 9.1 • Poncho Sánchez. Courtesy Jim Cassell, Berkeley Agency.

of Poncho Sánchez, which are based on the traditional Cuban son and incorporate various elements of the jazz tradition. Such change, or innovation, becomes an essential feature of Sánchez's recognized style, asserting him as an individual identity among the public, the music industry, and the musicians' community. It also reflects the artist's and the public's perceived need for innovative yet qualitative change within the context of tradition.

Analysis based on the musical/social matrix should be considered interactive and interdependent. Although many studies in ethnomusicology have focused on these analytical interrelationships, various shifts in such practices have emerged, and many studies borrow more from social science paradigms than stylistic analyses. Thus, in many studies, the "juncture" of the musical and social remains elusive. In noting the significance of this issue, Porter and Gower posit that analyses of music

encompass more than simply a concern for musical organization.

Structural analysis of music may answer such questions as these: how

does a particular style or piece work? how is it structurally successful? . . .
Analysis of traditional repertoires, for instance, as one strategy in scruti-
nizing whole bodies of music or song, can uncover the concepts, preferences, and ordering systems that musicians or singers bring to their overall
style, as well as changes they make under certain circumstances.
(1995:278–79)

Porter and Gower also posit that "transformativity of form and content
in songs is bound up with their arrangement by the singer [or other musi-
cian]. Such form and content are verbal and musical" (278). They define
transformativity as "the capacity to stimulate change [and] best understood as an artistic process. In sure hands, it is a powerful tool for influencing perception of the world" (276). Porter and Gower thus
conceptualize transformativity as a form of creation that can help change
the world, improve it, if the art is truly creative and positive.
"Transformativity connotes the active, transitive capacity of a skilled performer (a singer, say) to bring about qualitative change" (277). Adapting
such concepts to the study of Poncho Sánchez's role in Latin jazz and the
Cuban son, we can learn how tradition, structure, and innovation vary
from one artist or performance to another. We may thus shed light on the
direct interrelationships between the musical and the social.

The two models presented for analysis are "Este Son," from
Sánchez's *Sonando* album, and "Bién Sabroso," the title track of his
1985 Grammy-nominated album. Both examples represent adaptations
of the Afro-Cuban son form, which became an integral part of the for-
mulation of various salsa styles in New York City and Puerto Rico and
elsewhere. The concept of son implies more than a particular rhythm or
dance. In Cuba, it is a word that describes a particular sound, structure,
and instrumentation, characterized by a certain rhythmic and stylistic
complex. It originally emerged from the population of African heritage
in the rural districts of Cuba as a vehicle for entertainment at informal
gatherings. In the early 1900s it migrated to the urban sector, eventually
molding the entire landscape of Cuban popular music.

Sánchez's interest in Afro-Cuban music is illustrated by the two
examples selected here in addition to the majority of material on his
twenty recorded solo albums, which also include the Afro-Cuban genres
of mambo, *cha-cha-chá, son montuno,* rumba, bolero, *guaguancó,
guaracha,* and *danzón.* Brazilian rhythms such as bossa nova and samba
are also interpreted by Sánchez's ensemble.

MUSICAL STRUCTURE OF THE CUBAN *SON*

The traditional son form is composed of two major sections. The first
part, or verse, is a solo melody sung by the lead singer, usually compris-

FIGURE 9.2 • Anticipated bass pattern in Cuban *son*.

FIGURE 9.3 • Reverse (2-3) clave.

ing a maximum of eight measures. The second part, called a *montuno* or *estribillo*, demonstrates a denser rhythmic character and a more sharply defined melody than the first part. The montuno, or estribillo, normally does not encompass more than four measures per phrase. The term "montuno" is also commonly used for the piano rhythmic-harmonic pattern constructing this section. The meter of the son is most frequently in cut time, or, as in the case of Sánchez's "Este Son," 4/4.

One of the son's more outstanding rhythmical characteristics is its use of a highly anticipated bass pattern of unique character (fig. 9.2). Borbolla (1975) notes that this compositional formula, representative of son, is unique among popular music and dance. Although other musical forms may demonstrate elements of anticipation, they are not as calculated or of such definite character as in son. Borbolla defines this characteristic in terms of musical structure. As illustrated in the sample above, the dominant accent of the son rhythmic patterns falls on the upbeat of the second count. Both this anticipated bass pattern and also the pattern performed on the congas are commonly referred to as *tumbao*.

The son has retained its strong tradition and vigor since its emergence in Cuba in the early part of this century. It has been a vehicle for a constantly evolving landscape of Cuban musical forms including the bolero, the *conga* (dance), the rumba, and the guaracha, among others, as exemplified through the efforts of Arsenio Rodríguez in the late 1930s. Since its inception in Cuba, the innovative quality of the son has been its unique use of anticipation. For this reason it has not dissipated as a tradition; it has constantly conformed to the offbeat rhythms common to the wide array of Afro-Cuban genres and has proved to be a Cuban expression of musical, poetic, and social innovation. Its influence has penetrated musical culture throughout the Americas, Africa, Europe, and Asia. Poncho Sánchez dynamically symbolizes that influence within the Chicano musical culture of Los Angeles and the U.S. Southwest.

"ESTE SON"

"Este Son" was composed by Poncho Sánchez and the frequent *sonero* (vocalist) of his early group, José "Perico" Hernández, of Cuban birth. The arrangement of the composition is a modern interpretation of son structure, basically conforming to a guaracha-son form. Guaracha, a traditional, popular Cuban dance and musical genre, has become a frequently adapted form in modern salsa arrangements. Like son montuno, a *guaracha-son* employs the rhythmic base of reverse or 2–3 clave (fig. 9.3). The introduction consists of eight bars of an ensemble riff based on the basic verse melody, which is subsequently the main verse of the vocal part. An upbeat rim shot on the *timbal* (called an *abanico*) anticipates the ensemble's entrance on the first beat of the melodic phrase at measure 1. Measures 7 and 8 are an ensemble rhythmic break. The timbal player (*timbalero*) inserts a roll on the fourth beat of measure 8, anticipating the vocal entrance on the main verse at measure 9.

The verse structure of the piece adheres to the following scheme: ABCD/EFGH IJKL/ABCD (stanza 4 is a replica of stanza 1). The poetic stanza type of the text to "Este Son" is that of the *copla* (couplet), consisting of a paired rhyme scheme (ABCB). Such structure is quite typical of the Cuban son as previously outlined. Loosely structured in four octosyllabic lines, the texts of the four stanzas are as follows:

Oye china, este son	Hey pretty girl, this *son*
Ven y báilalo y verás	Come and dance to it, and you will see
Que gozarás tú conmigo	That you'll have a good time with me
Hasta por la madruga[da].	Dancing until dawn.
Mira que se pone bueno	Look how good it's getting
Ven y arrímate pa'cá	Come, get closer here
Si no te apuras, mi china	If you don't hurry, girl of mine
Este son se acabará.	This *son* is going to end.
Cuando tú bailas mi ritmo	When you dance my rhythm
En seguida aprenderás	You will then learn
Que tu cuerpo se menea	That your body shakes
Como el son y cha cha chá	Like the *son* and the cha-cha-cha
Oye china, este son	Hey pretty girl, this *son*
Ven y báilalo y verás	Come and dance to it, and you will see
Que gozarás tú conmigo	That you'll have a good time with me
Hasta por la madruga[da].	Dancing until dawn.

FIGURE 9.4 • Harmonic structure of "Este Son".

FIGURE 9.5 • Typical bass pattern in "Este Son".

Variation 1:

Variation 2:

FIGURE 9.6 • Piano *guajeo (montuno)* and variations in "Este Son".

Generically, the major requisite of the copla, the major assonance of the second and fourth lines, is generally adhered to in this son verse. As in the Mexican son, the number of syllables in each line may be less than eight; likewise, as in the latter, an extended syllable or pause in the text delivery adapts the rhythmic form to the length of the musical phrase.

The basic strophic melody of the verse structure based on the AABA form is notated in the transcription (measures 9–40). Stanzas 1, 2, and 4 conform to a common melody and harmonic progression. The text of stanza 3 is melodically and harmonically set to a different structure, although still in the copla poetic form, and can be considered as a "bridge." The overall nuclear harmonic pattern of the verse section of "Este Son" conforms to the schematic in fig. 9.4. This harmonic sequence can be perceived as a ii-V7–i in B minor (or the iii of G major) followed by V7/ii-ii V7–I in the tonic. The full progression is also built on a cycle of fifths (C#-F#-B-E-A-D-G). Such a cycle of fifths structure in the song bridge is somewhat unique for the son. It is, however, typical to jazz practice, especially bebop. As this son composition merges with jazz, it gains this harmonic feature.

Instrumentation of the piece includes congas, bongos, timbales, electric bass, acoustic piano, trumpet, alto saxophone, and trombone. Miscellaneous percussion utilized are *claves* and the cowbell (*cencerro*). As demonstrated in the previous analysis of son structure, the bass adheres to the rhythmic concept of anticipation so essential to the Afro-Cuban form. One of the typical bass patterns throughout the piece can be notated as in fig. 9.5.

One of the most important and distinguishing factors is the typical rhythmic structure of the piano patterns, which construct an organic framework of both the clave base and the syncopated tumbao of the bass and conga (as illustrated above in the typical anticipated quality of the bass contrasted with the clave). The rhythmic chordal structure of the piano part, referred to as *guajeo* or *montuno*, is thus syncopated through the utilization of broken, interlocking fingering patterns that can be played according to the following scheme with variations, two of which are also notated in fig. 9.6.

Following the vocal section of "Este Son," the piano and bass engage in a solo version of the composition's basic harmonic progression. This is accomplished through the use of a series of breaks contrasted with an interpolated conga solo (measures 41–44). The juxtaposition of a structured piano/bass framework against the conga solo dynamically demonstrates the extensive diversity of rhythmic variation that can be executed by the conguero (in this case, Poncho Sánchez) within a very typical style.

Next in the arrangement is a horn ensemble section juxtaposed with the same piano/bass series of breaks (measures 41–58). Arriving at this point, which has become a climactic juncture, is the *coro* (chorus) statement and response section traditionally called the *estribillo*, typically featuring a coro section of vocalists singing rhymed, responsorial phrases. Between the coros the sonero sings in improvisatory fashion a series of *inspiraciones*, thematically expressing the content of the son's text while creatively displaying rhythmic and melodic variation. The *bongosero* switches from playing bongos to the cowbell. The intersecting context of the estribillo manifests a constant, repetitive background of vocal and instrumental structure, thus highlighting the solo inspiraciones in a very driving, dance-oriented section. This is frequently the portion of a salsa- or *son*-structured arrangement in which the singer, other musicians, and dancers at large extensively embellish their music/dance movements in a free, expressive style. The estribillo section also refers to the traditional African practice of call and response.

It is also quite typical during coro sections for the instrumentalists to solo between the coros, usually in four- or eight-bar phrases. In the case of "Este Son," an additional instrumental section follows the coro section (measures 62–70) through a chordal progression that deviates somewhat from the basic nuclear harmonic pattern of the piece. Instead of the ii7–V7–iii7–V7/ii progression, the ensemble section alters the chord progression by flatting the iii7 and the V7/ii and then alternating it twice with the original chords b minor (iii7) and E7 (V7/ii). Immediately following the interlude, the montuno section arrives layered with piano and trumpet solos. Such improvisation is characteristic of the montuno section. During the piano solo the bongosero, in order to relax the rhythmic intensity of the montuno section, returns to the bongos. Culminating the piano solo are sixteen bars of horn figures (measures 75–81) leading to a climactic entry of the trumpet solo, structured on the repeated progression beginning at measure 71. The horn figures again signal the last sixteen bars of the solo, and the conjunto returns to the coro, interspersed again with inspiraciones by the sonero. The piece ends with a recapitulation of the introductory ensemble section (measures 1–8).

"BIEN SABROSO"

"Bien Sabroso" is a progressive interpretation of the son montuno rhythmic form. In deference to the use of a montuno section in other Afro-Cuban son forms such as the latter guaracha-son type analyzed, son montuno itself as a compositional form entails the adaptation of its rhythmic pattern throughout the context of a complete piece. Superimposed on the motivic base of the son montuno are the elements

FIGURE 9.7 • Piano pattern in "Bien Sabroso".

of instrumental sections, coros, and inspiraciones in a variety of applications. Rhythmically, reverse clave is employed as is standard in son montuno. The essential component, however, is the employment of a son montuno pattern; in the case of "Bien Sabroso," the piano pattern is notated in figure 9.7.

Progressive instrumental sections, as compared with more *típico* (typical) arrangements of son montuno such as those of early son innovator Arsenio Rodríguez, are illustrated by the ensemble orchestration in measures 1 through 8, which comprise the basic head of the composition. A unison instrumental break occurs at measures 32–36, and the use of extended chords is prevalent at measures 39–55. Also, melodic configurations are reminiscent of jazz phrasing and intervallic structures and relationships. Such stylized composition is common in the adaptation of Afro-Cuban rhythms to that of basically instrumental groups similar to Sánchez's octet format on the recording being analyzed.

The verse structure of "Bien Sabroso" consists of a simple unison vocal passage sung over the son montuno riff accordingly (fig. 9.8). Poetically, the verse structure adheres to the scheme of ABCD/ABCE. The text is as follows:

Para tí	For you
Mi son montuno está	My *son montuno* is
Bien sabroso	Really nice
Para bailar.	For dancing.
Para tí	For you
Mi son montuno está	My *son montuno* is
Bien sabroso	Really nice
Para gozar.	For enjoying.

In contrast to "Este Son," coplas are not employed, though the rhyme of the coro-styled verse occurs on the second and fourth lines of each stanza (albeit in an extended sense, adopting the rhyme of *está* and *bailar*). In more exact rhyme are the final words of the two stanzas, bailar and gozar.

Pa-ra ti   mi son mon - tu-no es - tá bien sa-bro- so   pa - ra bai-lar   pa-ra

FIGURE 9.8 • Vocal line (in chorus) of "Bien Sabroso".

THE ROLE OF JAZZ

The predominant influence of jazz in Latin jazz, as documented in the practice of Poncho Sánchez, lies not in the rhythmic or structural form, but more in phrasing and improvisation, specifically in terms of the piano and horns. The percussion section and bass usually conform to the traditional tumbao. Piano and horns vacillate from tumbao, clave, and "Latin" phrasing to instrumental "swing" or jazz riffs, especially when adapting a jazz standard feel to the Latin rhythm and arrangement. Improvised solos are especially the spaces in which instrumentalists venture into the incorporation of significant bop, cool, swing, and progressive jazz concepts influenced by performers from Charlie Parker to Woody Shaw.

The issue of phrasing is an essential link in conceptualizing the relationship of jazz and Afro-Cuban son. During the 1920s, the trumpet became one of the instruments of the early son ensemble in Cuba, and musicologists such as Olaro Alén have speculated that it was the influence of early New Orleans jazz that produced this innovation in the son.[2] On the other hand, early jazz artists such as W. C. Handy and Louis Armstrong were also being exposed to the Cuban son instrumental and improvisatory style. In "Este son," the montuno section solos by pianist Charlie Otwell and trumpeter Steve Huffsteter characterize a bebop influence that can be traced to the melodic/rhythmic syncopation of both the jazz and Afro-Cuban traditions. Thus the influence in solo phrasing has been a mutual one, and can be traced in jazz and son through instrumentalists such as Jelly Roll Morton and Thelonius Monk to Chucho Valdes, and from Louis Armstrong and Dizzy Gillespie to Chocolate Armenteros and Arturo Sandoval.

Interestingly, vocal style, which maintains an Afro-Cuban improvisatory element in the inspiraciones, has rarely (or at least not dominantly) adapted jazz phrasing (although Sánchez has adapted two rhythm and blues standards of James Brown to the Latin format). It should also be pointed out that Sánchez's group, unlike most Latin jazz groups, incorporates a good amount of solo vocals and inspiración. Additionally, the ensemble will at times interpret a typical salsa arrangement for dancing contexts or in club or concert settings.

Also of merit is the question of the Latin element in jazz, which can be traced back to the early creations of Scott Joplin, W. C. Handy, Louis Armstrong, and Duke Ellington's teaming with Juan Tizol. The "Cubop" experiments and success of Dizzy Gillespie and Chano Pozo consolidated the Afro-Cuban impact on jazz in a period and style development that intersected with the inversion of the equation—that of jazz-influenced Afro-Cuban music as personified through contemporary artists of the same era such as Mario Bauzá, Machito, Tito Puente, and Tito Rodríguez. In sum, Afro-Cuban music has "Latinized" jazz, but jazz also "jazzified" Cuban dance music.

In examining the role of Poncho Sánchez in this equation, it is interesting to note some of his own perspective in his own words.

> I play it the way I think it should be done. I'm a purist as far as the Latin jazz music goes, and I don't allow certain things in my band or certain sounds. I don't like loud guitars, rock drummers playing a backbeat to a Latin groove; I don't go for that at all. That's like having a rock drummer playing with a Latin band. That doesn't do a thing for me. I like a timbalero, a conga player, a bongo player, and that's it. I think it should be left alone that way. You always do your own thing, although I definitely follow the lines and the patterns and the roads that Cal Tjader, Mongo Santamaría, Tito Rodríguez, Tito Puente and guys like that have left for us, or have set for us. (Loza 1993:201)

Although claiming the purist philosophy, it is of interest that Sánchez has also accomplished some major innovation—for example, his adaptation of James Brown's R&B, soul/funk music to his Latin jazz format, interpreting with his ensemble and singing lead vocals to tunes such as "Cold Sweat" and "Funky Broadway" (see *A Night at Kimball's East*). Also, unlike many Latin jazz artists, Sánchez also sings both the typical Cuban son style and the traditional bolero, the slow-tempo romantic ballad style also of Cuban origin but highly popular and reinterpreted throughout Latin America. Another feature of Sánchez's style is his phrasing, an essential element to the Latin jazz concept since the innovations of the Machito Orchestra and the Gillespie/Pozo interchange. Sánchez's conga style is as informed by jazz and R&B phrasing as it is by typical Cuban rhythms. In its subtle presence and hybrid energy and form, Sánchez's Latin jazz/R&B equation is a grossly overlooked dimension of his performance style, interpretation, and ensemble.

JAZZ AND THE NEOCLASSIC STYLE

Within the past twenty years, a particular jazz movement or trend has occurred that has been referred to as "neoclassicism." The figure largely associated with spearheading this style has been trumpeter/bandleader

Wynton Marsalis. An interesting critique of this movement is included in Eric Nisenson's *Blue: The Murder of Jazz* (1997). As have a number of contemporary critics, Nisenson cites the music and attitude of Marsalis and the neoclassicists as one characterizing the gradual death of the spontaneous and culturally expressive nature of the jazz tradition. Marsalis, also an interpreter of Western classical music, has emerged as a symbol of both conformity and defiance. His historical place in music is a certainty; his place in jazz, to some, including this writer, is not so certain.

Does Poncho Sánchez represent for Latin jazz what Wynton Marsalis represents (to some) for jazz? I believe the comparison is incompatible. So why do I ask the question? Let me return to the "purist" philosophy of Sánchez that I previously referred to. In many ways it is not so different from Marsalis's musical philosophy of using only acoustic instruments in his ensemble (i.e., piano, string bass) and of reinterpreting a number of jazz standards from the past, in addition to his own compositions. Sánchez likewise refuses to use nontraditional instruments on his recordings and consistently reinterprets both Latin and jazz standards. Both have received major recognition from the mainstream recording industry, although Marsalis's business enterprise is undoubtedly much more lucrative.

But there are also many contrasts—contrasts that are perhaps much more meaningful. Marsalis is based in New York City (although born and raised in New Orleans), the recognized hub of jazz culture. Sánchez, ten years senior to Marsalis, is based in Los Angeles, a cultural hub of a number of Latin American musics (i.e., mariachi, banda), but unlike New York, not the "recognized" hub of "Latin music" (i.e., salsa and Latin jazz). Although both reinterpret jazz standards, Sánchez goes a step further and reinterprets R&B. Marsalis is classically trained; Sánchez only in recent years learned to read music. Marsalis writes his own compositions/arrangements; Sánchez composes tunes in his mind and orally and musically conveys them to his musical directors/pianists (who have included Clare Fischer, Charlie Otwell, and currently David Torres), who then orchestrate the arrangement. Marsalis was raised and trained in a musical family, his father being a renowned jazz pianist. He studied for a period at the Julliard School of Music. Sánchez was raised in a working-class environment where his immigrant parents listened and danced to Mexican music, and his sisters listened and danced to mambo. He learned guitar, vocals, and the conga drums by ear. His formal education never included studies beyond high school.

Can we draw relationships between one's musical, social encultura-tion, and the development of style? It is a hard question, but it is still a good question, for most creative musicians will tell us that music reflects the life and times of the artist making the music. In making comparisons of the musical and social enculturation of Wynton Marsalis and of Poncho Sánchez, I am not attempting to post a "Lomaxian" grid or formula for social/musical relationships;[3] but I am searching for relationships that possibly affect individuals in different ways for different reasons and in different contexts—and that in part can be informed and inspired by one's cultural, social, and psychological environment. Returning to Porter and Gower's concept of transformativity and to the jazz critique written by Nisenson, it might be insightful to reflect on the latter's thoughts as related to Porter and Gower's association of transformativity with qualitative change.

> If I think about what jazz has done for my own life, the one thing I would say is that, besides simply making living more enjoyable, it has given me courage. If the most profound representation of modern European culture is that of waiting hopelessly, and endlessly, for Godot, in this country I know that my life was made meaningful by waiting for Miles Davis's next album. Jazz gave those of us who loved it something to believe in—as a pointer toward community, understanding of self, the nature of compassion, ecstatic awareness and our deepest humanity. Jazz could even, as John Coltrane showed us, help us find the road toward God through looking within. (245)

THE GLOBAL AND THE LOCAL

From the Latin quarters of Los Angeles, where in his earlier days Sánchez performed in clubs and for Mexican weddings (I remember hiring him and his cousins Ramón and Tony Banda to play with my group) to his present international acclaim in Africa, the Americas, Asia, Australia, and Europe, Sánchez represents both the local and the global. He is locally identified as a Chicano and is recognized by Latinos and Angelinos in general as a virtuoso artist and a source of pride. But for many years, he has been and continues to be an individual with a global view. His readiness and ability to transform tradition into newness and freshness lie at the heart of his musicianship and style. His charisma and leadership skills place him in that special breed of musical transformers, of innovators that still manage to understand and respect tradition. It is for these reasons and others that his mentors such as Mongo Santamaría, Cal Tjader, and Tito Puente have looked to him as one of the major links to the present and future of their art form, and as a keeper of the flame.

Part of the global complex, of course, is that of the music industry, international marketing, and the industrial/public sphere of recognition.

This includes not only record sales, but also the formal recognition of the industry, such as the Grammy Awards presented by the National Association of Recording Arts and Sciences (NARAS). Critics have noted that the Grammy Awards, like the Oscars for film, are highly related to commercialism and the market. Nevertheless, such awards have had a profound effect on both artists' issues of integrity and the public perception. With the growing global popularity of Latin jazz, the question as to which category this style generically belongs in the recording industry has been a difficult one. For the past ten years, as a member of the Grammy Award National Screening Committee, I have continually witnessed debate in the Latin categories panel. This centers on the question of which category to assign artists such as Poncho Sánchez, Tito Puente, Eddie Palmieri, Pete Escovedo, Mongo Santamaría, and Jerry González, among many others. As panelists, we even requested that an additional category of "Latin Jazz" be added to the Grammy Awards competition. To the final satisfaction of many in the music industry, such a category was finally approved by NARAS for the 1994 Grammy Award competition, Arturo Sándoval being the first recipient in the new category (included in the general category of jazz).

Regardless of the question involving the formal recognition of Latin jazz, there can be no question as to the major impact that the style has generated among audiences and musicians in the domains of both jazz and Latin music throughout the world in the last five decades. Poncho Sánchez plays a vital role in the progressive integration and remarkable compatibility of these two rich traditions. He symbolizes both the local and the global dimensions of Latin jazz, the Cuban son, and the stylistic, social possibilities that these traditions of regenerative innovation represent.

NOTES

Acknowledgments. I extend my utmost gratitude to Daniel Castro for his complete critique of the article and his highly useful suggestion for the analysis and musical transcriptions. I also thank my research assistants, Jay Keister and Sarah Lee Peterson, for their editorial assistance and graphic formatting.

1. Both Charles Seeger (1997) and Kwabena Nketia (1979) used the term *juncture* in their critiques on the field of ethnomusicology and its relationship to the musical, the social, or to the field of musicology in general.

2. Alén offered this explanation in a public lecture he presented at California State University, Los Angeles, on March 3, 2001.

3. I refer to Alan Lomax's theory and method of his "cantometrics" project. See Lomax 1968.

BIBLIOGRAPHY

Borbolla, Carlos. 1975. "El son exclusividad de Cuba." *Anuario Interamericano de Investigación Musical,* Vol. 2, pp. 152–56.

Lomax, Alan. 1968. *Folk Song Style and Culture*. New Brunswick, N. J.: Transaction.

Loza, Steven J. 1993.*Barrio Rhythm: Mexican American Music in Los Angeles*. Urbana: University of Illinois Press.

Nisenson, Eric. 1997. *Blue: The Murder of Jazz*. New York: St. Martin's Press.

Nketia, Kwabena. 1979. "The Juncture of the Social and the Musical: The Methodology of Cultural Analysis." *World of Music* 23(2):22–35.

Porter, James, and Hershel Gower. 1995. *Jeannie Robertson: Emergent Singer, Transformative Voice*. Knoxville: University of Tennessee Press.

Seegar, Charles. 1977. "The Musicological Juncture: 1976." *Ethnomusicology* 11(2):179–88.

DISCOGRAPHY

Sánchez, Poncho. 1983. *Sonando*. (Concord/Picante CJP-201.)

———. 1984. *Bien Sabroso*. (Concord/Picante CJP-239.)

———. 1991. *A Night at Kimball's East*. (Concord/Picante CJP-472C.)

———. 1999. *Latin Soul*. (Concord/Picante CCD 4863–2.)

Part 3

RELOCATING SALSA

Chapter 10

LLEGÓ LA SALSA: THE RISE OF SALSA IN VENEZUELA AND COLOMBIA

Lise Waxer

first came across a copy of Federico Betancourt's *Llegó la Salsa* in a Caracas record shop. When I initially purchased the album, I was unaware of its significance. With its campy jacket cover depicting affluent young adults dancing what appears to be more like the twist than salsa, the record simply entered my growing collection as another curio. Later, the album's importance became clear. Produced in June 1966, *Llegó la Salsa* (Salsa arrived) was the first salsa recording ever made by a South American salsa band (fig. 10.1). Notably, it is also the first salsa album ever to use the actual term "salsa" in its title (Rondón 1980:33). The title of the release is particularly suggestive, for "llegó la salsa" points not only to the arrival of a new sound, but also to the development of a new social reality that was emerging in both Venezuela and neighboring Colombia. When I later shifted my field research site from Caracas to Cali, I discovered that many salsa fans in Cali had original copies of *Llegó la Salsa* and remembered Federico and his eccentric vocalist, Calavén, with great fondness.

In Venezuela and Colombia, countries distinguished by a wealth of local musical traditions, salsa began to articulate a new, commonly experienced urban reality in a way that individual local styles—each associated with a distinct town or region—could not. Although salsa did not originate on South American soil, it became strongly localized in these countries, a style with deep affective power that Venezuelans and Colombians consider to be "legítimamente *nuestra*, ni más ni menos" (legitimately *ours*, no more, no less) (Rondón 1980:6). By the late 1970s, Caracas had emerged as an international center of salsa per-

219

FIGURE 10.1 • *Llegó la Salsa* (1966). Courtesy of El Palacio de la Música S.A., Venezuela.

formance, production, and consumption, and Venezuelan artists such as Oscar D'León had acquired international stardom. Colombia soon followed, with the city of Cali becoming a so-called "world salsa capital" by the mid-1980s, boasting renowned salsa orquestas such as Grupo Niche and Guayacán. Farther to the north, Barranquilla-based Joe Arroyo also formulated an eclectic style of Colombian salsa that has become internationally popular.

The importance of Venezuela and Colombia as international sites of salsa activity has been given scant recognition in the main body of salsa research, which has concentrated on developments in New York City and Puerto Rico (e.g., Singer 1982; Duany 1984; Boggs 1992). Salsa's development in Caracas and Cali, however, provides a particularly clear illustration of local-global relationships in terms of concrete cultural practices. This history is also recent enough to shed light on the links between local cultural practices and transnational cultural formations that have shaped contemporary urban culture around the globe. Surprising parallels mark the adoption of salsa in both cities. Although distinct in terms of their historical significance—Caracas is a national political and economic capital, while Cali is a regional center that only blossomed into national prominence during the 1980s—salsa music has played a singular role in the popular identity of each city. As case studies, Caracas and Cali each provide a striking template for understanding how urban audiences in Latin America have responded to the increasingly deterritorialized flows of culture and commerce in the twentieth century. The rise of salsa in Caracas and Cali clearly illustrates the conjunctures of popular culture, urbanization, economic growth, and cultural production and reception at several levels: barrio, citywide, national, and hemispheric.

Salsa now boasts an ardent following in Ecuador, Peru, and other South American countries, but Venezuela and Colombia remain the most *salsero* nations on the continent. In the following pages, I focus on Caracas and Cali as two parallel cases in salsa's spread to South America, basing my analysis on a pilot study conducted in Caracas during the summer of 1992 and extensive field research conducted in Colombia from 1994 to 1996.[1] My work in Colombia has concentrated on Cali, despite the importance of other cities in Colombia as sites in salsa's transnational development, particularly Barranquilla and Cartagena. Geographically and culturally, Barranquilla and Caracas share many similarities: they are both tied closely to the Caribbean and have been important economic centers. The reason for concentrating on Cali, however, is related to the singular role that salsa and its roots have played in the development of local popular culture in that city, and the city's subsequent role as a magnet for national and international salsa artists during the 1980s. Despite its location far from the Caribbean, Cali is a more significant center for salsa consumption and performance in Colombia.

URBAN DEVELOPMENT AND WORKING-CLASS COSMOPOLITANISM IN CARACAS AND CALI

The rise of salsa in Caracas and Cali must be seen within the context of socio-economic transformation and hyperurbanization that shaped both of these cities during the twentieth century. In the case of Caracas, this expansion is related to the discovery of huge offshore petroleum reserves in the 1920s, which stimulated economic growth in the Venezuelan capital. Economic growth and urban construction in Caracas spurred migration from rural areas, as well as immigration from other countries in Latin America, the Caribbean, and Europe. By 1958, the urban sector of Venezuela had swelled to nearly 70 percent of the total population, rising to 85 percent by 1988 (Hellinger 1991:75). Although official census figures stake the population of Caracas at a conservative 1 million in 1971, growing to 1.8 million in 1981 and to more than 3 million by the mid-1990s,[2] other sources claim figures that are double or even three times larger: between 4 million and 6 million (Hellinger 1991:5).

Cali, now Colombia's second-largest city after Bogotá, began to mushroom after the 1950s, with a population of nearly 1 million by 1973, and just under 2 million by 1997.[3] Current unofficial estimates place the city's present population at more than 2 million. While spurred in part by the influx of rural migrants fleeing La Violencia (a bloody civil war that lasted from 1948 to 1964), Cali's rapid expansion was based primarily on the growth of the sugar industry, which boomed after the United States ceased trade links with Cuba following the 1959 revolution. The fertile lands surrounding Cali are ideal for sugarcane cultivation, and as the center of the Colombian sugar industry, Cali became an important supplier for the U.S. sugar market during the 1960s and 70s. Another white powdery substance is believed to have been the basis for Cali's second urban explosion during the 1980s, as the Cali cocaine cartel grew in power and began to pump inordinate sums of money into the local economy.

Perhaps the most significant factor in the adoption of salsa and its Cuban and Puerto Rican roots in Caracas and Cali, over and above regional or national musical styles, was the symbolic significance this music had as a transnational, and hence, *cosmopolitan* style. The diffusion of this music coincides with the rapid urban growth of these cities, and their increasingly strong ties to world markets. By "cosmopolitan," I refer to the ways in which increased transportation and communications links, colonialism, mass media, and other channels have helped to spread practices and values around the globe, so that they can no longer be linked to a specific place of origin (Turino 2000). The term is more useful than the Eurocentric notion of Westernization in understanding issues of globalization and modernity.

Especially in the case of Cali, much of the music disseminated on recording was unavailable through local distribution networks. Rather, recordings were introduced by black Caribbean sailors who brought the latest sounds from Cuba, Puerto Rico, and New York to sell at their ports of call, or to accompany their jaunts to local bars and brothels. The role of these sailors in helping to forge the cosmopolitan sensibility surrounding the local consumption of salsa and its Afro-Cuban and Puerto Rican antecedents cannot be overestimated. Although certainly not from the elite socioeconomic ranks of those usually considered to be "cosmopolitan," sailors have shared a similar position of moving between different cultural spheres and locations. By the very nature of their work, they have been central to processes of commodification, commerce, and the movement of international capital that has shaped contemporary globalization and cosmopolitan technologies. Connected to multiple localities and distinguished through particular codes of dress, physical bearing, talk, musical taste, and manner of dancing— themselves adapted and resignified from other cosmopolitan styles— sailors transmitted an alternative "working-class" cosmopolitanism to urban, working-class black and *mestizo* (mixed-race) Venezuelans and Colombians. While economic growth and technological developments were tying these people to international markets and cultural flows, they were blocked for reasons of socioeconomic status, ethnicity, and lack of resources from accessing the elite spheres of cosmopolitan culture. Salsa and its roots became accessible signifiers for worldliness, adopted from sailors. As such, they became central expressions of urban working-class identity, a sensibility that was simultaneously local but also connected to the larger world.

The cosmopolitan meanings ascribed to recordings had a particularly strong impact on the development of local urban sensibilities and cultural practices. Recordings acquired great value among members of the Caracas and Cali working class during the 1960s and '70s, in part because of their ties with the sailors who brought them. Being relatively expensive investments for people who barely earned enough to pay for basic necessities, they acquired status as symbolic capital. The difficulty of obtaining recent albums further heightened their desirability as luxury items. In the case of Cali, for instance, dealers and record collectors had to travel six hours to the port of Buenaventura in order to purchase the latest records.[4] Venezuelan fans had to rely on friends visiting Barranquilla and Cartagena in order to get the most recent sounds, since salsa records from New York and Puerto Rico usually arrived on Colombian shores months before they got to Caracas.[5]

Most importantly, the new sounds contained within these acetate grooves emerged as a sort of musical lingua franca for burgeoning working-class communities in which migrants from distinct regions of Venezuela and Colombia poured into Caracas and Cali, seeking a better way of life (Rondón 1980; Baéz 1989; Ulloa 1992). Some migrant communities maintained regional traditions, but none of these styles was capable of representing the diverse and rapidly shifting urban environment as a whole. Salsa and its antecedents, hence, were adopted as representative styles of the new urban and cosmopolitan context of the city.

Indeed, even when groups such as Madera (Caracas) and Bahia (Cali) have gained strong recognition for their performance of Afro-Venezuelan and Afro-Colombian traditions, these sounds have been fused with elements of salsa in order to give them a more polished, urban sound.[6] Betancourt's album *Llegó la Salsa* hence became a metonym for the profound transformations in urban life and social identity that shaped Caracas and Cali during the 1960s and '70s.

SALSA IN CARACAS

In *El vínculo es la Salsa* (1989), the only book-length social history of salsa in Venezuela, Juan Carlos Baéz divides the rise of salsa in the country into three periods: (1) the initial phase, 1962–1968; (2) its decline and resurgence between 1968 and the mid-1970s; and (3) its maturation and internationalization from the mid-1970s to the early 1980s, when he concluded his research. I follow Baéz's framework, adding a fourth period, from the mid-1980s to present; this brings Baéz's trajectory up to date, and also covers the transnational revitalization of salsa with the commercial *romántica* style promoted in the late 1980s. As with any historiography sensitive to the ebb and flow of cultural practice, these periods overlap in terms of stylistic developments, and should not be seen as rigid codifications.

From 1962 to 1968

Salsa's early formation in Caracas has its roots in the local popularization of Cuban *son* beginning in the late 1920s. Cuban music, through recordings and films, enjoyed a large following throughout Latin America and the Caribbean. The commercial spread of Cuban music linked Caraqueños to the burgeoning transnational communications industry through which salsa was later diffused. More important, however, it established a social identification with the Afro-Hispanic Caribbean, underscoring the city's close geographic proximity to Venezuela's Caribbean coast. This was articulated not only in the rhythms and lyrics of son, but also in the racially mixed constitution of most Cuban bands. Through the 1930s to to 1950s, Cuban son *conjuntos* (combos) and dance orchestras toured regularly to Caracas, and their music was enjoyed by working-class Caraqueños via records, radio, and film.

Through the 1960s and '70s, salsa became increasingly prominent among the large Caraqueño working class. Salsa fans in Caracas shared many socioeconomic conditions with salsa's progenitors in New York City: crowded living conditions, poverty, unemployment, urban crime, race/class discrimination, and so forth. Predominantly young, of African and mestizo heritage, the Caraqueño aficionados of salsa found something in the New York sound that resonated with their own experience. Unlike its Cuban prototypes, salsa is identified with the street, with life in the urban barrio. Aggressive lyrics, rugged trombones, and heavy percussion became sonic indices for the accelerated pace and harsh edges of city life.[7]

In 1962, Radio Difusora began broadcasting a midday radio show featuring the latest New York hits by artists such as Tito Puente and Eddie Palmieri. Called *La Hora del Sabor, la Salsa y el Bembé*[8] (Rondón 1980:33), some pinpoint this radio program as one of the first cases in which the term "salsa" was ever used as a stylistic label. As in New York City, salsa was primarily youth music. *Bugalú* (boogaloo) a commercially oriented fusion of salsa and African-American rhythm and blues (see Flores, this volume), was quite popular between 1967 and 1969— indeed, audiences still respond with delight whenever a band renders its version of Joe Cuba's "Así se Goza (I'll Never Go Back to Georgia)." During this period, local salsa bands emerged. Among the better known were Federico y su Combo (Betancourt's group), Los Dementes, and Sexteto Juventud. Most of these groups performed cover versions of hits by New York artists, older Cuban classics and originals in straight-ahead Cuban *guaracha* and son rhythms, and tunes in the new booga-loo style. The influence of North American 1960s youth culture prevailed: for example, Federico's *Llegó la Salsa* was followed by an album titled *Psicodélico con Salsa* (Psychedelic with salsa).

Through the late 1960s, salsa remained largely a working-class musical expression in Caracas. While working-class Caracas youth enjoyed salsa, middle- and upper-class teenagers listened to British–North American rock styles.[9] Looked down upon by many of the city's middle and upper class denizens, salsa was perjoratively referred to as *música de malandros* or *música de monos* (music of lowlifes or music of apes). Such labels highlight the manner in which class and race in Caracas have usually been collapsed within the official Venezuelan ideology of racial democracy and *mestizaje* (cultural mixing). Though the liner notes to *Llegó la Salsa* merely assert that the public wasn't ready for the "modernist tropical sound" promoted by Federico and his contemporaries, the underlying reality pointed to the refusal of middle- and upper-class defenders of "public taste" to admit music of African origins into the dominant cultural purview. Salsa was denigrated not only because it was lower class but because of its unmistakable associations with Afro-Caribbean culture and the full or partial African heritage of many salsa fans and musicians.[10]

1968 to the mid–1970s

In the mid-1970s, salsa began to move out of the working-class sectors of Caracas into the middle class, primarily through contacts made with leftist intellectuals at the Universidad Central de Venezuela and other circles where working- and middle-class intellectuals found common ground on political and social issues. As an emblem of urban working-class popular culture, salsa was adopted by middle-class intellectuals as an "authentic sound of the people" and a vehicle of "pan-Latino identity" that crossed geopolitical boundaries in Latin America (see Rondón 1980). The social messages of much 1970s New York salsa (e.g., Willie Colón, Rubén Blades, Ray Barretto) underscored this ideological position. A similar process happened during this time in Cali and in other Colombian cities.

Although local salsa suffered a brief decline in the early 1970s owing to the commercial incursions of Venezuelan rock music, it resurfaced in 1974 when the Fania All-Stars gave its first performance in Venezuela. Comprising some of salsa's foremost artists, this band was considered to be the apex of the New York sound, and its visit had a great impact. The concert's success encouraged the formation of several new bands in Caracas. Previously undistinguished local groups such as Dimensión Latina began to acquire a widespread public profile. Caracas began to establish a reputation as an important site in the transnational salsa scene, holding international salsa festivals at the geodesic-domed Poliedro Theater that not only brought together the top performers of New York and Puerto Rico, but also highlighted Venezuelan talent.[11] Most important, salsa was recognized as a commercially viable product by the Venezuelan music industry, and the local market was opened to the New York–based Fania label, which by that time had established a virtual monopoly on salsa production in the North (Baéz 1989:83). The impact of the Fania All-Stars' visit to Caracas is a particularly clear example of the ways in which transnational and local music scenes have been intertwined in salsa's development.

In Caracas, Dimensión Latina played a significant role in the transformation of salsa from an expression of the barrio population to a widespread urban musical form. Its founders, among them vocalist/bass player Oscar D'León grew up in the city's west end. According to Rondón, D'León drove a *por puesto* minibus on the route that trombonist José Antonio Rojas took to work. Listening to salsa cassettes every day in the bus, they would try to figure out the polyrhythms of the music and tap along. From this came their inspiration to form a salsa group, during 1972–73 (1980:229). The sound of the group, with only two trombones and no trumpets, was clearly modeled after the New York barrio sound of Willie Colón and Héctor Lavoe (see Valentín, this volume). The early *malandro* (lowlife) image of the group—album covers depict members in dark glasses, long sideburns, patterned shirts, and flared pants—was also influenced by Colón and Lavoe. The name of the band, "Latin Dimension," also followed the New York term *latino* (ethnic Latin American), which had pan–Latin American connotations particular to the melting pot environment of that city. The concept of latino had little meaning in Latin American countries, where specific nationalities defined social identity—but, as Rondón points out, the influence of New York salsa as a transnational style was key in the emergence of a pan-Latino identity in Venezuela (1980: 229). Dimensión Latina's first international hit came in 1975 with "Llororás" (You will cry), which remains a classic today. The band promoted itself throughout the city, not only through recordings and television and radio appearances, but also by performing at hotels, discotheques, bullfights, and baseball games (Baéz 1989:120). During this period, the band also performed for parties and dances in the middle- and even upper-middle-class sector, a position enjoyed previously only by Billo's Caracas Boys and Los Mélodicos—groups that played the cumbia-based style of Colombian *música tropical* and were considered by salsa fans to be *gallega* [literally, "Galician" or white Spanish, i.e., corny, old-fashioned). Subsequently, other local salsa groups began to perform for middle-class audiences.

Mid-1970s to Early 1980s

Through the mid-1970s, Venezuelan salsa bands were strongly influenced by New York and Puerto Rican bands. As salsa became more firmly entrenched in Caraqueño popular life, however, local bands began incorporating national and regional musical traditions. Some attempts, such as the salsa-*joropo* hybrids of Dimensión Latina, were dismal flops. Others, especially those fusing salsa with Afro-Venezuelan styles from the Barlovento region east of Caracas, enjoyed some success. "El cumaco de San Juan," performed both by Grupo Mango and El Trabuco Venezolano, is based on a Barlovento song that is traditionally accompanied by *culo e' puya* drums.[12] "El muñeco de la ciudad," in a 1980 arrangement by El Trabuco Venezolano, fuses *merengue caraqueño* with salsa percussion and elements of jazz, incorporating these cosmopolitan traditions in an attempt to create a truly Venezuelan urban sound. Alberto Naranjo, the leader of El Trabuco, insists that his project was never to reproduce the salsa sound, but rather to experiment with a number of urban musical traditions and thereby extend the trajectory of salsa-based musical styles.[13] "El muñeco de la ciudad" was later popularized on the international circuit as a straight-ahead *salsa dura* (hard/heavy salsa) number by Puerto Rican bassist Bobby Valentín.[14]

In turn, some traditional music groups began to "salsafy" their sound. Un Solo Pueblo, for example, added brass and electric bass to its ensemble in the 1980s, incorporating salsa-like horn lines into its arrangements. In Maracaibo, to the west of the country, the musical group Guaco transferred the Afro-Venezuelan *gaita* to a salsa-type ensemble—brass, piano, bass, percussion—and added salsa horn lines, piano *montunos,* and salsa-style arrangements to its sound (see Berríos-Miranda, chapter 2). After relocating to Caracas, Guaco incorporated cosmopolitan urban styles prevalent in Caracas, such as rock, pop, funk, and jazz, but its sound through the late 1980s and '90s retained the central fusion of traditional Afro-Venezuelan rhythms with salsa-based elements.

Through the late 1970s, salsa bands blossomed in the working- and middle-class sectors of Caracas. In addition to Dimensión Latina, important groups include Grupo Mango, whose vibraphone-based sound was inspired by 1960s boogaloo star Joe Cuba. The lead singer of this group, Joe Ruíz, was hailed as the country's greatest *sonero* (improvisatory vocalist), whose vocal range and skill at inventing *pregones* (sung improvisations in the vocal call-and-response section of Cuban music and salsa) were compared to the great Cuban and Puerto Rican soneros of the 1940s and '50s.[15] Another successful salsa orchestra was La Nueva Salsa Mayor, which had a dynamic rhythmic drive and polished trumpet-and-trombone horn section that ranked with the best New York and Puerto Rican bands. Older bands such as Federico y su Combo, Los Dementes, and Los Satelites also gained a new lease on life, finding work in the several new clubs, restaurants and salons that opened their doors to salsa (Rondón 1980:238). During this same period, a traditional Cuban-style conjunto called Sonero Clásico del Caribe emerged, reviving the classic 1940s and '50s Cuban *son* that predated salsa's popularity in the city. The name of the group reaffirmed a strong identity with the Spanish Caribbean and with the Cuban roots of salsa. Among the group's members was percussion maker Carlos Landaeta (known as "Pan con Queso" [bread and cheese]), whose congas, bongos, and cowbells were sought after by visiting New York and Puerto Rican salsa musicians.[16]

Generally, Venezuelan salsa groups of this period were distinguished by a preference for many trombones in the brass section, and a tight rhythmic swing similar to that of New York and Puerto Rican salsa bands, where the beat feels like it is propelled from behind. Although Venezuelan salsa arrangements from the 1960s and early 1970s were relatively simple, by the late 1970s charts by local salsa composers and arrangers rivaled—and in some cases surpassed—their New York and Puerto Rican counterparts in terms of complexity, harmonic color, textural shifts, melodic lines, polyphonic arrangements, orchestral breaks, and overall execution. Jazz-influenced instrumental solos also came to characterize the best Caracas bands, following the sound of New York bands such as Ray Barretto and Eddie Palmieri, or Puerto Rico's La Sonora Ponceña. Grupo Mango's recordings from the late 1970s, for instance, are filled with some of the most interesting musical ideas and playing in the international salsa scene of the time, with brilliant salsa/jazz vibraphone solos by Freddy Roldán and virtuosic timbales riffs by Cheo Navarro. Given the position of Caracas as a vibrant center of cosmopolitan culture, with some of the best schools for formal musical training in Latin America, it seems only natural that as salsa's local popularity grew, highly skilled musicians and arrangers allied themselves with this new idiom. Grounding the international influences in Venezuelan salsa, however, were the frequent references to Caracas barrios and other Venezuelan towns in local salsa lyrics, and also the use of Venezuelan slang expressions.

Following the model of 1940s and '50s Cuban dance orchestras and mambo bands, Venezuelan groups of the 1970s tended to place more emphasis on uniforms or costumes than did their New York counterparts. Tight choreography also received prominent attention, influenced by Puerto Rico's El Gran Combo.[17] Rondón reports that when Dimensión Latina first performed in New York City in 1978, audiences were greatly impressed by the slick routines of the band (1980:232). Anyone who has seen Oscar D'León can testify to the importance of stage presentation for his group—indeed, good choreography and stylish uniforms are now the norm for most salsa bands, and top groups from San Juan to Cali pay close attention to these aspects of performance.

On the international stage, Venezuela emerged as the principal center for salsa production and reception. The country's petroleum reserves not only provided steady foreign income (by this time Venezuela was a member of OPEC), but also the raw material with which to manufacture vinyl records, resulting in a flourishing music industry. Combined with Mexican production, Venezuela's industry usurped New York's control, via Fania Records, over the Latin American popular record market (Manuel 1991:109). According to Rondón, salsa sales in Venezuela alone tripled those of New York and the Caribbean combined (1980:227). In 1977, the monthly salsa magazine *Swing Latino* commenced publication in Caracas. Enjoying a run of three years, *Swing Latino* was the primary transnational print vehicle for salsa in the late 1970s.

By the late 1970s, Caracas was a regular spot on the touring circuit of international salsa performers such as Willie Colón, Celia Cruz, and Johnny Pacheco, with a local scene powerful enough to make or break careers. The regrouping of Los Hermanos Lebrón (the Lebrón Brothers) after its Caracas performance in 1981, for example, highlights the influential status of Caracas in the transnational salsa scene. The Lebrón Brothers was an early 1970s salsa band, based in New York, that was heavily influenced by the "bad boy" sound established by Willie Colón and Héctor Lavoe. In Caracas the group was enormously popular, owing in part to the extensive airplay of its songs by radio deejay Héctor Castillo.[18] In 1981, when Castillo contacted the Lebrón Brothers to do a concert in Caracas, he discovered that it had disbanded owing to lack of success up north. He persuaded band members to regroup for the concert, where they were overwhelmed by the enthusiastic reception of thousands of fans—apparently they had no idea they were so popular in Caracas. Their sold-out performance, one of the biggest salsa concerts ever held in Caracas, had as many people outside the hall as inside (Baéz 1989:217). As a result of this concert, the Lebrón Brothers regrouped again. Ironically, mirroring the way in which Cali replaced Caracas as the South American salsa capital, in 1989 the Lebrón Brothers was brought to Cali, allegedly via the patronage of a local drug baron, and band members ended up living there through the early 1990s.

Despite the spread of salsa across class boundaries, and Venezuela's prominence in the transnational salsa scene, salsa did not lose its street identity. From 1977 through 1980, a loosely organized movement called La Descarga de los Barrios was formed, performing salsa for free in the barrio streets. These presentations were primarily jam sessions[19] that brought together Venezuela's best salsa musicians as well as artists from abroad and provided an alternative outlet for salsa performance, as the record industry fell under increasingly rigid corporate control. As a cultural phenomenon, the Descarga de los Barrios illuminates the tension between local musical practice and transnational cultural commodification that constitute the arena in which salsa musical culture has emerged. Furthermore, it points to the contradictions between salsa's barrio origins, the affective power of its roots in street culture, and the reality of corporate control by the record industry (see Wallis and Malm 1984).

Social distinctions began to be marked through dance styles. Musicians told me that they could tell, from onstage, which barrio someone came from by the way he danced; the difference between the working and middle classes was fairly marked, but stylistic differences also existed among all the working-class barrios.[20] Such contrasts suggest that dancing to salsa was a way, virtually, to tell someone "where you were from." Thus, at the same moment that salsa was consolidating its trajectory as a hemispheric, pan-Latino musical expression, individuals were adapting salsa dance aesthetics to mark discrete social identities.

Mid-1980s to Present

During the mid-1980s, many Venezuelans abandoned salsa for the Dominican *merengue* craze that swept through Latin America (see Austerlitz 1997). The emergence of Puerto Rican *salsa romántica* in the late 1980s as a commercial response to merengue's popularity helped revive the flagging international salsa market, and this style competed with merengue for dominance of Venezuelan airwaves and record production. The late 1980s also witnessed the consolidation of corporate control over popular music interests in Venezuela, with the country's principal salsa labels, Rodven and Sonográfica, owned by the largest television and radio stations: Venevisión and Radio Caracas, respectively. Venevisión also owns the rights to Pepsi-Cola production in Venezuela, and bought out the Fania record label. The owners of Radio Caracas, on the other hand, own the city's largest central shopping mall, hence controlling what is sold in record stores inside.[21]

Instead of another Descarga de los Barrios, the response to such control in the early 1990s was the proliferation of street vendors selling pirated salsa cassettes. Indeed, with Venezuela's downward economic slide through the 1980s and early 1990s, the barrio streets became too dangerous for outdoor performances, although one musician, Gerardo Rosales, attempted to revive this ambience by performing municipally funded outdoor afternoon concerts in the city center during the summer of 1992. Salsa bands performed in sophisticated nightclubs in the eastern half of Caracas, which only the middle and upper classes could afford. The older venues in working class areas closed, owing to the dangers of mugging and holdups after dark. Whether such a shift in salsa's musical landscape has resulted in a fundamental transformation of the meanings and affective associations of salsa for Caraqueños remains an open question. Although the hub of transnational salsa had shifted to Cali by the mid-1980s, salsa was still an important part of daily life in Caracas in the 1990s. It could be heard everywhere, pouring out of radios, buses, corner stores. Salsa's barrio street identity continued to be a strong icon for Caraqueños, although it was nearly impossible to hear live performances of salsa in those streets.

SALSA IN CALI
Pre-1960s Roots

As in the case of Caracas, the Caleño passion for salsa has its roots in the popularization of Cuban son in Colombia in the 1920s. Recordings of Cuban music first appeared in Cali during the 1930s, introduced by black Caribbean merchant sailors, called *chombos*, who were docked at the nearby Pacific Coast seaport of Buenaventura. Cuban and Puerto

Rican sounds, referred to in Colombia as *música antillana* (music of the Spanish Antilles), caught on in the Buenaventura bars and brothels frequented by black Caribbean sailors. The sailors also introduced the dance style that went with this music (see Arias, chapter 11). The music and dance style also spread inland to Cali. Between the 1930s and the 1950s, the Zona de Tolerancia in Cali, a twenty-five block zone officially sanctioned for prostitution, became a hotbed for the reception of Afro-Cuban and Puerto Rican genres. Reinforcing the growing influence of recordings in local musical life were movie musicals from Cuba, Mexico, and Hollywood. While acetate recordings provided a key source of music, their celluloid counterparts played a critical role in providing images and models for dancing.

From Cali's red-light district, dancing spread to neighborhood parties during the 1940s and '50s. Key among these were informal weekend gatherings at which men would listen to 78 rpm records of música antillana, drink beer, and argue about their favorite soccer teams. As their wives and daughters finished household chores, they would join the gathering, and the soccer debates would shift to dancing.[22] Of particular significance is the way in which the boundaries between domestic and public spheres (house/street) in these working-class neighborhoods became blurred within the context of friendly social activity, hence reinforcing a sense of social collectivity and community that could be called upon in times of need. Through the 1950s and '60s, such gatherings gave rise to special neighborhood dance parties in Cali's newer barrios, held to raise funds for projects such as building a local school or church, or paving streets and sidewalks (Ulloa 1986:46). As an important point in the weekly cycle of work and leisure among Cali's working classes, dancing and listening to música antillana were not merely a routine way to pass time. Rather, they became cultural rituals in which recordings of Cuban and Puerto Rican music were intertwined with other important elements of local cultural practice—dance, drink, sport, and conversation—to establish and strengthen social ties.

1960s and '70s

The centrality of recorded music for Caleños challenges the privileging, in most scholarly work, of live performance as more "real" or "authentic" than its mediated versions. While recordings and other media are known to have contributed to new musical hybrids and identities around the globe (Lipsitz 1994; Taylor 1997), recent research suggests that the appropriation of such technology to local music practice and creativity is an area needing more attention than it has conventionally received (Manuel 1993; Mitsui and Hosokawa 1998; Kenney 1999). In contrast to Caracas, where live salsa bands emerged during the 1960s and blossomed during the late 1970s, Cali's local live scene remained dormant. During these two decades, local salsa activity centered on dancing to records of Cuban, New York, and Puerto Rican groups. Instead of taking up instruments and imitating the sounds they heard on records, Caleños poured their creative energies into dancing, using recordings as the primary source for musical sound. Owing to the significance of records as cultural objects whose local meaning and value extended far beyond the catchy rhythms in its grooves, not until the 1980s did Caleños actually witness the development of a significant live performance scene. The lack of resources for formal music training (the local music conservatory was geared toward the city elites) and the relatively high cost of obtaining music instruments contributed to this.

Through the 1960s, nightclubs (called *griles)* that specialized in música antillana opened up along the main road connecting the docks on the Cauca River to the railway station in town. The popular activity of dancing to recorded music shifted from neighborhood house parties to these clubs. The music featured in these establishments included recordings of 1950s Cuban son, guaracha, bolero, and mambo, as well as the newer rhythms of *pachanga* and boogaloo that began to emanate from New York City. At the same time, teenagers—barred from the nightclubs because of their youth—established their own public dance spaces, called *agüelulos*. Alcohol was not served at these events, and the dances were usually held on Sundays from 2 P.M. to 8 or 9 P.M. The name agüelulo derives from *agua 'e lulo,* or *lulo* fruit juice (made from an acidic fruit native to the region), but soda pop tended to be the main beverage provided at these dances, not juice. Attracting teenagers from throughout the city, the dances moved from barrio to barrio every weekend, and news of upcoming agüelulos spread by word of mouth. The youngsters who frequented agüelulos were called *agüeluleros,* or, since Coca-Cola was the main refreshment, *cokacolos.*[23] The agüelulos had become an important site for youth subculture by the late 1960s, where youngsters vied for prestige on the dance floor (Arteaga 1990:109). Through displays of physical stamina and competition for the most inventive dance variations, Caleño teenagers created their own public spaces, creating a fervor for dancing to salsa records that spread throughout local popular culture (see Waxer 1999 and 2001).

During the 1960s and '70s, Caleños developed a unique style of dancing, characterized by a rapid, "double-time" shuffle on the tips of the toes (fig. 10.2), combined with high kicks and rapid footwork. In Colombia, this idiosyncratic local style is still known as the *el paso caleño* (the Cali dance step). It is distinct from the way that salsa is

FIGURE 10.2 • Caleño salsa dancer. Photo by Lise Waxer.

danced in the rest of Latin America (and in other parts of Colombia, for that matter), where the basic "short-short-long" step derived from Cuban son is the norm. Caleño salsa dancing was a hybrid of elements from Cuban guaracha and mambo, along with North American popular dances such as jitterbug, twist, and Charleston. A unique fusion of these forms was introduced into Buenaventura by the chombos (sailors), and spread to Cali by influential local dancer Watussi (Hernández Vidal 1992:37).[24] As in the case of Caracas, distinctive styles of dance emerged in different working-class barrios, literally marking where one was from. These styles are still practiced in small barrio clubs.[25]

Fast dance tempos became key for Caleño dancers. The upbeat pachanga was ideal for this, but other rhythms were felt to be too slow—especially boogaloo. In a creative use of media technology, Caleño youth began playing their 33 rpm boogaloo recordings at 45 rpm![26] By the late 1960s, the practice of speeding up records had been adopted by deejays in the griles, becoming entrenched as a unique feature in Cali's dance scene. Indeed, when New York superstars Richie Ray and Bobby Cruz performed in Cali at the 1968 December *Feria* (carnival), they met with requests to speed up the tempo of their boogaloo numbers in compliance with local practice.[27]

Through the late 1960s and into the 1970s, dance competitions became a regular feature at many griles, which spurred dancers to further refine their moves and to invent new steps. The winners of such events usually received little more than a free bottle of *aguardiente* ("fire water," i.e., cane liquor) although some also received cash prizes,[28] but dancers competed mainly for enjoyment and social prestige (Ulloa 1992:411). Salsa floor shows also emerged in the early 1970s, with such groups as the Ballet de la Salsa performing choreographed salsa dance routines. During this same period, in a process similar to that occurring in Caracas, middle-class leftist intellectuals became attracted to salsa through contacts made with working-class friends at the local universities. Although most of the salsa dancers participating in competitions were from the working class, young middle-class Caleños also began participating in Cali's vibrant dance culture.

The local sphere of competitive salsa dancing reached its peak in the mid-1970s with the Campeonato Mundial de la Salsa (World salsa dance championship) held in 1974 and 1975. A grand prize of 100,000 Colombian pesos (equivalent to roughly U.S. $15,000) was awarded, making this a coveted local competition. Although nearly all the contestants were actually from Cali and no international dancers participated, these "world" dance competitions served as public spectacles that not only reinforced salsa's prominence in local popular life, but also underscored the cosmopolitan sensibility that was linked to salsa and música antillana. Dancing to salsa, in other words, became the expressive mode through which Caleños conceived of and projected their own position in the world at large. By the late 1970s Caleños proclaimed their city to be the "world capital of salsa." The significance of this claim lies not so much in whether it was true, but rather in Caleños' conviction that they were more passionate about salsa than anyone else on the planet. The emotional investment with which Caleños defined themselves as world-class salsa fans constituted a move to stake their position on the international popular cultural map.

1980s and 1990s

During the 1980s, the local record-centered dance scene declined. The teen agüelulos had ended in the early 1970s, and the nightclub scene shifted toward the growing class of new rich, associated with the rise of the Cali cocaine cartel. This period witnessed a new period of urbanization in Cali, marked by the rapid construction of luxury condominiums, shopping centers, and residential villages. The tendency toward material display and high spending in the new salsa nightclubs led to economic inflation throughout the local scene. As in Caracas, nightclubs in working-class neighborhoods folded in part because people did not want to be on the increasingly violent streets after dark.

As a result of the city's economic transformation, Cali's live salsa scene flourished, catapulting the city to fame as an important new site in international salsa, and consolidating its self-image as the "world capital of salsa." Local live salsa was galvanized by the appearance of the Fania All-Stars in 1980, who, in a process similar to that occurring after their Caracas debut in 1974, inspired younger musicians to take up instruments and perform. After this, international salsa bands were brought to the city on a regular basis. The late Larry Landa, a Robin Hood–like empresario said to have been involved in cocaine trafficking, was a key figure in this process. The marathon Festival de Orquestas, created in 1980 as part of the annual December Feria, became another showcase for international and local salsa bands. There was a constant demand for live salsa in the luxury nightclubs that appeared on the scene, and in lavish parties held at private mansions and country estates. Cartel bosses are said to have patronized local salsa bands, sponsored the formation of new groups, and provided instruments and uniforms. During this same period, new institutions opened that provided affordable music training for the working and lower middle classes, also contributing strongly to the growing pool of local musicians.[29] Between 1980 and 1990, the number of local salsa bands mushroomed, from only ten to almost seventy (see Waxer 1998). Even local businesses formed amateur salsa bands among their workers—the band formed by the municipal light and telephone company was particularly popular. The local army battalion also formed a salsa band, which performed in military fatigues. Just as Caleños had taken salsa dancing up with great fervor in the 1960s and '70s, so did they turn to salsa performance in the 1980s and early '90s.

Although most of these groups never gained any artistic distinction, two Caleño bands did achieve international prominence: Grupo Niche and Guayacán. Founded by two Afro-Colombian musicians born in Quibdó, the capital of Chocó province, Niche and Guayacán developed a distinct Colombian salsa that fused elements from Pacific Coast Afro-Colombian music with international salsa styles. Though Niche abandoned this sound for a more polished transnational style in the late 1980s, followed by Guayacán in the early 1990s, the early contributions of these orchestras were seminal in defining a new Colombian school of salsa. The only other Colombian artist to have made a comparable mark on the international scene is Barranquilla-based Joe Arroyo, who has forged a unique pan-Caribbean sound by fusing salsa with other Afro-Caribbean styles heard on Colombia's Atlantic Coast, such as cumbia, Dominican merengue, Trinidadian *soca*, and Martiniquen *zouk*.

When I asked local musicians, composers and arrangers, "What makes Colombian salsa sound 'Colombian'?" the unequivocal response from most was "su sencillez" (its simplicity). While New York, Puerto Rican, and Venezuelan bands are characterized by a driving percussive force and dynamic, complex arrangements, Colombian salsa owes much of its appeal to catchy melodies, piquant lyrics, and short, uncomplicated horn lines—elements that derive from cumbia, *currulao*, and other Colombian genres. As I discuss elsewhere in greater depth (Waxer 2000), the Caleño sound is characterized by a light texture, a crisp percussive attack, and an on-the-beat rhythmic feel. Interestingly, this manner of rhythmic phrasing is similar to the way most Colombians dance the basic salsa step, in contrast to Puerto Rican, New York, and Cuban dancers, who tend to step just slightly behind the beat. The heavy groove of New York, Puerto Rican, and Venezuelan salsa, as opposed to the sprightliness of Colombian salsa, is a central distinction between these different schools. During the late 1980s, several top Venezuelan salsa musicians relocated to Cali, including trombonist, producer, and composer-arranger Cesar Monge, a founder of Dimensión Latina, and pianist-arranger Felix Shakaito, founder of Los Bronco. Monge was contracted by Grupo Niche to tighten its arrangements, and he has played a critical role in the formation of younger Caleño musicians and arrangers since his arrival in Cali.

It is notable that the style of salsa performed by new local bands during this period was not 1960s/70s salsa dura, but salsa romántica. Following transnational commercial trends, local radio stations and luxury nightclubs also played salsa romántica instead of the classic sounds. In contrast to classic salsa, which had been strongly tied to the working class and to leftist university students in Puerto Rico, Venezuela, and Colombia, salsa romántica was marketed throughout Latin America as a glamorous product for the middle classes. Following this international vogue, much of the Caleño audience for this new style hailed from the city's growing new rich and from its Caleño middle-class youth.

In reaction to the live scene, diehard fans of the classic 1960s/70s sound established their own terrain. Record collectors opened small specialty bars called *salsotecas* or *tabernas,* where aficionados could gather to drink beer and listen to recordings of classic salsa and its Cuban and Puerto Rican antecedents (see Waxer 1999). Although there was virtually no room for dancing in these establishments, the salsotecas and tabernas flourished. Formed in part as an alternative to the flashy excess of the new live scene, Cali's salsotecas became an important "rearguard" in local popular culture, preserving and maintaining the sounds that had been popular in the earlier record-centered dance scene. Listening to records became an important new practice in local popular culture, and new codes of expertise replaced the earlier emphasis on virtuoso dancing, such as learning as many facts as you could about artists, recording dates, and stylistic developments, showing off records in your own collection, and so forth. Salsoteca and taberna disc jockeys emerged as metamusicians whose ear for selecting and mixing good salsa tunes paralleled the technical and expressive skills of actual musicians. Closely tied to this scene was the emergence of the subcultural *movimiento guatequero*[30] among working-class black and mixed-race male youth in the early 1990s. The rugged, inner-city sound of early 1970s New York salsa was favored by the *guatequeros,* where songs by Willie Colón and Hector Lavoe, the Lebrón Brothers, Orquesta Dicupé, and Frankie Dante y La Flamboyan, among others, were upheld by a second generation of salsa dura fans. Although recorded when some of these youngsters were barely born, these tunes of nitty-gritty barrio life resonated strongly with their own experiences of disenfranchisement in conditions that had not changed significantly from the time of their parents (see Waxer 1998:246–52).

Through the 1980s and '90s, the salsotecas and luxury nightclubs emerged as parallel salsa zones in Cali. With few exceptions, their physical location and the style of music they played mapped onto the socioeconomic stratification of Cali's neighborhoods. Luxury nightclubs featuring salsa romántica prevailed in middle- and upper-middle-class neighborhoods, while salsotecas and tabernas were concentrated in the working-class barrios. This dual salsa culture is unique in Latin America.

The fall of the Cali cartel in 1995 spurred a striking revival of the 1960s/70s record-centered dance scene. In clubs called *viejotecas* ("old-theques"), Caleños reaffirmed the sounds and moves that had accompanied the city's flowering into a major urban center (see Waxer 2001). The viejoteca revival can be seen as a grassroots response to the upheavals caused by the Cali cartel. In contrast to most cultural revivals, which tend to be romanticized middle-class appropriations of working-class expressions (Livingston 1999), the viejotecas are primarily working class, established by and for the populace who developed the record-centered dance culture in the first place. The economic boom associated with the cartel not only transformed the local scene—it opened the city to new cultural flows that threatened to displace the established image of Cali as a "salsa capital." The viejotecas, hence, mark a seizing back of local popular culture at the moment when the cartel's hold on the city was broken, before other factions that had entered as a result of the cartel's influence were able to dislodge salsa's primacy.

POPULAR CULTURE AND SALSA IN LATIN AMERICA

The cases of Caracas and Cali serve as clear illustrations of the process through which salsa performance, production, and reception have emerged in an arena framed by the interplay and tensions between salsa's multiple local, national, and transnational ties. As a localized music tradition, salsa has bridged distinctions of race, ethnicity, and class to become a widespread emblem of urban popular identity in these cities. As a transnationally disseminated commodity, on the other hand, salsa has joined Caraqueños and Caleños to hemispheric institutions of cultural production. Musicians and audiences alike have been subjected to mechanisms of commercial control and thereby challenge the construction, in much contemporary Latin American usage, of "popular culture" as a site of resistance to dominant socioeconomic processes (Rowe and Schelling 1991:97; Garcia Canclini 1982 and 1992). In response to shifting economic and social conditions, salsa's practitioners and aficionados have both opposed but also participated in salsa's production and commercial diffusion through the music industry, in the process of distilling, making sense of, and giving voice to the complex circumstances of their lives.

Most striking are the parallels that frame salsa's rise in Caracas and Cali—cities whose geographic locations, historical growth, and economic development are otherwise quite distinct. These parallels include the adoption of salsa by a large, mixed-race, working-class audience that identified strongly with salsa's Afro-Cuban and Afro–Puerto Rican roots, and with the themes of inner-city urban life contained in salsa's social image and lyrics. The localization of salsa and its antecedents was a direct result of the hyperurbanization that drew diverse migrant populations to Caracas and Cali after the 1950s. The regional traditions associated with these migrant communities could not represent this new heterogenous population, nor serve to express the experiences of a rapidly shifting urban environment. Tied to this process was the formation of a cosmopolitan sensibility through the adoption of salsa and its antecedents, which allowed Caraqueños and Caleños to position themselves in the complex transnational economic and cultural flows that were shaping their world. During the 1970s, leftist intellectuals from the Caracas and Cali middle classes adopted salsa, attracted not only to its exuberant rhythms, but also to the ideological possibilities of reframing salsa as an authentic vehicle of pan-Latino urban culture.

While Cuba, Puerto Rico, and New York remained the symbolic wellspring of salsa tradition, Caraqueños and Caleños affirmed their participation in the transnational scene by producing major salsa festivals that featured local and international bands. Perhaps most significant is the fact that Caracas and Cali were both home to a flourishing live salsa scene, in which local bands developed distinct Venezuelan and Colombian styles of salsa that subsequently flowed back into the transnational salsa market. Although Venezuelan salsa is closer to its New York and Puerto Rican counterparts in terms of rhythmic groove, arrangements, and execution, both the Venezuelan and Colombian schools contain distinct elements that mark these as important local styles. During this stage of localization, ironically, both Caracas and Cali became recognized as important *global* sites for salsa performance and reception.

One obvious question emerges in the comparison of salsa's adoption in Caracas and Cali. Even though salsa and its Afro-Cuban/Puerto Rican roots were introduced in each city during the same time period, why did prominent local salsa bands appear so much later in Cali? When I posed this question to Cesar Monge, the Venezuelan trombonist and salsa composer-arranger who moved to Cali, he replied that the pool of well-trained musicians was much larger in Caracas than it was anywhere in Colombia, hence stimulating the growth of local bands.[31] The lack of a strong local music tradition in Cali, however, led not only to the adoption of Cuban/Puerto Rican music and salsa, but also to the fetishizing of recordings in local popular culture—as concrete symbols of the working-class cosmopolitan identity. In Cali, records of Cuban/Puerto Rican music and, later, salsa became the central focus of expressive activities—they were more important as sources of musical sound than actually taking up instruments to play the new style. The sudden influx of money into Cali during the 1980s, however, stimulated local performance through the appearance of international bands and the creation of several new venues for live salsa.

Notably, Cali's live scene began to blossom during the same period that live salsa in Caracas declined. This is related in part to economic shifts in each city—Cali's local economy boomed in the 1980s, while that of Caracas began to crumble from the strain of an overburdened urban infrastructure and increasing graft and corruption in the national government (Hellinger 1991). It is also related to larger flows on the transnational Latin popular music market, as salsa's transnational prominence was strongly challenged by Dominican merengue. The consolidation of a "world salsa capital" image in Cali, on the other hand, insulated Caleños from these influences. By 1996, however, in the wake

of the cartel's collapse, merengue finally began to infiltrate local airwaves, nightclubs, and record stores. When I visited Caracas in 1992
and again in 1994, the city's struggle to redefine its identity within an
increasingly diverse number of urban popular styles was quite apparent.
Even though salsa remained important, several other sounds were
prominent, including merengue, techno-merengue, rock, *balada*, and
hip-hop. Similarly, in Cali during the late 1990s, diverse styles competed
for local attention: Colombian *vallenato* and *pop tropical* (currently the
national popular sounds), merengue, techno, rock en español, and rap.
Salsa-influenced arrangements of traditional Afro-Colombian currulao
and *chirimía* music of the Pacific Coast have also gained a growing presence. Within this milieu, salsa has remained emblematic of local popular identity, but its monopoly has become increasingly precarious.

For scholars of global popular culture, Caracas and Cali offer
potent illustrations of the articulation of transnational capital flows (as
manifest in the production and consumption of records and related
media) to local cultural practice and everyday experience. The local
salsa scene in each of these sites has been a product of, and a response
to, global forces of rapid technological development, urbanization,
industrialization, and social change in this century. In the diverse practices shaping salsa's local adoption, we can detect, as Arjun Appadurai
would say, "the workings of the imagination in a deterritorialized
world" (1996:63) through which Caraqueños and Caleños alike have
sought to reposition their sense of local identity at particularly unstable
moments in their recent history.

NOTES

1. Portions of this essay appeared previously in Waxer 1993, 1998, 1999, 2000 and
   2001. Financial support for this research was provided by generous grants from the
   Social Sciences and Humanities Research Council of Canada, the Wenner-Gren
   Foundation for Anthropological Research, the American Association of University
   Women, the Nellie M. Signor Fund, the Tinker Foundation, and the University of
   Illinois at Urbana-Champaign, all of which I gratefully acknowledge. I would like to
   thank Medardo Arias Thomas Turino, Charles Capwell, Alejandro Lugo, Deborah
   Pacini Hernández, and Paul Austerlitz for their helpful comments on earlier versions
   of this material.
2. Source: *The Statesman's Yearbook 1980–81,* ed. John Paxton, p. 1577; *The
   Statesman's Yearbook 1987–88,* ed. John Paxton, p. 1577; *The Statesman's
   Yearbook 1998–99,* ed. Barry Turner, p. 1931.
3. Source: *Anuario Estadístico del Valle de Cauca 1972–4* and *Statesman's Yearbook
   2000,* ed. Barry Turner, p. 473.
4. Personal communication from record collectors and dealers: Pablo Solano, February
   13, 1996; Cesar Machado, February 20, 1996, and Lisímaco Paz, February 19,
   1996.
5. Personal communication, Cesar Monge, August 14, 1995.
6. Madera was an important Caracas-based ensemble of the early 1980s, performing

Afro-Venezuelan drum traditions from Barlovento (the group dissolved when a car crash killed several of its key members); Grupo Bahia, based in Cali, is a 1990s ensemble that performs contemporary arrangements of *currulao* and other Afro-Colombian genres from the Pacific Coast. Both groups (have) gained national and international recognition.

7. Of the trombone, Baéz notes that it is "el instrumento que ha caracterizado desde sus inicios a la salsa, y que le confiere el carácter marginal del barrio" (the instrument that has shaped salsa from the first, and that has given salsa the marginal character of the barrio) (1989:88).

8. Literally, "The Hour of Taste, Salsa, and *Bembé*." Bembé is an Afro-Cuban term referring to a festive sacred/secular gathering to dance and sing for the *orishas* (deities) in the *santería* religion.

9. Such a social division finds a parallel in the antagonism between *cocolos* and *rocqueros* in Puerto Rico (Duany 1984). Rock and roll styles in Venezuela at this time were called *yéye* (Baéz 1989:115), in reference to the Beatles' well-known chorus, "yeah, yeah, yeah."

10. In recent studies, Winthrop Wright (1990) and David Guss (1993) suggest that poverty and blackness in Venezuela have a symbiotic relationship. Athough Venezuela has never suffered from the history of extreme racism found in the United States, Venezuelans of African heritage tend to be poor because they are black (Wright 1990:5).

11. According to Baéz, the artistic and commercial success of the first international festival, held in 1975, broke the stranglehold that rock had had on the music industry (1989:83).

12. *Joropo* is a tradition from the *llanos,* or grassy flatlands, of the Venezuelan and Colombian interior. Musical ensembles comprise vocals, harp, the guitar-like *cuatro, maracas*, and bass, and the musical style is characterized by a strong 2-against-3 polyrhythmic feel. The *culo e'puya* drums are long, cylindrical drums held between the legs and played with a hand-and-stick technique (right hand holds stick, left hand free). As in other drumming traditions of African origin, three drums are played, with the two larger ones providing a polyrhythmic ostinato over which the third drummer improvises. Both in playing technique and polyrhythmic patterns, culo e'puya drumming bears some similarity to Senegalese Wolof traditions (e.g., *sabar, kuotiro*).

13. Personal communication, June 19, 1992. The *merengue caraqueño* is part of the pan-Caribbean complex of merengue variants (Austerlitz 1997:15–17, 156).

14. Bobby Valentín, 1985, *La Boda de Ella* (Bronco 107).

15. Personal communication, Gerardo Rosales and Juan Carlos Baéz, on several occasions, June–July 1992. I had the opportunity to meet and talk with Ruiz throughout my field trip to Caracas, and was always impressed by the high esteem in which his musical peers held him.

16. Personal communication, Gerardo Rosales, July 21, 1992.

17. El Gran Combo's emphasis on choreography, in turn, was related to the band's former incarnation as a smaller group under Cortijo y su Combo in the 1950s (see chapter 1).

18. According to Gerardo Rosales, Castillo's radio airplay of the Lebrón Brothers was itself prompted by intense public demand—when people realized that he was willing to air *salsa malandra* (the "bad boy" sound ignored by other radio stations), they began calling the station en masse to request songs by the Lebrón Brothers (personal communication, July 16, 1992).

19. *Descarga*, literally meaning "discharge," refers to jazz-influenced ensemble improvisation in salsa. Descarga sessions originated in Cuban recording studios in the

1950s, and live sessions were popular in New York in the early 1960s (Salazar 1985).

20. Gerardo Rosales, personal communication, July 21, 1992.
21. Gerardo Rosales, personal communication, July 4, 1992.
22. Personal communication, Victor Caicedo, July 30, 1995.
23. Esneda de Caicedo, personal communication, July 30, 1995.
24. Watussi's influence on Caleño dancing has also been corroborated for me on many occasions by Medardo Arias, who was a boy in Buenaventura when Watussi emerged as a prominent local dancer.
25. Personal communication, Andrés Leudo May 6, 1996. Leudo, a dance teacher and avid gatekeeper of Cali's salsa dance tradition, proposed that we tour these clubs some weekend, but unfortunately we were unable to accomplish this before I left the field.
26. In a recent interview, Panamian reggae–dance hall artist El General notes that when he was growing up in the town of Rio Abajo during the 1970s, he and his friends would similarly speed up recordings of Jamaican reggae music, for a faster dance-hall feel (*Latin Music On-line,* May 27, 1997, front page).
27. Reported in *El Occidente* newspaper, December 29, 1968, p. 3.
28. Amparo "Arrebato" Ramos recalls winning as much as 500 pesos at one contest, a significant amount back in the late 1960s (personal communication, August 25, 1995).
29. These include the Instituto Popular de Cultura, the Universidad del Valle, and several smaller music academies. The regional Conservatorio de Bellas Artes also democratized its former elites-only orientation.
30. *Guateque* movement. *Guateque* literally refers to a raucous rural party in Cuba.
31. Personal communication, August 14, 1995.

BIBLIOGRAPHY

Anuario Estradístico del Valle de Cauca 1972–74. 1976. Cali: Gobernación del Valle de Cauca.

Appadurai, Arjiem. 1996. *Modernity at Large: Cultural Dimensions of Globalization.* Minneapolis: University of Minnesota Press.

Arteaga, José. 1990. *La Salsa.* Bogotá: Intermedio Editores. 2nd rev. ed.

Austerlitz, Paul. 1997. *Merengue: Dominican Music and Dominican Identity.* Philadelphia: Temple University Press.

Baéz, Juan Carlos. [1985] 1989. *El vínculo es la salsa.* Caracas: Fondo Editorial Tropykos.

Boggs, Vernon W., ed. 1992. *Salsiology: Afro-Cuban Music and the Evolution of Salsa in New York City.* New York: Greenwood.

Borregales, Alberto, ed. 1992. *Urbano demasiado urbano: un coloquio para la música urbana.* Caracas: Consejo Nacional de la Cultura.

Caicedo, Andrés. 1977. *¡Que viva la música!* Cali: Editorial Victor Hugo.

Duany, Jorge. 1984. "Popular Music in Puerto Rico: Toward an Anthropology of *Salsa.*" *Latin American Music Review* 5(2):186–216.

Garcia Canclini, Nestor. 1982. *Las culturas populares en el capitalismo.* Mexico City: Editorial Nueva Imagen.

———. 1992. *Culturas híbridas: Estrategías para entrar y salir de la modernidad.* Buenos Aires: Editorial Sudamericana.

Gonzalez, Enrique Ali. 1992. "La música urbana, sus protagonistas." In Alberto Borregales, ed., *Urbano demasiado urbano.* Caracas: Consejo Nacional de la Cultura, pp. 1–16.

Guss, David. 1993. "The Selling of San Juan: The Performance of History in an Afro-Venezuelan Community." *American Ethnologist* 20(3):451–73.

Hellinger, Daniel C. 1991. *Venezuela: Tarnished Democracy*. Boulder, Colo.: Westview.

Hernández Vidal, Fernando. 1992. "Bailadores." *Gaceta* 13:35–39.

Kenney, William Howland. 1999. *Recorded Music in American Popular Life: The Phonograph and Popular Memory, 1890–1945*. New York: Oxford University Press.

Lipsitz, George. 1994. *Dangerous Crossroads: Popular Music, Postmodernism, and the Poetics of Place*. London: Verso.

Livingston, Tamara. 1999. "Music Revivals: Towards a General Theory." *Ethnomusicology* 43(1):66–85.

Lombardi, John V. 1982. *Venezuela: The Search for Order, the Dream of Progress*. New York: Oxford University Press.

Manuel, Peter. 1991. "Latin Music in the United States: Salsa and the Mass Media." *Journal of Communication* 41(1):104–16.

———. 1993. *Cassette Culture: Popular Music and Technology in North India*. Chicago: University of Chicago Press.

———. 1994. "Puerto Rican Music and Cultural Identity: Creative Appropriation of Cuban Sources from *Danza* to *Salsa*." *Ethnomusicology* 38(2):249–80.

Mitsui, Toru, and Shuhei Hosokawa, eds. 1998. *Karaoke Around the World: Global Technology, Local Singing*. New York: Routledge.

Paxton, John, ed. 1981. *The Statesman's Yearbook 1980–81*. London: Macmillan.

———. 1988. The Statesman's Yearbook 1987–88. London: Macmillan.

Roberts, John Storm. 1979. *The Latin Tinge: The Impact of Latin American Music on the United States*. New York: Oxford University Press.

Rondón, Cesar Miguel. 1980. *El libro de la salsa: crónica de la música del caribe urbano*. Caracas, Venezuela: Editorial Arte.

Rowe, William, and Vivian Schelling. 1991. *Memory and Modernity: Popular Culture in Latin America*. London: Verso.

Salazar, Max. 1985. "La Descarga Cubana." *Latin New York* 13 (June):42–47.

Singer, Roberta. 1982. "'My Music Is Who I Am and What I Do': Latin Popular Music and Identity in New York City." Ph.D. dissertation, Indiana University.

Stigberg, David. 1982. "Mexican Popular Musical Culture and the Tradition of *Música Tropical* in the City of Veracruz." *Studies in Latin American Popular Culture* 1:151–63.

Taylor, Timothy. 1997. *Global Pop: World Music, World Markets*. New York: Routledge.

Turino, Thomas. 1988. "The Music of Andean Migrants in Lima, Peru: Demographics, Social Power, and Style." *Latin American Music Review* 9(2):127–50.

———. 1993. *Moving Away from Silence: Music of the Peruvian Altiplano and the Experiment of Urban Migration*. Chicago: University of Chicago Press.

———. 2000. *Nationalists, Cosmopolitan and Popular Music in Zimbabwe*. Chicago: Univesity of Chicago Press.

Turner, Barry, ed. 1999. The Statesman's Yearbook 1998–99. London: Macmillan.

———. 2000. *Statesman's Yearbook 2000*. London: Macmillan.

Ulloa, Alejandro. 1986. *San Carlos, te acordás hermano: historia del barrio San Carlos*. Cali, Colombia: Editorial Feriva.

———. 1992. *La salsa en Cali*. Cali, Colombia: Ediciones Universidad del Valle.

Wallis, Roger, and Krister Malm. 1984. *Big Sounds from Small Peoples: The Music Industry in Small Countries*. New York: Pendragon.

Waxer, Lise. "*Llegó la Salsa*: Thirty Years of Salsa in Caracas." Presented at the 38th Annual Meeting of the Society for Ethnomusicology in Oxford, Mississippe.

———. 1998. "*Cali Pachanguero*: A Social History of Salsa in a Colombian City." University of Illinois at Urbana-Champaign.

———. 1999. "Consuming Memories: The Record-Centred *Salsa* Scene in Cali." In

Cameron McCarthy et al., eds., *Sound Identities: Popular Music and the Cultural Politics of Education*. New York: Paul Lang, pp. 235–52.

———. 2000. "En Conga, Bongó y Campana: The Rise of Colombian Salsa." *Latin American Music Review* 21(2):118–68.

———. 2001. "Record Grooves and Salsa Dance Moves: The *Viejoteca* Phenomenon." *Popular Music* 20(1):61–81.

Wright, Winthrop R. 1990. *Café con leche: Race, Class, and National Image in Venezuela*. Austin: University of Texas Press.

SELECT DISCOGRAPHY

Dimensión Latina. 1974. *Dimensión Latina '75*. (Top Hits 100–07019.)

Federico y su Combo. 1966. *Llegó la Salsa*. (Palacio 6171.)

———. 1967. *Psicodélico con Salsa*. (Gilmar 110.)

Grupo Mango. 1980. *Mango*. (YVKCT 012.)

Grupo Niche. 1981. *Querer es Poder*. (Codiscos 22200347.)

———. 1984. *No Hay Quinto Malo*. (Codiscos 22200462.)

———. 1988. *Tapando el Hueco*. (Codiscos 29821260.)

Guayacán. 1985. *Llegó la Hora de la Verdad*. (Sonolux 01031301418.)

———. 1992. *Sentimental de Punta a Punta*. (FM Discos.)

La (Nueva) Salsa Mayor. *Nuestra Orquesta . . . ¡De Frente y Luchando!* (Velvet 1787.)

Sonero Clásico del Caribe. 1981. *Lo Mejor del Sonero Clásico del Caribe*. (Sonográfica 20009.)

El Trabuco Venezolano. 1979. *El Trabuco Venezolano*. (YVLP/YVKCT 005.)

———. 1980. *El Trabuco Venezolano*. (YVLP/YVKCT 013.)

Chapter 11

SE PROHÍBE ESCUCHAR "SALSA Y CONTROL": WHEN SALSA ARRIVED IN BUENAVENTURA, COLOMBIA

Medardo Arias Satizábal
Translated by Lise Waxer

The following memoir is a personal account of salsa's arrival and reterritorialization in the Colombian Pacific Coast port of Buenaventura, from where it spread to Cali. Although it is Colombia's principal port, Buenaventura is also a small town—Arias grew up here and his everyday experiences as a boy and young adult brought him into direct contact with the individuals (or comments about them) mentioned in the chronicle below. Their idiosyncratic activities and involvement with salsa and its roots form part of daily life in this Latin American port. This narrative complements and grounds some of the historical material outlined in chapter 10.

At times I ask myself how it was that from one moment to another the southwest Andean region of Colombia became inflamed with the rhythm of Salsa, especially since I come from a generation that began to dance not to Cortijo and his Combo, but rather to the *música tropical* bands that flowered in my country, almost as an extension of agrarian and urban life, in cadences that followed the beat of *porro* and *cumbia* from afar. That sound, which wasn't really cumbia or porro, came to be known as *chucu-chucu* or the *sonido paisa*—in other words, that degeneration of the cumbia produced in Colombian Andean cities, which would successfully enter the popular sectors of Mexico and a good deal of Central and South America.

But what did we dance to then?

I was twelve years old and had a tremendous desire to kill the photographer who came to our house with the purpose of perpetuating in his camera the instant of my First Communion, that second vow of religious duty that we Catholics make after baptism. The man, in the midst of children who milled about me trying to get into the photo, insisted that I smile at the same time as holding the mother-of-pearl missal in my right hand, leaving free, for his lens, the holy sash that hung over my left shoulder, upon which shone the insignia of a golden cup with the consecrated host.

Looking at that photograph today, I can see in the background, on the wall, a banner that says "Miami 1965" and displays some flamingos at rest, with their legs making the number 4. The banner, like the music that would later come to our house in Buenaventura, had arrived across the waves, in the ships of the Flota Mercante Grancolombiana [Greater Colombia Merchant Marine], where my father's brother worked as a steward.

During the time this photograph was taken, in 1968, my father used to drop the needle of our Phillips radiola on records of popular dance tunes of the time. These included "La mecedora," "La pata pelá," "Domingo por la mañana," "Los sabanales," "El pájaro amarillo," "El professor Rui Ruá," and "La maestranza," played by Colombian groups who called themselves Los Diplomáticos [The Diplomats], Los Hispanos [The Hispanics], Los Corraleros de Majagual [The Cowboys of Majagual], Los Bobby Soxers, Los Teenagers, and Los Speakers. We listened to porro, cumbia, chucu-chucu, *gaita, merecumbé* and the first *pachanga* tunes.[1] The bands with English names were part of the so-called "New Wave," that tide that came from Liverpool, London and the big cities of the United States. They were kids, all of them, who clearly wanted to look like the Beatles and the Rolling Stones. So they had longish hair, cut in a straight bang across their forehead, dark jackets, buttoned up the middle, cigarette-leg pants, and boots with high Cuban heels. Some lead vocalists in Colombia were already famous at nineteen years of age, interpreting *baladas* with a broken voice, like Paul Anka, chewing gum twenty-four hours a day and pushing back the hair that fell over their eyes. The radio and television were full of them: Oscar Golden, Harold, and Vicky sang Spanish versions of songs by Anka and The Beatles. The guys that followed the New Wave were the "Go-Go" crowd, and the girls followed the "Ye-Ye" style.[2] Their dress code included fishnet stockings pulled up over the knees, and miniskirts. On the radio, the nation was paralyzed by the New Wave[3] program "Milo a Go-Go," sponsored by a company that manufactured a chocolate powder drink. Television had a daily program dedicated to this music: "El Club del Clan." The hit tune by the singer Harold was a twist called "Mickey Mouse," and the theme song of this generation was "Boca de chicle" [Chewing-gum mouth], sung by Oscar Golden:

Que sea mi cuerpo alegre carrilera	May my body be a happy train track
Por la que corran tus manitas frías,	Along which your cold little hands run,
Que pasen palmo a palmo por mi tierra	That pass hand over hand through my land
Hasta que se confundan con las mías . . .	Until they merge with my own . . .

This was the first verse of a song dedicated to "a girl in Los Angeles," who told "pequeñas mentiras con su boca de chicle" [little lies with her chewing-gum mouth].

The stronghold for these songs was the upper-middle class of Cali, Bogotá, and Medellín, who read North American and European magazines and traveled every year to San Francisco in PanAm jets. But for kids from the provinces, removed from these privileges, we received echos of a world that was changing through a new and revolutionary music, mixed with the *puyas, paseos*, the *vallenato* of the Caribbean Coast, and chucu-chucu, known as música tropical, which came from the Andean region of Antioquia province. Our idols were Alejo Durán, Juancho Polo Valencia, Alfredo Gutiérrez [vallenato artists] or Gustavo "El Loco" Quintero [from the interior]. Their songs spoke of familiar or foretold lands, in verses that privileged brooks, valleys, banana plantations, or rodeos in Sincelejo. The record company in Medellín, Discos Fuentes, owned by Antonio Fuentes, played a fundamental role in the diffusion of musical trends back then, including some from abroad. Every year, even to this day, they released a record called *14 Cañonazos Bailables* [14 Danceable Sensations], in which the best música tropical of the previous year was included. It was released, obviously, in the month of December, and its jacket cover, without fail, depicted a nubile model in a bathing suit, posed on the Colombian beaches of Santa Marta or Cartagena de Indias. The album covers of these hit re-releases acquired this tendency for commercial reasons, since the first productions were rather conservative. One of the early ones showed a pirate lighting a cannon in the Fortress of San Felipe de Barajas in Cartagena. With one hand he held the fuse, while the other covered his ear.

For those of us from the Pacific Coast of Colombia, the appearance of the first LP by Peregoyo and his Combo Vacana in 1968 came like a revelation of our local identity. Recorded by Discos Fuentes, our musicians had gone to record for the first time in Medellín, and appeared on the back cover of the album lined up on a bridge in Medellín, dressed in jackets and ties, with their shoes propped up on a railing, and sporting Pepsodent smiles. So, along with the arrival of Puerto Rican Salsa, incubated in New York at the end of the 1960s and beginning of the '70s, the parties in Buenaventura and a good deal of the Pacific littoral were livened by the dance band of that musician from our own backyard, Enrique Urbano Tenorio, known as "Peregoyo." What he did was as important as the innovations of Ignacio Piñeiro in Cuba in the 1920s, who led the transformation of the traditional *son* from Oriente province into a national dance style. Peregoyo allowed *currulao,* our native folkloric music, to pass into the party salons. He converted it into popular dance band music. Peregoyo, furthermore, was our drawing and calligraphy teacher at Pascual de Andagoya High School in Buenaventura, an institution declared to have the highest level of educational achievement in the entire republic of Colombia during the 1950s. Thus, the invasion of Salsa in Colombia through the port of Buenaventura was accompanied by the festive currulaos of Peregoyo.[4]

Caribbean music was known in Buenaventura and Cali as "music from the other side," a widespread way of recognizing those harmonies that were not part of the Colombian context but which came from over there, from the north, the other side of the map of the Caribbean Basin. Moreover, the avalanche of music that emerged in the transition from the 1960s to the '70s, principally from New York, was nothing new. Sailors from Buenaventura had brought Caribbean music since the 1950s, when the ships of the Flota Mercante still docked in Cuba.

Before our beloved Phillips radiola, we had a *picó* ["pick-up"] record player at home, on which we listened to 78 rpm discs of Cuban groups such as the Sonora Matancera, the Orquesta of Enrique Jorrín and the Orquesta Casino de la Playa, along with Mexican *boleros* and *rancheras* featuring the voices of Lucho Gatica, Leo Marini, Toña La Negra, María Luisa Landín, Agustín Lara or Jorge Negrete. This picó also resounded with compositions by Colombian bandleaders Lucho Bermúdez, Pacho Galán and Edmundo Arias. Galán, in the 1950s, created the *merecumbé,* a mix of Colombian *merengue* and cumbia.

When Salsa arrived, the port of Buenaventura and a good part of Colombia was already familiar with Cuban *guaracha,* the Puerto Rican *bomba* and *plena,* the new pachanga rhythm, the *Watusi* of Ray Barretto, and the new sounds of boogaloo and *jala jala* coming from New York City (see Flores, chapter 4). At parties, we greatly enjoyed the tongue-twisting tunes of Mon Rivera ("Karakatisti" among them), the productions of Joe Cuba and his sextet, and the happy melodies of Cortijo y su Combo. Our affinity for the voice of Ismael Rivera grew with the presentation in the port of the film *Calipso,*[5] featuring Harry Belafonte, in which Cortijio's band appears. The title of the film was billed as *Calipso, Bomba, y Plena* in the Teatro Caldas, and the film was screened every second Sunday of the month, to a full house, until the theater's copy was consumed in a fire.

It is important to recognize that Hispanic Caribbean music began to be called "Salsa" only after the arrival, from Venezuela, of an LP titled *Llegó la Salsa*, by Federico y su Combo (see Waxer, chapter 10). On the jacket cover of this production appears a group of dancers, white, dressed in the style of the upper classes. In the foreground, a blond woman, with her leg extended and silver high heels, lets her hair fall to one side, in what appeared to be a step from the twist. Moreover, this manner of projecting popular music, "upwards" and not toward its true origins and protagonists, had to do with the misguided mentality of some record producers who were convinced of the need to put "formal clothes" on black rhythms. This thinking gave birth to those photographs of Caribbean musicians packaged in evening dress or tuxedos, looking pensive in salons of walnut and marble, lounging by fantasy swimming pools or white pianos. The tendency to present Caribbean music like this has been more or less maintained even to the present.

Curiously, after that LP and with the homogenization of Caribbean rhythms into a commercial formula that allowed for a rapid identification from this part of the world, everything was converted into "Salsa." Mon Rivera, Joe Cuba, Pete Rodríguez, the pachangas of Johnny Pacheco, the first releases of Celia Cruz in New York, Eddie and Charlie Palmieri, Ricardo "Richie" Ray, Frankie Dante, and Marcolino Dimond all suddenly appeared on the marquee with flashing lights that was "Salsa." In this transition, many of the specific names and labels that identified several musicians and dance orchestras were lost. In this regard, Tito Puente said, "Salsa is something that I eat on my spaghetti—what I play is mambo, son, chachachá, boogaloo, guaguancó . . ."

Via maritime migration, Pete Rodríguez, one of the first proponents of boogaloo, introduced a record in Buenaventura that—unfortunately—is little known today in the generalized tradition of Salsa. Titled *La Reencarnación* [The reincarnation], it gathered together *bombas* and *plenas* of the late 1960s—one of them, the most celebrated, was titled "Bomba de corazón" [Bomba from the heart].[6] The piece that gave the LP its name, "La Reencarnación," had a streetwise voice that spoke, between the lyrics:

Dicen que se mueren,	They say they die,
Y cuando reencarnan,	And when they reincarnate,
Vuelven como perro, como gato,	They come back as dogs, as cats,
Hasta como caballo	Even as horses
Que tú los ves por la calle.	That you see on the street.

| *Y no ves nada más que eso:* | And you don't see any more than that: |
| *¡Un caballo!* | A horse! |

But Colombian sailors didn't bring music just to their homes in Buenaventura. They also distributed them in the bars of the Zona de Tolerancia ["Tolerance zone," the red-light district] of this town, the major port in the country. This zone was known as "La Pilota," a barrio named in homage to the lover of a *piloto* or *prático* [pilot], that expert in winds and tides who accompanies ship captains when they cast anchor at Buenaventura's bay. He is the one who knows where a large freighter should navigate, to avoid running aground on the abundant sandbars and shallow mudbanks in the area.

In the mid-1960s, La Pilota had at least fifty brothels of high renown among the international sailors who docked there, and a similar number of tenement houses, small bars, and dance halls. It was legend that sailors saved all their money to place it in the hands of peasant girls from the Andean zone who came to Buenaventura seeking a better future. They abandoned their destiny as coffee gatherers and sowers of sorghum and wheat, to come dream in the perfumed beard of some English captain who promised them a castle of gold, nights of dancing, and many dollars. Some of them became prostitutes for two or three years and at the end of this time returned to their lands in Quindío, Risaralda, Tolima, or the eastern *Llanos* [prairies], to lead a "decent life." They bought a house for their parents and patiently awaited an honorable man who would take them to settle down discreetly. In the nights of La Pilota they learned to dance Charleston, foxtrot, the twist, boogaloo, pachanga, and, finally, Salsa. Their expertise in the basic vocabulary of various languages was also famous: English, French, German, Japanese, and Greek.

These goddesses of the "short time" and the "twenty dollar" not only knew the lyrics to Elvis Presley songs, but also the verses that came from the orchestra of Chorolo, the Chilean cumbias of the Sonora Palacios, and the Spanglish of boogaloos by Pete Rodríguez and Joe Bataan. In places like the Bamboo Bar, El Shangay, Tropicana, La Barata, Puerto Rico, Fantasio, Isla de Capri, Guillermo, El Bar de Próspero, and Aurora, the fashions of the day were flaunted: tight pants with bell bottoms, blouses tied above the navel, hair fluffed and toasted during the slow hours beneath beauty salon dryers, which at that time emulated deep-sea diving helmets. There, while they read illustrated romantic novels by Corín Tellado, recently declared the most popular writer in Spain, they prepared themselves for the night of dimmed lights, soft cushions, metallic chairs, fans, and big posters of *Playboy* divas, the Beatles, Tom Jones, Barry White, Raquel Welch dressed as a cowgirl, or

Burt Reynolds, naked. Lounging in easy chairs, they wore white boots, sequined shorts, and knew the latest fragrances from Paris, smoking Lucky Strikes, Chesterfields, or Kools while awaiting their lover of the moment, singing "It's Now or Never," Ray Barretto's "La hipocresia y la falsedad," or Benny Moré's bolero, "Camarera."

La Pilota, situated on one of the three hills on the island of Buenaventura,[7] began on Calle de los Alemanes [Street of the Germans] and ended at Garrido Street, on a dead end facing the sea, on which was located the Yellow Butterfly, a brothel reserved exclusively for white sailors and crewmen of rank: captains, first mates, and other officials. The doorman, an Afro-Colombian native, had the job of detaining sailors of color and stevedores who wanted to enjoy themselves there. The owner, a German woman who played the piano every midnight for her audience, offered an exotic cartel of French prostitutes from Guyana. The famous MPs, or military police, guarded the apartheid on this street, paid for by a bribe from this house. At the helm of an MP squadron that moved about in an army jeep was "The German," a young white Colombian born in earlier days to one of the women who had come to La Pilota in search of a better life. A deputy of the secret police, he wore black cowboy clothes, a wide-brimmed hat, and always carried a Colt .45 tied to his leg with a leather belt. He rode about the port on a German motorcycle with a sidecar, for which he earned the nickname "The German." Malicious tongues said he was the son of a German sailor.

Those police pursued thieves to the point of killing them; they corralled them beneath the port's wooden houses and lit into them with revolver shots. They were Afro-Colombian boys who snatched watches from the sailors and then ran to hide. They feared The German like the plague. Beneath La Barata, a brothel inflamed with the rhythms of boogaloo late into the night, he murdered various pickpockets. The German committed suicide in the early 1970s, after his legs were amputated, following a fatal injury in a motorcycle accident.

Cuban son, Puerto Rican plena and bomba, and Salsa music reverberated through all of La Pilota. Próspero, a retired engineer of the Pacific Railroad, had at the time—in the 1960s and the first glimmer of the '70s—one of the most complete collections of Caribbean music in the world, since the sailors—mostly Afro-Caribbean—of the Flota Mercante and companies like the Grace Line, the Likes Lines, and Gulf, always brought their music to him to listen to when they came from a voyage, accompanied by a rum and coke, "Cuba Libre." Próspero not only supplied music to the entire zone of La Pilota, but also dispatched ice to all the bars, carried on carts of sawdust which left blocks of ice at each door every evening at sunset. From Cali, then a distance of six hours by road and twelve hours by train, came the proprietors of bars such as Mis Noches, Costeñita, and Fantasio, to buy music from Próspero. This same music was heard in Cali's red-light zone and on some radio stations.

The black Caribbean sailors who worked for the North American shipping companies that docked in Buenaventura were known in the port as *chombos,* and their principal trait was the bilingualism they demonstrated. Most of them were Puerto Rican, and they performed the lowest jobs on the steamships. They were waiters, oilmen, cooks, carpenters, and sailors, and had learned English in New York, in Baltimore, in Jacksonville, Chicago, and other ports and cities of the United States. They had a refined way of dressing, flaunting linen *guayaberas* [long open shirts], two-tone shoes, English umbrellas, gold watchchain and fob, like the black zoot-suiters of Harlem or the Mexican *pachucos* of Los Angeles, straw Panama Hat with a colored band and cocky *buscapleito* [literally, "seeking a fight"] feather, with the inevitable pack of Juicy Fruit chewing gum in their shirt pocket. Some of them smoked a pipe, while others were irredeemable marijuana smokers. They also stamped the aroma of Vetiver on the port, a cologne bought in the stores of Panama and New York.

These sailors had a different way of dancing, which they had learned from their parents and grandparents. Black American sailors from U.S. warships also went to La Pilota. They danced according to the steps of Fred Astaire or Gene Kelly in the film *Singing in the Rain,* interspersed with twirls from the jitterbug. From this fusion of Cuban, Puerto Rican, and Afro-American dances came the dance style of Watussi, the first Salsa dancer in the port, who would later teach his method of dancing in Cali, Bogotá, and other Colombian cities. Watussi, a child of the streets, used to dance on the sidewalk in front of La Barata for the sailors who tossed coins and chewing gum at his bare feet. From those rapid, elastic feet arose beautiful movements that followed the rhythm of the piano or conga drums, or which jumped at rapid intervals, as if hopping through hot coals. Already at the end of the 1960s Watussi did the "Paso del tren" [Train step], the same dance step, imitating a locomotive, that Michael Jackson would make famous two decades later.

It must be noted that the choreography of this new dance lit up the multitudes in the city of Cali, then the third-largest city of the country. The appearance of Ricardo "Richie" Ray here, in the capital of the province of Valle del Cauca, also in 1968 (the year of my First Communion photo), signified a historic moment for the music of that region of Colombia and for the entire country. The *Ferias* [carnivals] with bands like Los Hispanos or Los Diplomáticos stayed behind. The young people of the barrios demanded Salsa from New York and imitated the steps of Watussi, who founded an entire school of dancers in Cali, a style of dancing that has survived and been enriched with time.

The last five years of the 1970s and the first years of the 1980s were a golden time for Salsa in Colombia, since that was the epoch in which Larry Landa, the promotor and empresario of Salsa orchestras and shows, appeared in Cali. A charismatic *salsero*, friend of each and every member of the Fania All-Stars, and a lover himself of New York and Puerto Rican *Salsa dura,* he had spent his adolescence in Cali as a disc jockey at *agüelulos,*[8] baptism celebrations, and weddings. He came to be known as "Lalá," and in the metallic box on wheels in which he carried his music to parties, attached to his small-cylinder motorcycle, he had had painted various notes in "La," his trademark.[9]

Some said he had been born in Buenaventura, but early on his family settled down in Cali. In 1978 he opened a boutique called "Los Baúles" in New York City, on the Avenue of the Americas, from which he organized parties and concerts with New York Salsa bands, since he was already prosperous by that time and had permanent residency in the Capital of the World. Sometime later, in 1983, I saw him there, in New York, in what was his element. He cruised along Park Avenue in a limousine, with a chauffeur in cap and uniform, and in September of that year he organized a grand Fiesta Colombiana at Studio 54. In Cali, his automobile attracted much attention: a Mustang Match-1 with a huge marijuana leaf, phosphorescent, painted on the hood, and blaring pachangas at top volume. Lalá was an old-time *pachanguero.*[10] The first orchestra he brought to Cali was the Yambú, and afterward came the Típica Novel, Héctor Lavoe, Cuco Valoy, Alfredo de la Fé, Eddie Palmieri, Los Rodríguez, Cheo Feliciano, Johnny Pacheco, la Sonora Matancera, Daniel Santos, and Celia Cruz. He had the idiosyncrasy of first presenting the bands in Buenaventura and then in Cali, an attitude that underlined the legend of his origins in the port. In organizing shows in Buenaventura, he had the backing of Chencho Trompeta, a music aficionado who roamed the streets to put up the posters for concerts, accompanied by a small troop of boys. When Landa brought Eddie Palmieri to Buenaventura for the first time, around 1978, the inhabitants of the city didn't believe this event was actually happening, since sailors had spread the news that Palmieri played only in the sacred temples of Latin music in New York and Puerto Rico, and that besides it was "expensive to bring him, since he had a gold piano . . ."

At the time, I was a writer for the daily newspaper *El País,* in Cali, and I traveled to the port to cover the concert. Seeing that it was already 8 o'clock at night and the Coliseum was empty, I recommended to

Landa that he hire one of the engines from the Fire Brigade to go around the city with the musicians, so that people could see for themselves that it was true, Palmieri and his boys were there. They did this, and in the photo, now historic, in a truck designed for putting out blazes, up front in the place traditionally reserved by the firemen for beauty queens appear Eddie Palmieri, Ismael Quintana, and Alfredo "Chocolate" Armenteros, with his trumpet held high. The fireman who drove the engine put the siren on full blast, and this pulled the Buenaventurans out into the street. In minutes, the Coliseum was packed full to bursting, and Eddie tapped his shoe to count off "Bilongo," with the inimitable voice of Quintana: "Estoy tan enamorao/ de la negra Tomasa/ que cuando se va de casa/ que triste me pongo . . ." [I'm so in love/ with the black woman Tomasa/ that when she leaves the house/ how sad I become . . .]. In the chronicle I wrote for the entertainment review of *El País,* I put the title: "Si el piano dice Kikiribú Mandinga, ése es Palmieri" [If the piano says Kikiribú Mandinga,[11] that's Palmieri] next to a photograph where Eddie appears, sweating buckets, with his left hand on the keyboard and his right hand in a fist punching upwards, like a leftist politician.

Along with Chencho Trompeta, another promotor of Salsa in Buenaventura was Walter Aspiazo, a character known as "La Logia." He was a stevedore for Puertos de Colombia, the company that administered the docks. He was in charge of managing the *winche,* or crane, for which his job was known as the *winchero.* A collector of Caribbean music, he defined himself as a man of the left. In fact, he was a permanent fixture and spokesman at strikes and petitions, likewise at student demonstrations and anything that gathered the people around some cause. He liked to flaunt clothes with an African cut, and book covers displaying the thoughts of Malcolm X, Franz Fanon, or Stokely Carmichael. He was also a reader of poetry by Leopold Senghor. He loved both the Black Panthers and the Cuban Revolution, and in the early 1980s founded the first Black Muslim congregation of the Colombian Pacific Coast, in company with a shoemaker, in the barrio of Viento Libre, the same neighborhood where Yuri Buenaventura, now known as "El Sonero de Paris" [The *sonero* of Paris] was born.

Among those of the port, La Logia spread that salute of grasped hands, feints, embrace to the left, embrace to the right, saying "mi sangre, mi sangre" (my blood, my blood). On his small motorcycle, he traversed the port at 25 kilometers [15 miles] an hour, like an African prince who had forgotten to buy bread at the corner store, and thus took advantage of any opportunity to come down and chat about the last concert, while tossing bread and strings of fish or plantain into the basket of his motorbike. "Clear-headed people don't have to go very fast," he affirmed, at the same time as he asked himself why such a beautiful race (the African) had to bust up their noses "for the pleasure and applause of some fiends." For this motive, he religiously carried bouquets of flowers for boxers before their matches, and also for Salsa musicians who came through Buenaventura. His salute, before presenting the flowers, consisted in throwing himself to the ground, as if to do some physical exercises, and from there he raised his joined hands: "mi sangre, mi sangre . . ."

Logia was struck and killed by a baker's truck one dawn in the month of July in the mid-1980s, when he was leaving his favorite dance club, El Caney, a place on the outskirts of Buenaventura in the sector known as "the highway" for being the road that leads to Cali. El Caney had inherited the music from the Bar of Próspero, and was close to Camaguey, the Monterrey, and the Boulevard of Rum, places that were legend in the port. El Caney is mentioned in a verse of the song "Buenaventura y Caney" by Grupo Niche of Colombia: "Del Caney al Boulevard/ camino dos pasos/ luego vamos al Piñal/ luego nos tapiamos . . ." [From Caney to the Boulevard/ I walk two steps/ then let's go to the Piñal[12]/ then we'll get soused . . .]

Even now, when I write this chronicle, I can remember Logia crossing the whole island with his new trombone, an instrument that he bought from a German ship, because he wanted to learn how to play "La Murga" [a famous salsa tune by Willie Colón]. From the balconies and windows of Buenaventura, when Logia had parked his motorcycle and advanced with the trombone on his shoulder, people shouted: "La Murga, Logia, La Murga!" and the man put his newspaper and books down on the pavement, and began blowing like a ship, emulating Willie Colón. "Purunpunpun . . . Purumpunpun," that was all he knew, those few lines which he had learned how to blow with some of his musician friends, but it constituted all his joy, the sole reason for which he had bought this costly instrument.

Now that Salsa is no longer a marginal music in Colombia, of sailors thirsty for sex and liquor, of the zones of prostitution and marijuana addicts, I can remember the day in 1981 when I began to write a twelve–chapter essay for the daily paper *El Occidente* in Cali, which I titled "Esta es la verdadera historia de la Salsa" [This is the true history of Salsa], a work which in the end won me the 1982 Simón Bolívar National Journalism Award for Best Investigation. I didn't have to research much, since a good deal of that extensive, reflexive chronicle was my own life. Even after receiving the award in the Teatro Colón of Bogotá, many of my media colleagues asked what the hell this thing about Salsa was, and if maybe it had to do with some revolutionary cooking method, since at that time, outside of Buenaventura, Cali, and the Caribbean Coast, "this thing about Salsa" was still the music of hooligans. And of course, I also remember when *Salsa y Control* by the Lebrón Brothers began to play on our radiola, and in my house we were forbidden to listen to this, since it was an "attempt against decency," all that "uproar" that we dared to consider "music." It was understood that for a good upbringing, softer rhythms were more suitable, such as the *tropical* songs, between city and country, of Los Corraleros de Majagual or Los Graduados.

Now, when we Colombians of the Pacific claim not only currulao but also Salsa as part of our identity, I think that it is worth embracing, from the bottom of our souls and also as ours, the music of the Caribbean that, for reasons outlined above, already also belongs to us by tradition and by history.

EDITOR'S NOTES

1. With the exception of the Cuban *pachanga*, these are all Colombian dance genres based on traditional rhythms from the Colombian Caribbean Coast.
2. "Ye-ye," a popular term in both Colombia and Venezuela for cosmpolitan rockers of the era, derives from the Beatles' chorus "yeah, yeah."
3. In Colombia, "New Wave" refers to the sounds of international rock and pop that entered the country in the 1960s (rather than the British punk-ska movement of the late 1970s that was marketed as New Wave in the United Kingdom and North America).
4. Peregoyo's transformation of the Afro-Colombian *currulao* must be seen in the context of the primarily black population of Buenaventura and of the Pacific Coast in general, who before this time had never before been recognized by the white/mestizo producers and audiences of mainstream Colombian culture. Arias and his contemporaries in the port of Buenaventura personally knew Peregoyo—he lives only a few blocks away from the Arias household, and many of Arias's contemporaries studied calligraphy and art with Peregoyo in the local high school.
5. Released in English as *Island in the Sun*.
6. This song was also recorded by Eddie Palmieri, in two different versions. See *Lo Que Traigo es Sabroso* (Alegre 8320 [1964]) and *Palo Pa' Rumba* (Fania ML 56 [1984]).
7. The main port and urban center of Buenaventura is on a small island that was connected to the mainland by a ferry until a permanent bridge was built in the 1980s. Although several neighborhoods have since sprung up along the mainland road leading to the island, the original town was contained entirely on this island.
8. Afternoon dances for teenagers, an important part of Cali's dance scene in the 1960s. See Waxer, chapter 10, this volume.
9. Arias knew Landa from the late 1970s in Cali, when Landa began bringing the first New York salsa bands to Colombia. As a young reporter at the time, Arias covered these concerts for *El Occidente* and *El Pueblo* daily newspapers, and often traveled with the bands when Landa took them out to do shows in Buenaventura.
10. Indeed, Landa built a legendary nightclub in Juanchito, a party spot for Caleños, called "Juan Pachanga," named after the famous song by Willie Colón and Rúben Blades.
11. The *coro* or refrain from "Bilongo."
12. Ferry dock, now a permanent bridge, that connects the island of Buenaventura to the mainland. See note 7 above.

Chapter 12

THE MAKING OF A SALSA MUSIC SCENE IN LONDON

Patria Román-Velázquez

In narrating the development of a local salsa music scene in London, this chapter focuses on the construction of Latin identities across salsa clubs. Salsa clubs are approached not as contained and bounded sites for social interaction, but in relation to broader spatial practices and power relations that play an important part in the construction and embodiment of particular Latin identities. This approach is an attempt to move beyond research on dance clubs that has tended to focus on audiences as subcultures and the production of the event. Although these perspectives are useful for exploring how salsa is appropriated so as to communicate Latin identities, and how audiences participate in the production of a music event along with various music industy interests, they provide little possibility for exploring the processes through which salsa comes to be present in London. They neglect how practices within the clubs are constituted out of wider social processes and relations of power.

By focusing on the salsa music scene in London I wish to account for the processes through which a local salsa music scene developed at a particular place-time in London. Narrating this process might be useful for understanding how a salsa scene was constituted out of spatial relations and how these played an important role in the construction and communication of Latin identities in London.

I emphasize that clubs need to be understood as part of wider social processes that I relate to the movement of people and cultural practices into London. These processes are constituted out of different power relations that at the same time contribute to the identity of a place at a particular moment. Thus, places here are studied not as the context in which events occur, but as constituted out of power relations and directly related to the construction and communication of cultural identities. Thus, at a theoretical level this discussion might further advance research on the relationship between cultural identities and places.

This chapter considers the different elements through which salsa comes to be present in London. Salsa's presence in London is related to the music industries' commercial interest in distributing and promoting its artists and products around the world; to the interest of non–Latin American people in salsa; to the commercial interest of individual entrepreneurs; and to the immigration of Latin Americans into London.

I will start by discussing the routes of salsa into Britain and concentrate on the movement of salsa as a marketable category from the Caribbean and New York City to London. Referring to the marketing, distribution and promotion of salsa, I will trace the routes of salsa into London and highlight how music industries have influenced the development of a local salsa scene. I then build up an account of the different clubs that have existed in London and pay particular attention to those issues that have contributed to the identity of some of the most prominent clubs. From there I will move on to consider how clubs communicate a particular type of Latinness. I discuss how club owners, promoters and disc jockeys construct and communicate the identity of the clubs while positioning themselves against or among existing clubs. The last section focuses on the routes and routines being created by participants, bringing in dancers' voices and considering how participants create spatial movements across the salsa clubs while contributing to the creation of different networks of clubs. This approach allows me to discuss the various elements through which relations of power develop from within and between the different types of salsa clubs. I suggest that the processes through which the identity of places is constructed play an important part in shaping the routes and routines that people develop across particular networks of salsa clubs in London. Through these movements, participants are also contributing to the identity of the clubs.

MUSIC SCENES ACROSS PLACES

Most recent research dealing with music clubs has been concerned with what is defined as "dance music" by North American and European recording industries.[1] The focus of this type of research has usually been on audiences as a subculture—either involved in appropriating symbols and constructing a distinct sense of alternative style (McRobbie 1991; Readhead 1990; Chambers 1985; Willis 1990; Gilbert and Pearson

1999), or in using various types of "cultural capital" and knowledge as markers of distinction (Thornton 1995). This research has been mainly concerned with distinct groups of young people, and the emphasis on youth subcultures has tended to maintain the idea of self-contained groups defined by musical taste and alternative means of symbolic resistance (to dominant culture).

In an attempt to move beyond music audiences as contained subcultures and in order to understand musical practices across space, Will Straw (1991) has introduced the concept of "music scene." For Straw, a music scene is "that cultural space in which a range of musical practices coexist, interacting with each other within a variety of processes of differentiation, and according to widely varying trajectories of change and cross fertilization" (1991:373). Straw's approach suggests the need for understanding musical scenes as "a larger international musical culture." Although Straw acknowledges the diversity of a group by recognizing the possibilities for regional variations, he also tends to emphasize the unity of a group through the notion of "alliances." The importance of Straw's approach is that he introduces theoretical debates about space and place to studies of popular music practices. However, as Hesmondhalgh (1996) points out, by privileging positive interactions across space Straw's conception of music scene lacks any sense of the way in which relations of power operate unequally across spaces.

Thus, Straw's notion of "scene" is useful for understanding how salsa clubs in London are part of salsa's movement around the world. Although I do not discuss in detail how salsa clubs in London interrelate with other localities as part of an international salsa scene, by focusing on salsa clubs across London I wish to consider the relations of power developing from salsa club practices in London.[2]

I have developed the idea of "routes and routines" as a way of discussing the geographical location of the clubs (whether permanent or moving from place to place) and as a way of understanding the movement of participants across these locations. I argue that as people develop spatial patterns across places these routes are converted into routines, which at the same time contribute to the development of different networks of salsa clubs. As new clubs open or as clubs reopen or move from venue to venue, participants' routines can be disrupted. The idea of routes and routines allows for considering the relations of power developing from people's movements and spatial practices.

A local music scene, I argue, develops as part of a wider set of relations that cannot be solely understood with reference to an audience group, the particular clubs or an international music scene, but through quite specific processes that cut across space-time and cultural practices.

Thus, the idea of routes and routines challenges the notion of self-contained musical events, as it allows for considering the relations of power of an international music scene (in the sense that salsa has reached major cities across the world) at a local level in London. In this way the local is not treated as self-contained and bounded, but is understood in terms of its interaction with global processes.

THE PRESENCE OF SALSA IN LONDON

Salsa's routes around the world are in part related to media exposure and distribution, and through them salsa has been incorporated into international music networks, while creating (as in the case of London) a local salsa scene. Hence, as salsa is placed geographically in different locales around the world, different localized identities are created, represented, and experienced. It is my intention, in this section, to explore how one element of the "global" movement of salsa involves commerce and industry as well as the movement of people who bring the music with them as part of the process through which they re-create, in London, part of the cultural practices they experienced in the Latin American countries from which they migrated.

Although for many Latin Americans in London a sense of Latin identity has been articulated through salsa, it is also important to recognize that there are differences among Latin American groups. Although there are cultural similarities, there are also political or geographical rivalries and economic and cultural differences. Hence, the Latin American groups I refer to in this chapter are those for whom music, particularly salsa, is part of the cultural repertoire through which they have developed and maintained a sense of identity.

The emergence of salsa music clubs did not happen in isolation, but occurred along with an increase in the number of Latin Americans migrating to the United Kingdom, a growing interest of non–Latin American people in the music, promotions by the music industry, the interest of record labels and the sponsorship of borough councils and embassies.

Latin Americans have played an important role in the spread of Latin music to and across London. The contact between Britain and Latin music started many years ago, and was apparent during the 1920s with the popularity of tango. However, the popularity of salsa music is related to the immigration processes of the 1970s. Different groups of immigrants brought with them, or asked their relatives to send them, the music they listened to in the countries they came from. They started organizing house parties, or getting together in community centers to share food and music with other Latin Americans.

At the same time, interest in the music was growing among the music industries and non–Latin American people. The routes of salsa music into London can be related to simultaneous efforts among music industries, record shops, magazines, radio stations, embassies, solidarity campaigns and clubs. Although acting for their own objectives and purposes, at the same time these were also developing links with one another. The networks developing from these relationships have contributed to the routes of salsa into London and to the development of a local salsa scene that is part of wider international networks.

Representatives of the music industry have explained their interest in Latin American artists as a source of "repertoire" for global markets. The music industry is recognizing the potential of Latin American music as a market, and not only in Spanish-speaking countries (Negus 1999; Scott 1994; Bourne 1993). Several articles in trade magazines like *Music Business International* and *Billboard* point to the importance of Latin American popular music as a market in Europe, and specialized magazines like *Latin Music Magazine* and *Latin Beat* have been distributed in Britain. In addition, world music magazines, for example *World Music* and *Global Music and Culture: Rhythm Music Magazine,* have included articles on salsa music. These magazines are addressed to a world music audience, and within this context salsa is referred to as "world music," a term created for specific marketing reasons that is sometimes an inclusive label for all non–English-language foreign music. Radio broadcasting of Latin, Caribbean, and African music coincided with the emergence of world music as a category with the launch of World Beat Box in 1988. Transmitted through Greater London Radio, this program catered to people who have "eclectic taste."[3] This program has played an important role for those people in London who do not necessarily attend the clubs. That program and these magazines provide their audiences with information about new releases, which not only contributes to knowledge building but establishes a link between salsa and an international world music network.

Major record shops like Tower Records and HMV have also contributed to the development of a salsa music scene in London. Some of these have created a new category and section for Latin music and even subsections for specific genres such as salsa and Latin pop, suggesting a more specialized audience of Latin music.

The first specialized record shop in Latin music, Mr. Bongo, started operating in London during the summer of 1990. This was followed by Latino Records in May 1991, but the shop ceased operations in January 1992. Dave Buttle, owner of Mr. Bongo, pointed out that local Latin music sales were not high and that major profits came from distribution to France, Holland, Spain, Greece, and especially Japan.[4] Mr. Bongo operated as a mediator and distributor for salsa to markets outside the United States, excluding Latin America. Reissuing special collections was one of the initial strategies adopted by record companies in England, and Charlie Records was the major reissue label for Latin music.

The beginning of the 1990s also saw the emergence of independent mail order services and local market stalls. For example, Latin Music operated mainly through individual orders. In March 1992 it launched *Latin Music Magazine*, each issue promoting a resident salsa band, a club, or an artist. Los Salseros also operated by mail order or to personal callers and usually had a stall at Salsa Fusion, a fortnightly club at Notre Dame Hall in Leicester Square. Individual CDs and tapes were also available in shops selling products from Latin America, such as La Tienda in Paddington and La Bodeguita in the Elephant and Castle shopping center.

The music industries have also contributed to local music scenes by promoting bands around the world. During the early 1990s, two production companies—Salsa Boogie and Tropicana Productions—started promoting salsa events in London. Previous to this, events were mainly organized on individual terms. These companies jointly organized and promoted their first mega-concert with the Oscar D'León concert at Hammersmith Palais on April 24, 1994. The organization of this concert was their first attempt to extend and expand their operations in London. Salsa Boogie was set up by Dominique Roome during the summer of 1992, and Tropicana Productions was set up by Ramiro Zapata at the beginning of 1993.[5] These two production companies managed to get support for the Oscar D'León concert from various sources connected with Latin America. The concert had the support of most salsa music clubs, restaurants, and Latin-owned shops in London; it was also sponsored by record shops, a Venezuelan airline, a travel agency, and a liquor company. The popularity and success of salsa concerts increased, so that by the summer of 2000 BBC London Live was promoting an all-day festival featuring Rubén Blades, Celia Cruz and Oscar D'León.

While promoters, record shops, magazines, and radio programs contribute to the development of a local salsa scene, the music industry-related networks have contributed to the presence of salsa in London and to the development of a local salsa scene which at the same time has led to routes beyond London, particularly to other European and Asian cities. Although the emerging local salsa scene in London is constantly building up through its interaction with what is occurring in New York, Miami, Puerto Rico, Cuba, and Colombia, local circumstances are important for the continuation of salsa in London. It is in this sense that the growing presence of Latin Americans, the interest in salsa among non–Latin Americans and the support of embassies and clubs play an important role in the development of a local salsa music scene.

The presence of Latin Americans in London has been recognized by embassies that have supported music festivals, Latin fiestas, and concerts in London. The Gran Gran Fiesta, one of the biggest festivals organized in London, is one of those events that has received support from local boroughs, embassies and private enterprises. The Gran Gran Fiesta is organized every two years, with the major events usually held at open-air parks in South London and music halls in Central London. A Pequeña Fiesta (small fiesta) is organized in the year between. The Colombian Carnival was sponsored by the Colombian Embassy and local boroughs. The interests of other local institutions—different from music-industry related ones—also contributed to the creation of a local salsa scene in London.

Musicians' interest in the music is also important for salsa's continuation and routes throughout England and beyond. However, regular venues for live music have often been limited to the weekends at a small number of clubs. This meant that larger bands would also play as trios or duos, mainly entertaining diners in small restaurants. In addition to clubs and restaurants, musicians occasionally played private parties, and in this way they contributed to spread salsa music to a public that was not confined to a bounded Latin club scene. Musicians also created routes and routines that transcended their gig circuits in London. By playing at different venues across Britain and Europe, musicians not only contributed to salsa's continuation in London but developed a wider network of salsa music beyond the United Kingdom.

Clubs have played the most important role in spreading salsa music in London, particularly through disc jockeys' growing interest in the music. When acquiring recordings for their performances, most of the disc jockeys preferred to get direct information from music magazines and international music charts. They have also traveled to New York or Miami (where many Latin music releases are launched) and attended music carnivals or festivals (those held in Colombia and Tenerife were usually mentioned). Dave Hucker, for example, had received inquiries from people in Japan who wanted to know what was happening in London, and had been invited to work as a disc jockey in France and Japan. Networks across the world developed from this interest, and through this process disc jockeys contributed to strengthening a local salsa scene in London.

SALSA MUSIC CLUBS IN LONDON:
A BRIEF ORAL HISTORY

Building up an account of the different clubs that have existed in London is a difficult task. I have had to rely on oral history along with information from the London-based Latin American press, which established a presence in 1984. Because most of the promotion for clubs was done by leafleting, it was difficult to find exact details. Leaflets are ephemeral, and hardly anyone collects them. Hence, this section relies mainly on oral history, with the inaccuracies or ambiguities that are part of narrated memories. My intention is not to present a chronological account, but to differentiate among the types of clubs that have existed and to highlight how this contributes to the routes that people take across salsa clubs in London.

From the beginning, two different forms of commercial gathering could be distinguished, articulating the differences or interests of the different groups of Latin Americans that first arrived in London. Many one-off clubs were organized by and for Latin Americans in London, and a *peña* was organized by a Chilean political refugee. A *peña* is a bohemian type of bar at which poets gather to read poetry or sing protest songs.

Toward the end of the 1970s the tendency was to rent church halls and community centers in South London. These parties were organized by a group of five or six people who took turns renting the same church hall or community center each week for a period of five to six weeks or until they were discovered to be operating clubs by the managers running these halls. The church halls and community centers rented space for private parties as a strategy to raise money, but they did not anticipate that the space would be used for clubs. That is why Amigo Hall in Lambeth and Saint Matthew's Hall in Brixton were the most popular ones. These clubs were located away from the center of the city and in places where they were less exposed to the police. As Hugo Benítez explained, "people tend to look for places around here (South London). The problem in the north is that the authorities have more control, and it is more difficult to manage. That is why Latinos do not like to go over there."[6] Some of the "clandestine clubs" were also organized in the center of London. This meant that maintaining publicity within close circles was important for their continuity.

Another tendency during this period was to organize clubs by hiring bars and restaurants. One of these was El Escondite (the Hiding Place), which ended in a tragic incident in which seventeen Colombians died. El Escondite, organized by Lubín Reyes and located in Soho, Central London, was considered clandestine because it operated without a license.[7] Juan Salgado tells how it ended:

It was in 1980, I think it was in August. With people in there at around three in the morning. In the same place as this *metedero* (clandestine spot) was a bar run by a Jamaican on the first floor that was frequented by a Scottish drunk. That night they did not allow him to go in, he might have done something wrong. The entrance was the same for both places. As he was not allowed to go in he went to a petrol station, bought a gallon of petrol and burnt the place, and seventeen people along with around twenty members from the other club died.[8]

This incident was remembered by many people I spoke to, particularly when recalling how clubs were organized in warehouses or underground floors of restaurants.

Many of these clubs were considered clandestine because they operated without a license or because they were open until six or seven in the morning.[9] In England it is established by law that it is necessary to obtain various licenses in order to keep a place open after eleven at night, the time at which all pubs should close. Clubs are allowed to open, once the licenses are granted, until two or three in the morning, depending on the area in which the club is located. In the center of the city, the license is granted until three in the morning, outside the center until two. The requirement of a license is a way in which the state (as a governmental apparatus) regulates and controls public spaces. This is an important point because it politicizes the geographical location of these clubs in London—their organization and distribution in the city.

At the beginning of the 1980s, Nacho Gálvez, a Chilean political refugee, organized the first *peña*, which met once a week above a bar in Soho. The idea was to create a meeting place for Chilean exiles, but it also attracted many other groups. Poets and songwriters gathered to share their poems, or to sing Cuban or Chilean "new protest songs." The *peña* became very popular and in six months moved to a bigger place in Brixton. This time salsa was played between the poets' sessions. Soon the peña changed character because the people who came were more interested in salsa than in listening to poets. The *peña* was transformed little by little into a Latin club, although it kept its name, but ended because the place was sold, and the new owners did not extend the lease.[10] Nacho, the organizer, later established a very successful Latin club, Club Bahia.

Sol y Sombra in Charlotte Street was one of the first Latin clubs in London to be in the same location for a relatively long period. This differentiated it from those with very short lives that were organized in different locations such as church halls or community centers. Sol y Sombra was organized by a Colombian in 1982 and burned down in 1986. The cause of the fire was not clear, but Dave Hucker, the disc jockey of the club, said that it could have been a "deliberate incident."[11]

Bass Clef, another club mentioned by most people interviewed, played an important role among musicians; for a long period it was the main venue for live music, the focal point for the Latin scene in London.[12] Although recognized by musicians as the first venue for live music, all of the musicians I interviewed considered the conditions and payment at the club to be poor, and they had boycotted it by refusing to play there. Bass Clef closed for refurbishment and opened under a new administration that no longer promoted Latin nights.

Aside from these two clubs, many other were mentioned to me but in an indiscriminate order and with a vaguer idea of when they started. Names like La Plaza, Yo te Amo, Costa Brava, Changó, Chicagos, La Clave, Tunel del Tiempo, and Jacqueline's were mentioned.

These clubs moved to and from different places all the time, or they rapidly disappeared. Most of them operated until they were discovered by the police or changes were made in the initial agreements. Some of these clubs ended, others opened in other places, perhaps with the same name or under another name. The ephemeral characteristic of these clubs brought them a negative reputation. These "clandestine clubs" were shadowed by fights, the constant intervention of the police, and by fires. All these incidents contributed to the construction of a Latin identity as violent, aggressive, illegal, and drug related. These images and conceptions had influenced some of the people I interviewed as to the routes they took to different places. Here the identity given to these places was constructed through a series of specific incidents and practices rather than through visual and verbal representations alone.

CONSTRUCTING AND COMMUNICATING THE IDENTITIES OF SALSA CLUBS

In this section I explore how Latin is signified through the location and decoration of the clubs, and through advertisements, marketing strategies and the music played. For example, those clubs that operated in leased properties tended to emphasize their Latin identity through the decoration, music, and food. However, others that operated at rented venues, where restrictions forbid altering the property, would build an identity mainly through the name of the club, which was usually promoted by the disc jockeys. These clubs were characterized by their mobility. In the following section I will profile some of the clubs and pay particular attention to how the promoters of these places positioned their clubs among or against existing clubs as a way of creating and communicating a unique identity. I shall highlight various issues that have an impact on the routes and routines of participants and hence their participation at any event.

Short-Lived Clubs

During the early 1990s, when I was conducting detailed research, most of the Latin nights were organized in venues with proper licenses. These were rented to different people throughout the week, and one night would not necessarily be related to the other; perhaps just one day of the week was a Latin night. The place was prepared to operate as a club and decorated to accommodate the different interests operating in that venue. When operating in hired or rented premises, the notion of a club can be fluid and mobile, not tied to a particular place. Because a club was usually built upon disc jockeys' names and music collections, it could move from venue to venue. Most of the clubs in these venues ran according to verbal agreements, and they were characterized by mobility or short existence because the owner of the place could change the initial arrangements at any moment. In many cases, the club would cease operating after a short period. This was the case of Chicagos, a South London club that organized Latin nights during the weekends for about four months (August to December 1992) under the same administration. Hugo Benítez, who rented the club, ended the agreement because of a dispute with the owner, who changed the initial agreements on the rent and deals regarding the entrance fee. After Chicagos closed, Hugo Benítez and Guillermo Norton opened Copacabana in the Old Kent Road, traditionally a working-class neighborhood, again in South London. This club operated without a license for almost three months, from December 1993 to February 1994, before it was discovered by the police.

Copacabana aimed to attract Latin American workers. The identity of Copacabana as a working-class salsa club for Latin Americans in London was established by the entrance fee, the method of selling drinks, and the use of recorded music rather than bands. In addition, the publicity for the club was restricted to Latin American circuits in London, such as the Elephant and Castle Shopping Center, Clapham Common football league, and advertising in the Latin American press. It would not promote in magazines such as *Time Out,* as this reached a wider public that Hugo Benítez did not wish to attract. The aim was to attract the "Latin worker and charge a reasonable price because we have to pay the rent and staff, but not an exaggerated cost, and not to exploit."[13] This was so because, as Hugo Benítez pointed out, "Latin Americans in this country only go out at the weekends. It is not like in our countries, partying every night of the week. Here, the Latin American does not have the money. Latin Americans are just working, and working very hard."[14] Clearly positioned against Club Bahia, a club also run by a Latin person, Hugo said:

I think the entrance fee is six pounds, it is too expensive. They sell drinks, not the bottles [of liquor]. If you start buying by drinks it is too expensive. They have bands. Also, the people there are selective. Not everyone can go, first because it is too expensive, second because it is calmer. It is not for "the people," it is for people with a slightly higher level, those who earn more. Not just anyone goes there.[15]

These two clubs, although part of the growing salsa scene in London, were positioned by their owners as belonging to different networks and different social classes. Club Bahia aimed to attract a different audience. On this point, Nacho Gálvez, the owner of Club Bahia, commented:

These small clubs are oriented, basically, towards the Latin American immigrant. These are places of entertainment for them. I think that from that point of view they carry out a social function, by offering a cheap and popular place of entertainment for Latin American immigrants. . . . I have to recognize that in a certain way they have a social function, at least they are a place of escape for large numbers of illegal Latin American immigrants who have nowhere to go and who are looking for the cheapest entertainment, and for the cheapest Latin American club. A relief from those weeks in which they work almost twenty hours daily. But these clubs are completely different to what we try to do here. We aim at a completely different clientele.[16]

The distinction made by Nacho is of class, but one that relates to the legal status of immigrants. Those whose visas have expired or were working early morning or late evening shifts and were usually badly paid, had less access to salsa clubs in London, limited to certain clubs that operated outside of standard licensing hours.

These two clubs operated in completely different ways. The owner of Bahia had a lease on the place, while Copacabana was operating without a license. Copacabana was positioned among Latin American workers in London, while Club Bahia positioned within the "cultural variety of London."[17] These clubs occupied different positions according to economic and social differentiation, a fact that both owners were aware of.

Club Bahia

Club Bahia was opened in March 1990 on the ground floor of the Gallery, a Spanish restaurant. Although near Vauxhall underground station and a short distance from the center of London, it was located in an area where there was little night life and few pubs or shops. Thus those who visited Club Bahia did so because they knew of its existence.

Club Bahia was mainly visited by middle-class Latin Americans and Europeans.

Bahia was decorated with signed photos of famous jazz musicians like Dizzy Gillespie and Duke Ellington, and some top Latin jazz musicians in London, including Roberto Plá. The tables were round and covered with red gingham tablecloths. Latin American handicrafts and wooden parrots hung on the columns of the club. Nacho Gálvez, the owner, explained that with the mixture of objects he intended to signify both Latin and jazz, simultaneously.

The club established a direct link with its audience through a mailing list and the distribution of a professionally produced program, rather than photocopied fliers distributed randomly on the street. Apart from promoting bands in a prominent way in each leaflet by placing a photo on the front page, Nacho was also attempting to position Bahia's presentation of salsa within London's jazz music scene by advertising Bahia as the "Home of the Latin Beat."

Nacho was interested in attracting an audience that would not be limited to Latin Americans. As he pointed out: "In London there are British people as well as different ethnic minorities. . . . Basically, it is towards this variety that our publicity is directed and open to."[18] Although aiming at a mixture of people, Bahia was mainly frequented by middle-class Latin Americans. This type of audience was maintained through the cost of the entrance fee (which was £ 7), the quality of the service (tablecloths, drinks served individually and not as bottles of liquor), and through the centrality of live music as something to be appreciated as well as danced to.

Nacho Gálvez positioned Club Bahia outside of and against those clubs that offered what he considered to be cheap entertainment for Latin American immigrants. He wanted to get away from what he called "the Third World image"[19] of Latin America, which he thought many clubs contributed to. In this context salsa in Club Bahia was presented as part of a Latin identity that was constructed in a deliberate contrast to those clubs frequented by working-class Latin Americans and the clubs that draw on tropical and tourist images. A more subtle and sophisticated appreciation of music was privileged over dancing, drinking, and eating, and this was reinforced through the decoration and construction. Visually, Club Bahia placed an emphasis on musicians, and it was constructed and organized in a way more akin to jazz clubs than to disco dance clubs.

Barco Latino

Barco Latino, a boat located on the River Thames (Temple Pier, Victoria Embankment), opened in November 1990. During the day it was a

Colombian restaurant, and it became a Latin club from 9 P.M. to 3 A.M. Because of its location, during the day Barco Latino was visited by tourists who stopped for a beer or a glass of wine, and by those working nearby for their lunch. As a club, Barco Latino was frequented mainly by Colombians, particularly on Saturdays. Among Colombians, this was one of the most popular clubs that operated with a license.

Barco Latino was a small boat limited by the licensing authorities to seventy-five people and was decorated with some Colombian motifs. The wall near a small dance floor area was decorated with a collection of postcards from the varied regions of Colombia (the mountainous Andean region, the urban cities of Bogota, Cali, and Medellín, and the Caribbean coastal area of Cartagena and Baranquilla). The back walls of the boat were painted with a mural of a bright blue sky and a sunny beach with palm trees. Some toy parrots hung near the bar area, but most prominent were stickers over the frames of the bar with proverbs (refrains) of Latin sayings, many sexist, for example, "Mother in laws are good, but when buried like *yuca* root." Barco Latino was managed by Camilo Pereira, a Colombian who had been living in Britain since 1974.[20] He started at the boat in November 1990, when he hired the place on Sunday nights. After a year he bought the lease for the business of the boat and converted it into El Barco Latino, a Latin bar-restaurant. He also changed the music, by playing Latin music all the time and included a menu that had a selection of Latin American dishes like tamales, *sancocho*, *tostones* and *chicharón*.

Contrasting with Bahia, as a club, Barco Latino attracted mainly working class Latin Americans. Camilo said that this was a matter of self-selection and that he was "not interested in attracting people by race or social position. They can wear a tie or not, they could be blacks or not; this is a Latin place for everyone."[21] "Smart" dressing codes were specified in Bahia's promotion, while Barco Latino had no specification. There was no entrance fee at Barco Latino until eleven, when 3 pounds (approximately $5 U.S.) was charged. The club offered a selection of Latin American drinks and beers, sold individually and by bottles (more economical for those wanting to spend a longer time at Barco Latino), in contrast to Bahia where drinks were sold only individually.

Barco Latino started with a license to open until eleven as a bar-restaurant, but without a license to operate as a club. Despite this, it was open until very late. Although it did not have a license to operate as a club, Barco Latino advertised itself as a club in the Latin American press and leaflets that were distributed at Clapham Common and Elephant and Castle Shopping Center. In time, the authorities caught on. "The place became very popular," Camilo said, "and the police and fire brigade started to notice that there were many people coming onto the boat and that it was open until late. We are in the center of town, that it is where the police and the council have a stronger enforcement policy, thus from February 1993 until November we had to start closing at eleven and the business went down."[22] When it reopened in November 1993, Barco Latino was advertised in the Latin American press as "a Colombian patrimony at the service of all the 'Rumberos' (partiers) of the world," opening its doors "to the rest of the Latin American community and to the world in general."[23] As Camilo explained, his new license, along with club's location and the fact that Latin American food and music had become more recognized prompted him to seek to appeal to a wider audience. Despite this change, Saturday nights continued to be frequented mainly by Colombians.

A short walk from the Houses of Parliament, this club had always been very visible for the authorities and was raided by the police and by immigration officers many times. Camilo explained how the police were alerted after an article published in *City Limits* described dancing in Barco Latino as like "dancing in the underground trains at peak hours." A further example occurred during the football World Cup of 1994 in which Colombia went into the finals, and when the boat had a large screen transmitting the games. Just after the first match in which the Colombian team lost, an article was published in the *Guardian* (Chaudhary 1994) about Colombians watching the match at Barco Latino. Three days later the police raided the boat, but no other Latin club transmitting the games was raided by the police during that period.

Camilo acknowledged that at the beginning it was fair enough because he had opened without the proper license. But after obtaining the license he continued to be visited by police who insisted on seeing the license. Camilo said:

> I was getting tired. They would come every eight days and ask me to show them the license, or to see whether there was control over the number of people allowed into the boat. One day I was a bit rude and told them, "This is racism. I bet that you are not checking out English discos as much as you do here." That time they even took me to talk to the superintendent. But since then they have not come anymore. It has already been three months since that incident.[24]

The case of Barco Latino, in which the owner had to negotiate the club's position with the licensing authorities and the police, brings me back to an important dimension—that of the hierarchies established by the state. Through the process of regulating licensing times for bars and restaurants in the city and by granting licenses, the state has the power to regulate public space. Thus, in the case of Barco Latino, relations of power were established not necessarily with entrepreneurs who changed the cost of the place or the initial agreement at any time, but in relation to state regulations and licensing authorities.

BAR CUBA AND BAR RUMBA

At the beginning of the 1990s, another type of club started becoming visible in the West End. The physical presence of these clubs was more visible in the city because these were created and promoted as Latin places through the names and menus offered, although each night could change depending on the disc jockeys' or musicians' ability to attract a greater public and therefore, their ability to be economically successful for the owner of the club. This was the case of Bar Rumba and Bar Cuba.

Dave, the owner of Bar Cuba, recalled that in 1988 a small group of entrepreneurs co-ordinated the opening of several clubs at the same time in order to start building up a scene. They started opening Spanish *tapas* bars: Bar Madrid, Bar Seville, Grey Camino, and Bar Escoba. These tapas bars began with Flamenco nights and little by little incorporated salsa nights. This proved to be economically successful, and so Latin nights started taking over Flamenco nights. Some of the people involved in the creation of the Spanish bars started selling them and opening places in which the setting was Latin, instead of Spanish, although in many cases both concepts were mixed. Most notable, because of their geographical location, were Bar Cuba (January 1992) in Kensington High Street, Bar Rumba (September 1993) in Shaftesbury Avenue, and Salsa in Charing Cross Road (March 1993).

Dave was involved in the group who started Bar Madrid, Bar Seville, and Grey Camino; eventually these were sold, and he started Bar Cuba. He said he was trying to move away from the Spanish bars that he had started by creating a new concept of a bar with a Latin identity. Regarding the process of creating Bar Cuba he told me the following:

> I wanted to do something Spanish, but a bit different because everybody was catching on the same. . . . So I took it from a Spanish idea to a Caribbean idea. What can be Spanish Caribbean? Puerto Rico, well, no. Cuba, well, that is a good idea, it is basically Spanish. Not Puerto Rico, because it normally reflects fairly violent images. Puerto Rico is *West Side Story*, things like that, Puerto Ricans in America, and I did not want to have that sort of image. I wanted a mysterious image of the Caribbean extended in the food, be a little more competent in the food, rather than just the tapas.[25]

Cuba was taken as a theme to construct a very specific Latin identity, one that attempted to re-create the style of prerevolutionary Cuba that the immigrant community had built up in Little Havana, Miami, rather than what he found in present-day Cuba. The Latin identity that was being constructed and communicated here was a "mysterious" and nostalgic Cuba of the 1950s that drew on the way that such an identity has been maintained by Cuban exiles and Cuban-Americans in Miami.

The other elements taken into consideration, after the decoration, were the type of people he wanted to attract, the location of the club, and finally the music. The people whom Bar Cuba aimed to attract were "casual smart . . . upmarket, anywhere between the age 20 up to 40." This was a middle-class clientele for whom this idea of Cuba was presented in a particular location, Kensington High Street, where the idea of a restaurant and club were combined. Music was one of the last considerations in constructing the identity of the place, "You can get away with any type of music as long it has the right atmosphere," Dave said. "The main thing is the decor, then the people and then the music. What if you have the right music if it is in bad surroundings."

Bar Rumba was constructed following a process similar to that of Bar Cuba: first, elaborating the concept of the club, then constructing the place according to the concept. Eric Yu, the owner of Bar Rumba, explained that the idea behind it was to construct "a modern and trendy place that attracted trendy people."[26] The idea of a Spanish tapas bar was mixed with Latin food. The menu was a version of Spanish tapas with Mexican food (or "Mexican tapas") and Spanish or Mexican beers. Although it was seeking to appeal to a similar type of person to Bar Cuba, and while people tended to visit both clubs, it was constructed with a more generic Spanish-Mexican themed Latin identity, which drew on the food and beer rather than the decor.

Unlike Bar Cuba, Bar Rumba operated as a club with a snack bar rather than a restaurant. In addition, music was far more important to the way that the club was given a Latin identity on specific nights. Bar Rumba was a tapas bar located in a corner of Trocadero Shopping Center in Shaftesbury Avenue, central London. The decoration of the place was based on body shapes in movement so as to accommodate the different clubs that operated in Bar Rumba during the week. When it opened in September 1993, Bar Rumba started with two Latin nights, Sundays and Tuesdays.

Maintaining the commercial success of these clubs relied on the entertainment manager who was in charge of organizing each night. Chris Greenwood, the entertainment manager of Bar Rumba and Bar Cuba, was responsible for making decisions in these clubs that would not antagonize the owners' objectives. His interests and aims shaped each night of the place:

> What I try to do is fuse things. I don't like being a purist. I mean there are Colombian clubs where the girls all sit on one side and the guys on the other, and they will wear a lot of gold. You know, like in Colombia. But our idea was not to duplicate what is happening over there and bring it here. You have to adapt it. We do dance classes to try to get people into it, and it has been a great success.

Greenwood used a stereotyped version of Latin identity to differentiate the clubs he was managing from those frequented by working-class Colombians, by referring to the separation of men and women in the clubs and the wearing of exaggerated gold jewelry. This emphasis on being different from "Colombian" clubs highlights the way in which these two clubs (Bar Rumba and Bar Cuba) were not aiming to attract Colombians in London; although as Eric Yu mentioned, having some Latin Americans in the club "gives authenticity," because after all "it is a Latin bar." Within this context, it is worth noting that these clubs were promoted as Cuban (or with Cuban signifiers such as "rumba"), for example, rather than as Colombian.

In addition to the entertainment manager, disc jockeys publicized their club while also promoting the venue, and this had to be done according to the owners' aims. In Bar Rumba, Saturday nights were reserved for "trendy people . . . for the people who like Soho and Covent Garden."[27] The following advertisement for one Saturday night includes almost every element the owners were interested in attracting. "Dress up and be grown up, as this is likely to draw an older (20– and 30–something) good-lookin' crowd."[28] Near Piccadilly Circus, this tapas bar also attracted passing tourists.

Although selling Mexican and Spanish food and beer, the Latin identity of Bar Rumba was largely constructed through the music played on these two nights and the way these were promoted to a particular type of audience. One night aimed to attract a more cosmopolitan audience for whom salsa might be a part of "world music," whereas the other attempted to attract those more interested in salsa as a dance. Both nights were organized within the context of the owners' strategy of positioning Bar Rumba in relation to a wider network of popular dance music in London.

FROM PLACES TO ROUTES AND ROUTINES

In moving from the club's identities to the routes and routines of dancers I intend to highlight how the movements of those who participated at these clubs were as important in the making of Latin identities as the aspects mentioned above, such as decoration, geographical location, advertising strategies, and publicity. I will use the idea of routes and routines to refer to the specific movement and patterns that dancers create by participating at certain clubs and not others. More than concentrating on participation at the event, which I consider to be that particular moment in which participants come to be together, I wish to concentrate on the specific dynamics through which the intersection of participants occurs. I argue that understanding participation across the Latin clubs in London requires an awareness of how the routes of some might limit the movement of others who are involved in similar processes and movements—that is, through the specific dynamics that affect the co-presence and exclusion of those who participate in salsa music clubs in London.

My argument here was initially developed from my observation of the absence of Latin Americans in many of the Latin music clubs that I visited, and the fact that when Latin Americans were present, the absence of non–Latin Americans was often noticeable. This was not the case in every club, bar, restaurant or event—there were occasions when Latin Americans and non–Latin Americans were both present (particularly at political solidarity events and fiestas supported by local borough councils, and at the Gran Gran Fiesta). I do not want to reduce participation in the construction of Latin identities to the issue of presence or absence, but suggest that this idea is useful for thinking about the movement of people around the city. The routes and routines created by people as they move between different places are important for understanding the power relations within which individuals locate themselves and move across space and in doing this contribute to the making of Latin identities in London.

The routes and routines created by dancers can be influenced by the days of the week that clubs operate, the band performing, the disc jockeys playing, and the policies and practices of club owners or promoters. The movement of dancers can also be related to their economic situation and employment conditions, especially their work schedule. The location of the club was also significant in influencing the intersection of participants at any particular club.

The movement of participants occurs across a network of particular clubs; some will regularly visit one club, others will go to different places every week and some would even have a routine of visiting various clubs throughout the week. One such person is John Madison, an Englishman whom I met at the London School of Salsa and who participated at different salsa clubs. John, who was a self-employed graphic designer, started dancing to salsa and visiting clubs in August 1993 through a friend who first invited him to one of the many salsa clubs in London. John developed a network of friends with whom he would arrange to meet at the clubs. When I asked him which clubs he visited most, he said:

> Oh, I can give you a list. It almost works like a routine now. Everybody goes to certain places on certain nights. There are slight variations, obviously. Starting from Monday night it is Cuba in Kensington, on Tuesday it would probably be Bar Rumba. Wednesday nights could be at La Finca the early part of the evening and take the lessons, then go to a place called the Rocket in Holloway Road. On Thursday nights it is obviously here (Latinos), and the routine now is to meet down in Salsa in Charing Cross Road. Sometimes we go to Palladium as well, we go there for an hour and then go to Salsa, because Salsa gets very packed about 11 PM. So we go to Palladium, spend an hour there and then go back to Salsa. Friday nights, possibly I would not go anywhere. If I am taking somebody out maybe I'll go to Club Bahia. Saturdays, I used to do a class at La Finca on Saturday evenings, but that now has stopped. So, every fortnight I go to Salsa Fusion. Obviously the Saturday in between if I was doing salsa I maybe go to HQs or Mambo Inn at Loughborough Hotel, or maybe to Club Bahia if there is a good band. Sometimes there is a good band at HQ, although you don't get many serious salsa dancers there. Club Bahia is more a kind of place where you take somebody out, rather than a club you just go to dance. You take somebody to dinner and then go down to the club, sit and listen to the band. That is basically it.[29]

John had developed a routine according to the days of the week on which each club operated; whether he was going to meet some friends, if there was a band he preferred and if he knew he was going to find good dancers. The clubs he frequented were different from those mentioned by Latin Americans. Club Bahia presented possibilities for meeting points as it was mentioned by Latin Americans and non–Latin Americans.

Although John had developed a network of friends through the clubs, he mentioned that he had not met many Latin Americans in these clubs: "Obviously Elder, the guy teaching, and Xiomara; one or two people I know, but I do not know their names and can't regard them as friends." Though he was expecting "the clubs to be full of people from South America, I was surprised how many Anglos were there." Through these routes and routines John narrated how he was involved in specific spatial practices across salsa clubs in London. He also noticed the visible separation of Latin Americans and non–Latin Americans at the salsa clubs that he regularly visited.

Lily, an Israeli woman I met at the London School of Salsa and who first arrived in England in 1987, developed a similar routine to that mentioned by John. They were friends and had met through the clubs. She described her activities in the following way:

> I think I have checked almost every club that existed. Not really, I haven't been to Chicagos. But, it is very Latin, they said, not our people the ones who go out there so much. Clubs, our clubs obviously, Bar Tiempo, the Rocket, Cuba, I have been to Bar Rumba a couple of times, Barco Latino, Bahia and Salsa Palladium. I find the Latin people kind of stick to each other, in a way. I have heard of Chicagos, there have been quite a few places that I don't go to. I know them, but I don't go there because there are mainly Latin people. I tend to mix with Latinos that like to meet with foreign people. I want to go to places where I know people, and then also the Latin mentality can sometimes clash. It is like, if you go here, you know Western people go on their own and you don't have to go with a man, you go to these places and if you want to dance with somebody you just go and ask them. Latin places, they tend to go in couples, from what I have heard, I have never been; and you might be considered like looking for it. If you go and ask them to dance, they get the wrong idea, you know. Hey, you just want to have a good dance, nothing to do with them, and they can get pretty sticky, and thinking "Oh she wanted to dance with me, maybe she wants something else." I can't stand it. So unless I go with somebody, I wouldn't go to these places. I've heard that they tend to have a lot of fights, and they get carried away.[30]

In the case of Lily, an idea based on assumptions of a Latin identity influenced the routes she took and the routines she developed. In this quote, two types of assumptions about Latins arose, the first one related to the role of men and women in the clubs, and the second to a perceived threat of violence. Even though, as she acknowledged, she had never been to these places, her considerations were based on a particular version of Latin identity. Some of these ideas were related to incidents that she had heard of. The sharing of accumulated meanings about clubs, through word of mouth, played an important part in shaping the routes and routines that Lily developed. Although this is an individual's experience, the identity of the clubs had an influence on her routes and routines.

Referring to those clubs that were frequented by Latin Americans, Miguel,[31] who had been in England for five years and whose visa had expired, thought that these clubs were reproducing the image of a "ghetto." He was doing various types of jobs, like cleaning offices and restaurants and washing dishes. He was actively working with a solidarity campaign group for a Latin American country. He used to visit these clubs during his first year in England but not anymore. "It is like extending the ghetto, and you never can get out of it; you live, talk, work, and also have fun with them; it is like a circle from which you never escape."[32] The image of Latin places as reproducing the "ghetto" is another version of Latin identity, this time based on the differences among the Latin American groups in London.

The clubs that were most mentioned by Latin Americans were Barco Latino, Club Bahia, Rumberos, and La Gota Fría in Bootleggers. This last club was located near Oxford Circus, and it operated on those premises on Saturdays and Sundays and was frequented by Latin Americans. The advertisement for this club was published in the Latin American press, and leaflets were distributed at the Elephant and Castle Shopping Center. Although many non–Latin Americans know about this place, the ones I talked to did not visit this club.

Diego Medina, a Colombian man who was involved in organizing cultural events for the Latin American Association, did not visit most of the salsa clubs mentioned by non–Latin Americans because he believed that these were reproducing stereotypical images of Latin America. As he explained:

> If I go to any it is to Bahia . . . I do not go regularly, but I think it is important. I would go at least every three months. Sometimes I go to new places to see how they are. But generally I don't like them because they represent precisely the exoticism of our culture. If you go to places like Down Mexico Way, you don't see any Latin people around, but you are listening to salsa music, seeing Mexican food, and perhaps the only Latin is washing dishes. Then, I prefer not to go.[33]

Although salsa clubs, as I explained in the previous section, were constructed in a way that communicated various Latin identities, Diego thought that most of the salsa clubs that he had visited were reproducing images of Latin America as a tourist site or as an exotic culture, and this affected the routes that he chose to adopt. However, the fact that Diego's participation was limited to Bahia was also a sign of class difference among Latin Americans. In Club Bahia, the entrance fee was higher than any other Latin club in London, so even when this club was included in the routes of dancers, it was not part of their weekly routines. The identity of Club Bahia was also created through the sharing of accumulated meaning about the owner. The owner of Bahia was the same person who started the first *peña*, which was initially set up as a response to the interests of a particular group of political refugees, articulating the differences of Latin American groups in London. Thus, in this case the knowledge about the owner's previous clubs and practices contributed to the identity of the clubs, while having an impact on the routes and routines of some participants, particularly along the lines of political consciousness and class differentiation.

Diego worked as an organizer of Latin American cultural events in London, and Miguel was involved in a solidarity campaign group for the country he is from. Like all participants, they perceived the different clubs according to their own experiences and commitments. Although both were labor immigrants, their political commitments made them more critical of Latin clubs that they thought represented a stereotype of "ghetto" or the "exotic."

For Carmen and María,[34] two other labor immigrants, different considerations were taken into account. They would not visit Club Bahia or Barco Latino. In the case of Club Bahia the cost was a strong consideration; in the case of Barco Latino possibilities of being raided by the police were a major concern. There were other considerations taken into account when visiting salsa clubs. Carmen had been living in England since 1984 and María since 1989. María's visa expired in 1990. Both were doing domestic labor during the week, working all day, from eight in the morning to seven in the evening. They lived on the outskirts of London and did not earn much money. Thus, the idea of going to a club was a big economic investment; they could visit clubs only once a month and on Saturday nights. In addition, they went to clubs where María could go without the fear of drawing attention to her legal status. Most of the time they invited people over to their flat or went to one-off parties organized by different organizations, such as the Latin American football league. Thus, for those Latin Americans whose situation drew them to operate underground, the routes had to be negotiated across places where they become less visible for the policing authorities. The routes and routines of Carmen and María are an indication of how presence and absence in the intimate setting of a bar or club is influenced by broader patterns. The possibility to participate in the making of Latin London is shaped by macro power relations involving the regulation of space, particularly the policing of immigration controls at certain salsa clubs.

The geographical location is a strong element influencing participation. However, the location alone was not the only element influencing the movement of participants across the salsa clubs. For example, Barco Latino and Bar Rumba were both located in the center of London, and entry was free or minimal. Although geographically located in areas of major economic investment and activity in London, there were similarities and differences among those who participated in creating the event at these clubs. I would like to draw attention to some issues regarding these two clubs as up to now I have made contrasts between clubs located in different geographical areas of the city. This might lead to the assumption that those clubs that are located in the center of London are mainly frequented by British, other Europeans, and tourists passing by, and that those away from the center by Latin Americans. Although I have mentioned a number of clubs that would counter such an assumption, I will now consider these two clubs (Bar Rumba and Barco Latino) and their interrelation to extend the discussion of routes and routines.

In Bar Rumba, Saturdays were for what the owner considered to be the most "trendy" clubs, attracting middle-class people, ages twenty-five to forty who could spend money. This was maintained through the entrance fee, which could range from 10 to 12 (about $15 to $18 U.S.) pounds on Saturdays, in contrast to Latin nights, which started with free admission and then charged 1 pound (less than $2 U.S.). Despite this low cost, there were not many Latin Americans in this club during the week. It is worth noting that, first, the owners of Bar Rumba were not interested in attracting Latin Americans and, second, that Latin nights were held on Tuesdays and not on Fridays or Saturdays, when most Latin Americans had the time to go out. Thus, for many Latin Americans it was often not possible to go to places like Bar Rumba during the week. Those who participated in creating the event in Bar Rumba did not necessarily include Barco Latino in their routines. The opposite also happened: those who participated at Barco Latino would not necessarily include Bar Rumba in their routines.

Hence, there was not a unified salsa scene. In this example, Barco Latino was part of a different network of clubs to that of Bar Rumba. Barco Latino was frequented mainly by Colombians, and it encountered several problems with the licensing authorities and was forced to close in February 1993, reopening with the proper license during November of the same year. When closing and reopening, the routines of those participating at Barco Latino were disrupted. But by then Barco Latino was operating semiclandestinely, and therefore included in a network of clubs different from those of Bar Rumba's network. Thus, although routines were disrupted, the movement of participants did not shift to Bar Rumba, but to other salsa clubs that were within similar social positions, often clandestine. It is in this way that those clubs with a short life, those constantly changing venues or operating half clandestinely, come to have an important role in disrupting and creating new routes for participants. Thus, although participation may be disrupted, a certain degree of continuity is guaranteed through the process by which participants are moving around certain salsa clubs and not others.

FINAL REMARKS

Focusing on salsa as a "dislocated" cultural practice usually associated with Latin Americans has allowed me to raise questions about the movement of Latin Americans to London, their relationship to music and the activities and practices that contribute to the making of Latin London. This is not to say that salsa and the presence of Latin Americans in London directly correspond in a straightforward way, but that these are related. In this sense, then, Latin Americans do not simply move to London carrying a unified culture but attempt to construct, within the local circumstances and geography, and interacting with various inhabitants of London, an environment that provides a sense of identification. In the same way, salsa is not simply "flowing" across space and reaching the entire world to the same degree but moving in specific ways and undergoing particular processes of transformation. Throughout this chapter, I have also tried to demonstrate how the construction of Latin identities is not an exclusive practice of Latin American groups.

I have argued that Latin identities across salsa clubs cannot solely be understood through a focus on the clubs alone but by adopting an approach that takes in to consideration macro as well as micro elements. Hence, I have focused on the routes and routines created by participants, the monitoring of licensing authorities and policies, and the practices of club owners and promoters. From this I suggest that the degree of participation in the making of Latin identities in London has to be understood in relation to these ongoing practices and relations of power across and between different salsa music clubs in London. Hence, Latin places are not contained and bounded sites for social interaction, but constituted in relation to broader spatial practices and power relations that play an important part in the construction and embodiment of particular Latin identities. In discussing Latin identities, this chapter is also embedded within my sense of identities as both Latin American and Caribbean. Having grown up mainly in Puerto Rico, and for periods in the United States, I participated in salsa clubs and other cultural activities organized by Latin Americans in London with some knowledge, preconceptions and presumptions, with similar cultural knowledge and also with the personal experience of migration. Thus, as a Puerto Rican who completed research on Latin American identities in London, issues of authority and knowledge cannot be underestimated, as these present a potential dichotomy between identification and ethnographic authority. Identifying as a Puerto Rican had implications for the practice of fieldwork and of writing this account. First, my knowledge about salsa was either overestimated, tested, or taken for granted by participants. Second, the way in which an ethnographer positions her- or himself in the writing has implications for the constitution of ethnographic authority. In presenting myself as both Latin American and Puerto Rican I ran the risk of implying that I was a complete insider (which was not the case) and that this provides me with an authoritative voice. However, this has another side to it: by claiming that I was not an insider and that I had to become one I run the risk of assuming a naive position as if my prior knowledge and views were not affecting the research or the ethnographic writing. Thus, my sense of identity and identification with Latin Americans cannot be separated from my participation and my account of the making of Latin London.

Although my research might suggest that there are many narratives, experiences, and meanings of Latin identities and that these are always in the process of formation, it is not my intention to celebrate multiplicity. Not everyone participates in all Latin expressions in London or is exposed to them to the same degree or even experiences them in the same way. Although I acknowledge this multiplicity, my intention has not been to privilege or celebrate this diversity. Rather it has been to stress how Latin identities developed from the ways in which different groups occupy different positions, and how certain cultural practices are positioned in terms of power relations in the city of London. Thus, I have stressed that multiple Latin identities are realized through specific relations of power at particular times and places.

NOTES

1. It is important to clarify that "dance music" and dance events are not limited to music clubs. See, for example, anthropological research on dance events in Greece by Cowan (1990), and the discussion of performance dance events by Hanna (1988).
2. For an example of this, refer to Hosokawa (1999).
3. Personal interview with Jo Shinner, producer of *World Beat Box*, November 8, 1993.
4. Personal interview with David Buttle, owner of Mr. Bongo, November 4, 1993.
5. Personal interview with Ramiro Zapata, March 22, 1994.
6. Personal interview with Hugo Benítez, February 21, 1994. Interview was held in Spanish. Original text follows: "La gente tiende a busar a sitios en esta área (refiriéndose al sur). El problema en el norte es que las autoridades controlan más alla. Es más controlado por las autoridades, son lugares difíciles de manejar, a los latinos no le gusta ir alla por eso."
7. Personal interview with Juan Salgado, November 30, 1993. Juan Salgado is Colombian and was involved with Latin American groups since his arrival in London and was also the founder of the first Latin American newspaper, *Crónica Latina*.
8. Personal interview with Juan Salgado, November 30, 1993. Interview was held in Spanish. Original text follows: "Eso fue en 1980, el mes creo que fue en agosto. Estando ellos ahí a las tres de la mañana. En el mismo sitio donde quedaba este metedero, había un bar de un jamaiquino en el primer piso y a ese bar lo frecuentaba un

escosez borracho. Lo hecharon esa noche, algo hizo mal. La puerta era común para ambos sitios. Como no lo dejaron entrar arriba se fue a una surtidora de gasolina y le echó fuego y quemó 17 y veinti algo de miembros del otro club que era un club privado."

9. To open a club it is necessary to obtain various licenses. One allows selling liquor after 11 PM; another, called an "entertainment license," allows dancing. There are further regulations stipulated by the fire department and other security bodies.

10. Interview with Nacho Gálvez, Saturday, October 30, 1993.

11. Personal interview with Dave Hucker, February 22, 1994.

12. Personal interview with Dominique Roome, November 16, 1993.

13. Personal interview with Hugo Benítez, February 21, 1994. Interview was held in Spanish. Original text follows: "Lo que nosotros tratamos es de atraer al latino trabajador y cobrarle lo que es razonable. Porque hay que pagar renta y 'estaff,' pero tampoco una cosa exagerada, tampoco explotar."

14. Personal interview with Hugo Benítez, February 21, 1994. Interview was held in Spanish. Original text follows: "El Latino aquí no funciona sino el fin de semana. No es como en los países de nosotros que toda la semana, todas las noches estamos rumbeando. Aquí no, el latino no tiene plata para eso. Está trabajando solamente y trabajando fuerte."

15. Interview with Hugo Benítez, February 21, 1994. Interview was held in Spanish. Original text follows: "La entrada creo que vale seis libras, es muy caro. Venden por trago, no botellas. Si usted comienza a comprar por tragos es muy caro. Ellos tienen orquestas. Inclusive la gente alla esta seleccionada. No dejan entrar as, primero porque es muy caro, segundo porque es, (pausa) es más calmado. Es como para la gente más, no es pa' pueblo, es para gente que tienen un nivel más altito, ganan más plata. Allí no va cualquiera."

16. Interview with Nacho Gálvez, October 30, 1993. Interview was held in Spanish. Original text follows: "Estos clubes pequeños estan orientados básicamente al inmigrante Latinoamericano. Son lugares de distracción para ellos. Pienso que cumplen una tremenda función social desde ese punto de vista. La función social que cumplen es la de ofrecer un lugar de distracción barato y popular para el inmigrante Latinoamericano. . . . No puedo dejar de reconocer que cumplen de una manera una función social, de darle a lo menos un escape a una gran inmigración Latinoamericana ilegal que no tienen a donde ir y que busca la diversión m·s barata y el club Latinoamericano más barato. Desahogarse de las semanas en las que trabajan hasta casi veinte horas al día. Pero son clubes totalmente distinto a lo que tratamos de hacer nosotros. Apuntamos a una clientela totalmente distinta."

17. Personal interview with Nacho Gálvez, October 30, 1993.

18. Personal interview with Nacho Gálvez, October 30, 1993. Interview was held in Spanish. Original text follows: ". . . y en el gran Londres hay británicos y distintas minorías étnicas. . . . Eso es a lo que la publicidad va dirigida, básicamente abierta a la variedad."

19. Personal interview with Nacho Gálvez, October 30, 1993.

20. Personal interview with Camilo Pereira, March 31, 1995. Camilo was also well known amongst Colombians because he used to play football at Clapham, where he then started selling food and drinks.

21. Personal interview with Camilo Pereira, March 31, 1995. Interview was held in Spanish. Original text follows: "no me interesa atraer a gente por raza o posición social, pueden tener corbata o no, pueden ser negros o no, es un sitio Latino para todo el mundo."

22. Personal interview with Camilo Pereira, March 31, 1995. Interview was held in Spanish. Original text follows: "Comenzó a hacerse popular y la policía y los

bomberos comenzaron a notar que venía mucha gente y que abría hasta tarde. Como estamos en el centro que es donde la policía y el 'council' ataca más desde Febrero de 1993 hasta noviembre tuvimos que cerrar a las 11 pm y el negocio se nos cayó."

23. *Noticiero Latinoamericano*, November 16–December 15, 1993, p. 28.
24. Personal interview with Camilo Pereira, March 31, 1995. Interview was held in Spanish. Original text follows: "Un día ya me tenían cansado, venían cada ocho días a pedirme que le enseñara la licencia, o a ver si se tenía el control en la entrada. Un día me le puse un poco grosero y les dije 'eso es racismo, a que a las discos inglesas no las estan chequeando tanto.' Esa vez me llevaron a hablar con el superintendente y todo. A partir de eso ya no vienen, y de eso ya van tres meses."
25. All quotes from personal interview with Dave, October 12, 1993.
26. All quotes from personal interview with Eric Yu, October 22, 1993.
27. Personal interview with Eric Yu, October 22, 1993.
28. *Time Out*, March 16–23, 1994, Clubs section, p. 50.
29. All quotes from personal interview with John Maddison, June 30, 1994.
30. Personal interview, May 2, 1994; name has been changed.
31. I met Miguel in a club, when it was closed to the public. I was waiting for an interview, and he was rehearsing with other musicians.
32. Conversation with Miguel, while waiting for an interview, February 13, 1994. The conversation was in Spanish. Original text follows: ". . . porque eso es extender el gueto y nunca sales de él. Vives, hablas, trabajas y también te diviertes con ellos, es un círculo del cual nunca sales."
33. Personal interview with Diego Medina at the Latin American House, August 17, 1994. Interview was held in Spanish. Original text follows: "Si voy es al Bahia. . . . No regularmente, pero pienso que es importante, cada tres meses voy. A veces voy a lugares nuevos para ver que tal son. Pero en general no me gustan, no me gustan porque representan justamente el exoticismo de nuestra cultura. Si tu vas a lugares como el Down Mexico Way no ves un latino en ninguna parte; de pronto estas escuchando salsa, ves la comida Mejicana y a lo mejor el único latino que hay está lavando platos. Entonces prefiero no ir."
34. I met them in a club and met with them several other times outside the clubs. The names have been changed.

BIBLIOGRAPHY

Bourne, John. 1993. "Sound Stirrings in Latin's Giant Market." *Music Business International* 3(3):25–28.

Chambers, Ian. 1985. *Urban Rhythms: Pop Music and Popular Culture*. London: Macmillan.

Chaudhary, Visram. 1994. "Up the Creek with Conspiracy Theories. Why Did the Much Fancied Colombia Do So Badly at the World Cup?" *The Guardian*, June 28, p. 19.

Cowan, Jane. 1990. *Dance and the Body Politic in Northern Greece*. Princeton, N.J.: Princeton University Press.

Gilbert, Jeremey, and Ewan Pearson. 1999. *Discographies: Dance Music, Culture, and the Politics of Sound*. London: Routledge.

Glasser, Ruth. 1990. "Paradoxical Ethnicity: Puerto Rican Musicians in Post–World War I New York City." *Latin American Music Review* 11(1): 63–71.

———. 1995. *My Music Is My Flag: Puerto Rican Musicians and Their New York Communities, 1917–1940*. Berkeley: University of California Press.

Hanna, Judith Yume. 1988. *Dance, Sex and Gender: Signs of Identity, Dominance, Defiance and Desire*. Chicago: University of Chicago Press.

Hesmondalgh, David. 1996. "Popular Music after Rock and Soul." In J. Curran, D. Morley, and V. Walkerdine, eds., *Cultural Studies and Communications*. London: Edward Arnold.

Hosokawa, Shuhei. 1999. "Salsa no tiene fronteras. Orquesta de la Luz and the Globalisation of Popular Music." *Cultural Studies* 13(3):509–34.

León, Argeliers. 1991. "Of the Axle and the Hinge: Nationalism, Afro-Cubanism, and Music in Pre-Revolutionary Cuba." In Peter Manuel, ed., *Essays on Cuban Music. North American and Cuban Perspectives*. Lanham, Md.: University Press of America, pp. 267–82.

Manuel, Peter, ed. 1991. *Essays on Cuban Music. North American and Cuban Perspectives*. Lanham, Md.: University Press of America.

McRobbie, Angela. 1991. *Feminism and Youth Culture: From "Jackie" to "Just Seventeen."* London: Macmillan.

Negus, Keith. 1999. *Music Genres and Corporate Cultures*. London: Routledge.

Readhead, Steve. 1990. *The End-of-the-Century Party: Youth and Pop Towards 2000*. Manchester, U.K.: Manchester University Press.

Roberts, John Storm. 1975. "¡Salsa!" *Stereo Review,* March, pp. 64–68.

———. 1979. *The Latin Tinge: The Impact of Latin American Music on the United States*. New York: Oxford University Press.

Robbins, James. 1990. "The Cuban *Son* as Form, Genre, and Symbol." *Latin American Music Review* 11(2): 182–200.

Rondón, César Miguel. 1980. *El libro de la salsa: crónica de la música del caribe urbano*. Caracas: Editorial Arte.

Scott, Ajax. 1994. "Latin America and the Focus in the Nineties Swings South." *Music Business International* 4(6):11–13.

Straw, Will. 1991. "Systems of Articulation, Logics of Change: Communities and Scenes in Popular Music." *Cultural Studies* 5(3):368–88.

Thornton, Sarah. 1995. *Club Cultures: Music, Media, and Subcultural Capital*. London: Polity.

Willis, Paul. 1990. *Common Culture*. Milton Keynes: Open University Press.

Ulloa, Alejandro. 1992. *La salsa en Cali*. Cali: Ediciones Universidad del Valle.

Chapter 13

SALSA NO TIENE FRONTERAS: ORQUESTA DE LA LUZ AND THE GLOBALIZATION OF POPULAR MUSIC

Shuhei Hosokawa

> Q. What exactly is salsa?
> A. I never liked that adjective. It was used for identifying a series
> of rhythms coming from the Caribbean area in order to sell it to
> North Americans and the rest of the world. That is to say, to
> simplify a form of musical information that is really complex. . . .
> It came to obtain the pejorative acceptance of a spoiled genre in
> the most hidden part of Latin American culture.
>
> Rubén Blades

The interconnectedness of the world often reveals spectacles of cultural combination unimaginable even a short time ago. The all-Japanese salsa group Orquesta de la Luz is one such wonder. Popular both at home and in Latin American countries, Orquesta de la Luz (hereafter "OL") presented an opportunity to explore key dynamics in the globalization of popular music. OL is a vivid demonstration of the intertwined nature of the global and the local, and illustrates how Japanese culture is shaped by global power and aesthetic relationships. At the same time, enduring Japanese modes of response to the external world exhibit "Japaneseness" in specific ways that must be interpreted in light of cultural practice and history. OL, as an example of the cultural transfer of salsa to Japan then back to the world, reveals key factors in the articulation of popular music across national and ethnic boundaries. I argue that the global and local cannot be considered as a pair of opposites but rather as an interwoven nexus shaped by the contours of history.

OL began performing in the mid-1980s. It achieved a number one album on the Billboard's Tropical Chart in 1990 (*Salsa caliente del Japón*) and toured the Americas and Europe between 1989 and 1994. It even received the United Nation's Peace Award in 1993. The group disbanded in 1997 after releasing five albums. As a Japanese salsa band, OL faced criticism of merely imitating the sound without grasping the deeper roots of the music, and this criticism opens many of the larger issues of this article. Philip Sweeney, a well-known author of a world music guide, mocks a kind of hyperrealism of OL: "the bright, CD-polished gloss of their music lacks the soulfulness and depth of great Latin originals" (1993). He is not the only one to accuse Japanese foreign-music players of being mere copycats who emphasize technique over feeling. Yet it is precisely this assumed dichotomy (mastery of technique versus depth of feeling) that cuts to the core of Western stereotypes of the Japanese.

In part, this shows how national identity arises from a mix of internal history and external comparisons, whether they are well grounded or prejudiced. It also raises the question of how to theorize the relationship between music and place. The musicologist Richard Middleton rejects the dichotomy between appropriated copy and authentic original, and offers instead a spectrum between these notions because "there are always limits to appropriation":

> Within cultural production in capitalist societies, musical objects, however integrated into particular social practices, always carry the marks of their (contradictory) origins and of other (real or potential) existences. And this then raises the whole question of how they relate to particular social locations. (1990:140)

This article intends to answer this question by positioning OL in the world atlas of salsa and in the sociohistorical context of Japan. As the consequences of time-space compression become increasingly clear, many cultural theorists question the conventional assumption of cultural homogenization and exploitation under an assumed Western hegemony. A growing number of voices defend the active role of local actors in producing a variety of cultural mixtures. They tend to regard the global and the local not as opposites but as complementary categories. Music is easily displaced and disseminated around the world by means of recording technology, transnational music video channels, and multinational corporations that are connected to worldwide booking, advertising, and distribution networks.

It is important to recognize that the displacement of music often highlights "consumable" idioms, that is, styles and expressions, sound and vision, dance and outfits, that become largely abstracted from the context of the "original" culture. This effect of abstraction tends to be attenuated, if not erased, by the purist aesthetics. As a result, this movement situates them in a new complex of interpretive meaning and social organization. It is the premise of this chapter that processes of globalization, of which music is a prime example, cannot be discussed in the abstract but rather demand a precise articulation of the particularity of the contexts in which they occur. We should view our band both from home and abroad to examine how the "home" conditions frame the basis for their music production and how the conditions "abroad" intervene in it.

THE SALSA DIASPORA

The genesis of salsa and its meaning for Latino people have been extensively studied (e.g., Boggs 1992; Quintero Herencia 1997). Yet, except for a few cynical notes about gringo audiences, there has been little examination of the significance of its spread outside Spanish-speaking communities. The movement of salsa clearly forces a reconsideration of its meaning. As Hannerz notes, we can appreciate the staged performance of faraway people even when their words are "only gibberish." This means "we have to draw different boundaries of intelligibility for each symbolic mode" and redefine the "notion of the boundaries of a culture, as a self-evident package deal, with a definite spatial location" (1996:22). For example, outside the Latino community, salsa is likely to be less participatory; no longer a stream of sound that triggers spontaneous bodily response, it instead becomes a background metronome for social dancers or an object for armchair melomania. There are degrees of intelligibility among the components of the cultural complex called salsa. This does not mean that outsiders necessarily "exploit" and "commodify" an exotic culture, or at least no more than the commodification of music that occurs even within its original context. The economic conditions that convey salsa to faraway places like Japan and Europe also affect life in the Latino community and alter the music itself. Conversely, the distance between Japan and the Americas reduces the risks for groups like OL to produce salsa, and perhaps eases the dissonance likely to be caused in a Latino audience by hearing a Japanese salsa group. In a way, the expanse between Japan and Latin America encourages, rather than blocks, musical communication at both ends by allowing the undisturbed sound production of OL in Japan and the curious reception and consumption of them abroad.

The Puerto Rican poet Mayra Santos Febres discusses the ways this cultural product (salsa) takes advantage of an international market economy, the ways this economy transforms salsa's inner structures, and finally, the ways salsa relies on two mutually exclusive modes of access (direct participation and indirect consumption) and how this access is navigated by salsa musicians, artists, and a vast Latino community (1997:177). She calls salsa "translocal" rather than multinational because it "cuts across national boundaries to create a community of urban locations linked by transportation, communication technologies, and the international market economy" (180). This way of conceiving salsa as "translocation" fits well the fluid boundaries separating contemporary musical products, though her ideas are still limited to "a vast Latino community." What I hope to highlight here is a much more long-distance transfer of salsa (in terms of geography and culture) and the "local" (Japanese) conditions that enabled such a far-reaching move.[1]

ETHNIC VERSUS INTERNATIONAL SALSA

Music offers a powerful case study for globalization in part because it is regarded both as a universal language and as a particular expression of certain groups of people. There are interesting parallels between salsa and jazz in this regard. Ingrid Monson explains the rhetorical positions of universality and cultural particularity implied in jazz musicians' aesthetic and political stances. The two apparently contradictory positions ("jazz is universal" and "jazz is specifically African American") can coexist in the same person and are dependent upon the context: Since whiteness tends to be a sign of inauthenticity within the world of jazz, the appeals of white musicians to universalistic rhetoric can be perceived as power plays rather than genuine expressions of universal brotherhood (1994:203). Although the racial implications of being a non-Latino *salsero* and of being a white jazzman are not identical, the invocation of a universalist rhetoric to justify their marginality shares some common features. The "universal brotherhood" imagined by OL when they address "todos somos hermanos" to the Latino audience arises from the conviction that the band's "Latin flavor" can appeal to a kind of sameness despite the difference in ethnicity.

OL blesses the universality of salsa in the title track of its second album, "Salsa no tiene fronteras":

La salsa no tiene fronteras,	Salsa has no frontiers,
no, ni barreras	no barriers
Queremos agradecer a todo	We thank all the
público oyente	listening public
Que abrieron nuestras	Who opened our
puertas . . .	gates . . .

Esta música es para todos	This music is for everybody
Baile conmigo, pueblo latino	Dance with me, Latin people

This seemingly innocent verse spotlights the tension between the Japanese Latin band and the ethnic identification of the listener. The message, "this music is for everyone," is in fact addressed to *pueblo latino*, "Latin people." Who is this *todos* [everybody]? Are Japanese included? Which frontiers and barriers are they singing about?[2] It seems likely that the "todos" in this song is concerned less with the euphoria of fraternity than with the concealment of *real* frontiers and barriers inside and outside the salsa community. It is through an alleged *sabor latino* ("Latin flavor") of the members that they seek to construct a universal (or at least "translocally" Latino) fraternity:

Tú sabes que somos de Japón	You know we are from Japan
Pero tenemos sabor latino.	But we have a Latin flavor.
Todos somos hermanos	We are all brothers
	("Arroz con salsa," *La aventura*)

Just as they extract a characteristic sound from a collection of expressive styles and modes, they construct a "Latin flavor" from what they believe to be real. This flavor is synthesized primarily through their sound but also via choreography, costumes, stage names (e.g., *Carlos* Kanno) and other ingredients. But despite these moves to associate themselves with a kind of Latino identity, there are other indications that their style of salsa is removed from the particularities of place. International salsa, according to the lead singer Nora, should not adhere too much to the *barrio* (street) aesthetic but rather must satisfy an international aesthetic standard. There is no global "street" but only global images of it.

> After all, salsa cannot continue any longer as street music. Both the melody and the words of salsa were born in the street and it still carries a strong influence of street. [Its roots in the street] are advantageous and a joy. But in the process of internationalization, salsa must naturally strive for extraordinary quality in its lyrics and melody. That is what we have done. And I do wish that salsa will be international as we become internationalized. (Quoted in Sato 1993:10)

It is easy to understand why OL has neither voiced "the problems of this [Caribbean] disadvantaged class," that is to say, "scarcity, violence, inequality, marginality, and desperation" (Duany 1984:206) nor alluded to the reality of Latino community. These issues may provide substance to Latino salseros but they seem to be too close to the political reality of the barrio for OL. All the messages they convey are neutral and abstract, issues like peace, love, and ecology.[3] For example,

"Los niños" on *Sabor de la luz* sounds like a UNICEF version of "Salsa no tiene fronteras":

Para todos los niños del mundo que lindo son!	For all the beautiful children around the world!
Para los niños del mundo	For the children around the world
Cantamos de corazón	We sing from our heart
Son ustedes el futuro de nuestra generación	You are the future of our generation
No importa de dónde vengan	No matter where you come from
No importa raza ni color	No matter your race or color
En su mundo no hay fronteras	In your world there is no frontier
Ustedes alumbran la tierra con amor . . .	You light up the earth with love . . .

OL has globalized salsa at the cost of eliminating a key element in the original context: ethnopolitical expression. Such depoliticized salsa sounds so smooth that critics may well call it "commodified." But what matters for Japanese salsa musicians and audiences is the "hipness," the groove, or the feeling of "globality"; that is, the experience of listening or dancing to a faraway cultural product.

Another direction in which OL de-ethnicizes salsa appears in its distancing itself from so-called *salsa romántica*; that is, salsa with sensual lyrics and bolero-influenced arrangement. For example, Nora was reluctant to sing "Tú eres el hombre" of María Teresa Diego and María Luisa Diego ("Kiss me, burn me. . . . You excite me, you conquer me"), a *salsa erótica* piece as she saw it, when her producer, Sergio George, proposed recording it on their first album (quoted in Maho 1990:164). For OL as well as for many Japanese fans and critics, salsa romántica sounds too feminine to be real salsa, or what the Latinos call *salsa dura*, even though it is the salsa romántica that is currently more commercially successful. Both politics and sentimentality appear to be too closely associated with ethnic particularity for the Japanese group. OL, instead, depoliticizes as well as de-eroticizes salsa for the purpose of international reception. Singing in English offered another avenue for producing international salsa. For a Japanese reviewer of *La aventura*, the two English covers ("Time after Time" by Cyndi Lauper and "I Can Only Be Me" by Stevie Wonder) reveal "a shift [in the history of salsa in Japan] from 'salsa of Latino, by Latino, for Latino' to a globalism [*gurobaru shugi*] originating from Japan" (Kihara 1993). This celebration of the "globalness" of OL is central to the band's popularity in Japan because it allows Japanese, at least ideally, to "participate" in a global salsa village. Speaking of these same songs, Nora, in turn, remarks that singing in English is in some ways comfortable, in other ways discomfiting.

> We intended [while recording] to address the public outside the salsa scene we had not yet targeted. To tell the truth, it is more relaxing for me to sing in English [note that she sang soul music before converting to salsa]. Singing in English, I can sing in my own way. Salsa sung in Spanish is inseparable from the *clave* rhythm—it's limited. At first, you must get in the groove [*nori*] and you must sing on clave. Sometimes it makes me feel uncomfortable, because we don't have the clave rhythm in our bodies. For example, when Adalberto Santiago sings, he never misses it. That is the royal road of salsa. It's beautiful. But sometimes we think that it's also good to get out of clave. . . . I have a feeling that getting out of clave is somehow tied with the internationalization of salsa. Well, it's a contradiction. (Quoted in Uemura 1993:11)

Her discomfort is understandable because Spanish, inextricably linked with the culminating rhythm of salsa and with the oral poetry that grounds the music, is not her native or daily language. Nor is English, for that matter. Yet English is easier for her to express herself, probably because it is her first foreign language. The "bilingualism" of OL is quite different from that of people like Gloria Estefan and Rubén Blades, for whom the constant pendulum between two languages is a basic condition of life and song. Nora is aware of the contradictions of being a non-Latina and a *salsera*, but she also feels the excitement of the "royal road of salsa" and the need to move beyond routinized patterns. Even so, the band has generally not ventured in new directions (except for a hip-hop flavor in a few tunes) and have basically maintained a preference for the classic format of salsa, perfectly in line with the Japanese cultural hierarchy associated with niche musics.

Despite the band's universalist conviction, the multinational record industry first underlined their ethnicity, as is obviously seen on the original jacket of their first album, *Hot Salsa from Japan* (fig. 13.1). It featured a half-naked, muscular *taiko* percussionist posing in front of a Chinese gong with an Asian conga performer by his side. The models were not even members of the band. Spanish and English titles are written in bamboo lettering over a Japanese title. Although this went against the desires of the band members, OL first appeared as a picture of exoticism in the West.

This orientalist design was soon judged too blatant, and before long

FIGURE 13.1 • *Salsa caliente de Japón* (1990). Courtesy of RMM Records.

an exoticism-free design was substituted. The original was never used by the Japanese distributor, who exchanged it for neutral artwork. Although that jacket design was too "exotic" for the band, they do not always hide their ethnic difference. We must recognize the game of sameness and difference that OL plays in the parallel process of ethnicization (or self-orientalization) and de-ethnicization (or universalization):

No sabíamos nada sobre el mundo latino	We knew nothing about the Latin world
Como tocar la salsa	How to play salsa
Como bailar guaracha.	How to dance *guaracha*.

                    ("Descarga de la Luz," from *Salsa caliente del Japón*)

Somos diferentes   We are different

al público que nos quieren . . .	from the public who want us . . .
No importa que me critiquen	It does not matter if they criticize me
Al son del oriente	To the sound from the Orient
	("Somos diferentes," from *Somos diferentes*)

The latter song is interesting, since it was originally a song about dissonance between two lovers, but OL also alludes to a "difference" of race. A notable aspect of their success is that they are sensitive to a "difference" that is less audible than physical. A Latino, surprised by their Manhattan performance, says, "If I turned my back, I'd never know that they were Japanese. They really proved themselves" (quoted in Watrous 1990). CDs are certainly good for "color-blind" consumption.

"Arroz con salsa" ["Rice with salsa"], from *La aventura,* is the only piece in which OL uses Japanese symbolism:

Arroz con salsa es	Rice with salsa [sauce] is a
tremenda combinación	tremendous combination
Un buen arroz oriental y	Good Oriental rice and
la salsa latina con sabor.	Latin salsa with flavor.
Si tú unes sabores de	If you mix flavors from
lugares diferentes	different places
La armonía especial se siente	The special harmony fills the air
en el ambiente.	with fine smells.

Rice is more than a daily staple for the Japanese: it is symbolic of the Japanese nation, its pride, its sentiment, and so forth (Ohnuki-Tierney 1993). Gastronomic metaphors are not uncommon in salsa, as the very name of the genre indicates. "Arroz con salsa" follows this tradition, but the emphasis is on compatibility despite differences between Japanese and Latino. The band sings,

Tremenda combinación, salsa y	Tremendous combination, salsa and
arroz oriental	Oriental rice
Y ahora que está de moda,	Now it's fashionable,
tú la puedes saborear	you can taste it
. . . Arroz con salsa es como la	. . . Rice with salsa is like
Orquesta de la Luz porque tenemos	Orquesta de la Luz because we have
"SALSA GOHAN*" en nuestra barriga	"SALSA GOHAN" in our stomach

*Gohan means "white rice" and also "meal" in general.

Thus they eat, digest, and probably conquer salsa. The lyrics on difference, in turn, follow:

Comimos [sic] Sushi, Sukiyaki,	We eat sushi, sukiyaki,
Teriyaki, Teppanyaki	teriyaki, teppanyaki.
Allá comen Cuchifrito,	There they eat cuchifrito,
Mondongo, Tostones,	Mondongo, tostones,
Bacalaitos . . .	Bacalaitos . . .

The four rhyming Japanese dishes are notably among the most popular
Japanese foods abroad (the middle-class dishes). OL clearly recognizes
that these are sufficiently Oriental for Spanish-speaking audiences to
grasp their meaning. To distinguish themselves from mainstream
Japanese popular music, they choose to play as thoroughly authentic a
salsa sound as possible, while distinguishing themselves from Latino
bands through self-orientalized lyrics.

COMPARTMENTALIZATION AND CULTURAL HIERARCHY IN JAPAN

It is likely that the first question a non-Japanese would ask about OL is
simply, why does it play salsa? The question belies an assumption about
the relationship between salsa and locale. No one would wonder why a
Chinese plays Bach or why a Dane plays bebop. Universalized—"international"—types of music can cut across ethnic and geographical
boundaries without raising questions about for whom, of whom, and by
whom the music is being played. Yet because salsa is still so exclusively
associated with specific groups and experiences, it is generally conceived
as "local" or "ethnic" music, though more recently it might fit under the
rubric of "world music." OL is not the only example of Japanese musicians who play "local" music. Ska Flames, Lisa Ono (bossa nova), and
Ranko Fujisawa (Argentine tango) are but a few examples of the wide
range of Japanese "mimicking" foreign genres (Bhabha, 1995:85–92). It
is significant that they all share a strict approach whereby they remain
extremely faithful to the original aesthetic model. Indeed, their domestic
appeal is premised on their ability to perfectly (re)produce an authentic
sound. This inclination to purism and orthodoxy leads them to a kind
of "hyperrealism." It is important to recognize that their approach to
musical aesthetics owes much to the nature of small music scenes, "niche
scenes," if you will, in Japan. We need to examine the array of assumptions governing this compartmentalized world in order to grasp OL's
musical upbringing.

In part, the purist approach relates to an attempt on the part of the
performers and the audience of the many small niches in Japan to dis-

tinguish themselves from mainstream pop genres, which tend to be heavily influenced by Western styles. When mainstream artists produce domesticated versions of foreign genres, they are shunned by the niche audiences. Japanese fans and artists of *tango argentino* (or country and western) usually see Japanese-written tango-like (or C&W-like) pieces as inauthentic. The coexistence of syncretic mainstream and purist niche alone is not specifically a Japanese phenomenon. Curational efforts to preserve the authenticity of imported music are found in many countries. What we have to see in the coexistence mentioned above is its relationship with the process of modernization. From the dawn of the Meiji era in 1868, when Japan ended more than two centuries of virtual isolation, an idea of cultural "exclusivity" in many ways guided Japan's rushing modernization. The modernizing effort posited Western superiority and Japanese inferiority. To be superior in the cultural hierarchy one should keep the Western Western, and avoid contamination with Japaneseness. The lack of interaction with the vernacular limited the range of diffusion and increased the cultural status of the Western in the society. It is usually apt for elite adaptation.

In some cases, this hierarchy is applied to other foreign (for example, Latin American) cultures, too. Kôsaku Yoshino calls this reverence for the foreign "exocentricism" (1997:105). This has always been in conflict with the ethnocentrism since the beginning of modernization. To put it differently, the friction between these two directions is constitutive of and complicit in Japanese modernity. Certainly, the boundaries between "ours" and "theirs" are as fluid as the concept of authenticity of cultural products. Therefore what is at stake is an epistemological differentiation from the Other. One consequence of such exocentricism is that it sometimes produces a sense of rootlessness among Japanese. OL's trombonist, Taisei Aoki, for example, contrasts Latin American people's love of salsa with Japanese people's disdain for their own musical roots.

> The Caribbean people are proud of their own music. Salsa is to them what *min'yô* [folk song] is to Japanese. But Japanese are not proud of their own music. There is no proper music to us. . . . Japan has no music rooted upon life, does it? (Quoted in Ohta 1991:5–6)

This sense of being without roots, and of being alienated from the continuity of tradition, often evokes among urbanites a nostalgia for "roots music," music that is closely attached to the "heart" of the people. *Min'yô* is a generic term for rural folk song and has been systematically excluded from the modern education system. It is the urban intellectuals and their rural sympathizers who institutionalized those songs in the 1920s by establishing preservation societies of local amateur singers.

The regional societies are affiliated with national associations, and the various competitions that they organize are the main focus for the min'yô scene (see Hughes 1990, 1992). For the trombonist, min'yô represents authentic Japan, and what we can proudly call our music. It is intriguing that min'yô symbolizes a type of "music rooted upon life" despite its unpopularity among urbanites. But it is important to recognize that Aoki uses "life" and "roots" as no more than romantic tropes with which to assert salsa's emotional commitment within a (trans)local community and to emphasize its continuity from generation to generation. Certainly salsa is part of his and his Japanese fans' lives, although it is more a "flavor"—and never *nuestra cosa* (our thing)—for them.[4]

His regret at the absence of roots may come partly from the modernizing project's effect on music culture in Japan. The disappearance of min'yô from urban youth life is related to an ideology of exocentricism, that has introduced a kind of purism in musical production and consumption. It is this ideology that prevents niche musicians from interacting with Japanese music, especially with the declining min'yô style. This may explain why members of OL, feeling the loss of their own folk tradition, search instead for the roots of the Other. Authenticity for them is more closely linked with the groovy flow of the sound itself than with its relationship to the musicians' own upbringing. At the same time, one reason that Japanese audiences are especially receptive to Japanese musicians performing exotic music may be the country's relative ethnic homogeneity. It allows Japanese to freely choose foreign music for performance or appreciation without questioning the racial/ethnic background of the artists. They are color-blind in the realm of aesthetic production. Moreover, the relatively large music markets in Japan allow ambitious musicians of niche genres to become professionals in Tokyo and Osaka. Elsewhere, non-Latino musicians, if they want to be socially recognized as *salseros*, must survive tough competition with a number of Hispanic fellows. They must live—physically and economically— inside the barrio if they want to be professionals, just like Larry Harlow, a Jewish salsero in New York (*el judio maravilloso*). Salsa provided him with a "powerful critique of mainstream middle-class Anglo-Saxon America as well as with an elaborate vocabulary for airing feelings of marginality and contestation." Their "conversion" engages in "indirect expression of alienations too threatening to express directly" (Lipsitz 1994:55). This is not the case for OL because they are geographically and socially disconnected from the Latino community in terms of race and geography. For the Latino, a Japanese band is nothing but "foreign guests," and an all-gringò salsa band, if any, would probably be less surprising but more threatening and scandalous than OL.

In sum, the geographical location of Japan, its relatively homogeneous ethnic makeup and its large urban markets for niche musicians work in tandem to create a space for groups like OL to grow and be nurtured. Moreover, a defining feature of niche music producers and audiences in Japan is a commitment to purism that eschews contamination by Japanese elements. This aesthetic approach relates partly to Japanese history, which from the early days of modernization denigrated Japanese folk styles or relegated them to the status of museum pieces. The purism is also a means for niche musicians to distinguish their works from the indiscriminately syncretic blends that dominate the mainstream pop music world. This gives us a sense of OL's position in Japan. We must next consider how OL deals with the tensions raised when Japanese *salseros* begin to transfer their music overseas.

CLASSICIZING SALSA

If OL avoided the sweetish styles of salsa most popular among Latin audiences, how did it achieve a strong international following? There were two advantages in the timing of OL's international appearance. One relates to the world music boom. The European and Anglo-American acceptance of salsa changed the social status of salsa in Puerto Rico (and probably in other parts of Latin America as well). Before then, discotheques appealing to the middle and dominant classes rejected the music because of its association with an undesirable sector of society. Later, however, they welcomed *salsa blanca*, a salsa style acceptable to the white audience and the sophisticated class of Latino society (Roman-Velásquez 1995:288; see also Manuel 1991). OL showed people that salsa could even reach the antipode. Another factor was the relative stagnation of salsa dura, which had largely been replaced by salsa *romántica*, and the decline of the band format, which was eclipsed by solo singers. OL's success partly derived from its attempt to return to classic salsa, an orthodoxy coming directly from the Fania All-Stars, El Gran Combo, Sonora Ponceña, and other bands of the 1970s. OL declares its debt to such groups in the songs "Salsa caliente del Japón" and "Salsa es mi energía" from its first album. Japanese commentators Yasuo Ohta, in his flattering report on OL's 1991 tour in Latin America, is optimistic about the classicized salsa as well as being sentimental about life in the barrio:

> Orquesta de la Luz is especially popular among the poor classes living in the barrio. They say, "their salsa has a different style from ordinary salsa." . . . Their salsa is not the same as contemporary salsa called *salsa erótica* or commercialized salsa. They name with pride in their songs powerful musicians in the 1960s and 70s, as if singing "here are our heroes."

> Those musicians were heroes of the poor but now are seemingly forgotten. Salsa is music born from the life of the poor and is a part of their life. The music of Orquesta de la Luz has penetrated this scene rooted on life and has become a part of the life of the poor people. (1991:5)

Two points should be noted. First, the authentic salsa that OL plays is contrasted to "ordinary" salsa or commercialized "salsa erótica." Second, the barrio as well as its "poor" inhabitants are idealized as the legitimate makers and audience of real salsa, what the Japanese press often identifies as the "origin" (*genten*) of salsa (Sawamura 1994). Whereas Rubén Blades, as shown in the epigraph of this chapter, denounces the usurpation of salsa by gringo mass media, the non-Latin purists are trying to authenticize it by returning to the supposed origin. Ohta assumes that excessive romanticism and commercialism, two forms of temptation, spoil salsa as a true reflection of the "poor" life in the cradle of salsa; in contrast, OL reminds the Latino people of their true tradition, he claims. Ohta, along with other Japanese commentators, imagines the barrio in an ambiguous way: it is the most authentic space for salsa, but it also suffocates real salsa. The contradiction is obvious. Ohta knows that salsa is rooted in the everyday life of the barrio; yet he prefers " real" salsa to the commercialized forms more popular there. The purists, by definition, rejecting the commercialism, keep their taste away from mass consumption.

OL members believe that their "foreign" position is more privilege than defect. They see themselves as the ones who could set salsa free from its ethnic fetters. Carlos Kanno, the front man for OL, suggests that because many Latino musicians are under strong commercial pressure, they cannot help but perform syrupy music for a quick profit (quoted in Sato 1993: 11). He believes that favorable conditions of work and OL's commitment to technical perfection allowed the band to rejuvenate, if not innovate, classic salsa. Being outsiders allowed OL members to return to the classic style of salsa that is respected but untrendy. According to a Japanese review,

> As time goes by, salsa has changed, turning out to be different from what it initially was. It may be shocking and fresh [in such a moment of salsa transition] that a group stoically loyal to the aesthetics and basis of the Latino world suddenly appeared from the Orient, a place with nothing to do with Latin history and problems. Without this factor, no one could explain their extraordinary Pan-Latin popularity. . . . What we find [in Sabor de la Luz] is nothing less than the royal road of Latin music, *the authentic product*. They offer a new development in some ways but still express the perennially new and old—timeless—Latin world. (Fujimura 1995:248, my emphasis)

The same reviewer elsewhere views the actual salsa scene as entering a phase of "revitalization by the periphery" because the center is so stagnant (Fujimura 1992: 310). He justifies this periphery-strikes-back theory by summoning a long history of worldwide diffusion and stylistic hybridization in Latin American music such as beguine and rumba. Still, one may doubt if OL can be compared to rumba in Congo (*soukous*), for example, because their performance has nothing to do with fusing a foreign sound with the vernacular. It is dubious for Fujimura to link OL to the arcana of worldwide Afro-Caribbean music. One wonders whether he considered that Japan had also domesticated rumba tunes in mainstream popular songs since the 1930s (Hosokawa 1999). OL's "classicization" of salsa is partly concerned with the compartmentalization mentioned above. The compartmentalized foreign certainly stresses the foreignness, that is, its difference from Japaneseness. This process of cultural remake can also be seen at Tokyo Disneyland, as Mary Yoko Brannen writes:

> Here [at Tokyo Disneyland], Japan appropriates a cultural artifact from America (Disneyland) and uses it in relation to its Western and Asian Others in such a way as to retain its own unique identity. This Japanese form of cultural imperialism operates by continually reinforcing the distinction between Japan and the Other, by keeping the exotic exotic. (1992:227)

By the same token, Japanese keep the Latino Latino. In other words, to copy a foreign artifact is, at least in the world of niche musicians, to domesticate it for Japanese society.

Japanization therefore does not necessarily imply mixture or synthesis with vernacular elements, at least for niche musicians. It was fortuitous that this style of appropriation spoke equally to Japanese and to Latin American consumers, if for different reasons. In Japan, a commitment to authentic, not syncretic, salsa appealed to niche audiences in large cities. In Latin America, the appearance of salsa dura by OL achieved a certain kind of distinction in the context of the more commercially successful salsa romántica. OL also benefited from a concurrent world music boom that raised the social status of salsa. Thus in a variety of ways the globalization of popular music opened doors for a Japanese group, while at the same time their approach to the music created a space for a non-Latino salsa band to achieve worldwide acclaim. It is important to recognize, however, that OL's brand of salsa is perhaps less a savvy response to market conditions than it is an outgrowth of a Japanese approach to learning. Borrowing is not as superficial as it appears. More important, it is intrinsic to the Japanese sense of self.

HYPERREAL SALSA THROUGH *KATA* LEARNING

Learning (*manabu*) is imitating (*manebu*). This oft-quoted saying in the Japanese traditional arts highlights the value ascribed to copying perfectly the works of past masters. Moreover, this approach can apply equally to salsa as to flower arranging, and OL is no exception. Gen Ogimi, OL's bandleader, said: "We copied everything off records. . . . At first we transcribed everything except the percussion. We'd do the horn section, the piano, the chorus and the vocals. We'd sit there and write it all down. And nobody spoke Spanish" (quoted in Watrous 1990). Imitation is certainly fundamental to all cultural transmissions and the basic *modus operandi* for the early phase of any band. Regardless of locale, one can find semiprofessional salseros attempting to be the Tito Puente or the Ray Barretto of their small scenes. What characterizes Japanese imitation may be their "high fidelity" to the model (a question of degree and technique) as well as the value ascribed to mimesis (question of aesthetics). The tireless pursuit of technical mastery is an aesthetic ideal closely held by Japanese musicians. In contrast to Sweeney's criticism of OL's hyperrealism as "the bright, CD-polished gloss," a Japanese reviewer ascribes a higher value to their sound.

> Nora's vocals in Spanish have a slightly different flavor [from that of native singers]: *the mood is somehow more authentic than the native singer.* Just like *enka* [Japanese romantic baliads] sung by Teresa Ten [a Taiwanese singer with Pan-Asian reputation]. It is something like "the more phony, the more real," the very charm and essence of people's music. (Fujimura, 1995: 248, my emphasis)

Simulacrum is more authentic than the authentic—OL is more Fania (of good old days) than Fania today: *hyperreal salsa.* Hyperrealism, according to Jean Baudrillard, neither reflects nor represents the object nor the referential illusion (so-called "reality") but rather is constitutive of simulation. It is the "hallucinating resemblance of the real to itself" (1976:112). It is phantasmic because it evacuates the subjectivity in favor of a "pure gaze." This purely "optical" representation effaces the illusions of relief, perspective, and depth that are tied in with the conventional perception of an object. In the hyperreal paintings or novels, he continues, "the contradiction between the real and the imaginary is effaced." OL simulates, rather than imitates, the classic style of salsa in the sense that all the band desires is a "Latin flavor." OL's hyperrealism is intimately linked with the high-fidelity sound enabled by digital technology. Furthermore, the immaculate nature of their CD fits the high-tech image of contemporary Japan. OL's squeaky-clean sound coincided with the rise of digital sound as the dominant recording technology, and globalized images of Japan as a hotbed of high technology probably encouraged curious listeners to give the music a try. It is no coincidence that OL's recording debut (1990) was concurrent with the CD's substitution for the LP in the world market.

To be more real than the real, it is logical that OL canonize the classic styles. This canonization includes freezing, authenticating, and packaging every detail of existent musical patterns. Their way of learning is crystallized in the traditional Japanese notion of *kata*, a term difficult to translate, but which can be thought of as a pattern-form-shape-model complex. Christine Yano, in her treatises on a popular music genre called *enka* (romantic ballad), identifies six faces of kata:

> For one, kata emphasizes surface form and its beauty of effects. . . .
> Secondly, kata emphasizes detail, which makes of a knowledgeable audience a highly refined one, acute to the finest differences and their aesthetic effects. Third, as a system of theatrical display, kata places emphasis on technique, on the process of doing. . . . The fourth aspect of kata . . . is that kata separates the whole into discrete, patterned units. These units create a recognizable code of the performance action, a code whose goal is beauty. It is through patterns that beauty and emotions are created, perceived, and evaluated. Fifth, kata is important as a means by which art forms are taught and handed down from generation to generation. . . .
> Kata becomes a distillation of not merely one individual way of doing things, but an historic panoply of teachers present and past, embedding the doing and the doer in a thick diachronic context. . . . [Kata] also spiritualizes. This sixth aspect of kata may be the most crucial. Working on the external through kata transforms and defines the internal. The two are interrelated parts of the same whole. What is important for this study is that unlike much Western thought which gives primacy to what is below the surface and behind the mask as somehow truer and more significant, a theory of kata gives the surface its due. (1995: 18–19)

These six faces of *kata*—the surface aesthetic, the attention to detail, the process of performance, the code-orientedness, the rote learning, and spirituality—are all relevant to OL. These aspects can be observed in OL's sound perfection, conservatism, conventionalism, excellence in technique, mimicry as ultimate goal. The band members' sincere respect for the "original" model, their strict discipline and their keen sense of authenticity—can be seen as evidence of the lingering practice of *kata*, even beyond traditional Japanese arts. Kata is still very prevalent in the Japanese education system, which is largely based on rote learning that allows pupils little room for deviation from the norm. Without a doubt this affects the mimetic practices of Japanese musicians. It also gives them confidence in their own "dexterity" (*kiyō*) as an aspect of their self-image as Japanese. Carlos Kanno says:

> Sergio George [their record producer] said, "Why can the Japanese master everything so quickly?" If such dexterity [or versatility] is specific to the Japanese, they had better make use of it. Latinos have played salsa for such a long time and they cannot get out of it. We have no such yoke and have the dexterity to use the varied stimuli we live with. (Quoted in Hirai 1990:18)

The "dexterity" of Japanese in adopting foreign cultures may be related, on the one hand, to the type of rote learning that keeps each imported style separate from all others and, on the other hand, to the temporary bracketing of "identity" that constitutes the Japanese self. Frederick Buell wonders whether the "capacity for inauthenticity, simulacra, theater" might be a Japanese characteristic (1994:58). This functionality and elusiveness in Japanese identity is constructed both by simulacra of what they want and imagine (occidentalization) and of what the Other (West) wants and imagines them (orientalization).

What I want to emphasize is that the Japanese are fully capable of pretending to be the imagined Other and do not limit themselves to an identity in opposition to non-Japanese. But beyond that and perhaps more important: they can also recognize themselves as Other. In other words, "we" and "they" are sharply distinguished at some times, and at other times are ambiguously interchangeable. This is what Joseph Tobin calls a parallel capacity of self-occidentalization and self-orientalization. The former is concerned with "becoming Other" (occidentalization, Caribbeanization), while the latter "occurs when Japanese consciously or unconsciously make themselves into, or see themselves as, the objects of Western desire and imagination" (Tobin 1992:30). This slippery construction of self is closely linked with the "dexterity" that Kanno identifies as a unique feature of Japaneseness. It is a seeming paradox: the better they play non-Japanese music, the more they become "Japanese." The fluidity of identity makes it difficult to answer a question of whose music OL plays, a question central to the cultural identity and aesthetic expression.

CONCLUSION: GLOBAL SALSA, LOCAL MEANING

Where is Japan in the theory of globalization? According to Roland Robertson, Japan is important because of its "globally oriented gesture" despite a long period of isolation from the outer world (1992:85). Japan, in its process of modernization over the past century, negotiated efficiently with the West in terms of economy and culture. Robertson wonders why "Japan exhibits a particular proclivity for adopting and adapting externally generated ideas for its own specific purposes" (93). OL is a graphic example of this proclivity, and its "Latin-oriented gesture," I argue, has much to do with the production of difference resulting from a cultural hierarchy that places a high value on appropriating foreign objects without allowing any contamination by Japanese elements. This disciplined learning by simulating the Other is a characteristic feature of Japanese modernity. Hence the paradox of Japan's globally oriented gesture (cultural openness) and its inwardly oriented gesture (social closedness) reveals itself to be based on a mistaken premise. Or rather, the paradox misreads the meaning of Japaneseness in appropriating the foreign. This interlocking pair of the global and the local operates at the heart of cultural practice of OL. This band, through its seemingly non-Japanese performance—rather than despite that performance—is related more to the cultural conditions of Japan than to those of Latino society. Simulating is intrinsic to the Japanese sense of self. OL is first and foremost a Japanese band. Whatever and however it may play, its members are conditioned by their national culture. In many ways, however, this national culture is itself shaped by global forces and the history of modernity in Japan. As a result, any discussion of the processes of globalization must be grounded in such a way as to articulate the particularity of the contexts in which they occur.

What makes OL such a vivid illustration of globalization is not only that Japanese approaches to learning and self are embodied in their music, but also that these aesthetic principles are caught up in a global nexus that gives such approaches a certain weight beyond Japan's national borders. I am thinking particularly of changes in recording technology, as well as high-tech images of Japan in the West and New York's appeal as showbiz capital in Japan. It should be noted that OL first recorded not in Tokyo but in New York, under the auspices of RMM, a venerated label in the Latino music industry. Since the band had no basis in the Latino (and world) market, this label devised a meticulous strategy of selling the Asian band on the clear-cut quality of the recording. In the Japanese press, their success was at first reported as a "sensation in New York." The artistic aura of New York contributed to the instant fame of OL within the Latin music niche in Japan (the "How to Dance Salsa" video with Carlos Kanno takes on a form of his semitouristic guide to a New York dance school and Latino clubs). Thus OL's success cannot be understood apart from its ability to ride a wave of globalization in popular music. At the same time, denigrating the band's high-fidelity imitation misses a key aspect of Japaneseness in OL's musical aesthetics; band members' approach to the music must be understood in the context of Japanese approaches to learning and performance. There is a kind of convergence at work that harmonized OL's brand of hyperrealism with an emerging global market in CDs, both of which fed into an image of Japan as an epicenter of high-technology development. Furthermore, the band's recording and reported success in New York aided its rise as an "international" star.

In this article, I have focused upon a process of globalized intercourse between music makers and consumers, and between technologically mediated sounds and local milieux, in an effort to show what Hannerz (1996:20) calls a multilayered "interplay between technology, social organization, and particular meaningful forms." The starting point is to recognize that the global and local are not paired opposites, but are intertwined to form a nexus. This perspective shows how it is important to grasp salsa not merely in terms of the vast Latino community, but also the vast body of listeners who are not themselves Latino, including Japanese. In Japan, the audiences in niche markets display a marked preference for the "authentic" even when it is played by Japanese musicians (and note that Japanese ethnic homogeneity makes such audiences more color-blind in their receptiveness to Japanese musicians performing ethnic music). This purism is characteristic of the compartmentalization of such music, in contrast to mainstream syncretism, and also relates to a long-standing understanding of cultural hierarchy that denigrates Japanese folk music while elevating the foreign. OL benefited both at home and abroad from their performance of a depoliticized style of *salsa dura*. It is tempting to proclaim that OL's international success derives from its triumph in playing the global markets masterfully, but the reality appears more complex. OL members' rejection of politicized salsa and the more sensual (and commercially popular) "salsa erótica" seems to have more to do with their understanding of their own limitations as Japanese salseros than an attempt to profit from a market opening. Finally, OL's efforts to distinguish themselves as Latin musicians from Japan epitomizes their liminal position. They proclaim a kind of difference in their lyrics, yet, as the words are in Spanish, few in their Japanese audience catch the references. It is a game of sameness and difference, and their aesthetic choices reveal key dynamics in the globalization of popular music. It is important to examine "a plurality of practices within popular music to understand how *popular culture contains different meanings in different countries*" (Lipsitz 1994:17, my emphasis). OL has achieved a following within Japan and abroad by moving agilely among these different contexts, yet it is also clear that its success owes much to the fortunate turns that the salsa market has taken. For it is not that salsa has no borders, but rather that some groups can cross over them more easily than others.

NOTES

The epigraph is taken from an interview that appeared in the September 16, 1995, issue of *El Pais*. The translation and all other translations in this chapter are by the author.

1. OL was not the first salsa band in Japan. As early as the 1930s, Japanese Latin American bands (*tango* and *rumba*) were active (see Hosokawa 1995,1999). After the war, almost all the Latin fads (mambo, *cha-cha-cha*, boogaloo, *pachanga*, to name a few) reached the niche fandom in Japan. Salsa was not an exception to the rule. Imported salsa albums appeared in local record shops around the early 1970s, and the Japan tour of Fania All-Stars in 1976 was fervently received. The late 1970s and early 1980s saw the emergence of some Japanese salsa groups such as Orquesta del Sol and Orquesta 246. Many of the members had a jazz, soul, or Latin background.

2. Compare this song with "Montuno" by Gloria Estefan in her million-selling album *Mi tierra*: "[Montuno] No tiene fronteras! Es libre/No tiene banderas! De Todos/Es tumbao de calle y de hermandad." ([Montuno] has no frontiers! It's free/It has no flags! It's of everyone/It's drumbeat of street and of fraternity). Here, *fronteras* and *banderas* clearly refer to those of Cuba and of the United States for the singer and the audience.

3. Soon after the band was awarded the prize by the United Nations, she remarked, "so far we have mostly sung some romantic things in romántica numbers or if the words are good with a bit of sensuality. Simple. But with this [award], we think that we might sing some songs with stronger lyrics, not just romántica but more tunes with a message. Profound lyrics. Sure, a love song can be profound . . . "La aventura de vivir" [from the album, *La aventura*] is . . . a peace song. The lyrics are profound. This song, I hope, will get especially conveyed to the Latin market. It's a song of love, the most important thing for humanity" (quoted in Uemura 1993:11). "La aventura de vivir" sings: "Hoy ya no tenemos solución/Solo nos queda el amor/Con amor todo es posible" (Today we have no solution/All that remains to us is love/With love everything is possible). It is difficult to distinguish the "salsa romántica" she rejects from the "message salsa" she wants to sing.

4. Compare Aoki's remark with the following statement by a Japanese aficionado of Latin American music after he was overwhelmed by the Fania All-Stars' performance in Tokyo: "Japanese are argumentative about music. This may be because they don't have music in everyday life and have had little bodily experience of music" (Koyama 1976:134). The emphasis on bodily feel in Japanese salsa discourse often complements criticism of intellect-centered interpretation of the music. For example, Yasuo Ohta, exaggerating the spontaneity of the Latin American audience, closes his OL report as follows: "Music is not theory, not analysis. It is 'what one feels in one's body'" (1991:7).

BIBLIOGRAPHY

Baudrillard, Jean. 1976. *L'échange symbolique et la mort*. Paris: Gallimard.

Bhabha, Homi. 1995. *The Location of Culture*. New York: Routledge.

Boggs, Vernon, ed. 1992. *Salsiology: Afro-Cuban Music and the Evolution of Salsa in New York*. New York: Excelsior Music.

Brannen, Mary Yoko. 1992. "'Bwana Mickey': Constructing Cultural Consumption at Tokyo Disneyland." In J. T. Tobin, ed., *Re-Made in Japan*. New Haven: Yale University Press, pp. 216–34.

Buell, Frederick. 1994. *National Culture and the New Global System*. Baltimore: Johns Hopkins University Press.

De Mente, Boye L. 1991. *"Kata" Nihon no Himitsu Heiki* . Trans. Masao Tazuki.

Tokyo: HBJ Shuppan. [*Japan's Secret Weapon: The Kata*, n.d., Phoenix, Ariz.: Phoenix Books].

Duany, Jorge. 1984. "Popular Music in Puerto Rico: Toward an Anthropology of *Salsa.*" *Latin American Music Review* 5(2):186–216.

Erlmann, Veit. 1993. "The Politics and Aesthetics of Transnational Musics." *World of Music* 35 (2):3–15.

Feld, Steven. 1994. "Notes on 'World Beat.'" In Charles Keil and Steven Feld, *Music Grooves*. Chicago: University of Chicago Press, pp. 238–46.

Fujimura, Toshiyuki. 1992. "Orquesta de la Luz: Orquesta de la Luz at Madison Square Garden." *Music Magazine,* February, p. 310.

———. 1995. "Orquesta de la Luz: Sabor de la Luz." *Music Magazine,* June, p. 248.

Hannerz, Ulf. 1996. *Transnational Connections: Culture, People, Places*. London: Routledge.

Hendry, Joy. 1997. "Who Is Representing Whom? Gardens, Theme Parks, and the Anthropologist in Japan." In Allison James et al., eds., *After Writing Culture: Epistemology and Praxis in Contemporary Anthropology*. London: Routledge, pp. 194–207.

Hirai, Tadashi. 1990. "Orquesta de la Luz gaisen interview" [Interview with the triumphal Orquesta de la Luz]. *Latina*, December, pp. 16–19.

Hosokawa, Shuhei. 1995. "Le tango au Japon avant 1945: formation, déformation, transformation." Trans. Pierre Monette. In Ramón Pelinski, ed., *Tango nomade*. Montreal: Triptyque, pp. 289–323.

———. 1999. "Strictly Ballroom: The Rumba in Prewar Japan." *Perfect Beat* 5 (in press).

Hughes, David W. 1990. "Japanese 'New Folk Songs,' Old and New." *Asian Music* 22(1):1–50.

———. 1992. "'Esashi Oiwake' and the Beginnings of Modern Japanese Folk Song." *World of Music* 34(1):35–56.

Kihara, Tambo. 1993. "Orquesta de la Luz: La Aventura." *Latina*, December.

Koyama, Takeshi. 1976. "Nihon de sakuretsu shita salsa" [Salsa Explosion in Japan]. *Chûnanbei Ongaku*, November, p. 134.

Lipsitz, George. 1994. *Dangerous Crossroads: Popular Music, Postmodernism, and the Politics of Place*. London: Verso.

Maho, Miyuki. 1990. "Orquesta de la Luz." *Music Magazine*, November, p. 164.

Manuel, Peter. 1991. "Salsa and the Music Industry: Corporate Control or Grassroots Expression?" In Peter Manuel, ed., *Essays on Cuban Music: North American and Cuban Perspectives*. Lanham, Md.: University Press of America, pp. 157–80.

Massey, Doreen. 1994. "Double Articulation: A Place in the World." In Angelika Bammer, ed., *Displacements: Cultural Identities in Question*. Bloomington: Indiana University Press, pp. 110–21.

Middleton, Richard. 1990. *Studying Popular Music*. Milton Keynes: Open University Press.

Minamoto, Ryôen. 1989. *Kata*. Tokyo: Sôgensha.

Monson, Ingrid T. 1994. *Saying Something: Jazz Improvisation and Interaction*. Chicago: University of Chicago Press.

Ohnuki-Tierney, Emiko. 1993. *Rice as Self*. Princeton, N.J.: Princeton University Press.

Ohta, Yasuo. 1991. "Latino tachi wo nekkyo saseta Orquesta de la Luz" [Latinos get crazy for Orquesta de la Luz]. *Latino*, July, pp. 4–7.

Pacini Hernández, Deborah. 1993. "A View from the South: Spanish Caribbean Perspectives on World Beat." *World of Music* 35(2):48–69.

Quintero Herencia, Juan Carlos. 1997. "Notes Towards a Reading of Salsa." In Celeste

Fraser Delgado and José Esteban Muñoz, eds., *Everynight Life: Culture and Dance in Latin/o America*. Durham, N.C.: Duke University Press, pp. 189–222.

Robertson, Roland. 1992. *Globalization: Social Theory and Global Culture*. London: Sage.

Roman-Velásquez, Patria. 1995. "Discothèques in Puerto Rico: Salsa vs. Rock." In Will Straw et al., eds., *Popular Music: Style and Identity*. Montreal: Centre for Research on Canadian Cultural Industries and Institutions, pp. 285–91.

Santos Febres, Mayra. 1997. "Salsa as Translocation." In Celeste Fraser Delgado and José Esteban Muñoz, eds., *Everynight Life: Culture and Dance in Latin/o America*. Durham, N.C.: Duke University Press, pp. 175–88.

Sato, Ayumi. 1990. "Orquesta de la Luz Nichibei Dôji debut no Keii" [How Orquesta de la Luz made a debut in Japan and the U.S. simultaneously]. *Latina*, July, pp. 52–53.

Sato, Yumi. 1993. "Salsa market kara sekai eno hiyaku wo hakaru Orquesta de la Luz no Shin'i wo Tou" [The true intention of the leap of Orquesta de la Luz from salsa market to the world]. *Latina*, September, pp. 8–11.

Sawamura, Wataru. 1994. "Salsa no genten motto tsuikyû" [Searching further for the origin of salsa]. *Asahi Shinbun*, November 1.

Sweeney, Philip. 1993. "The Sincerest Form of Flattery." *Independent*, June 10.

Tanaka, Katsunori. 1993. "Orquesta de la Luz: La aventura." *Music Magazine* December, p. 331.

———. 1995. "Orquesta de la Luz: Sabor de la Luz." *Music Magazine,* June, p. 268.

Taylor, Timothy D. 1997. *Global Pop: World Music, World Markets*. New York: Routledge.

Tobin, Joseph T. 1992. "Introduction: Domesticating the West." In Joseph Tobin, ed., *Re-Made in Japan: Everyday Life and Consumer Taste in a Changing Society*. New Haven, Conn.: Yale University Press, pp. 1–41.

Uemura, Toshiaki. 1993. "Orquesta de la Luz: sekai market eno shinkijiku" [Orquesta de la Luz: Their new devices for world market]. *Latina*, December, pp. 9–11.

Watrous, Peter. 1990. "New York Says konnichiwa to a Hit Salsa Band." *New York Times*, September 11.

Yano, Christine Reiko. 1995. "Shaping Tears of a Nation: An Ethnography of Emotion in Japanese Popular Song." Ph.D. dissertation, University of Honolulu.

Yoshino, Kôsaku. 1997. *Bunka Nationalism no Shakaigaku [Sociology of Cultural Nationalism]*. Nagoya, Japan: Nagoya Daigaku Shuppankai.

DISCOGRAPHY

Orquesta de la Luz. 1990. *Salsa caliente del Japón*. (BMG Ariola 17953.)

———. 1991. *Salsa no tiene fronteras*. (BMG Ariola 17592.)

———. 1992. *Somos diferentes*. (BMG Ariola 10674.)

———. 1993. *La aventura*. (BMG Ariola 17399.)

———. 1995. *Sabor de la luz*. (BMG Latin 28063.)

Glossary

afinque: The tightness and groove of a good salsa band, the band members' ability to lock together and drive the music forward.

aguinaldo: A secular religious song sung in Puerto Rico and other Latin American countries at Christmastime.

agüelulo: In Cali, a popular afternoon dance context for teenagers in the late 1960s, with no alcohol served. These were usually held on weekends. Athletic prowess was emphasized, and dances would last from 3 to 8 P.M. The agüelulos died out by the mid-1970s.

balada: Spanish-language sentimental pop ballad.

batá: Hourglass-shaped, double-headed drums used in Afro-Cuban *santería* religious ceremonies. Performed in a group of three differently sized drums: *okónkolo, itótole,* and *iyá.*

barrio: Working-class neighborhood; ideologically tied to the roots of salsa

bolero: Cuban lyrical song form developed in the late nineteenth century, popularized internationally during the 1920s, '30s and '40s. Characterized by a slow tempo and poetic lyrics of lost love and heartbreak.

bomba: Afro–Puerto Rican genre dating back to colonial days, developed by slaves on the sugar plantations of eastern Puerto Rico. Performed on three barrel-shaped drums called *barriles,* and accompanied by vocals and small percussion. Bomba features a very volatile and kinetic dance style characterized by much interplay between the lead solo drum and dancers.

bongó: Set of two small single-headed hand drums, held between the knees.

bongosera/o: Bongó player.

Boricua: Term used to refer to Puerto Ricans, derived from the original Taino name for the island, *Boriken,* which became Hispanicized as *Borinquen.*

boogaloo/bugalú: Popular early salsa form of the mid- to late 1960s, fusing rhythm and blues elements with Cuban-based sounds. Characterized by slow to mid-tempo performance, I-IV-V-I progressions, and hand clap and/or percussion on beats 2 and 4.

campana: Large cowbell used during the *montuno* section of a son or salsa tune, plays downbeat accents.

cha-cha-chá: Variant of the *danzón*, uses a medium-slow tempo and is marked by a strong downbeat accent. Dancers' feet emphasize "cha-cha-cha."

charanga: Typical ensemble of Cuban music, associated with *danzón* and cha-cha-chá. Characterized by flute, violins, and timbales.

chombo: Local Buenaventura slang for black U.S. and Caribbean sailors who docked in the port.

clave: Central timeline of salsa and Cuban music. Can be phrased as 3–2 or 2–3:

conga: Large, conical, single-headed hand drum of Cuban origin, referred to in Cuba as *tumbadora,* featured in all salsa bands. In Cuba, the name refers to the carnival processional dance in which this drum was used.

conguera/o: Conga drummer.

conjunto: Literally, "combo." Small six- or seven-piece ensemble for Cuban *son,* emerged during the 1920s with the format of: *tres* (Cuban guitar), bongó, claves, maracas, bass, voices, sometimes with trumpet. During the 1930s this was enlarged with the addition of piano, more percussion, and more trumpets.

coro: Literally, "chorus." Refers to the backup chorus that alternates with the lead singer in salsa and Cuban music. The term also refers to the refrains sung by the backup chorus, in alternation with the *pregones* (calls) of the lead vocalist, or a solo instrumentalist.

cuatro: Small, sweet, ten-string guitar-like instrument with a notched waist (copied from the violin) that is an emblem of Puerto Rican national identity. The instrument is tuned in five double courses. Traditionally associated with *jíbaro* (peasant) culture, the *cuatro* is also used in *plena* and salsa ensembles. Colombian and Venezuelan *joropo* and other genres use a different form of *cuatro,* with only four strings (as the name implies).

cumbia: Colombia's national musical style, based on Afro-Colombian genres from the country's Caribbean Coast, strong pulse on 2 and 4, also characterized by a ♩ ♫ ♩ ♫ rhythm. Traditionally played by the *conjunto de gaita* ensemble. The term also refers to a simplified variant of this music (referred to as *raspa* in Colombia) that spread to Mexico, Central America, Ecuador, Peru, and Bolivia.

currulao: Afro-Colombian music from the Pacific Coast, traditionally performed on marimba with drum and percussive accompaniment.

danzón: Elegant salon dance of Cuban origin. Traditionally performed by the flute-and-violin *charanga* ensemble.

descarga: Literally, "discharge." In Latin music, an improvisatory "jam session" based on heightened energy and rhythmic drive.

fraseo: Musical phrasing, considered important for *soneros* and salsa singers.

gaita: An Afro-Venezuelan genre played on percussion. Not to be confused with the double-reed flutes that are used in traditional Colombian *cumbia* ensembles.

grill (pl. griles): In Cali, a salsa discotheque or nightclub.

guajeo: The catchy, repeated pattern played by a piano in Cuban music and salsa, also referred to as a *montuno.* Guajeo also refers to the rhythmic vamps played by the violins in a *charanga* ensemble.

guaracha: Light, uptempo Cuban form, emphasizing witty lyrics and a sprightly arrangement. Very popular among Caleño listeners.

güiro: A notched gourd scraper of indigenous origin (Taino and Siboney), used in Cuban and Puerto Rican musical ensembles and also in salsa bands.

jíbaro: In Puerto Rico, a peasant or rural person.

joropo: Harp-based style of the interior plains of Colombia and Venezuela.

kata: In Japan, a performance-oriented concept of learning based on imitation of a model as a path to aesthetic perfection, technical mastery, and spiritual transcendence.

mambo: Popular 1940s and '50s dance craze, emphasizing dynamic brass and energetic dancing. The term also refers to the flashy horn segments in the *montuno* section

melómana/o: A music aficionado who considers her-/ or himself to be a cultivated listener and knowledgeable connoisseur.

merengue: Principal popular dance genre of the Dominican Republic, characterized by a fast duple rhythm, sprightly horn choruses, and catchy refrains.

min'yô: Japanese rural folk song.

montuno: Second half of salsa tunes, and *son* and other Cuban forms. Features call-and-response and heightened rhythmic intensity; instrumental solos might also be played. Can also refer to the specific rhythmic pattern played by the piano in this section (also called a *guajeo).*

moña: Spontaneously improvised horn riffs that create excitement in the montuno; can also be thought of as a heightened mambo section.

música antillana: Literally, "Antillean" music, i.e., music from the (Spanish) Caribbean. In Colombia, this term refers specifically to Cuban-based styles of the 1930s, '40s, and '50s.

música jíbara: Traditional peasant or "cowboy" music from the rural interior of Puerto Rico. The principal musical genre of músial jíbara is the *seis.*

música tropical: Literally, "tropical music." In Colombia, *música tropical* denotes the cosmopolitan dance band style that emerged in the 1940s and 50s, featuring big band arrangements of cumbia and related genres.

orisha: Yoruba deity worshipped in Afro-Cuban *santería,* also disguised as a Catholic saint.

orquesta: Literally, "orchestra." Refers to dance band with brass/wind instruments, piano, bass, and percussion.

pachanga: A genre of 1960s salsa form, popular during the early part of the decade. Characterized by an uptempo, "on the beat" feel, with a $[\downarrow \, \vphantom{}_\uparrow \, \downarrow \, \vphantom{}_\uparrow \, \downarrow :]$ pattern emphasized.

panderetas: Small round frame drums used in Puerto Rican *plena.*

plena: A Puerto Rican style mixing African and European elements, developed in the working-class neighborhoods of Ponce during the early twentieth century. Played on small round frame drums called *panderetas,* plena is characterized by topical and satirical lyrics—it is sometimes referred to as the "singing newspaper."

plenero: Plena musician or singer.

porro: A variant of *cumbia,* developed by the town bands of the Atlantic Coast and then further taken up by 1940s and '50s dance bands.

rumba: In Latin America, *rumba* is generally used to denote a party or festive outing. Among musicians, references to *rumba* as a musical form follow specialized Cuban usage of the term, which denotes an Afro-Cuban folkloric style performed on conga drums. Afro-Cuban rumba is subdivided into three main subgenres: *yambú* (slow), *guaguancó* (mid-tempo), and *columbia* (fast).

rhumba: A watered-down North Americanized version of Cuban *son,* for ballroom audiences. Not to be confused with Afro-Cuban *rumba.*

salsa dura: "Hard/heavy" salsa. Refers to the rougher-edged sound of the 1970s, with driving rhythm section, punchy brass, usually some kind of social message in the lyrics.

salsa romántica: Fusion of pop balada with salsa rhythm. Less intense musically, but with intensely romantic or even erotic lyrics. Main commercial style on the international scene since the late 1980s.

salsera/o: Salsa fan, aficionado, or musician.

salsoteca: Found in Colombia and especially Cali, a *salsoteca* is a place where you go to drink and listen to records of salsa, particularly *salsa dura* (hard/heavy salsa). The term *salsoteca* is a cognate derivative of *discoteca,* or discotheque.

santería: Afro-Cuban religion in which Yoruban *orishas* (deities) were masked as Catholic saints during slavery, in order to preserve African religious practices. Characterized by a rich musical liturgy that uses *batá* drums and other percussion.

santera/o: Initiate and practitioner of santería.

seis: One of the most typical genres of traditional Puerto Rican *jíbaro* (peasant) music, often featuring a *décima* (ten-line verse) that is typically improvised, and which is accompanied by guitar, Puerto Rican *cuatro,* *güiro* (gourd), and the Afro-Cuban bongos.

son: Predominant form of Cuban music, characterized by two-part verse/montuno structure. Traditionally played by small *conjuntos,* son has become the main basis for salsa.

son montuno: Slow-paced *son,* without verse section; has a very compelling feel.

soneo: An improvised verse in the call-and-response section of Cuban *son* and salsa.

sonera/o: Typical singer of *son,* characterized by thick, expressive voice, ability to improvise words and melody.

songo: A Cuban dance rhythm invented in the late 1960s, fusing elements of Cuban *son* with Afro-Cuban *rumba,* funk, and rock. Popularized by Los Van Van.

tango: Important Argentine dance style from the first decades of this century. The *canción*-tango [song-tango] emerged during the 1930s, and became popular throughout Latin America.

timba: Cuban dance style derived from *songo,* developed toward the end of the 1980s. Sometimes referred to as "Cuban salsa." Strongly influenced by funk and hip-hop rhythms, and a freer, more improvisatory approach to the percussion, piano, and bass patterns played in typical Cuban ensembles.

timbal(es): Set of two toms, mounted on a stand, played with thin sticks. Used traditionally for the *charanga* ensemble, then was adopted into the *mambo* bands and, later, salsa groups.

timbalera/o: Timbales player.

tumbadora: Cuban term for *conga* drum.

tumbao: Rhythmic pattern played by the conga drum. Also refers to the line played by the double bass or bass guitar in salsa music.

Contributors

Frances R. Aparicio is author of *Listening to Salsa: Gender, Latin Popular Music and Puerto Rican Cultures* (Wesleyan/ University Press of New England, 1998), and is currently Director of the Latin American and Latino Studies Program at University of Illinois, Chicago. She was formerly Associate Professor of Spanish and American Culture at the University of Michigan. She has authored *Versiones, interpretaciones, creaciones* (Hispamérica, 1991), was coeditor of *Tropicalizations* (Dartmouth/ University Press of New England, 1997) and editor of *Latino Voices* (Millbrook, 1994).

Medardo Arias Satizábal is a Colombian writer and journalist. A winner of numerous literary and journalism awards, including the prestigious Simon Bolívar Award in Colombia for best investigative series in 1982, he is the author of *Luces de navegación* (poetry, 1985), *Las nueces del ruido* (poetry, 1989), *Esta risa no es de loco* (short stories, 1992), *Jazz para difuntos* (novel, 1993), and *Que es soplo la vida* (novel, 2001), recently published in Spain. He is also editor of *De la hostia y la bombilla: el pacífico en prosa* (1992), an anthology of literature from the Colombian Pacific Coast. Arias Satizábal is currently the New York foreign correspondent for *El País* and *Cambio* in Colombia, and is a columnist for *Hoy* newspaper and various other Hispanic newspapers in the United States.

Marisol Berríos-Miranda is currently a University of California President's Postdoctoral Fellow. She has conducted field research on salsa and other Caribbean musics in her native Puerto Rico, Venezuela, Trinidad and Tobago, the San Francisco Bay Area, Central Florida, and Seattle, Washington. She is the author of "The Significance of Salsa Music to National and Pan-Latino Identity," (Ph.D. dissertation, University of California, Berkeley, 1999), *The Influence and Reception of Puerto Rican Salsa in Venezuela* (forthcoming with St. Martin's Press) and articles on salsa, dance, and their relationship to the Latino diaspora in the United States.

Catalino "Tite" Curet Alonso is one of the best known salsa composers. He has written songs for virtually every famous performer in salsa history, and is considered by many to be salsa's elder statesman. His skilful lyrics and incisive social commentary frame such hits as "Anacaona," "Las caras lindas," "Pueblo latino," "Plantación adentro," "La Oportunidad," and many, many more. In addition to his career as a composer, he has also been a successful journalist, sociologist and postman. He is a recipient of two honorary doctorates and numerous awards and accolades.

Juan Flores is Professor in the Department of Black and Puerto Rican Studies at Hunter College (CUNY) and in the Sociology Program at the CUNY Graduate Center, and is also Director of the Mellon Minority Fellowship Program at Hunter College. From 1994 to 1997 he served as Director of the Center for Puerto Rican Studies at Hunter, and has served on numerous editorial boards. He is the author of *Poetry in East Germany* (*Choice* magazine award), *The Insular Vision* (winner *Casa de las Americas* award), *Divided Borders: Essays on Puerto Rican Identity*, and *From Bomba to Hip-Hop: Puerto Rican Culture and Latino Identity*. He also is the translator of *Memoirs of Bernardo Vega* and of *Cortijo's Wake* by Edgardo Rodríguez Juliá, and co-editor of *On Edge: The Crisis of Latin American Culture*.

Shuhei Hosokawa is Associate Professor of the Department of Humanities and Social Sciences at the Tokyo Institute of Technology. His research interest includes the history of Japanese popular music and Japanese-Brazilian culture. His English publications are found in *Popular Music, Japanese Studies,* and *Perfect Beat,* among others. He is co-editor of the book *Karaoke Around the World: Global Technology, Local Singing* (Routledge, 1998).

Steven Loza is associate professor of music at the University of California at Los Angeles and is a performer and producer of Latin jazz. He is the author of *Barrio Rhythm: Mexican American Music in Los Angeles* (University of Illinois Press, 1993) and *Tito Puente and the Making of Latin Music* (University of Illinois Press, 1999).

Robin Moore conducted dissertation research in Havana, Cuba from 1992-94 and received his doctorate from the University of Texas at Austin in 1995 with an emphasis in ethnomusicology. He is a performer and scholar of Latin American music and has received numerous awards including a Rockefeller postdoctoral research grant and fieldwork support from the MacArthur Foundation. He is the author of the book *Nationalizing Blackness: Afrocubanismo and Artistic Revolution in Havana, 1920-1940* (Pittsburgh: University of Pittsburgh Press, 1997) as well as various articles on music of Cuba. He is currently an Assistant Professor in the College of Music at Temple University, Philadelphia.

Patria Román Velázquez is a Lecturer in Media and Communication studies, Dept. of Sociology at City University, London. Prior to teaching at City University, she taught at the University of Puerto Rico, where she completed her BA and MA in Communication Studies. Her Ph.D., also in Communication Studies, was completed at Leicester University, England. She is the author of *The Making of Latin London: Salsa Music Place and Identity* (Ashgate, 1999).

Wilson A. Valentín Escobar is a Doctoral candidate in the Program in American Culture(s) at the University of Michigan. He holds a Master's degree in Sociology and is currently an Andrew W. Mellon Fellow conducting dissertation research on the Latin Jazz scenes in New York City. In press is a co-authored essay with Frances R. Aparicio on Héctor Lavoe and La Lupe. His research interests include oral history, memory, performance studies, Latino/a popular cultures and music(s), and cultural theory.

Christopher Washburne has been called "one of the best trombonists in salsa" by Peter Watrous of the *New York Times*. He has performed and recorded with Tito Puente, Eddie Palmieri, Celia Cruz, Mark Anthony, and La India. He received his doctoral degree from Columbia University in 1998. His dissertation, "New York Salsa: A Musical Ethnography" will be published by Temple University Press in 2002. He currently is a Visiting Assistant Professor at Columbia University in New York City.

Lise Waxer is assistant professor of music at Trinity College in Hartford, Connecticut. A Canadian-born ethnomusicologist, she has conducted extensive ethnographic and historical research on *salsa* music, its Cuban and Puerto Rican roots, and transnational spread. Her book *The City of Musical Memory,* a social history of salsa in Cali, Colombia, is forthcoming with Wesleyan University Press.

Index

KING ALFRED'S COLLEGE
LIBRARY